D1479673

635.977 M575
Meyer, Jeffrey G.
The tree book

MID-CONTINENT PUBLIC LIBRARY
Colbern Road Branch
1000 N.E. Colbern Road
Lee's Summit, MO 64086 **CR**

WITHDRAWN
FROM THE RECORDS OF THE
MID-CONTINENT PUBLIC LIBRARY

ALSO BY JEFF MEYER

America's Famous and Historic Trees:
From George Washington's Tulip Poplar to Elvis Presley's Pin Oak

The
Tree Book

*A Practical Guide to Selecting and Maintaining
the Best Trees for Your Yard and Garden*

Jeff Meyer

A Lark Production

SCRIBNER

New York   London   Toronto   Sydney

MID-CONTINENT PUBLIC LIBRARY

3 0001 01092788 9

MID-CONTINENT PUBLIC LIBRARY
Colbern Road Branch
1000 N.E. Colbern Road
Lee's Summit, MO 64086 **CR**

SCRIBNER
1230 Avenue of the Americas
New York, NY 10020

Copyright © 2004 by Jeff Meyer

All rights reserved, including the right of
reproduction in whole or in part in any form.

SCRIBNER and design are trademarks of Macmillan Library Reference USA, Inc.,
used under license by Simon & Schuster, the publisher of this work.

Illustrations by Robin A. Jess, Lori McBride, Dick Rauh, and Elayne Sears

For information about special discounts for bulk purchases,
please contact Simon & Schuster Special Sales:
1-800-456-6798 or business@simonandschuster.com

DESIGNED BY ERICH HOBBING

Text set in Adobe Caslon

Manufactured in the United States of America

1   3   5   7   9   10   8   6   4   2

Library of Congress Cataloging-in-Publication Data

Meyer, Jeffrey G.
The tree book : a practical guide to selecting and maintaining the best trees
for your yard and garden / Jeff Meyer.
p. cm.
1. Ornamental trees. 2. Ornamental trees—Identification. I. Title.
SB435.M525 2004
635.9'77—dc22
2004045283

ISBN 0-7432-4974-7

For my friend
MIKE VENEMA,
who left us too early

ACKNOWLEDGMENTS

Special thanks to all my "tree people," including Susan Corbett, Michelle Robbins, Holly Shimizu, Gary Moll, and Deborah Gangloff. Thanks also to those nice, smart, energetic people at Lark Productions, including Sulin Carling, Robin Dellabough, Lisa DiMona, Lauren Kanter, Marjorie Waters, and Karen Watts. And many thanks to our enthusiastic editor, Beth Wareham—as well as her energetic young cohorts, Brant Rumble and Terra Chalberg—without whose highly motivating encouragement this book would never have seen the light of day.

CONTENTS

THE TREE BOOK

INTRODUCTION

Other than my wife, Anne, I can say with all honesty that trees have been the love of my life. Playing in them, planting them, and ultimately making them my life's work—trees are my personal passion.

Most trees live longer than people do, and planting one is an act of faith, a gift of hope for the future, and a powerful gesture. I look at a tree and see history—my personal history, as well as my connection to all that's gone on before me and what will happen long after I'm gone. Watching a tree grow is like watching time pass—barely perceptible, yet happening all the same. Trees change with gentle seasonality, reminding us of the invisible hand of nature. And losing a tree makes us realize our own vulnerability, marking a permanent shift in time and place.

When I chose to center my career on trees, it was simply because I hated to see trees cut down and run through a chipper, simply for the crime of being in the way of development. Also I grew up in a family deeply involved with trees, and the cavalier destruction of trees made no sense to me. "Why can't they figure out a way to *move* the tree instead of cutting it down?" I thought many times. That's when I discovered the tree spade—a huge truck with a hydraulic digging mechanism that can move a large tree to another location—and bought one. I started The Big Tree Company in 1983, and we were busier than I had ever dreamed possible, saving big trees from the woodchipper by digging them up with a tree spade and transplanting them in a new location. And who knew there would be such a thriving market for big trees? Several years ago I sold The Big Tree Company so that I could concentrate on growing historic trees.

There is a gentle giant of a honey locust that "heard" Lincoln deliver the Gettysburg Address; a towering tulip poplar that George Washington planted; the last living apple tree planted by John Chapman aka Johnny Appleseed; a southern magnolia planted at the White House by Andrew Jackson in 1829; and a Kentucky coffee tree that stood for years like a marker over the amputated arm of Stonewall Jackson. In a poignant way, these trees connect us to those who forged the path that made this country what it is. When you stand in the shadow of one of these silent and knowing trees, our nation's collective history runs right through you. It was this connection that I wanted to extend to anyone, anywhere, who loves trees and history as much as I do.

In the mid-1980s, I founded the Historic Tree Nursery in Jacksonville, Florida, with American Forests, the oldest nonprofit conservation group in the country. We collect seeds or take cuttings from historic trees at national parks, presidential homes, battlefields, and landmarks. The historic tree saplings are sold in our catalog and on the Internet (www.historictrees.org); the proceeds allow American Forests to plant more trees to restore damaged ecosystems.

Growing the direct offspring of trees that witnessed famous people and historic events has put me in touch with the natural world in such a unique way, and I have had the privilege of seeing so many amazing trees that my job doesn't even seem like work. Many of these historic trees appeared in a 1999 public television documentary called *Silent Witnesses: America's Historic Trees,* narrated by actor James Whitmore. That broadcast led to my own weekly show for public television, *Tree Stories,* and now I host *Tree Stories: Leaving a Legacy,* on which celebrities talk about their connection to trees.

Every individual tree we plant is an expression of the relationship between man and planet, time and place. Like others, I plant trees to mark important personal moments or events in my own and my family's life. I also plant trees as part of a personal and professional goal to reforest on a massive scale. I have kept track of the number of trees I have planted in my life, and I am up to 623,000, including seventy-three different species. Of course, a few of these trees stand out in my memory more than others.

In 1988 American Forests announced a project known as Global ReLeaf, which included an initiative to plant 20 million trees for the new millennium. That was a nearly outlandish goal—who could even mentally picture 20 million, let alone make it happen! Global ReLeaf gained tremendous momentum, involving countless volunteers, foresters, everyday citizens, children, and corporations. Trees were planted in more than five hundred ecosystem restoration projects across the United States as well as in Czechoslovakia, Russia, Africa, Indonesia, and South America. By the spring of 2003, the count stood at 19,999,999.

It was a pretty nasty day when I met Val Kilmer at his ranch in New Mexico. We were bundled up in jackets and gloves, but Val had on his flip-flops—my kind of guy! We drove out to Los Alamos, an area ravaged by a fierce wildfire in 2000, and an area that American Forests was trying aggressively to reforest. There we planted Tree Number Twenty Million—a sawtooth oak—and shook hands, beaming from ear to ear. A distant cousin of poet Joyce Kilmer, Val appropriately recited his poem "Trees." Everyone present was humbled by helping bring the area back to life.

Global ReLeaf launched another big chapter in my life in 1991. I was asked to join the delegates to Moscow for the first Peace Victory Parade. The Soviets had always celebrated May Day with a huge marching display of powerful weapons and thousands of troops. On May Day 1991, however, a post–Cold War Russia wanted to show solidarity with the world's peace-loving nations.

American Forests, of course, wanted to plant a tree—an international symbol of peace. We chose a sycamore that I had grown from seeds collected from the tree that had shaded George Washington's headquarters at White Plains, New York, during the American Revolution. That was the easy part—getting a plane ticket for the tree was *not*, and the regulations were unbelievable! We had to clear all the soil from the roots, carefully wrap them in sterile sphagnum moss, and burlap the root-ball—and still keep the tree alive. The tree had to be inspected, certified, reinspected, and recertified about a dozen times. All these expenses meant that tree flew one way for twice as much as my round-trip ticket.

When the plane landed in Moscow, a contingency of armed guards was waiting on the tarmac—not for us, but for the tree! They stood guard over the sycamore until we planted it on the lawn of the government building known as the Russian White House, and then assigned an armored tank patrol to twenty-four-hour guard duty. But the glasnost-paved road to democracy was bumpy; ironically, about two years later there was rioting in Moscow and our tree was flattened by a tank protecting Russian President Boris Yeltsin.

On the immediate horizon, we are working on planting Liberty Forests—environmental restoration projects that will match one tree for every current active duty member of the United States armed forces—1.384 million new trees. When that goal is met, we will count back, planting a tree for every person who has worn a uniform for our nation; a total of more than 40 million trees to eventually stand in honor of America's veterans.

Historic trees are usually America's native species—many were here when settlers arrived. They are survivors of natural disasters, in most cases improving their genetic toughness with each new generation, going the way of the dinosaur in others. I believe species diversification is critical in order for trees to survive development, clear-cutting, pollution, global warming, and their most threatening predator—man.

At the same time, man can work some magic when it comes to breeding tree species that can tolerate today's harsh conditions. Cultivars and hybrid trees fill a necessary and important need—they can flourish despite pollution, root compaction, and urban stress. They are bred by dedicated horticulturists and arborists to improve on the native species, making them more resistant to pests and disease, hardier in a compromised ecology, or simply more beautiful or fragrant. Developed cultivars and hybrids are often better to plant for a specific purpose or condition than the native original, as certain natural weaknesses in the native have been minimized or eliminated in the cultivar. It is rare for a modern home landscape to not have native trees and cultivars growing side by side. When it comes to native versus cultivar, I guess you could call me a "Republocrat"—some of both makes the balance interesting.

I wrote this book to bring attention to my favorite trees in the American landscape—their beauty, their utility, and their history. I also wrote this book to take the mystery out of the process of choosing and planting these trees, so you'd have the tools to make confident choices about which trees to plant in your yard from among more than sixty of my favorites, as well as where and how to plant them and how to care for them over time. Every tree you plant will bring added enjoyment and value to your home. It is my hope that you'll become as big a tree booster as I am, starting right in your own yard.

PART ONE

The How-To

CHAPTER ONE

Trees in the Yard

For a lot of people, trees are like the stars—there are so many of them, and they are always right there in view, it's easy to stop seeing them altogether. We see trees only when they become a problem; when they've been damaged in a storm, losing a limb on the road. Or when they drop their leaves, which we resign ourselves to raking up. We may give them a moment's notice in the spring when they're in flower or in the fall when their dramatic foliage demands our attention. But in the regular day-to-day, trees often make up the nonspecific background to everything else in our yards and gardens and lives.

You know the saying "You can't see the forest for the trees"? Well, I see the forest *and* every single one of the trees—all the time. Whenever I look at a landscape, my eyes search for the trees. To me, they're the most important plants on earth, producing most of the oxygen we need to live and punctuating our surroundings in the most meaningful way possible. I want you to see trees—really see them—the way I do, each as individual, valuable assets.

What can I say? I'm a tree guy. I see every landscape in terms of how well it incorporates trees, how well they are cared for, how dynamic or appropriate they are by

species. I say this to make clear that I'm not a shrub man or a gardener, although I do grow shrubs and keep a garden in my own yard. For me, being a tree guy means I see trees as the big important pieces of furniture in each outdoor environment. And I leave the decorating, if you will—the shrub and garden planning—to the landscape designers. The balance of lawn to garden to shrubs to trees is important in your home landscape, to be sure. But I'm here to talk about your trees—where and how to grow the best trees for your yard.

In the home landscape we're generally looking for a few simple things from trees. Curb appeal is one. A well-cared-for property with mature, healthy trees gives the best kind of first impression as a car pulls up to the house—an appearance of long-term value. Indeed real estate professionals claim that established, healthy trees in the yard are worth $2,000 to $3,000 apiece when setting a price for a property. That's worth paying attention to, isn't it?

More than that, though, trees make your house a home and anchor it in the world. Every time you pull into your own driveway, the trees subtly remind you that this is your homestead. The old trees are saying, "Hey, we've been here all along!" while the young trees are saying, "Welcome to the future." Like songs on the radio, trees can snap us back to who and where we were at defining moments of our lives. The slightest whiff of the season's first dogwood blossom transports me to my freshman year of college and the little cluster of dogwood trees on the edge of the college green. When I hear the rustle of maple leaves, I can close my eyes and be lying in my childhood bed, listening to the breeze through the window, thinking about fishing. Hate to sound like a commercial, but you can't put a price on that powerful quality.

You can, however, quantify the benefit of a well-placed, well-cared-for tree—shade. An unshaded house, wide open to the summer sun, can be a mighty uncomfortable place. One or two trees strategically situated to provide shade when you need it most can make a huge difference in your quality of life (and your air-conditioning bills)— home as cool refuge versus blazing inferno. Likewise, in certain situations, trees planted in rows can serve as a visual or sound screen from traffic or neighbors, or as protection against tough winter winds.

Then there's the beauty benefit. You have the obvious spring blooms and fall color. But there's also the aesthetic appeal of a spectacular specimen tree—say a delicate flowering almond—placed just so in your yard. Or the contrast provided by the dark blue-green needles of a spruce against your house in winter, the bright red berries of a holly adding interest outside your kitchen window. Or consider the architectural drama of a single giant oak holding court over your entire property.

Certain trees are favorite habitats for songbirds, hummingbirds, and other small animals. And all trees and their soil, if well maintained, are home to tremendously beneficial insects, the kinds that keep your soil healthy *and* minimize nuisance pests. A smattering of trees attractive to wildlife is an invaluable gift to your little backyard eco-culture. You help them, they help you.

Finally—though we may not consider this benefit constantly or consciously— there is the oxygen factor. We've got to breathe, and every tree we plant or care for helps us do that. And the leaves and needles they drop in the fall, as pesky as they seem when we're raking them, add critical organic matter and microbes to the earth. If the soil is healthy and vital, the trees will be healthy and vital. And so goes the cycle.

As I have noted, my main passion is planting trees for the future. Every tree you plant is for those who will follow you— your children and grandchildren and great-grandchildren. Plant for the other reasons—the value, the shade, the beauty. But also plant for the most important reason—the future.

ALL SHAPES AND SIZES

Lesson One in seeing trees is to consider the general shapes you will find among familiar trees.

A tree's shape is an important practical and aesthetic consideration. For example, some more natural, informal shapes, such as round, weeping, or spreading trees, offer the most shade. Trees with more distinctive shapes, such as columnar or conical, make a more formal impression. Having familiarity with a tree's shape, along with the characteristics of its leaves, is one of the best ways to identify a tree you've just met.

Size is the other side of this particular

The Future of Trees

I'm a tree farmer and a serial tree planter. But though I've planted more than 600,000 trees in my lifetime, believe it or not, I'm hardly putting a dent in the attempts to reforest for the future. Trees growing in the cities, suburbs, and small rural towns of America are suffering, their numbers are decreasing, and we're not doing nearly enough to make up for the losses.

Trees planted in the parks and streets of our towns and cities are particularly imperiled. Soil compaction, pollution from cars, factories, and airplanes in urban areas, as well as the long-term effects of global warming, cut short the lives of many trees. A tree that might grow two to three hundred years in an ideal environment may have a life span of only twenty-five years in a town or city. And when these trees die, they are not vigorously replaced, even though the urban environment truly needs them.

Economic globalization is taking its toll as well. Our nation's already stressed trees are increasingly exposed to exotic insects and diseases brought over inadvertently through world trade and travel. We lost most of our elms to Dutch elm disease, many chestnuts were lost to an imported blight, and oak trees in the Northeast were assaulted by the wandering gypsy moth. Each of these particular problems developed over almost a hundred years, but today new serious pest infestations seem commonplace. The emerald ash borer is destroying the ash trees of Michigan even as you read this, with over 5 million lost in just three years. And the Asian long-horned beetle is destroying otherwise healthy trees at an alarming rate in big cities like New York and Chicago.

The best, most honorable thing we can do is to plant trees, as many as we can, to replace those that have been lost. And we have to plant varieties that are not vulnerable to these pests—here's where hardy modern varieties developed to resist infestation come in. Both American elm and chestnut trees are making a comeback, thanks to new varieties that have been developed. And you can help in other ways. Plant trees for the public good somewhere in your town every year. Plant disease resistant trees to strengthen the species where it once faltered. Plant trees to celebrate birth, memorialize a loved one, or just for the fun of it. Do your part for the future of trees.

coin. If a tree is seventy-five feet tall with a fifty-foot spread when mature, it might be gigantic compared against a small lot and home. Conversely a larger property might look silly planted only with dwarfs or other diminutive specimens. Young trees are like puppies—they're cute and little when you first get them, but then they grow up. Figure out how tall and wide a tree will be when mature so that you can keep your property in scale. When considering trees for your yard, think of the shape and ultimate size of the tree as important factors in the balance of your landscape.

Beyond shape and size, let's look at three practical groupings of trees as they will contribute to your home landscape. Obviously trees can be categorized in dozens of different ways, but for our purposes—how they will contribute to the home landscape—our groups are shade trees, evergreen trees, flowering and fruit trees. Part two of this book serves as a reference to more than sixty of my favorite trees, as well as hundreds of varieties and cultivars, organized according to these three groups.

Shade Trees

I loosely describe a shade tree as any tree that will have enough size and canopy spread when it's ten to fifteen years old to block out most direct sunlight. Of course, the bigger the tree, the more shade it will create. Shade trees can be beautiful specimen trees with big star appeal, such as red maple, or solid, dependable workhorses like live oak. Most shade trees are deciduous, meaning they drop their leaves or needles every autumn. So their spread and leaf coverage shades and cools during the growing season, and, minus leaves or needles in the winter, allows in the sun's warmth.

A shade tree doesn't have to be large. If you're looking for some shade over a patio, or on the edge of a deck, a tree that matures to, say, twenty feet can provide plenty of shade to keep you comfortable. If you are impatient to begin enjoying some shade, in whatever areas, look for a fast-growing tree. Or consider paying extra for a more mature tree so you can cool off sooner than if you were to buy a smaller tree and wait ten years for it to grow.

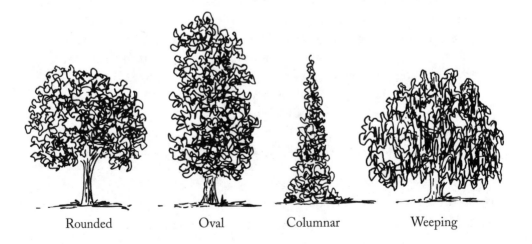

Rounded   Oval   Columnar   Weeping

When considering which shade trees to buy, note the position of your house in relation to the sun. If the front of your house bears the brunt of the heat from the summer sun, obviously that's where a big, generous shade tree will do you the most good.

Evergreen Trees

Evergreens are trees that retain their leaves or needles all year long, even in winter. Many evergreens are conifers, which are trees with needles, such as pines and firs. Larger evergreens can provide shade, but they are usually planted for visual interest or as a screen to block wind, noise, or an unwanted view.

Flowering and Fruit Trees

Flowering trees can also provide shade, but their primary appeal comes from their breathtaking blooms. Most flowering trees bloom in the spring and serve as a harbinger of warm days after a long, gray winter. Some, however, bloom in the summer, and a few more even bloom in the fall. Often flowering trees have lovely, colorful berries or fruit that follow the flowers, providing food for birds that bring their own beauty to your yard.

Fruit trees are backyard favorites that we plant for their edible fruit. Apple trees, citrus trees, peach trees, pear trees—all require a bit more care than other landscape trees, but the bounty of their harvest makes the extra work worthwhile.

Of course, these three distinctions

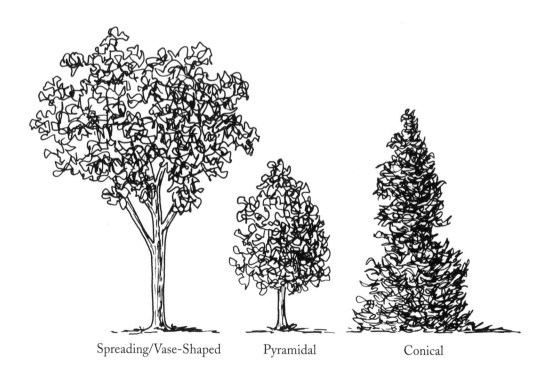

Spreading/Vase-Shaped   Pyramidal   Conical

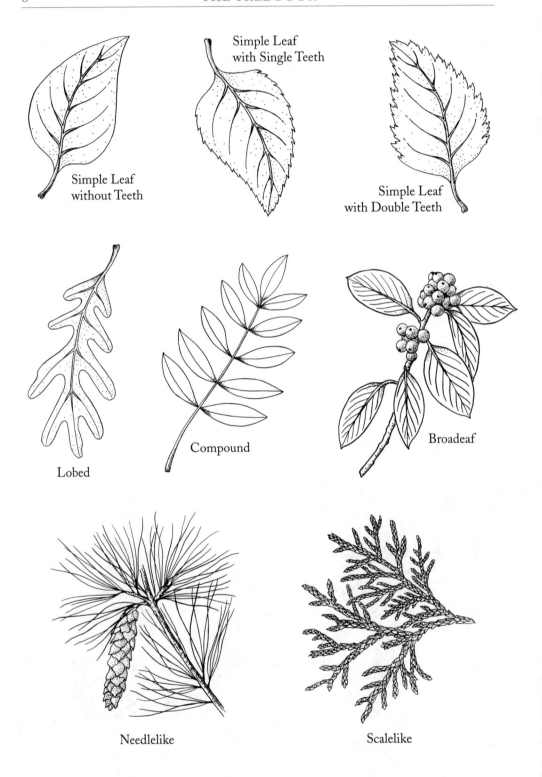

Simple Leaf
with Single Teeth

Simple Leaf
without Teeth

Simple Leaf
with Double Teeth

Lobed

Compound

Broadeaf

Needlelike

Scalelike

(shade, evergreen, flowering and fruit) are not the only factors to bear in mind when choosing trees to plant in your yard. The up-close details are interesting, too, like the shape or nature of the leaves, seeds, or flowers. Or the appearance of the bark or fall foliage. Or whether the tree adds beauty to your winter landscape with its silhouette, bark, or fruit. Throughout the reference section of this book, I will bring your attention to these features when they make a particular tree remarkable. I will also note examples of good specimen trees for your yard.

Leaves

Some trees have simple leaves, called whole, undivided, and unlobed.

There are also trees with lobed leaves and compound leaves.

Finally, evergreens and conifers feature broad-leafed foliage and narrow-leafed foliage, including needlelike leaves and scalelike leaves and cone seeds.

Specimen Trees

Certain trees beg to be in the spotlight. Though they may offer some of the ordinary benefits of a tree, such as shade or screening, they're primarily planted for effect. Specimen trees are meant to be a

Love Those Trees

Once you step into the world of trees, you realize you can become irrationally partial to certain of them. A friend of mine would give anything to line her driveway with tall, lean cypresses in the Tuscan style, but unfortunately she lives too far north to actually do this. She's tried many alternatives, and now enjoys a row of Lombardy poplars that remind her of her beloved Tuscan cypresses. As for myself, the Iowan in me loves the solid, hardworking trees like buckeyes or walnuts that you see on so many farms in the Midwest. But as a longtime resident of the Deep South, I've fallen in love with the big, deep green, leathery leaves of the southern magnolia.

Become a connoisseur of your favorite kind of tree. Learn its history, explore its varieties and subspecies. Find ways to use different types of the tree in your home landscape, creating a kind of collection. Look for new varieties—there's no end to them—in annual nursery catalogs. Or showcase historic varieties as I do.

focal point, a real show-off in the context of your yard and garden. Is it spectacular fall foliage or unusual bark you want to draw attention to? Or perhaps an extraordinary flowering fruit tree deserves center stage. Weeping and wide-canopied trees are great specimens, as are delicate-leafed beauties such as the Japanese red maple.

Your specimen tree will want to grow in a relatively open space, easily seen and not crowded by other trees or elements of your landscape. It may call for an uncluttered background that provides contrast against its distinctive features. Not every home landscape needs a specimen tree, but you may have a spot in your yard that cries out to serve as a focal point. That's where a specimen tree comes in.

Water Warning

Before you start making big plans for planting a bunch of trees, take a moment to think about water. Sure, common sense tells us we'll have to be conscientious in watering the tender young trees we plant. And we know to water our gardens and lawns. But how many of us think about the water needs of a large tree?

Ponder this: A large shade tree can transpire—lose water through its leaves—up to one hundred gallons or more a day. A medium-size maple tree, for instance, will lose about twenty gallons of water through leaf evaporation during an average eight-hour period. On a hot day, this loss can reach forty gallons. A soaking rain that deposits an inch of water over the area of the tree's root system (about 1,200 square feet) will provide the tree with seven hundred gallons of water. When there is a dry spell, however, it doesn't take long for the tree to suffer.

In the last few years, more than half the United States experienced drought conditions that necessitated water-use restrictions, sometimes severe. If you live in an area that regularly has dry summers, you may want to plant modestly to ensure your trees will get enough water. Or plant drought-resistant trees, especially native trees, which require less water than some non-natives and cultivars. There are ways to water in water-restricted times, but your first line of defense is not to bite off more than you can chew—or water, to be precise. And pay attention to whether your trees will be close enough to your source of water, should it be necessary for you to water them. Carrying bucketfuls of water to a tree where your hose (and water pressure) won't reach isn't the easiest thing to do.

Trees in Containers

Like specimen trees, trees planted in containers serve a certain purpose. For one thing, they allow you to place a tree where trees don't normally grow, such as on a patio or at the bottom of your front steps. There are obvious limitations to planting in containers, including climate and the size of the tree and roots that a container can accommodate. But when you work within those restrictions, container trees can be an effective part of your treescape. Citrus trees, figs, and many dwarf or naturally small varieties of deciduous or evergreen trees work well in pots. Container trees require special care—and they can be heavy and difficult to move once planted and settled in their pots! But you should definitely consider them as you landscape your home.

Native Trees and the Benefits of Diversity

I am inclined toward native trees—that is, trees that have evolved as a part of the natural landscape in North America. I like to see native trees in the home landscape where they are appropriate, because it is often the only natural home to many native birds, insects, and animals as well.

The non-natives that are so popular in this country, like the Kousa dogwood or the Japanese maple, are often wonderful in appearance, hardiness, and have the same maintenance requirements as do natives. They're beautiful and grow happily here.

My Favorite Trees

I've been loving all kinds of trees since I was a boy, but there are a select handful that I can easily call my favorites.

Live Oak—For its humbling size and longevity . . . and how much it means to my personal history with trees.

Bur Oak—I love those acorns. Love them.

Blue Spruce—For the sheer beauty.

Sugar Maple—The syrup!

Sycamore—The white bark gets me every time I see it.

Black Gum—The honey!

Flowering Crab Apple—My all-time sentimental favorite flowering tree.

False Cypress—If this tree were a person at a party, he'd be the most interesting guy in the room.

Southern Magnolia—Each elegant flower is like a gift.

But the ecological health of your property is related directly to the percentage of native plants; in short, native trees support songbirds, good insects, and microbes, while non-native trees may not. It's a basic ecological truth, so I stress the practical value of having a balance of native and non-native trees in your home landscape.

There will always be a case in which the non-native tree or cultivar is the best choice to serve a particular purpose in the home landscape. Where a native variety, for instance, has fallen victim to disease, a hardy non-native can step in to save the day. The message here is simply balance.

Diversity is also important to the overall health and value of your property. A yard that is all lawn and one pine has little diversity. A yard that has, for example, some lawn, some flowers, some shade trees, some flowering trees, and an evergreen or two offers tremendous variety to that ecosystem you call your yard.

Now that I've shared my worldview on trees—how essential they are, how beautifully and dramatically they punctuate our environment, how much value they add to your property—I hope you're beginning to see trees the way I do. The trees you already have, as well as the trees you hope to see growing in your yard, will benefit from your thoughtful planting and care. Use this book to choose, plant, and care for trees that will reward you and future generations many times over.

CHAPTER TWO

Choosing Your Tree

LOOK BEFORE YOU LEAP

Before you set foot in a nursery or dig a single hole, you need to think about two things: what do you already have in your yard to work with, and what is your goal in planting a tree? Take a walk around your yard and look at your trees. Are they close to your house or do they define the perimeter of your property or both? Are they integrated naturally into your landscape, or does it feel like the trees were planted as one-offs without a thought for the whole? Do the trees feel proportional to your house as well as to the property? On an older property, have the trees matured in balanced relation to one another; in other words, have they crowded each other or does each grow easily and well in relation to the other? On a newly developed property, are there young or mature trees in place or are you starting from scratch?

As you ask yourself these questions, draw a rough sketch of your property, noting the location of the house, driveway, garage, gardens, patios, etc.—and, of course, marking where the trees are. When you look at your situation in black and white, it's easier to begin assessing your goals for planting.

So why do you want to plant another tree? Having a clear, specific idea of why you want to plant makes it more likely you'll end up planting the right tree to satisfy that desire. In fact, by determining why you want to plant a tree, you begin to answer the question of which tree you should plant. For instance, you might want to:

- Shade the yard or house in the summer.
- Protect the yard or house from seasonal winds.
- Give focus to a certain part of your property.
- Add beauty to the yard—spring blooms, fall color, attractive bark, or unusual tree shape.
- Establish a barrier to screen out sights or sounds that you wish to minimize.
- Add financial value to your property.
- Attract birds, squirrels, and other wildlife.

Knowing that one or more of these factors is important to you automatically begins to narrow down your tree prospects—which is

features. Or they can serve a purpose independent of the rest of your yard or home, enjoying a spotlight effect as a specimen tree.

Is the style of your home and property ordered and formal? If so, you may lean toward columnar or tightly conical trees, perhaps along a driveway or as an accent near the house or garden. A tree like a big, stately oak is never a mistake, if you have the space and scale to your home and property to pull it off.

Perhaps your home is more informal, such as cottage- or ranch-style. Looser and more irregularly shaped trees may be more suitable for your property. A weeping tree might add a soft stroke to the scene for a period home, such as a Victorian, especially in the background.

Think about what you have, in terms of a house, property, and existing trees. Now think about what assets in a new tree might appeal to you most. Consider overall shape, size, and habit; the texture of foliage, branches, and bark; and the color of foliage, branches, fruit, and bark. Do you daydream about something simple, like the fragrance of a blossoming tree wafting through your kitchen window in springtime? Or do you prefer elegant old trees that suggest a permanence and history? Maybe all you want is a tree that shades your backyard in summer and will support a tire swing for your far-in-the-future grandchildren to play in. When you

good. So does considering your potential trees in relation to the size of your house and property. A small, one-story house might be dwarfed by a hulking elm but framed nicely by a modest Eastern larch. A two-story house with all the fixins would easily share the stage with a larger tree, while a smaller tree would seem off in the same spot.

Trees can enclose, broaden, or help define your home landscape. They can create distinct boundaries between one property and another or between one part of the yard and another. They can accent a spot in the landscape to bring out your home's best

PRACTICAL MATTERS

Whether you want to plant just one tree or you intend to plant several, the same basic truth applies: every tree has its own environmental needs that dictate its viability and proper location in your landscape. In other words, your goals can't come before the needs of the tree. Think of it this way: 25 percent of young tree failures are due to poor planting—letting the roots dry out, planting too deeply or too shallowly, and so on. The other 75 percent fail because they have been planted in the wrong location for their needs.

So don't dash off to the nursery until you've accounted for certain practical matters—your growing zone, your light and soil factors, how close your site is to a building, driveway, or other trees, or the height and spread of the tree you are considering. Carefully assessing these issues won't lengthen your list of tree options, but it will make it stronger, because you will be narrowing down your choices to trees that are truly suitable to your location.

can describe clearly what you've got and what you want, it's time to figure out what specific trees might work for you.

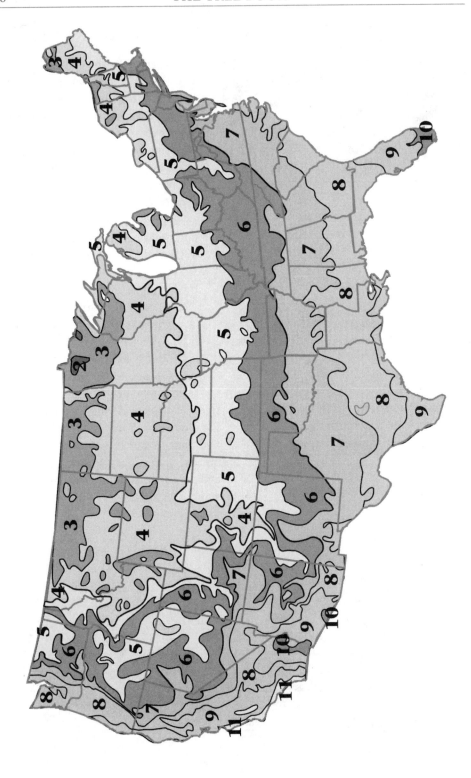

KNOW YOUR ZONE

The USDA hardiness zone map (on the opposite page) carves up the country into eleven regions according to how cold (in increments of 10°F) it gets during an average winter. So, for instance, it can get as cold as –40°F to –50°F in Zone 2 (which amounts to two little pockets at the top of Wisconsin) or as cold as 30°F to 40°F in Zone 10 (the southern tip of Florida and a sliver of southern California). These ranges define how much a plant can take—if a plant is designated safe to grow in Zone 2, it can withstand a winter during which several –35°F days are not uncommon.

Gardeners are notorious for stretching and testing their growing zones when they plant, but I always advise people who are trying to grow healthy trees not to be such daredevils. Trying to grow a tree that isn't totally comfortable in your zone will put it at an immediate disadvantage, vulnerable to stress and disease and the vagaries of weather. There are plenty of trees highlighted in this book that are hardy across several zones, so even if you're at a given end of the zone spectrum, you will have many terrific zone-appropriate trees to choose from. Know your zone—and stick to it.

THE SOIL FACTOR

Trees have different preferences and tolerances regarding the acidity or alkalinity of the soil they're planted in. *Acid* and *alkaline* refer to the pH level of the soil, which indicates the availability of nutrients to plants on a scale that ranges from 1 (highest acidity) to 14 (highest alkalinity). Soil at a pH level of around 7 is considered neutral; most trees are happy in soils that are somewhat acid to neutral (pH 5.5 to 7), although there are exceptions. Hollies and some oaks, for example, like a more acidic soil, while the European beech prefers a somewhat alkaline soil.

Test your soil to determine its natural pH level, and keep that figure in mind when you're considering trees for your yard. You can take steps to increase the acid or alkaline levels of the soil, but it's best to stick with trees that suit your soil naturally.

TRUE LIGHT

The same gardeners who try to cheat on zone hardiness recommendations when they plant have also been known to try to cheat on sunlight requirements. As with the zones, I say don't cheat or otherwise kid yourself about sunlight in your yard. **Full sun** is full sun—a minimum of six hours of direct, unobstructed sunlight per day. If that's what a tree requires, that's what it must have, no more and no less. **Full sun/part shade** means a minimum of four to six hours of direct sun. And **shade** means no direct sun, a condition very few trees can tolerate.

Look at your property and try to determine the level of exposure to the sun in the area where you'd like to plant a tree. It may take a few days or weeks (or a whole season!) of observation to get an accurate sense of your sunlight status, but knowing—and sticking to—the truth about your sunlight will be a big boost for your tree.

Testing Your Soil

Professional soil tests can tell you the levels of pH, phosphorous, potassium, and organic matter in your soil, as well as the percentage of sand, silt, and clay. Your local agricultural extension office can usually perform this soil test for a modest fee. You can also use a do-it-yourself home soil test kit available at garden centers that will tell you only the pH of your soil, which is all you really need for the purposes of your tree search. To get a clean, accurate soil sample for either kind of test, follow these steps:

1. Use clean tools. A rusty or otherwise caked-up tool or bucket can contaminate your soil sample. Clean your tools and buckets thoroughly or start with new ones. You'll also need a clean core sampler, trowel, or shovel, and a clean container to hold the soil.
2. Using the core sampler, trowel, or shovel, take a thin slice of the soil at least six inches deep. Take samples from eight to ten different areas around your yard, including near where trees are already growing. Get at least two samples from every 1,000 square feet of lawn space. Remove as much grass as possible from the soil, and mix together your samples. Take a cup or two of this soil mixture and place it in the test container provided with your kit or by the test lab.

That's all there is to it. When you get the results of the soil test back, you'll have a critical piece of information in hand to help you choose trees that will thrive in your yard.

PHYSICAL FACTORS

Note your desired planting site's proximity to things like utility lines (overhead or underground), sewer and septic pipes, sidewalks, driveways, buildings, and even other trees. Some trees have aggressive roots that can wreak havoc on these systems or fixtures. These are very important, very practical considerations that are easy to neglect when you're looking at a small, young version of the tree you're in love with—it'll grow into a full-sized, mature tree that'll be wrestling with the pipes and sidewalks if you don't play your cards right.

THE MATURE TREE

Speaking of your full-size, mature tree, what exactly will that tree look like? Specifically, what will its height and spread and root reach be—and how will that affect your home, landscape, and those so-called physical factors we just discussed? A tree needs to have room to grow to mature size without crowding its neighbors, obscuring other important landscape features, growing too close to your home or other buildings, or buckling your sidewalk or driveway. Pay careful attention to the projected height and reach of the tree you are considering in order to avoid problems down the road.

A rule of thumb is that you should plant **large trees** (50 feet or taller at maturity) at least 35 feet away from your house to allow healthy root development and to minimize risk to your home. There should also be 12 square feet of area around the mature tree where there are no competing trees or shrubs.

Medium trees (30 to 50 feet at maturity) should be planted 20 feet from the house and anywhere they will have room to spread unhindered. There should be eight square feet of unplanted area around the mature tree.

And **small trees** (15 to 30 feet or less at maturity) can be safely planted near most utility lines, with at least four square feet of unplanted area around the tree. Some of these trees can also be planted in large containers.

TREE SHOPPING

For the same reason you shouldn't go grocery shopping when you're hungry, you shouldn't go tree shopping without knowing what you're looking for. Sure, browsing is fun, but without a particular tree in mind or a short list of trees you've already determined are viable choices, you might fall in love with the first tree that catches your eye. And that tree may not suit your landscape goals or physical requirements. So do your homework in advance, and go out with a clear vision of what you want to accomplish in your yard.

WHERE TO BUY

After doing your at-home research, a visit to your **local garden centers or nurseries** is the best way to start shopping for a tree. You can get a good sense of what's available, what grows well in your area (presumably a neighborhood nursery wouldn't be selling a tree that isn't a good local fit), and what some of the trees you might be interested in look like up close. You might not buy anything yet, having determined that prices or availability or selection are better elsewhere, but you've informed yourself about the process by having a good look around. Then again, you may very well find just what you want, so be ready to inspect the tree and roots carefully before buying. Ideally you'll be consulting with a knowledgeable nurseryman, which will increase your chances of ending up with a tree that is both appropriate for your purposes and well cared for. At a nursery, you can buy small, very young, and relatively inexpensive trees or else mature trees that can represent an investment of hundreds or thousands of dollars.

You may also live near a **tree farm,** which is an excellent place to look at trees that grow well in your area. Tree farms grow tiny seedlings until they are big enough to be packed up and sold to the consumer. Many tree farms deal only with wholesalers or retailers, and not directly with home consumers, but some have their own retail outlets or catalogs, which can be an excellent source of high-quality, inexpensive (if young) trees. If there is a tree farm near you, visit it, even just as a field trip.

You can also buy trees through **mail-order or Internet catalogs,** in which case you'll usually be buying very small plants. This isn't helpful if you're looking for larger-scale, instant gratification in your yard, but the upside is that catalogs usually offer many interesting varieties of the tree you are considering, and for a lot less money (say $30) than the more mature tree you'd buy at the nursery (maybe between $300 and $3,000). The varieties and cultivars can be very enticing; just be sure you've determined that the features of the variety or cultivar (which can vary greatly from what you know about your species) match your needs and requirements. The disadvantage of mail order is that you cannot inspect the plant before you buy it. So if you're purchasing through a catalog, be sure you're working with a reputable company that takes care of its plants and meets your expectations. Our catalog on historic trees, *Famous and Historic Trees* (www.historictrees.org), is a comprehensive source of distinctive, reasonably priced seedlings, but there are many catalog companies that grow and sell good trees. See the resources section at the back of the book for catalogs to order.

Note: As elsewhere in life, you get what you pay for. If you pay too little for a tree

from a catalog or a discount retailer, there's a good chance it won't be in the best shape. A low price is hard to resist, but it'll catch up to you in time and resources and likely in disappointment when your bargain tree fails.

GOOD TREE, BAD TREE

When you buy a tree, it will be either bare-root, in a container, or balled and burlapped. When you shop in person, have a good, close look at the root system or root-ball of the tree you are considering. Learn to recognize the sure signs of a tree that will have trouble once you plant it.

Bare-root plants should be damp, with plenty of strong, evenly spread roots. Roots that seem overly lopsided or have a wadded up, too-crowded appearance are bad prospects. Be prepared to get your bare-

root plants straight into a bucket of water after you buy them.

Container plants should also be damp—all the way through to the bottom of the container—as proof they've been regularly watered. Before purchasing, hold the tree firmly at the base of the trunk and gently nudge it out of the container to get a look at the roots. The root system should appear evenly distributed and well established. If roots have begun to encircle the form of the root base, and roots are sprouting out the bottom of the container, this plant is pot-bound and you don't want it.

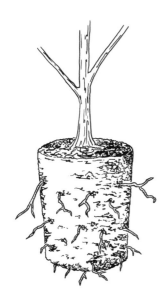

Because you can't actually see the roots of **small balled and burlapped plants,** you have to look for different clues to their health and well-being. The leaves should be green and robust, not skimpy and tentative. The way the root-ball is wrapped is important; it should be enclosed surely in burlap with ties made of organic material. If the ties or the burlap is loose, it may indicate that some roots are dried out or damaged.

Beware also of plants choked at the trunk by ties.

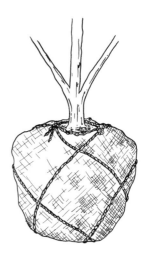

You shouldn't try to plant most large **balled and burlapped trees** on your own—plan to get the big guys with the heavy equipment to help. But as with all other types and sizes of trees, inspect the condition of the root-ball when you purchase the plant and again when it is delivered by the nursery. It should be wrapped securely, preferably with natural fiber ties and burlap, and with no signs of choking at the trunk. The root-ball of a bigger tree may well be supported at the bottom with a sturdy metal cage that has wide spaces for roots to grow through. This metal netting is intended to be planted with the tree, as the roots will grow easily around and through the wires. As with small-balled trees, loose wrapping materials may be a hint that the roots are in bad shape.

A word to the wise: don't buy a tree that doesn't have all the signs of a healthy and promising future. A bad tree is not like a stray from the pound that you can save and rehabilitate and turn into a great dog. If the tree is not thriving when you put it in the ground, its chances of surviving are slim. Put your chips on the good trees, especially when you're paying good money for them

BUYING A MATURE TREE VERSUS A YOUNG TREE VERSUS A SAPLING

Buying and planting a mature tree is an appealing notion because you'll have instant enjoyment of the features you bought the tree for in the first place—shade, color, shape, etc. It's an exciting prospect if you just don't want to wait the years it takes for a young tree to grow. And it's an exciting process—I know because it's how I started my career in trees—awe-inspiring, like watching a building go up. Buying a mature tree can be expensive, though, into the thousands of dollars; the additional cost of transporting and planting the tree can cost hundreds more. Also, healthy mature trees aren't always easy to find—certain companies specialize in them—so you'll have to do some hunting.

A young tree could take five or ten years to begin contributing to the enjoyment and value of your home, but it's a much more economical option than mature trees, with handsome, healthy, high-quality young trees costing less than a hundred dollars.

Planting saplings calls for patience and an ability to nurture that not everyone has. But the extremely low cost would enable you to plant more trees and stay within your planting budget. You could plant a veritable forest if you'd like!

Your decision to plant a mature tree, a young tree, or a sapling boils down to whether, as a tree planter, you're the hare or the tortoise—and how much cash you've got in your wallet.

QUALITY AND CONDITION CHECKLIST FOR BUYING A TREE

The ideal tree should have at least five of these features to qualify as a good prospect.

TREE CHARACTERISTICS
- Growth is compact.
- Leaves are plentiful, with good color.
- Flowers (if present) are of appropriate size, color, and number.

Ask the Nurseryman

Ask your nurseryman for a written guarantee on your tree, especially if you enlist his help in planting a larger tree. You will have spent too much money on your tree to risk a bad planting experience. Usually a tree is guaranteed for a year, long enough to ensure its success. If the nursery won't guarantee your tree, you're working with the wrong nursery.

- Fruits or berries (if present) are of appropriate size, color, and number.
- Overall size and form are appropriate for this tree.
- Tree does not look leggy or unkempt.

TREE CONDITION
- No evidence of insect or disease problems.
- No evidence of aboveground damage, such as broken branches or bark wounds.
- Strong central trunk, few narrow

Ten Best Bang-for-Your-Buck Trees

These trees give you a little (or a lot) of everything you could hope for in a tree: hardiness, adaptability, flexibility in the landscape, beauty, shape, comfort. You can't go wrong with these trees.

Bur Oak—This tree has good range, beautiful bark, the traditional massive oak shape, and large acorns for squirrels.

Red Maple—Beautiful spring and fall colors, easy to grow in a wide variety of soils, tolerates variables in sunlight.

Sargent Crab Apple—Lovely color of the leaves and blossoms, a good small tree for small yards.

Fraser Fir—This is a great living Christmas tree for the yard. It has soft needles and is a truly haunting shade of green.

River Birch—The wind sounds beautiful when rustling the leaves, and it has lovely bark. It is sleekly upright, making it ideal for narrow areas.

Japanese Maple—Splendid shape, leaf color, and bark. Can be trained and sculpted and loves shade. What a good sport!

Bald Cypress—This is a fast-growing tree with an upright, triangular figure. It can grow in moist areas, and has lovely soft green foliage. A solidly consistent tree.

Lombardy Poplar—Has an elegant, European shape, beautiful fall color, and intriguing winter structure.

Norway Spruce—Has a terrific vertical shape that can really frame a home. Great windbreak, remarkable winter color—the colder it is, the bluer the needles seem to be.

Kousa Dogwood—Brilliant flowers, great fragrance, terrific for small yards.

crotches (areas where the limbs meet the trunk).

- A clean, undamaged container.
- Undamaged root-ball; roots aren't growing out of container or burlap wrapping.
- Base of tree does not wobble at soil line.
- Overall appearance is attractive.

TRANSPORTING YOUR TREE

Be careful when transporting your tree from the nursery home to your yard. Use an oversize vehicle, such as an SUV with a large open back section, a pickup truck, or a car that has a trailer attached to it. Gently but securely wrap the top of the tree in an old bedsheet or piece of canvas to protect it from the sun and wind. Even the shortest drive can harm and dry out an unprotected tree. Cushion the stem and branches with a blanket—and drive slowly!—to protect the tree from jostling and rubbing. When unloading the tree from your vehicle, be careful not to drop the root-ball, as this can tear roots and damage tissue.

Ideally you will plant your tree as soon as you get home from the nursery. If you don't, keep the roots moist, and store the tree away from direct wind and sunlight in a shady, shielded spot outdoors until you're ready to plant—as soon as possible!

Good Trees for Certain Conditions and Uses

TREES FOR ALKALINE SOIL

European Alder	Red Horse Chestnut
White Ash	Amur Chokecherry
Green Ash	Japanese Crab Apple
European Beech	Sargent Crab Apple
Ohio Buckeye	American Elm
Red Buckeye	Chinese Elm
Yellow Buckeye	Chinese Fringe Tree
Northern Catalpa	White Fringe Tree
Southern Catalpa	Ginkgo
Chinese Chestnut	Goldenchain
Horse Chestnut	Golden Rain Tree

Shagbark Hickory	Bur Oak
Katsura Tree	English Oak
American Linden	Eastern Poplar (Cottonwood)
Littleleaf Linden	Japanese Pagoda Tree
Silver Linden	Callery Pear
Amur Maple	Downy Serviceberry
Hedge Maple	American Smoke Tree
Norway Maple	Smooth Sumac
Paperbark Maple	Staghorn Sumac
Silver Maple	

TREES FOR ACID SOIL

American Beech	Eastern Redcedar (Juniper)
European Beech	Rocky Mountain Juniper
Japanese Birch	Austrian Pine
Paper Birch	Bristlecone Pine
River Birch	Himalayan Pine
American Holly	Red Pine
Chinese Holly	Scotch Pine
English Holly	Swiss Stone Pine
Honey Locust	Eastern White Pine
Chinese Juniper	Japanese White Pine

TREES FOR FULL OR PARTIAL SHADE

American Beech	Kousa Dogwood
European Beech	Pagoda Dogwood
Ohio Buckeye	Chinese Fringe Tree
Red Buckeye	White Fringe Tree
Yellow Buckeye	Canadian Hemlock
Northern Catalpa	Carolina Hemlock
Cedar of Lebanon	Mountain Hemlock
Hinoki False Cypress	Western Hemlock
Flowering Dogwood	Amur Maple

Japanese Maple
Allegheny Serviceberry
Apple Serviceberry
Downy Serviceberry
Western Serviceberry
Fragrant Snowbell

Japanese Snowbell
Japanese Stewartia
Korean Stewartia
Tall Stewartia
English Yew
Japanese Yew

TREES THAT CAN SURVIVE DROUGHT

Green Ash
European Beech
Ohio Buckeye
Northern Catalpa
Southern Catalpa
Chinese Chestnut
Chinese Elm
Ginkgo
Golden Rain Tree
Cockspur Hawthorn
English Hawthorn
Lavalle Hawthorn
Washington Hawthorn
Winter King (Green) Hawthorn
Honey Locust
Littleleaf Linden

Hedge Maple
Silver Maple
Bur Oak
English Oak
Pin Oak
Japanese Pagoda Tree
London Plane Tree
Callery Pear
Sweet Gum
American Sycamore
American Smoke Tree
Common Smoke Tree
Smooth Sumac
Staghorn Sumac
Black Walnut
English Walnut

SMALL TREES (5 TO 30 FEET)

Apple
Oriental Arborvitae
Red Buckeye
Higan Cherry
Japanese Flowering Cherry
Nanking Cherry
Sargent Cherry

Japanese Crab Apple
Sargent Crab Apple
Kousa Dogwood
Pagoda Dogwood
Flowering Almond
Japanese Flowering Plum
Chinese Fringe Tree

White Fringe Tree
Goldenchain
Cockspur Hawthorn
English Hawthorn
Lavalle Hawthorn
May Hawthorn
Washington Hawthorn
Winter King (Green) Hawthorn
Saucer Magnolia
Star Magnolia
Amur Maple
Japanese Maple
Paperbark Maple

Peach
Common Pear
Allegheny Serviceberry
Apple Serviceberry
Downy Serviceberry
American Smoke Tree
Common Smoke Tree
Fragrant Snowbell
Japanese Snowbell
Japanese Stewartia
Korean Stewartia
Tall Stewartia

MEDIUM-SIZE TREES (30 TO 50 FEET)

European Alder
Italian Alder
Japanese Birch
Ohio Buckeye
Southern Catalpa
Yoshino Cherry
Chinese Chestnut
Japanese Chestnut
Amur Chokecherry
Flowering Dogwood
Chinese Elm
Golden Rain Tree
Black Gum

Honey Locust
Eastern Larch
Hedge Maple
Norway Maple
Osage Orange
Callery Pear
Ussurian Pear
Quaking Aspen (Poplar)
Sassafras
English Walnut
Babylon Weeping Willow
Corkscrew Hanklow Willow
Yellowwood

LARGE TREES (50 FEET AND TALLER)

Green Ash
White Ash
American Beech
European Beech

Paper Birch
River Birch
Yellow Buckeye
Northern Catalpa

American Chestnut   Sugar Maple
Horse Chestnut   Bur Oak
Bald Cypress   Chinquapin Oak
American Elm   English Oak
Douglas Fir   Live Oak
Ginkgo   Northern Red Oak
Canadian Hemlock   Pin Oak
Mockernut (Hickory)   Scarlet Oak
Pignut Hickory   White Oak
Shagbark Hickory   Japanese Pagoda Tree
Shellbark Hickory   London Plane Tree
Chinese Juniper   Eastern Poplar (Cottonwood)
Katsura Tree   Dawn Redwood
Japanese Larch   Sweet Gum
American Linden   American Sycamore
Littleleaf Linden   Tulip Tree
Silver Linden   Black Walnut
Southern Magnolia   Golden Weeping Willow
Red Maple   Zelkova
Silver Maple

TREES FOR A WINDBREAK OR SCREEN

Red Buckeye   Austrian Pine
False Cypress   Bristlecone Pine
Leyland Cypress   Eastern White Pine
Chinese Fringe Tree   Himalayan Pine
Cockspur Hawthorn   Japanese White Pine
Carolina Hemlock   Red Pine
American Holly   Scotch Pine
English Holly   Swiss Stone Pine
Eastern Redcedar (Juniper)   Lombardy Poplar
Rocky Mountain Juniper   Colorado Blue Spruce
Amur Maple   Norway Spruce
Hedge Maple   Japanese Yew

FAST-GROWING TREES

Green Ash	Quaking Aspen (Poplar)
Paper Birch	Eastern Poplar (Cottonwood)
River Birch	Lombardy Poplar
Northern Catalpa	Dawn Redwood
Deodar Cedar	Norway Spruce
Bald Cypress	Sweet Gum
Fraser Fir	American Sycamore
Golden Rain Tree	Tulip Tree
Honey Locust	Babylon Weeping Willow
Red Maple	Corkscrew Hanklow Willow
Silver Maple	Golden Weeping Willow
Eastern White Pine	Zelkova

TREES WITH SHOWY SPRING FLOWERS

Ohio Buckeye	Sargent Crab Apple
Red Buckeye	Flowering Dogwood
Yellow Buckeye	Pagoda Dogwood
Higan Cherry	White Fringe Tree
Japanese Flowering Cherry	Goldenchain
Nanking Cherry	Saucer Magnolia
Sargent Cherry	Callery Pear
Yoshino Cherry	Ussurian Pear
Horse Chestnut	Downy Serviceberry
Red Horse Chestnut	American Smoke Tree
Amur Chokecherry	Japanese Snowbell
Japanese Crab Apple	Fragrant Snowbell

TREES WITH SHOWY SUMMER FLOWERS

Northern Catalpa	Chinese Fringe Tree
Southern Catalpa	Golden Rain Tree
Kousa Dogwood	Cockspur Hawthorn

English Hawthorn
Lavalle Hawthorn
May Hawthorn
Washington Hawthorn
Winter King (Green)
   Hawthorn
Southern Magnolia
Japanese Pagoda Tree

Common Smoke Tree
Japanese Stewartia
Korean Stewartia
Tall Stewartia
Shining Sumac
Smooth Sumac
Staghorn Sumac
Yellowwood

TREES WITH GOOD FALL COLOR

Green Ash
White Ash
Japanese Birch
Paper Birch
River Birch
Ohio Buckeye
Sargent Cherry
Flowering Dogwood
Kousa Dogwood
Pagoda Dogwood
American Elm
Chinese Fringe Tree
White Fringe Tree
Ginkgo
Cockspur Hawthorn
Katsura Tree
Eastern Larch
Honey Locust
American Linden
Japanese Maple
Amur Maple
Hedge Maple
Norway Maple
Paperbark Maple

Red Maple
Sugar Maple
Bur Oak
Northern Red Oak
Pin Oak
Scarlet Oak
White Oak
Callery Pear
Allegheny Serviceberry
Downy Servicebery
American Smoke Tree
Common Smoke Tree
Japanese Snowbell
Japanese Stewartia
Korean Stewartia
Tall Stewartia
Shining Sumac
Smooth Sumac
Staghorn Sumac
Sweet Gum
Tulip Tree
Yellowwood
Zelkova

TREES WITH INTERESTING BARK

American Beech	Winter King (Green) Hawthorn
European Beech	Shagbark Hickory
Japanese Birch	Japanese Maple
Paper Birch	Paperbark Maple
River Birch	London Plane Tree
Higan Cherry	Japanese Stewartia
Sargent Cherry	Korean Stewartia
Yoshino Cherry	Tall Stewartia
Amur Chokecherry	Sweet Gum
Chinese Elm	Yellowwood
Chinese Fringe Tree	English Yew
Goldenchain	Zelkova

TREES THAT ATTRACT BIRDS AND OTHER ANIMAL LIFE

American Arborvitae	American Elm
American Beech	Balsam Fir
European Beech	Fraser Fir
Japanese Birch	White Fir
Paper Birch	Chinese Fringe Tree
River Birch	White Fringe Tree
Ohio Buckeye	Black Gum
Red Buckeye	Cockspur Hawthorn
Yellow Buckeye	English Hawthorn
Horse Chestnut	Lavalle Hawthorn
Red Horse Chestnut	May Hawthorn
Amur Chokecherry	Washington Hawthorn
Japanese Crab Apple	Winter King (Green)
Sargent Crab Apple	Hawthorn
Flowering Dogwood	Mockernut (Hickory)
Kousa Dogwood	Pignut Hickory
Pagoda Dogwood	Shagbark Hickory

Shellbark Hickory
American Holly
English Holly
Eastern Redcedar (Juniper)
Rocky Mountain Juniper
Southern Magnolia
Amur Maple
Hedge Maple
Norway Maple
Paperbark Maple
Red Maple
Sugar Maple
Silver Maple
Bur Oak
Chinquapin Oak
English Oak
Live Oak
Northern Red Oak
Pin Oak
Scarlet Oak
White Oak

Callery Pear
Austrian Pine
Eastern White Pine
Himalayan Pine
Japanese White Pine
Mugo Pine
Red Pine
Scotch Pine
Downy Serviceberry
Colorado Blue Spruce
Norway Spruce
Serbian Spruce
White Spruce
Shining Sumac
Smooth Sumac
Staghorn Sumac
Sweet Gum
Tulip Tree
Black Walnut
English Walnut

GOOD CITY TREES

Green Ash
White Ash
River Birch
Catalpa
Red Horse Chestnut
Japanese Crab Apple
Bald Cypress
American Elm
Chinese Fringe Tree
White Fringe Tree
Golden Rain Tree

Black Gum
English Hawthorn
Washington Hawthorn
Winter King (Green)
　 Hawthorn
American Holly
Honey Locust
Eastern Redcedar (Juniper)
Chinese Juniper
Katsura Tree
Littleleaf Linden

Norway Maple	Austrian Pine
Red Maple	Scotch Pine
Silver Maple	Allegheny Serviceberry
Sugar Maple	Downy Serviceberry
Pin Oak	Western Serviceberry
Red Oak	Shining Sumac
Osage Orange	Smooth Sumac
Japanese Pagoda Tree	Staghorn Sumac
Callery Pear	Zelkova
London Plane Tree	

TREES TO GROW IN CONTAINERS

Atlas Cedar	Golden Rain Tree
Red Horse Chestnut	Winter King (Green) Hawthorn
Citrus Trees	Amur Maple
Hinoki False Cypress	Japanese Maple

CHAPTER THREE

Planting and Caring for Your Tree

Now that you've picked your tree and decided on your site, you have to do what you can to give your tree the best chance of thriving in your yard. Prepare the site before you bring the tree home from the nursery so that your tree doesn't dry out as you prepare to put it in the ground. If planting immediately is not an option, prep the site and put the tree in the ground as soon as possible—waiting to be planted stresses it and may affect its ultimate success.

A PLANTING PRIMER

Planting a tree is actually very simple and requires only that you be attentive to some basic details about when you plant, how you plant, and what you do after you plant. Don't fudge the details—or cheat on any of the six simple steps for planting that follow—or your tree will be at a disadvantage from the get-go.

WHEN TO PLANT

The best time to plant any tree is in the dormant season where you live. In the deep South, that would be late fall to midwinter,

while in the North, it's early springtime, after the last frost and before buds have broken open and new growth appears on a tree. Bare-root trees are available only in the spring and that's when they should be planted. Balled-and-burlapped trees should be planted in early spring, before bud break, or in early summer (mid-Junish) when new growth has tapered off. Technically, container trees can be planted at any time during the growing season, but, as with any tree, they are best planted just before or after the new growth stage. Planting container trees—especially evergreens—in the fall can be risky if you live where there is the danger of early frost. If you want to get container trees in the ground before winter, do it in the early fall, well before any chance of a hard frost. And plan to mulch thoroughly to protect from early freezing of the soil.

Six Simple Steps for Planting Your Tree
1. Dig.

    For a balled-and-burlapped tree, loosen the burlap from the trunk so that you can determine the location of the root collar (where the roots begin to branch from the trunk). Dig a wide, dish-shaped hole that is at least three times wider than your root-ball, and just deep enough to accommodate the entire root-ball up to the trunk flare. Break up the compacted soil on the sides of your hole, but leave the bottom soil firm.

If you're planting a seedling or bare-root tree, dig a hole that is at least three times wider than the tree's straightened root system, and deep enough to accommodate the roots when you set the tree in the hole.

2. Prep it.

If you are planting a container-grown tree, remove all the container materials, including any netting, wires, or ties, just prior to planting. For trees in wire baskets, cut and remove all of the wire. If the roots are pot-bound, with a mass of roots encircling the root-ball, use a sharp knife to make four or five evenly spaced vertical cuts on the sides of the root-ball, about one-half-inch deep. When you set the tree in the hole, carefully spread the roots outward. Any time you cut the roots to prepare the tree for planting, you need to get the tree in the soil and watered quickly because the roots are stressed and vulnerable to drying.

For a balled-and-burlapped tree, remove all burlap wrap and twine after setting the tree in the hole. Prune dead or crushed roots and straighten or cut bound or circling roots, making clean cuts with a double-edged hand pruner. Again, work quickly if you have to cut.

Remove a seedling or bare-root tree from the tube, bag, or pot and carefully straighten and spread the roots. Place the roots in the soil immediately (so they don't dry out).

3. Set it.

Set your seedling or bare-root tree in the hole so that the root collar (where the roots meet the stem) is about two inches higher than the surrounding soil. This will allow the soil and roots to settle so that the root collar is eventually even with the surrounding soil. Spread the loose roots and begin to cover them with soil by hand, being careful not to

While It Waits

After all the researching, shopping, transporting, and prepping you're doing for your new tree, don't neglect to care for it in that crucial period just before you plant. Keep the material housing your bare-root tree moist, but not soggy, and store the tree in a cool, shady place. Your balled-and-burlapped and container trees need water and shade, especially just after you get them home. If you're not able to plant right away, keep the soil ball or container watered but not supersoaked, especially just before planting.

kink or sharply bend the roots. Add most of your backfill, going slowly so as not to unsettle the tree. Gently water, then add the remaining backfill and water again. Tamp the backfill lightly, not firmly.

Set a balled-and-burlapped or container tree in the center of the hole and make sure all container, wrap, or tie materials are removed completely. A large balled and burlapped tree can retain its metal netting. Fiddle with the tree's position by adjusting the rootball—tugging at the tree by the trunk can harm the roots. Put the backfill in the hole and then water slowly.

Arrange a little raised rim of dirt around the edges of your hole that will create a reservoir to help the soil hold water in the weeks after planting.

4. Water it.

Water your new tree slowly but thoroughly after planting, filling the reservoir and making sure the soil is watered deeply, not just on the surface. Water until air bubbles stop coming to the surface of the water; this means you have achieved a good integration between

Good Soil

The soil in which you plant your tree will be its home for several decades, if you make sure it's good soil. Good soil is not compacted and allows easy access for the tree's roots to grow in all directions. Good soil drains well but also retains water like a sponge. Good soil hosts an active population of creatures from earthworms to helpful bacteria that provide nutrients for the tree and improve the soil's ability to drain and store water. If the soil you remove when you dig the hole for your tree doesn't have these qualities, now's the time to make it good soil. Mix your backfill well with 30 percent potting soil and 30 percent rich compost, and after planting your tree, use an organic mulch. Gardeners know how important it is to work with good, healthy soil. Tree growers should, too.

the roots and the soil. When I water after planting, I like to give the soil a weak shot (10 percent to 20 percent strength) of Miracle-Gro, just as a kind of welcome-to-the-neighborhood gesture. Water again in a week, filling the reservoir slowly but thoroughly.

5. Stake it.

Many young trees need staking when planted, especially when they are at risk of not standing up to a strong wind. You should stake if you're planting in an undeniably windy area, if you're planting a tree that is top-heavy, or if you're planting a large evergreen (easy to topple) that might be roughed up by animals, equipment, or kids. The goal is to support the tree but give it enough flexibility to move and sway, acclimating to the rhythms of nature.

Old-school staking involved hoses, wires, and other restrictive materials that actually inhibited a young tree's growth. Today we use pieces of three-inch-wide soft rubber belt strapping,

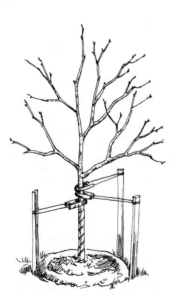

twisting them loosely at their midpoint around the tree and attaching them to a stake with a staple gun. Stabilize a tree with a trunk three inches or less in diameter with just one stake, positioned on the side facing the wind. A larger tree may need two or three stakes, positioned evenly around the tree. Hammer your stakes 18 to 24 inches into the ground, and make sure they're tall enough that no one will stumble over the stake strapping, which should be at least three feet off the ground. You may also need to protect your new tree with temporary fencing or tree shelters (see sidebar, p. 39) if you live in an area where deer are likely to help themselves to the tender plant.

You should be able to remove your planting stakes after a year or so, when the new tree has established a solid root system. Don't leave the stakes in the ground for longer than that because the tree needs to learn on its own to brace itself in the wind and inclement weather.

6. Mulch it.

Spread a loose three-inch layer of wood-chip or organic mulch over your entire planting area, being careful to leave about a six-inch ring of bare soil all around the trunk. The mulch is there to help your planting area absorb and retain moisture, reduce runoff in heavy rains, and slow the evaporation of moisture from the soil. Don't mulch too deeply or your tree will lose touch with reality! And don't even think about using landscape fiber or those polyethylene plastic sheets, which will cut off the air channel to the roots of the tree.

ROUTINE CARE OF YOUR NEW AND ESTABLISHED TREES

Your tree's in the ground, it's staked, watered, and mulched, and for the most part, you've done all you can to give your tree a good start in life. The maintenance requirements for your young tree—and the basic care of all of your trees—is simple, seasonal, and methodical. It pretty much amounts to mulching, watering, fertilizing, pruning, and protecting your trees from seasonal variables.

Mulching

The mulch you spread at planting will eventually decompose, so add more mulch from time to time to maintain a constant thickness of three inches, being careful to keep the mulch at an appropriate distance from the tree trunk.

The main reasons to continue mulching a tree after it has been established are to reduce evaporation, prevent erosion, control weeds, and, perhaps most important, to feed the earthworms and soil microbes that keep the soil healthy for the tree. A tree growing in healthy soil is less susceptible to disease and pests, as well as to environmental stresses such as heat, drought, and air pollution. The farther north you live, the more important it is to mulch—and stay mulched—to protect your tree.

Use chopped leaves for mulch, if possible. You can easily chop leaves with a mulching lawn mower or leaf shredder. Why chopped leaves? They cost nothing, the earthworms love them, and they don't mat up like whole leaves, preventing rainwater from saturating the area evenly. Avoid mulching with the leaves of black walnut, English walnut, or butternut trees, because these leaves contain juglone, a chemical that is toxic to many plants and trees. And never use grass clippings for mulch.

For the sake of convenience and aesthetics, most people use store-bought

Gimme Shelter

For small trees, an alternative to staking is the tree shelter. This is a photodegradable tube that gets placed over the newly planted tree and is staked firmly to the ground. The tube provides insulation from wind and temperature extremes, encourages a straight single trunk, and promotes growth because the tree reaches for the light at the top of the tube. The tube also prevents deer and rabbits from munching on your new tree and will remind the teenager mowing your lawn of the tree's presence—so it won't get mowed to the ground! Ask your nursery about tree shelters such as the brands Tubex or Blue-X.

Planting a Large Tree

As noted earlier, if you're planting a large tree, be sure you're working with professionals who have the equipment and manpower to make the planting a success. Planting like this (or transplanting, which is what it really amounts to) costs bucks—a couple hundred of them, on top of the considerable price of your tree—so choose a good planting site, a good, healthy tree, and work with a good company.

The nursery where you bought your large tree is likely to be the party transporting and planting it. So start by working with a top-quality nursery that is fully insured and offers a solid guarantee with the purchase of your tree. If the nursery is not doing the planting, work with an arborist who is fully insured, professionally certified, and highly recommended by his personal references.

Whoever is planting your tree will come with a giant tree spade that hydraulically forces blades into the ground to extract a big, conical plug of soil. There should be a 10-to-1 ratio between the diameter of the spade (anywhere from 20 to 96 inches) and the diameter of the trunk of your tree. This ratio is meant to ensure that the roots of your mature tree are undisturbed enough to spread in a new site.

Make sure the truck and equipment will have access to your site and room to maneuver—the trucks and equipment can weigh many thousands of pounds, and this operation should not, for instance, be trampling over your septic field. To increase your tree's chance of survival, you should plant in early spring, before its new growth begins, and giving time for leaves and roots to recover moisture lost during transplanting before the full heat of the season takes effect. Or plant in the fall, when cooler temperatures increase chances of the tree surviving and thriving.

Finally, double-check the location of your utility lines—and any other important site considerations—before the big dig begins, for obvious reasons. Now stand back and enjoy the spectacle of a big tree being planted. When your tree is in the ground, stake it broadly to stabilize for as long as a year or more, and water it generously. An hour before you plant, flood the hole one-third full with water to ensure a thoroughly watered soil. Then water again, per initial and long-term watering guidelines. Don't fertilize until the following growing season—now's the time for your mature tree's roots to heal and establish themselves, not for new growth.

wood chips or shredded bark as mulching material. These items are easy to get, not too expensive, and last about a year before needing to be supplemented. They're not quite as enriching to the soil as leaves, though, so you might want to put a layer of straw or pine needles underneath a top layer of wood chips to up the enrichment quotient. If you're lucky enough to have pine needles to collect in your yard, use them! Otherwise buy them at your garden center.

How much mulch? For young trees and smaller mature trees, the mulch should cover an area around the tree that is at least three feet in diameter. For medium-size trees (30 to 50 feet), the mulched area should be eight feet in diameter. And for large trees (taller than 50 feet), the mulch should be at least 12 feet in diameter. A layer of mulch three inches deep is plenty, though if you are using leaves, straw, or pine needles, you may want to start with four or five inches because the material

will compress by an inch or more after a few rains.

Be careful to keep the mulch at least six inches from the tree trunk, because the microbes and bacteria in the mulch may be great for the soil but are harmful to the tree's bark. And replenish your mulch before winter to buffer the soil from the effects of freezing and thawing, which disturbs shallow tree roots.

Watering

Newly planted trees need three inches of water a week for their first growing season, so pay attention to how much water the tree is getting from rain and supplement accordingly.

After your new tree's first growing season, water only when the soil feels dry at a depth of four inches. Just like your lawn, a tree doesn't appreciate frequent, light waterings; it much prefers deep, thorough soaks only when it needs them.

If you're getting plenty of rain (an inch or more a week), there's no need to supplement. But during a hot summer with no rain, a young tree will need water after a week or so without rain. A mature tree will begin to show signs of thirst in three to four weeks.

A sapling or small young tree can be watered with a hose or watering can. As the tree gets larger, you can water it more effectively with a soaker hose. To do this, spiral a soaker hose around the trunk of the tree, keeping about two feet between each hose loop for maximum coverage. Give the tree an inch of water per session. To determine when you've watered an inch, sink an empty tuna fish or cat food can into the soil and set the soaker hose on top of the

Fertilizing

Other than that shot of Miracle-Gro when you water after planting, you don't need to fertilize the tree during the first year because the starches already stored in the tree will stimulate most of its growing then. Extra fertilizing after planting only encourages leafy growth at a time when root establishment and development is most important.

Begin fertilizing in the late spring a year after planting. Some people like to fertilize once in the spring, but I prefer to fertilize regularly—from three to six times, depending on the length of the growing season. This fertilizing method provides the tree with a steady diet instead of an all-at-once feeding, which may not last the entire season. Trees are like people—they need a vitamin a day, not the whole bottle at a time.

can. Mark the amount of time it takes to fill the can an inch deep with water—the same interval will apply to the watering of your tree.

My fertilizing formula couldn't be simpler. For young trees, I use a liquid quick-release fertilizer like Miracle-Gro, diluted

Water Stress

Young trees, small mature trees, unmulched trees, and trees that grow in full sun or exposed to wind are more susceptible to water stress, which happens when the tree doesn't take up enough moisture from the soil to replace water loss from transpiration. Water stress can develop during long dry periods, severe hot spells, or after prolonged cold winds. Symptoms during the growing season include leaf droop followed by a drying of the foliage, especially at the leaf edges. You can stop water stress before it starts by paying close attention to your trees' water needs, especially the needs of those that are prime candidates for stress.

to 10 or 15 percent strength. For more mature trees, I use a water-soluble slow-release granular fertilizer, such as Osmocote, at 20 percent of the recommended dose. Some folks add biostimulants, which are shots of beneficial bacteria and organic nutrients you can feed your tree, from time to time. And there are species-specific mycorrhizal treatments you can use to promote root development and vitality. But I have too many trees to fuss with "snacks" like these, so I stick to my simple fertilizing formula for all my trees.

I truly believe that less food and more frequent feedings is the best way to have healthy, thriving trees. But if you have a lot of trees or are not up for multiple applications of fertilizer during the growing season, fertilize with Osmocote once a year in the North and twice a year in the South. Follow the directions on the bag for dosage, and spread the fertilizer using your hand or a drop spreader to within a few feet of the crown of the tree, never coming closer than a foot from its trunk.

Finally, don't think that just because your big old tree looks great that it's not hungry! Even the most mature tree welcomes the boost from annual feeding. If you're committed to fertilizing your trees throughout their lives, you'll make a big difference in their long-term health and happiness.

Pruning

There is rarely a need to prune a newly planted tree unless a branch has been injured or broken during planting. If, in the first year, any branches begin to cross or rub each other, bruising the tender bark, remove one of them.

After a year or two some structural pruning may be necessary. If your tree develops two competing leaders, or main stems, use a sharp pruning saw or loppers to cut off the weaker stem to encourage the development of a strong single trunk. Use hand pruners if stems or branches are no thicker than your thumb.

A homeowner should undertake the pruning of a mature tree under just a few conditions:

A Word about Tree Spikes

You may be tempted by the spike-form fertilizers that are so popular at your local garden center. Tree spikes may seem appealingly convenient, but they're most effective to use for younger trees because they can release fertilizer in a concentrated area. Tree spikes are not as practical for larger trees; to fertilize a mature oak tree properly, you'd have to use up to a hundred spikes. This could get expensive! My advice? Use spikes if you want to on younger or smaller trees and stick with the liquid and granular fertilizers for your larger trees.

- To remove damaged or diseased branches
- To remove lower branches that obstruct a view or path, as well as crossed or rubbing branches
- To thin the crown to allow for better light and air circulation and stimulate growth
- To shape the tree for aesthetic reasons

In the case of pruning a large, mature tree, always hire an arborist, who will have the right tools and technique for whatever is required. Even for smaller trees, it is best to attempt pruning only with the best tools and full confidence in your own judgment and abilities. Pruning is not that complicated, but I've seen too many trees suffer from overeager, uninformed pruning, especially in the thinning and shaping categories. You can either take a class to learn the art and science of that kind of pruning or let the professionals do it.

Except for emergencies, such as storm damage or disease, it's best to prune a tree in the winter or very early spring when it is still dormant. The trick to making a clean, effective cut when pruning is to use good tools properly. Wear gloves and goggles, and use sharp, clean tools. I use a double-edged hand pruner or a double-edged lopper for smaller branches, a pruning saw for larger branches, and a pole pruner for simple cuts that are beyond my normal reach.

PRUNING DECIDUOUS TREES

For a deciduous tree, pruning in winter, after the leaves have fallen, allows you to really see the shape and branching pattern of your tree in order to make effective

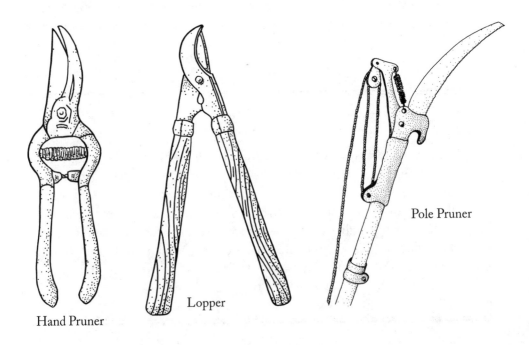

Hand Pruner

Lopper

Pole Pruner

choices about what to cut. It also allows the pruning wounds to heal faster during new spring growth.

There are two primary kinds of pruning cuts: *heading cuts* and *thinning cuts*. A heading cut shortens a branch by cutting off its tip and stimulates the dormant buds below that point to grow vigorously.

By using a hand pruner, you can cut the end bud off, cutting just to the point of the first lateral bud at an angle parallel to the bud. This will encourage growth in the direction of the first lateral bud.

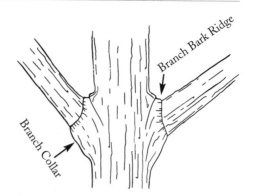

To make a heading cut on a branch with opposite buds, cut straight across just above the bud tips.

A thinning cut removes a whole branch at the point where it joins the main stem, larger branch, or trunk. You will use a thinning cut to remove dead, dying, or broken branches, crossed or rubbing branches, or a

branch with a narrow crotch angle, or to remove a branch that is too close to the ground. The key to a good thinning cut is to protect the stem and bark of the tree in order to promote effective healing after the cut. It is very important to make a thinning cut just *outside* the branch collar. The best way to do that is to use this three-cut method to remove a limb or branch:

1. With a pruning saw, make a small cut on the underside of the branch or limb you are removing, about 12 inches from the branch collar and not more than one-third of the way through the branch. This cut is intended to break the bark at this point to prevent a tearing of the bark and stem wood when you make your final cut.

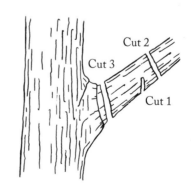

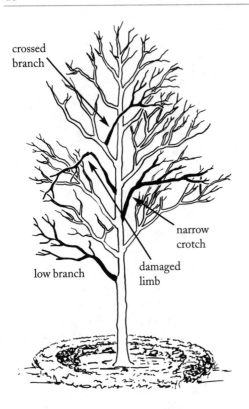

crossed branch

narrow crotch

low branch

damaged limb

2. Make a second cut a bit farther out along the branch or limb, starting at the top of the branch and cutting all the way through, leaving a stub end.
3. Make your last cut on the branch side of the branch collar, parallel and close to the stem collar but not flush with it.

This method protects the stem and any branches that might be growing from the stem, and it promotes effective healing after the cut.

PRUNING EVERGREENS AND CONIFERS

On a young evergreen or conifer, you can prune to encourage a strong, single leader and that characteristic pointed top. Unless you've trained evergreens into hedges that require trimming for shape, a large evergreen rarely needs pruning beyond removal of damaged or dead branches.

PRUNING FRUIT TREES

Techniques and tools for pruning fruit trees are the same as for all deciduous trees. Young fruit trees can be pruned for shape, either to have a central leader system or an open center shape in which the main trunk divides into three or four main branches. Fruit trees can produce a lot of sucker growth—those root shoots that come up from the ground not far from the trunk of the tree. Suckers need to be removed by pruning once a year.

To encourage growth, prune fruit trees in midsummer. Cutting stimulates the development of tissue at the wound site during the growing season. To thin a crowded interior and let some light and air circulate, remove branches that grow toward the inside of the tree.

A final word regarding pruning. Avoid "topping" a tree, or reducing its size by cutting back the trunk or major stems from the

How to Hire an Arborist

Whether planting, pruning, or removing trees, fertilizing or spraying insecticide, or cabling and bracing a tree, it's important to work with tree experts that are fully insured and have professional certifications, verifiable references, and good work they've done for someone else that you can check out for yourself.

When considering hiring an arborist, ask to see his or her certificate of insurance, including proof of liability for personal or property damage. Ask for proof of certification and membership in professional organizations such as the International Society of Arboriculture, the National Arborists Association, and the American Society of Consulting Arborists. Call references and inspect the contractor's work. Get estimates from more than one tree care company, not just to compare prices but to compare the companies' professionalism and the scope of their work.

When you've decided on a company, get a contract that spells out the start and end dates of the work, exactly what work will be done, descriptions of any pesticides or fertilizers that will be used, details on cleanup work for which the company will be responsible, details on what happens to any wood that is removed (cut and stacked for firewood, hauled off site, etc.), and whether the removal of a tree includes grinding out the remaining stump. And, of course, also find out the exact dollar amount you will pay for all this work.

An arborist's work is usually priced as a single fee for the entire job—per tree or per hour of work. If you're paying an hourly rate, be sure to get an estimate in writing of the time it will take to complete the job.

Good tree work can be expensive, but working with an excellent arborist is a good investment when you consider that fine, well-cared-for trees can contribute up to 15 percent to your property's value.

top. Topping can destroy the natural form of most trees, weakening them and making them vulnerable to decay, disease, and sunburn where the foliage has been shorn away. Topping is appropriate only for fruit trees, which may need to have their height contained, or for trees that are being trained to a specific shape.

TRANSPLANTING

There are times when moving a tree to a new location is the only way to save it from a bad site, relieve overcrowding, or simply to thoroughly enjoy its beauty.

For the most part, young trees tolerate transplanting well enough, especially if you do it in the fall after the leaves are gone and the growing period is over. This will give the roots some time to establish themselves before the tree pops back to life in the spring.

To prepare for transplanting, use a spade to cut the roots, cutting a circle around the tree roughly twelve inches in diameter for every inch of trunk diameter. Ideally this cut should happen a full year before you transplant, allowing new roots to grow inside that circle, which will reduce stress on the tree when you transplant it the following year. If you can't plan that far ahead, make your cut and follow the remaining steps.

Rake grass, mulch, and debris away from your site. Begin to dig out your tree, creating a root-ball 12 to 18 inches deep and at least 12 inches in diameter for every inch in diameter of trunk. Use your spade to cut roots on all sides of the root-ball. By now you should be able to tip and wiggle the loose tree. Lift the tree out of the ground and lay it on a good-sized sheet of burlap or tarp so that you can drag it to its new planting site. Use pruning shears to trim stray roots, then wrap the root-ball in burlap and twine to transport the tree to its new site.

Prep your new site in advance, and keep the root-ball moist until it gets settled into its new home. Then follow the "Six Simple Steps for Planting Your Tree" at the beginning of this chapter. Hire an arborist to transplant your mature tree, whatever the size, because he or she will have the equipment to give the tree a good chance for survival in a new location.

WINTER PROTECTION FOR YOUNG TREES

In northern parts of the country, some trees, especially young ones, are susceptible to damage from harsh winter weather, especially dry, cold wind and extreme freezing temperatures. Stress from rough winter weather can cause bark splitting, as well as dieback and the browning of evergreen leaves. Root systems can be damaged by soil that heaves as it freezes and thaws during a winter season that can't make up its mind. Branches often break under the weight of heavy snow or ice. And when spring comes, winter-damaged trees are more vulnerable to attack by insects and disease. Makes you want to hibernate, doesn't it?

There are a few things you can do to help your young trees make it through a tough winter. First off, mulch! As for all trees, a robust prewinter mulch is the best aboveground protection for the underground life of your tree.

To protect your trees from particularly fierce wind, you can set up wind barriers using stakes and natural burlap. Just be sure to leave a bit of space at the bottom to allow for air flow. Some people go even further and wrap evergreens such as juniper and arborvitae with burlap or a sleeve of netting and firmly wrapped twine (though with a generous bit of give).

Young, thin-barked trees such as ashes, honey locusts, lindens, maples, willows, and fruit trees are at highest risk for bark damage from extreme cold and sunscald during the winter. One way to protect the tree is to wrap the trunk with burlap or another natural tree wrap, all the way up to the area just below the lowest branches, securing the material with tape (be careful not to attach the tape to the bark). Remove

Winter Tree Prep

One warmish, sunny late autumn day is all you need to prepare each of your trees for winter weather. Inventory your trees, make a list of which needs what, and get to it.

Water. Give one last supersoak to any evergreens you feel are in danger of damage from a raging winter. After a summer of extreme heat or drought, also give a last watering to any mature trees you might be worried about.

Mulch. Spread a lush three inches of mulch—straw, chopped leaves, pine needles, or wood chips—to both feed and protect your beloveds in winter. Mulch will especially protect your trees from the cycle of freezing and thawing that so often disturbs their roots during the winter. As ever, keep mulch away from the trunks of the trees to prevent infestation and rotting.

Protect trunks. Surround your tree with wire mesh guards, pushed an inch or two into the ground around the trunk to prevent rodents and small animals from burrowing beneath it. Use tree shelters or wrap the trunks with burlap to protect against incursions by small animals and deer.

Establish windbreaks. Set up wind barriers with stakes and burlap to protect vulnerable trees. As with mesh guards and burlap wrap, this doesn't make for superior winter aesthetics, but if it's the only way to help your trees soldier through the winter, do it.

Spray. Spraying antidesiccants such as Wilt-Pruf on vulnerable evergreens will help prevent moisture loss from exposure to wind or winter sun.

What's in My Garden Shed

I'm often asked which products and tools I use in my work with trees. To be honest, my garden shed hosts a fairly simple array of items, nothing too fancy or expensive. My general rule of thumb is to spend good money on good pruning tools, and everything else can be as inexpensive as you like. Remember, I grew up in the Midwest where winterizing gear was important; but where I live now, in Florida, I just don't need burlap and the like, which you may very well need in your garage or shed. Here's the short list of good stuff I rely on when planting and caring for my trees:

- Double-edged loppers, for pruning branches
- Doubled-edged pruners, for work with small branches
- Pruning saw, for pruning large branches
- Pocket pruning knife, for cutting twine and trimming roots
- Hedge trimmer, for shaping my hollies
- 12-foot fiberglass pole pruner, for pruning high branches (I use fiberglass because it needs to be strong to do the job, and wood pole pruners are too heavy.)
- Garden spade
- Trenching shovel (with a long, narrow head) for planting and transplanting
- Post hole digger, for easy planting of ten-gallon trees
- Hard rake, for raking and loosening soil before planting
- Leaf rake
- Tree shelters for new plantings
- Cypress mulch
- Miracle-Gro and Osmocote

Note: The three things I advocate spending money on are your lopper, hand pruner, and pruning saw. There's a big difference between the cheap ones and the expensive ones, and in the case of these tools, it's worth it to pay more.

the tree wrap and tape in early April to avoid girdling (a bruising or pinching damage to the trunk) and insect damage. You may want to wrap your trees for several consecutive winters until the bark thickens and is less prone to winter damage.

Winter-hungry rodents and rabbits gnaw the bark near the bottom of a tree trunk, inhibiting the flow of nutrients up and down the plant, which can lead to the death of a tree. Deer will also have their way with whatever looks tasty on the surface of a young tree. A burlap barrier or tree shelter will protect your tree from all of these marauders.

Winter sun and wind are enemies of young (and mature) evergreens in the North, drying and burning exposed foliage. Screen and mulch your young evergreens, and water them deeply with a soaker hose before the ground freezes, enough so that the ground is wet to at least 12 inches deep, if possible. You can also spray your evergreen with an antidesiccant (ask for it at your garden center) to prevent moisture loss through the leaves during winter months.

CHAPTER FOUR

Handling Your Tree Problems

There are certain insect, disease, animal, and cultural problems that you may encounter with your trees, depending on what kinds of trees you have, where you live, and how you care for your trees. Young trees are especially vulnerable, so to protect your investment of time and money, watch your trees carefully, and attend to any problems as soon as you spot them. Mature trees are less vulnerable, but when you see a problem, bring in a tree professional to help you prune or spray, as Barney Fife would say, to nip the situation in the bud.

Before I start describing some common problems you may encounter with your trees, I must note that in many cases a tree is already in trouble before the insect or disease arrives. For many trees, the pest or disease is a symptom of some underlying stress or cultural problem that threatened the tree in the first place. So you can spray for the bugs or eliminate signs of disease, but you should really ask yourself what the root cause of the problem is. Has the tree been weakened by rough winters or dry, hot summers? Have you slacked off on mulching, fertilizing, and soil enrichment and now your tree is nutrient starved? The point is, if you're not doing basic ongoing

health maintenance for your trees, you're putting them at risk of inviting pests and disease further down the road.

By staying on top of annual fertilizing and, if necessary, supplemental watering, you can ensure your tree isn't hungry or thirsty. Mulching is an important part of thwarting a tree's hunger and thirst, but it's also key to nurturing the earthworms, microbes, and beneficial bacteria that keep your tree soil healthy. Good mulch also provides a critical habitat for the ground beetles, ants, and spiders that help control the bad kinds of insects on a tree. A healthy population of soil surface insects can control up to 50 percent of the pest insects that visit your tree.

WHAT'S YOUR TREE PROBLEM?

Even though there are hundreds of pests and countless diseases that might affect your trees, problems you will encounter fall into familiar categories (trunk or bark damage, leaf or needle discoloration or damage, etc.) that help you take corrective steps. The first thing to remember is that not all trees suffer from all pest insects and diseases. Each tree family (like people!) has its own problems, and usually a certain few insects and diseases are particular to that family. When your tree develops a symptom, refer to the Common Symptoms table in each tree profile in part two of this book and you'll get a good idea of the likely suspects for that particular tree.

PEST INSECTS

Specific symptoms will help you identify the pest insect you're dealing with. In most cases, pest insects attack the tree's youngest and newest growth, so examine the leaf surfaces and undersides (where most insects and their eggs are found), as well as the point where leaves are attached to the stem. Common symptoms of pest attack include:

- Leaves chewed on the outside edges
- Holes chewed in the middle of the leaf
- Defoliated branches
- Wilted, discolored, or speckled leaves
- Curled leaves
- Holes in bark

The Common Symptoms table in each tree profile will help you narrow down your possible culprits, based on the symptoms you observe.

Once you've determined that the cause of your tree problem is a pest, you want to move swiftly to control or eliminate it. I prefer to use insecticide as a last resort, but sometimes the only effective tool for dealing with pest insects is an insecticide that targets your particular pest. Whenever you encounter a problem with pests, you should first consult your local nursery to find out what products are most effective in your area, because what works in one location on a certain pest may not work as well in a different location.

Whatever product you decide to use, follow the directions for dosage and application very carefully for your own safety and to get the full effectiveness of the treatment. Never spray on a day when there is wind that might carry the chemical where it doesn't belong. Wear rubber gloves, goggles, and a face mask to protect yourself when working with insecticides.

Some people prefer to use natural insecticides, such as neem, dormant oil, Bt (*Bacillus thuringiensis*), or products containing rotenone and pyrethrin. Neem is

Feed the Birds!

Besides growing trees that birds like to visit, you can go further and encourage them to stay. Feed them, give them water, set up birdhouses in a variety of locations in your yard. A healthy population of songbirds can be a tremendous help in controlling the pest insects that show up in your yard.

an organic insecticide, insect repellent, and antifungal that is sprayed on a plant and works against many pests that feed on that plant. Dormant oil is a refined oil that is applied to the bark of trees and smothers dormant insects on the tree by smothering them to death. Bt is a biologically-based pesticide that kills insects that ingest it. And rotenone/pyrethrin-based products are contact insecticides, killing the pests with which they come in contact. I like a natural product called Sevin, which is mixed with a mild liquid soap like Ivory and applied by spraying.

Synthetic insecticides include those that contain permethrin and resmethrin. These are toxic contact insecticides, very effec-tive on certain pests, but to be used selec-tively and with care. Natural pesticides tend to be less potent than the synthetics, so it's important to get total coverage on both the tops and bottoms of the leaves, which is not always easy. Synthetic products pack a more powerful punch, and tend to have a residual effect. I don't endorse natural over synthetic or vice versa. I just use the prod-ucts that work to solve my problems.

COMMON TREE PEST INSECTS

Following are the most common pest insects that might attack your tree, listed

Cultural Conditions That Stress Your Tree

A tree under stress is the most vulnerable to pests and disease. Common cultural factors to be aware of that may affect your trees include:

- Soil compaction
- Soil that is either too wet or too dry
- Soil that is nutrient-deficient
- Overly acid or alkaline soil
- Too much nitrogen-rich fertilizer
- Too much or too little light
- Air pollution
- High winds
- Pesticide damage
- Winter damage
- Transplant shock
- Crowding within the structure of the tree, limiting air circulation and light
- Age

alphabetically, including details regarding symptoms and recommendations on solutions.

Adelgid, Woolly

Symptoms—White, cottony masses on branches, especially near young tips.

An aphidlike insect, the hemlock woolly adelgid is by far the most serious pest for Canadian and Carolina hemlocks, killing whole forests of them from New England to North Carolina. Adelgids feed on the sap at the base of hemlock needles, primarily on new twig growth beginning on the lower branches. Needles turn gray, then yellow, and then drop off. Branches die back, and growth is slowed. Untreated trees usually die after four to eight years, depending on their size, stress level, and location. Trees of all sizes and ages are attacked. Adelgids reach maturity between late winter and early spring at the base of individual needles, covering themselves with white, cottony wax for protection. Under the cottony wax, they lay brownish orange eggs that hatch from February through June. Wind, birds, and animals spread the eggs from tree to tree throughout the spring.

Solutions—Because these pests thrive

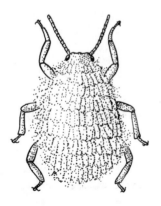

on trees rich in nitrogen, do not fertilize infested hemlocks. Up to twice as many adelgids survive on fertilized hemlocks as on unfertilized trees.

During the newly hatched nymph stage, the adelgid is very vulnerable to control by appropriate natural insecticide sprays, insecticide, insecticidal soap, or neem. Thorough coverage is important, so use a compression sprayer for good control. Some synthetic solutions are also appropriate. Consult your garden center on the best products for your area. If your tree is large, it's probably best to hire an arborist to spray to ensure total coverage. If you're doing it yourself, follow the label instructions carefully.

Special note—Avoid placing bird feeders near hemlocks, as birds pick up adelgid eggs and nymphs in their feathers and spread them to other trees.

Aphid

Symptoms—Pale or yellow spots, needles or leaves that are curled and distorted.

Aphids are soft-bodied, pear-shaped insects that cluster on growing tips, new leaves, and flowers of many trees. They may be green, brown, or pink, and while they are usually only about the size of a pinhead, aphids vigorously attack tree needles or leaves, sucking their sap and causing them to turn yellow and curl. These insects also secrete sticky "honeydew" that coats the foliage and encourages the growth of sooty mold fungus, which then coats the leaves in black.

Solutions—To control light infestations, spray the undersides of the leaves with a firm spray of water three times, once every other day, in the early morning. This knocks the aphids off the tree, making for

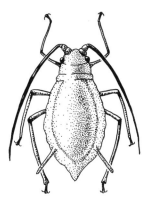

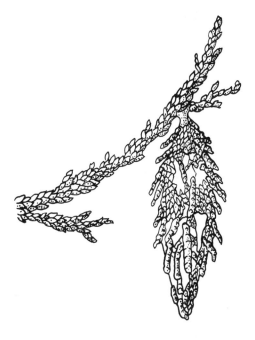

a very appealing lunch for ants and spiders in the grass.

For a light to moderate infestation, spray with insecticidal soap or neem every three to five days for two weeks. If the problem is serious, use an appropriate natural or synthetic insecticide every five to seven days until the pests disappear. Be sure the insecticide thoroughly covers the undersides of leaves and the area at the stems where the leaves connect to a branch.

Bagworm

Symptoms—Tiny "bags" hanging on branches, needles have been eaten, tree looks sickly.

Bagworms are little caterpillars that build their "houses" right around their bodies on the needles of your tree. Each casing is woven of silk and bits of needles. Dark brown with white or yellow heads, these bagworms carry their bags with them as they feed on foliage. They can kill a tree if left uncontrolled. A fully developed bag is about two inches long and protects up to one thousand eggs over the winter, which hatch the following spring.

Solutions—During the winter, handpick the bags from the trees and burn them.

In the late spring and early summer, after the caterpillars have emerged, spray evergreen tree foliage with natural Bt (*Bacillus thuringiensis*) just as the young caterpillars begin to eat the leaves. Repeat every ten days through mid-July so that as many caterpillars as possible ingest the bacteria as they eat and eventually die.

Beetle, Asian Long-Horned

Symptoms—Holes narrow and deep enough to accommodate a pen, occasional sawdust piles at the base of the trunk, dead branches.

The Asian long-horned beetle is a new introduction to American insect populations, currently seen in the eastern mid-Atlantic and around New York state. This large black beetle has white spots, and bores into the trunks of many kinds of shade trees. Larvae can be large (up to 1½ inches) but are never seen because they are con-

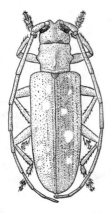

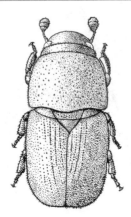

cealed as they bore through the wood. Unfortunately this borer attacks the tops of trees first, and the infestation spreads downward, making it very difficult to spot them early enough to control them. By the time you become aware of the problem, severe damage has been done and most trees that are infested will die. These beetles will attack almost any shade tree, especially maple, elm, ornamental cherry, beech, and ash trees.

Solutions—Because they are relatively new on the scene, little research has been done on how to control their damage, although Sevin and soap may be effective if your problem is detected early. When a mature tree has been infested with Asian long-horned beetles, the tree is usually removed.

Beetle, Bark

Symptoms—Holes in bark, bud and twig damage, needles or leaves that turn yellow.

Adult bark beetles are short-legged, stout, and about one-eighth inch long. The young beetles are soft and yellow and eventually turn dull brown. These pests are especially dangerous after a prolonged drought. Beetles attack trees in the spring, starting at midtrunk, working both up and down. They are attracted to trees already weakened by injury or other stressors. Their larvae, or grubs, bore through the outer bark and excavate tunnels in the sapwood. Emerging adult beetles leave tiny holes in the bark. The foliage on affected trees goes yellowish green from 10 to 14 days after an attack.

Solutions—There are no 100 percent effective controls for this problem. Your best defense is to keep trees in good health through proper feeding and watering. No natural products exist to help control bark beetles, though Sevin and soap can be somewhat effective. Remove severely infested trees.

Beetle, Japanese

Symptoms—Holes in leaves and flowers, usually on the inside of the leaf.

Japanese beetles converge in droves, skeletonizing the leaves of many trees and destroying their flowers when they are in bloom. Their grubs (larvae), called "white grubs," sometimes attack tree roots, which can be very harmful if the tree is young. Adult beetles are one-half inch long, with shiny metallic-green and copper-brown

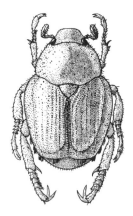

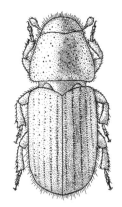

wing covers. Beetle larvae are grayish white, with dark brown heads. Fully grown grubs are plump, one-half inch to one inch long, and lie in the soil in a distinctive arc shape.

Solutions—Where possible, handpick the beetles from trees and drop them into a pail of soapy water. They are easiest to knock off the plant in early morning. Otherwise, these beetles can be controlled by neem or an appropriate natural or synthetic insecticidal spray.

Beetle, Pine Bark

Symptoms—Yellowish needles, tunnels in bark.

Adult pine bark beetles are stubby and about one-eighth inch long. The young beetles are soft and yellow, eventually turning brown. The beetles attack pine trees in the spring, starting at midtrunk, working both up and down. Their larvae, or grubs, bore through the outer bark and make tunnels in the sapwood. Emerging adult beetles leave holes in the bark. Affected trees show yellow-green foliage from 10 to 14 days after an attack.

Solutions—Keep trees in good health through proper feeding and watering. No natural products can control these beetles,

but appropriate synthetic insecticides can be effective. Check with your local nursery for the best product for your area. Remove severely infested trees.

Borer

Symptoms—Holes in trunk and branches, smaller limbs girdled, sawdust at holes.

Borers are the larvae of certain moths and beetles that tunnel under and feed off bark, causing girdling and branch dieback. Borers prey especially on trees that are weak due to drought, transplanting, bark wounds from yard-care equipment, or insect attack. Look for the telltale holes in stems, which may have sawdust around their entrance.

Solutions—The best preventive strategy against the borer is to try to maintain the overall health of your tree. Proper fertilization, watering, and pruning of damaged branches are important. Because newly transplanted trees are at risk, prevent borer attacks by wrapping the trunk and largest limbs with burlap or commercial tree wrap material for their first season. Insecticides can be effective, but the timing of your spraying is critical—insecticide must be on the bark for the small window of time (two weeks) between when the eggs hatch and

the borers enter the tree. Spray the trunk and main limbs (not foliage), especially in crevices or around bark wounds, where eggs may have been laid. Or wrap the affected area with burlap and spray the burlap with insecticide, as it will retain the insecticide longer than just spraying the trunk.

Budworm

Symptoms—Needles and buds eaten out, defoliation.

Larvae of this small moth are among the most serious pests of needled evergreens. The larvae grow to be inch-long caterpillars, brown with yellow stripes down the sides. In the spring they feed heavily on needles and then on the new buds, after which they weave messy silken webs and pupate inside. A serious infestation can defoliate an entire tree.

Solutions—Spray the foliage of affected trees as soon as young larvae appear with the natural insecticide Bt (*Bacillus thuringiensis*). Cover both sides of the needles so that the caterpillars will eat the bacteria and die in a matter of days. Spray two or three times at five-day intervals while the worms are eating. Sevin and soap or

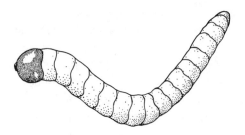

appropriate synthetic insecticides can also control these pests.

Carpenter Ant

Symptoms—Piles of wood fragments found beneath slitlike openings or nest entrances on a dead portion of a tree.

Carpenter ants are usually black and can be as large as one-half to three-fourths inch in length. Normally carpenter ants burrow into dead portions of standing trees, stumps, logs, or under fallen logs or stones. So if your tree has carpenter ants, you have a sick or dying tree. Carpenter ants can also invade a home structure and can cause serious damage to the wood portions of a building.

Solutions—Remove the dead parts of a tree that have become home to carpenter ants. Use synthetic insecticides designed specifically for carpenter ants. Check with your local nursery for the appropriate insecticide for your area.

Caterpillar, General

Symptoms—Leaves with holes or needles chewed at their edges or devoured completely, defoliation.

Caterpillars come in all sizes and colors since they are the larvae of many different kinds of butterflies and moths. When these hungry larvae emerge to feed on tree foliage, if present in sufficient numbers,

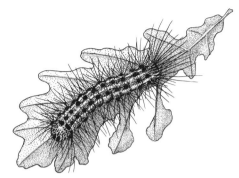

they are capable of doing serious damage to the tree.

Solutions—If the tree is not too large, handpicking can make an effective dent in most caterpillar attacks, especially if you catch the infestation at the outset. For larger infestations, spray foliage with the natural insecticide Bt (*Bacillus thuringiensis*), covering all the leaves or needles, especially the undersides, while the caterpillars are feeding. Spray every 10 to 14 days until the caterpillars disappear. Repeat spray if it rains just after spraying. The pests will ingest the bacteria and die within days. For overwhelming infestations, spray foliage with an appropriate synthetic pyrethroid-type insecticide. To be effective, this insecticide must contact the pest itself. Usually two applications, three to four days apart, are enough to reduce their numbers to the point where Bt can control them. Most appropriate synthetic insecticides will kill these caterpillars on contact.

Caterpillar, Gypsy Moth

Symptoms—Trees defoliated, tan egg masses on trunk.

Adult gypsy moth caterpillars can be more than two inches long, are covered with black hairs, and have five pairs of blue spots, six pairs of red spots along the back, and voracious appetites. In July they pupate by encasing themselves in brown shells attached to the trunks of trees. Gypsy moth larvae are often confused with the eastern tent caterpillar and fall webworm, both of

which make silken tents in trees. Gypsy moths do not make tents; look for the distinctive sawdust-colored egg masses on trunks, branches, under your roof eaves, and in other protected spots. The eggs look like little gold pearls. When infestations are heavy and uncontrolled, gypsy moth caterpillars can defoliate a tree completely.

Solutions—Young caterpillars emerge and start feeding in April and May, so do your best to catch them then. Spray the foliage of affected trees with Bt (*Bacillus thuringiensis*) every 10 to 14 days so that the caterpillars will ingest the bacteria and die. Gypsy moth caterpillars come down the trunk of the tree every morning to find a shady place to rest before returning upward in the evening for dinner. This makes them vulnerable to trapping. In June, when they are most active, trap the pests in burlap skirts wrapped around trunks, then scrape them into a bucket of soapy water. For large infestations, spray foliage with Bt, covering all the leaves or needles, especially the undersides, while the caterpillars are feeding. The pests will ingest the bacteria, sicken, and die in a matter of days. Spray every 10 to 14 days until the caterpillars disappear. Repeat spray if it rains just after spraying. If caterpillars become overwhelming, spray foliage with an appropriate synthetic insecticide. To be effective, this insecticide must make contact with the pests. Usually two applications, three to four days apart, are enough to reduce their numbers so that the Bt can then control them. Most appropriate synthetic insecticides will also kill these caterpillars on contact.

Caterpillar, Tent

Symptoms—Webbed nests in tree branches.

Tent caterpillars are black and hairy with white stripes and have narrow brown and yellow lines and a row of blue spots along their sides. These pests grow to be about two inches long in large silken nests in the forks of tree branches. They feed on tree foliage and, if left untended, can defoliate a small tree. Wild cherry trees are natural hosts for these pests.

Solutions—As with all caterpillars, your best strategy is to catch them early. If the tree is not too large, handpicking makes a sizable dent in most caterpillar attacks if you catch the infestation right away. You can wait until late evening or very early morning and, with a stick or pole, destroy the tents in which the caterpillars reside overnight. Dump the destroyed tents into soapy water. You can also spray tree foliage with the natural insecticide Bt (*Bacillus thuringiensis*) as soon as the telltale tents are visible. Continue to spray every five to seven days while the caterpillars are feeding so that they will ingest the bacteria and die. Most appropriate synthetic insecticides will also kill these caterpillars on contact. Check with your local nursery for the best insecticide for your area.

Lace Bug

Symptoms—Pale or mottled foliage.

Lace bugs suck sap from the undersides of leaves, causing the foliage to turn pale or mottled. The adults are small square-shaped bugs, three-sixteenths of an inch long or less, with elaborate wings that resemble lacework. This sucking insect appears in early summer. The good news is each variety of lace bug usually feeds on only one

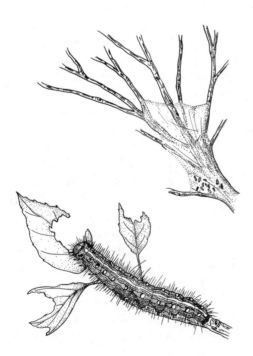

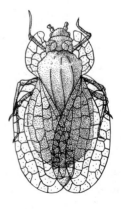

type of plant, so it's easy to isolate your problem.

Solutions—Control infestations by spraying the leaf undersides with a natural insecticide such as insecticidal soap, neem, or a locally recommended and appropriate synthetic insecticide spray.

Leaf Miner

Symptoms—Blistered and curled leaves, brown and dying leaves.

Leaf miners are tiny gray moths whose small greenish larvae overwinter in the "mines," or tunnels, they have eaten out between the upper and lower leaf surfaces. These "mines" look like squiggly white wandering lines on the outside of the leaves.

Solutions—Because the worms doing the damage are inside the leaf, common insecticides are not effective. Some systemic synthetic insecticides may be effective because they work inside the plant's leaves to kill the worms. Check with your local nursery for the best insecticide for your area. You can also trim out and destroy infested foliage. If necessary, prune back affected branches until only healthy growth remains.

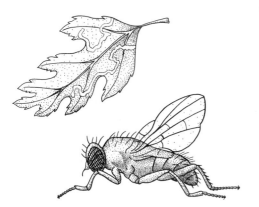

Mealybug

Symptoms—Cottony tufts on foliage and stems.

These insects gather in cottony white masses on a plant's roots, stems, and leaves, sucking sap and reducing plant vigor. As they feed, they secrete a sticky "honeydew" that attracts ants and encourages mold growth. Mealybugs are one-fifth to one-third inch long, oval, flattened, and covered with white, waxy powder. The telltale cottony tufts on leaves and stems are their egg sacs.

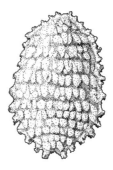

Solutions—Control mealybugs by spraying them with neem or the appropriate natural or synthetic insecticide.

Midge

Symptoms—Leaf tips die.

Tiny yellow maggots of a small fly

called a midge cause blisters at evergreen needle bases and kill leaf tips.

Solutions—Control midges by cutting off and destroying the affected plant parts. You can also spray the whole tree with a natural insecticidal soap, neem, or an appropriate synthetic insecticide. Spray trees with dormant oil in early spring to kill overwintering eggs.

Sawfly

Symptoms—Skeletonized leaves (only the midrib and veins are left), defoliation.

Adult sawflies are wasps but have thicker midsections and do not sting or bite. They are one to one and a half inches long, with two pairs of transparent wings. Their larvae, one-half-inch-long green caterpillars with black or white dots, devour needles and leaves and are capable of totally defoliating a tree. They are particularly devastating to young trees. Sawflies lay eggs on tree leaves in late spring. The larvae hatch and set to work eating the foliage from early to mid-summer.

Solutions—Try to catch an infestation of sawfly larvae in its early stages, when you can simply handpick the caterpillars and destroy them. With larger infestations spray the needles or leaves thoroughly with the natural insecticide Bt (Bacillus thuringiensis), as soon as you see the pests feeding. They will ingest the bacteria, which is lethal only to the caterpillars. Respray as necessary after rain. Some synthetic insecticides are also effective when used in direct contact with the caterpillars. Check with your local nursery for the best insecticide for your area.

Scale

Symptoms—Small bumps on needles or leaves.

Scale insects feed beneath the small bumps or blisterlike protective shells that they form as they crawl on stems and leaves. These shells may be white, yellow, or brown to black, and are about one-tenth to two-fifths inch in diameter. The first sign of a scale attack is often discoloration of needles or leaves, followed by needle or leaf drop. Some scale species also excrete honeydew, which coats foliage and encourages ants and growth of sooty mold.

Solutions—Control scale infestations by

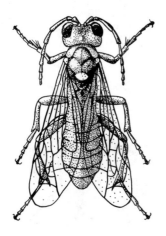

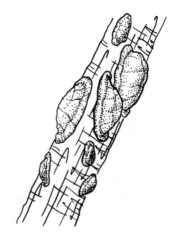

thoroughly spraying foliage with neem or an appropriate natural insecticidal soap or synthetic spray. In all cases, it may take two or three applications of any insecticide to solve the immediate problem.

Spider Mite

Symptoms—Needles or leaves discolored in summer; mini–spider webs evident where leaves join stems.

Spider mite damage usually shows up in the summer, when needles or leaves on affected branches turn bronze. Look for the tiny mites on the undersides of needles or leaves. Since mites are related to spiders, the presence of webs may also indicate mite infestation. Check for mites by shaking a branch over a white sheet of paper. If small, dark spots that move appear on the paper, you have spider mites.

Solutions—Mites can be very difficult to control, whether you use natural or synthetic products. You must use the insecticide several times if you hope to be successful. Spray foliage with an appropriate natural insecticide every three to five days for two weeks.

Webworm

Symptoms—Leaves and twigs webbed together.

Webworms are one-half-inch-long brown caterpillars with reddish brown stripes. The adult female moths appear in June and lay eggs that hatch in two weeks. The fully developed webworms appear in the late summer or early fall and spin webbed nests that enclose a tree's leaves and eventually kill them. Webworms are found on both the East and West coasts but

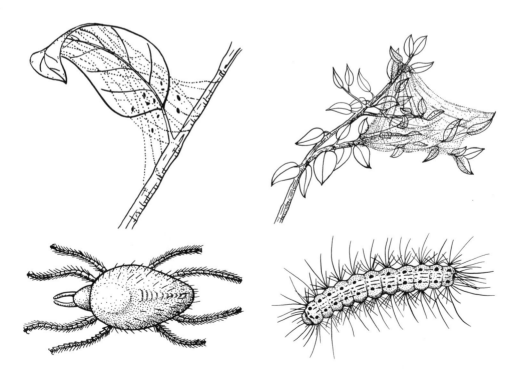

are most prevalent in the northeast and northwest.

Solutions—For a minor infestation, you can remove the nests by hand and destroy them by dropping them in a bucket of soapy water. For larger infestations, spray foliage with the natural insecticide Bt (*Bacillus thuringiensis*) when the worms begin feeding. Repeat sprays at weekly intervals for three weeks or more frequently if there is rain. Neem and certain natural insecticides can be effective, as can appropriate synthetic insecticides if sprayed directly on the worms.

Weevil

Symptoms—Needles turning yellow; weak, dying branches; leaves that are notched on the edges.

Black vine weevil adults are brown beetles with long snouts. They have tearshaped bodies with hard shells, averaging one-eighth-inch long. They feed on leaves and bark, leaving notches along the edges of needles or leaves. Weevil larvae, white grubs with brown heads, feed on roots deep in the soil. These pests are hard to

spot because they feed at night, living under tree bark and debris on the ground by day.

Solutions—Because these weevils "play dead" when disturbed, folding their legs and dropping from plants to the ground, they can be trapped easily. Go outside after dark and gently beat the branches of the infested tree, collect the weevils on a white cloth spread beneath the tree, and destroy them. You can also apply a sticky adhesive such as Tanglefoot to the trunk of the tree to prevent the adults from climbing up and eating the leaves. Make the sticky band about six inches wide and replace the material every week or so. Neem and appropriate natural and synthetic insecticides can be effective in dealing with weevils.

Whitefly

Symptoms—Weakened trees, yellow leaves.

Whiteflies are about the size of a pinhead. They are mothlike and have dusty white wings. These yellowish nymphs are legless, somewhat flat, and oval, and they resemble scale insects at certain stages. If you shake a tree infested with whiteflies, it

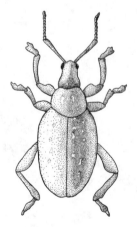 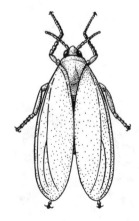

appears as though dandruff is flying off the leaves. Honeydew from the whiteflies drops on fruit and encourages fungal growth.

Solutions—Spray the whiteflies with a natural insecticide such as insecticidal soap or neem. Spray every two to three days for two weeks, making sure you spray the undersides of the leaves, where they reside. Certain synthetic insecticides are also effective in controlling whiteflies. Check with your local nursery for the best insecticide for your area.

DISEASES

The diseases you may encounter in your trees are caused either by a fungus, a virus, or a bacteria. Viral and bacterial diseases are virtually impossible to address, but they are not common in the home landscape. Fungal diseases are what you'll see and luckily, for the most part, they can be controlled effectively.

Fungi are plants that can't make their own food and so depend on organic matter for their nutrition. Fungi work with other scavenger organisms to break down organic matter and build the soil fertility that supports the plant life on which we all depend. The top foot of soil in a 1,000-square-foot planted area contains about 30 pounds of fungi, only a few types of which are harmful to trees. When you've ruled out pests as the cause of your tree problem, or if you have a kind of tree that is susceptible to fungus, consider whether your tree has a fungal disease.

Fungal diseases usually take several days or weeks to cause visible symptoms in your tree, your first clue it's not a bacterial or viral disease, which strikes very quickly and dramatically, in just a day or two.

WHAT DOES FUNGAL DISEASE LOOK LIKE?

A close look will usually reveal the following kinds of symptoms in one or more of these parts of your tree:

Roots: Root-infecting fungi usually live in the soil, causing decay of tree roots. Pale, wilted lower leaves signal roots that are swollen and discolored. Young trees displaying pronounced symptoms of this kind of fungal disease usually die.

Stems and twigs: Stem-infecting fungi cause blight, decay, dieback, and growths on the surface of the bark. Most of these fungi overwinter in dead stems or twigs and produce spores in spring or early summer.

Flowers, fruits, leaves, and needles: These fungi cause black spots, blisters, fuzzy white or orange coatings, or deformities on flowers and foliage.

For the most part, fungal-disease spores live quietly in balance with other organisms in your yard and soil. It is usually some kind of shift in conditions that triggers an attack on your tree. Typical conditions can include unusual weather, compacted soil, a change in available light or shade, even pesticide residue. Young or newly planted trees are particularly susceptible, as are most ash, hawthorn, magnolia, oak, and pine trees.

Once you've determined that the cause of your tree problem is a fungal disease, you should take action to control the problem. Fungal diseases are best managed with fungicides. Fungicides don't cure the disease; rather they allow you to stop its spread. When you spray healthy foliage with fungicide, spores have difficulty attaching themselves to it, and you've effectively prevented the spread of the disease. There are natural fungicides, such as neem, sulfur, and common baking soda, but only a few synthetic fungicides are available to the homeowner.

Whether you are using natural or synthetic fungicide, coverage is critical, because only those parts of the tree that are coated with fungicide are protected. Consult your local garden center about the best products to use for particular problems in your area. Follow directions carefully when preparing and spraying your tree, and plan to repeat treatments every week or ten days. For a large tree or a tree that exhibits serious symptoms of disease, consult a tree care professional.

COMMON TREE DISEASES

Anthracnose

Symptoms—Dead areas of the leaf along main veins, often in a V shape.

This is a leaf and twig disease, first affecting the leaf, then spreading to the twig. Several trees, including sycamore, maple, white oak, ash, and dogwood, are very susceptible to anthracnose. When the disease becomes severe, it deforms the tree, with the death of shoots and buds causing the plant to grow asymmetrically. When the fungus grows through the bud or down the leaf into the wood, it kills the branch. Inside the wood, the fungus grows as a canker. Each year's new buds, shoots, and leaves may become infected by spores on the cankered wood in early spring. The disease is most severe when springs are cool and wet.

Solutions—Ultimately the most effective control of anthracnose is to plant resistant trees in the first place. Otherwise, gather and destroy diseased leaves when they fall, replace your mulch, and prune away diseased branches, being careful to disinfect your pruning saw or loppers between cuts by dipping in a mix of hot water and bleach. Mature trees usually survive and regenerate leaves.

Fire Blight

Symptoms—Flowers and leaves wilted, bark cankered.

This bacterial disease is spread by insects and rain. Most prevalent in the Rocky Mountains and in western states such as Colorado and Nebraska, it is a major problem in certain types of fruit trees. New shoots may wilt suddenly in late spring,

encourages excessive growth and the spread of fire blight.

Leaf Spot

Symptoms—Dark spots and holes on leaves.

On the leaves of vulnerable trees, leaf spot fungi cause red spots that rot out and leave holes in the foliage. Heavily infected leaves turn yellow or brown and fall prematurely. Cool, moist spring weather encourages this disease when new leaves are developing. It is rather prevalent in ornamental cherry trees.

Solutions—Shake diseased leaves from the infected tree onto a disposable tarp and destroy them. Remove dead branches toward the center of the tree to allow bet-

turn black or brown, and die. The dead leaves hang downward on the affected twigs, giving the tree the appearance of having been scorched. It is a serious disease, capable of killing even a mature tree.

Solutions—Hire an arborist to treat a mature tree by pruning and spraying with a professional bactericide, rather than attempt to treat the problem yourself. In small trees, cut off affected branches at least three inches below the infected area between November and March. Before making each cut, disinfect the pruning saw or shears by dipping them in a solution of hot water and bleach. Control insect pests that carry the bacteria by spraying the tree with insecticidal soap or an appropriate insecticide. Do not fertilize a tree with fire blight; the nitrogen in the fertilizer ter aeration. Mulching helps prevent this disease from splashing up from the ground and infecting the tree. Spray weekly at ten-day intervals with sulfur or copper fungicide, starting when the blossom petals fall. Remove seriously infected trees, including the root system and soil ball.

Powdery or Downy Mildew

Symptoms—Leaves covered with white powder.

Powdery mildews and downy mildews are caused by fungi that live on the surface cells of the infected tree's leaves, not inside the leaves. Infected leaves are covered with a white or ash-gray powdery mold. Badly infected leaves become discolored and distorted, then drop off. This may be unsightly, but is not life-threatening to mature trees. Powdery mildews thrive in either very humid or very dry weather and on foliage that does not enjoy good air circulation.

Solutions—Spray the healthy foliage of affected trees thoroughly with sulfur fungicide. Collect and discard all tree debris in the fall. Prune out extra branches within the tree canopy to promote good air circulation.

Rust

Symptoms—Powdery orange spots on leaves.

Cedar-apple, cedar-hawthorn, and cedar-quince rust are common fungal diseases of apple and flowering crab trees. These fungi spend part of their life cycle on hosts such as apple, flowering crab, and hawthorn trees, and the other part on junipers, including eastern redcedar. Rust can cause defoliation and fruit damage on the flowering trees, while the effect on junipers is minimal.

Solutions—If you have redcedars in your area, pay attention to your susceptible flowering trees. Since rust grows wild all over parts of the central and eastern United States, this can be tricky. You can spray healthy foliage on crab apple trees with garden sulfur to protect them from the spread of the fungus.

Witches'-Broom

Symptoms—Shoots branch from lateral buds.

This odd viral disease causes clusters of two to six or more slender shoots on a branch, forming a "broom." These shoots branch freely from the infection point, producing leaves and sometimes blossoms. Small brooms may erupt all over the tree, killing the main branches and eventually

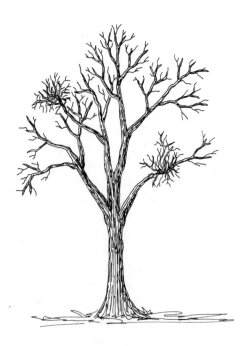

the entire tree. The disease may spread by means of grafts.

Solutions—Prune away and burn the brooms and injured branches. Spray the tree with fungicides recommended by your local nursery in the fall or early spring.

PEST ANIMALS

Pest animals are seldom as much of a problem for trees as are pest insects and other diseases. But try to tell that to someone who lives in deer country. Deer can be the most destructive animals you encounter in a lifetime of trying to grow things—and homeowners can spend a lifetime (and a fortune) just trying to thwart the deer. Though rabbits and mice can be a problem over the winter, they are much easier to manage than those pesky deer.

Deer

There are only two schools of thought about deer. You either love them, and make peace with their constant snacking in your yard. Or you hate them, and spend more time and resources than you probably ought to trying to thwart their behavior. I personally prefer a Zen-like approach to deer. Although that's easy for me to say, living where I won't see a deer—ever—munching on my trees and garden.

Unfortunately, in many areas of the country, deer, which are increasingly deprived of their traditional habitat, are devouring local landscape foliage as fast as it is planted. It is important to discourage deer immediately, because it is much harder to evict them once their feeding habits are established.

Symptoms of deer damage include:

Young trees nibbled to their base overnight.
Tender new growth at tips of small trees and shrubs nibbled off.
The lower stems of shrubs, trees, and woody vines stripped of foliage.
The bark on trunks of small trees torn and abraded by bucks rubbing off the velvety covering on their antlers in the fall.

When pressed with extreme hunger, deer will eat anything, including plants that are supposed to be "deer resistant." Trees that are ordinarily most appealing to deer include arborvitae, fir, certain types of holly, juniper, Leyland cypress, pine, and yew.

Deerproof Plants

Nothing is truly deerproof, but in general deer tend to ignore trees that are prickly, aromatic, or have hairy foliage. There is no guarantee that the deer in your neighborhood won't develop a taste for these trees, but historically some seem to be deer resistant, including black locust, false cypress, golden chain tree, maple, oak, and smoke tree.

Deer Strategies

Fences are about the only way to guarantee preventing deer damage to a yard, garden, and trees. Because deer are able to jump as high as six feet from a standing start, to be truly effective, a fence must be higher than eight feet. Fences are expensive, often unsightly, and just send the deer to forage more aggressively in your neighbor's yard.

Beyond fencing, most successful strategies for handling deer involve subjecting the animal to systematic aggravation. In essence, you insult the different senses of the deer (smell, taste, hearing, sight, touch) on a rotating basis. You can use a smell repellent for two weeks, then use a taste repellent for two weeks, and then use a motion repellent for two weeks. Many find that it takes a course of three to five different repellents, applied in different areas of your yard over a period of six to eight weeks, before seeing the deer move on. Unless of course the deer are starving, in which case no repellent is going to work for very long.

Deer Repellents

There are a number of repellents that may help you protect your trees from deer. Products advertised as "taste repellents" use various ingredients including rotten eggs, hot peppers, garlic, and a chemical called Bitrex, one of the most bitter substances known to man. You don't have to spray the whole yard, just a few strategic areas to upset the deer's feeding patterns. There are also smell repellents, mostly home remedies, including human hair, Irish Spring soap, and blood meal. Motion detector–activated floodlights and watering devices are effective in startling deer into moving on. And nothing beats the family dog, which can give chase and leave unpleasant doggy smells around the yard.

Mice and Voles

Roots of young trees, especially newly planted trees in the home landscape, are fair game for mice and voles. Voles leave holes in the surface of the soil that are about the size of a quarter. Mice and voles are known to move into mole tunnels and use them to gain access to tree roots. If there are no mole tunnels, mice will make their own. They can also gnaw at the ground-level bark of young shade or fruit trees, sometimes girdling and killing the trees. Tree-girdling usually occurs between October and April. Mice are generally active all year round. Commercial plastic tree shelters, tree bark guards, and tree wraps are effective in protecting tree bark from mice and voles.

Rabbits

The eastern cottontail and desert cottontail are the rabbits most likely to be found nibbling in residential yards. Rabbits favor a wide variety of perennial and annual flowers, vegetables, shrubs, berries, and clover. Unfortunately they also love tree bark, especially young tree bark.

Trees that have been damaged by rabbits have tree stems and leaves near the ground that have been nibbled down to the base. The lower bark and branches of certain trees may be chewed, sometimes damaging the tree enough to cause girdling and eventually kill it. Rabbit damage is easily distinguished from that of other pest animals by the type of cut on the nibbled branch or stem. Severed ends look as if they were cut with a knife, and the cut is diagonal rather than straight across.

Tree guards are an essential piece of equipment in the effort to fend off rabbits. To protect orchard or ornamental trees for the winter, wrap the lower portion of small tree trunks with commercial tree wrap, burlap, aluminum foil, or plastic cylinders. The wrapping or cylinder should be at least

18 inches above the height of the deepest expected snow.

After a snowfall, pack down the snow around the trees so that rabbits can't reach to chew on low limbs.

CULTURAL PROBLEMS

The trees in any home landscape can from time to time be vulnerable to problems caused by the weather or other physical conditions. These problems are known as cultural problems, some in your control, others not, but all responsive in some way to certain remedies.

Drought

A large shade tree can lose up to one hundred gallons or more of water a day through its leaves. Tree experts estimate that a large tree, when it experiences just one summer of drought with no water, will take five years to recover from the stress induced. After two years of drought, you can worry about some of your trees dying in three to five years because the tremendous, prolonged stress of drought has created an environment perfect for the invasion of pest insects and diseases.

If you live in an area that experiences drought, take steps right in the beginning to help a new tree prepare itself. Make sure the soil in which the tree is planted has lots of good organic material. That organic content will help hold more water in reserve when a drought hits. Having a three-inch layer of organic mulch around a tree will ensure that the organic content of the soil continues to be high.

When your area has had enough dry periods for the government to declare it to be experiencing a drought, you need to begin providing your trees with additional water, assuming your community allows you to do so. Often watering lawns is prohibited during periods of drought, but watering trees and shrubs may be allowed. Use a soaker hose to provide regular and thorough watering during dry periods. Remember that the younger the tree, the more vital it is to avoid drought stress.

Finally, if you can't water during hot, dry spells, then don't fertilize, prune, or apply pest controls. And resist disturbing the soil, as this will increase moisture loss.

Equipment Damage

Few homeowners realize how harmful a little nick from a lawn mower can be to the bark of a young tree, particularly during the late spring or early fall. Even the smallest wound in the thin, tender bark can cause its premature death in the years that follow. Wounds and abrasions weaken the tree, allowing disease and insects to gain access to the inner wood.

Avoid touching your trees with your lawn mower, your string trimmer, or other yard-care equipment. Mulching around the tree (which you should be doing anyway!) is the best possible way to keep these mechanical dangers to a minimum. Tree shelters also protect young trees from errant equipment.

Mistletoe

Broadleaf mistletoe is an evergreen parasitic plant that grows on a number of landscape trees, especially on the East and West coasts and throughout the South.

Ash, alder birch, live oak, silver maple, walnut, and zelkova are among the common hosts of mistletoe. Leafy mistletoes have green stems with thick, oval leaves and develop a roundish shape two feet or more in diameter. Evergreen clumps of mistletoe are easy to see on bare deciduous trees in winter.

Mistletoe robs both water and mineral nutrients from its host trees. Healthy trees can withstand a slight mistletoe infestation, although individual branches might suffer. Heavily infested trees may even die, especially if they're weakened by other problems like stress or disease.

To treat mistletoe, remove it before it produces seeds in the fall and spreads to other limbs and branches or other trees. Pruning is the most effective method for control, but complete removal is the only option for severely infested trees. Using thinning cuts, prune infected branches back to their points of origin. Severe heading cuts are used to remove heavy infestations, but this kind of pruning can weaken the tree's structure and ruin its natural form.

You can also treat dormant trees by spraying the mistletoe clumps with a plant growth regulator containing ethepon. Because this method only causes some of the mistletoe plants to fall off, this is not a comprehensive or permanent solution, but it may be a way to put a dent in the problem before it gets out of hand.

Salt Spray

Trees don't like the salty spray that's kicked up by cars on nearby roads in winter. When the water evaporates, it leaves a salt residue that can kill buds and twigs and damage your trees. Salt accumulation in the soil can cause early fall color, needle-tip burn, and browning on the leaves' edges.

There is not much you can do to protect your trees from such a spray of salt. But you can do something about the salty runoff that accumulates in the root zones of trees growing near the road. As soon as the soil thaws in the spring flush the soil with water. This should send salt deposits beyond the trees' root zones, where they can't harm trees.

Tree species vary in their susceptibility to salt injury. A vulnerable species such as the white pine should not be planted near roadsides where salt may be applied. For your own driveway, use sand or calcium chloride instead of salt, so you're not adding to the threat of salt harming your trees.

Sunscald

In cold-winter areas, the warmth of the sun on brilliantly sunny and clear days in January and February activates growth cells on the trunk of a tree. When the sun goes down, the temperature plummets, and the cold ruptures those cells and dries them out, causing the tree the equivalent of our skin swelling and peeling after a nasty sunburn.

To prevent sunscald from happening, wrap the trunks of trees exposed to southwestern sun with strips of burlap or commercial tree wrap and secure with twine. This will help reflect the sun and protect the tree from dramatic fluctuations in temperature. In March or April, when the weather turns milder, remove the wrap.

Surface Roots

Large trees in your yard often exhibit roots exposed above the surface of the soil, or

surface roots. These roots often get skinned by the lawn mower; they also buckle sidewalks, trip people walking in the yard, and look unsightly.

Surface roots are usually the result of heavy, poorly drained, or shallow soils that have low oxygen content. Because roots need oxygen to grow, these oxygen-deprived roots tend to form near the surface of the soil, then grow above it as they become larger. Surface roots can also become exposed by soil erosion.

Pruning surface roots can be dangerous to your tree and should be attempted only by a professional in the event that the roots are damaging driveways or sidewalks. Otherwise, cover the surface roots with no more than two inches of light soil (topsoil mixed with peat moss or sand). You can also plant a ground cover that hides and protects the roots from traffic, or apply mulch that extends to the area where surface roots appear, but never too close to the trunk.

How to Know When It's Got to Go

Usually you can tell when a tree is dead and needs to be taken down; it has no leaves and the bark is flaking off like dandruff. Other times it's not so clear, and it's good to get a diagnosis from an arborist (often free of charge). If the arborist says the tree is sick but might be saved, you have to decide how much effort and expense you're willing to put into saving the tree. Compare the proposed cost of treating the tree with the cost of taking it down.

If the tree is a sentimental favorite, you may well treat it, even if there's no guarantee it will be saved. But if it's not a favorite tree, and removing it will not devastate your landscape, taking it down may be the right thing to do. It's certainly the right thing to do with a diseased or dying tree that might imperil people or buildings if it falls in a storm. Save a tree if you can, and if you can't, plant two to replace it!

Winter Storms

Winter snow and ice storms can dramatically damage the trees in your yard. Snow accumulation on trees, especially evergreens, can build up and cause breakage. The more snow you can remove from endangered trees during and after a storm, the better. It is the accumulated weight that will cause the damage. The main rule is to never brush snow off a shrub or tree with a downward motion, because this may break the branch. Use a careful upward motion with your arms or a broom to relieve the plant of the excess weight.

When a major sleet or ice storm leaves a coating of ice on all branches of all trees and shrubs, the rules are different. First, do not try to remove any accumulated ice on branches of trees and shrubs; simply leave the ice alone. If the branch is not already broken, then it will be fine when the ice melts naturally. If you try to remove ice from the limbs of trees and shrubs, you will certainly cause more breakage and increase the existing level of damage. Even if the tree or shrub is bent all the way to ground under the weight of the ice, leave it alone.

Cleaning up the damage to large trees after a winter storm is dangerous under any circumstances. Do not try to remove damaged limbs from large trees. A tree that has fallen is often balanced on branches still underneath; only a tree professional should remove a large fallen tree, even if it is sitting on top of your house. A large branch that is broken but still hanging in the air is also dangerous and should be dealt with by a professional. These hanging branches are called "widow-makers" for a reason.

When a snowstorm is over or the ice has melted from the trees (or later, just before spring), remove all small branches that have been damaged on trees and shrubs that you can easily reach from the ground. Make a smooth cut, away from the damage, where good wood starts again. Hand pruners and loppers will handle most problems on branches up to two inches in diameter. Anything larger than two inches usually needs a pruning saw or a chain saw.

PART TWO

The Trees

As homeowners, we've never had a better, more vast selection of trees to choose from to plant in our yards. The last thirty years have seen an extraordinary increase in the numbers of new species and new cultivars of traditional species readily available through catalogs and nurseries. As with many situations in consumer America—which of the fifty cereals on my grocer's shelf should I choose?—sometimes too many options makes it harder, not easier, to decide.

It's for that reason this book is meant above all to be a practical resource, one you use when you plant and care for your trees and when considering tree possibilities for your yard. It is a guide not to every possible tree you could plant but to solid choices among those that are:

Available: No sense falling in love with some little-known, hard-to-get variety your local nurseryman has never heard of and you'll never find for sale. If you can't find it, you can't plant it, can you?

Viable: These are solid species, varieties, and cultivars—native and non-native—that can and do grow well in the home landscape. You don't want to spend time and money on temperamental, hard-to-grow trees when there are so many beautiful—and agreeable—alternatives.

Geographically representative: Excepting some extreme climates, such as the truly desert southwest, the tropical Deep South, and the harsh northernmost reaches, there are trees in this book that you can find and grow in your zone.

Following is a selection of practical profiles of my favorite trees for use in the home landscape, organized by shade trees, evergreen and conifer trees, and flowering and fruit trees. Each tree profile includes a description of the tree's appealing features, varieties and cultivars to consider, particular requirements for the tree (sun, soil, etc.), how to plant and care for it, special problems to look for, and at-a-glance details about height, spread, and zone requirements.

Note regarding height, spread, age, and zone data: there is little consensus among horticulturists on these kinds of details. It is not unusual to find, for instance, three different zone ranges cited in three different highly credible references. I represent as realistic an expectation as possible, taking into account modern environmental stresses, regarding height and age in the tree profiles that follow. In addition, the northernmost zone and the southernmost zone in the ranges I've suggested are the conservatively reasonable edges of the tree's comfort level.

Shade Trees

Shade trees have it all—the height, the shape, the structure. They've also got the leaves that give us the splashy show of yellows, reds, and oranges in fall. These wide-branching trees represent a tremendous variety, from medium to large trees in a range of shapes, from broadly rounded to vase-shaped and pyramidal. Think oaks and maples for their beloved traditional shapes. Or honey locust for its graceful spread and dainty leaves, giving a dappled shade. Or willow for its signature drooping branches.

Shade trees need space to spread and do their shade thing, so even if you crave a big shade-tree umbrella to cool your house in the summer, pay careful attention to your shade tree's space requirements for its canopy and roots. A well-placed, well-cared-for shade tree will be worth many times what you paid for it in comfort and added value to your home.

ALDER (*Alnus* sp.)

Top Reasons to Plant

- ᄵ Does well in moist, even wet, soil
- ᄵ Grows rapidly
- ᄵ Stabilizes wet soil
- ᄵ Is pest and disease resistant

The alder is a spectacular tree surrounded by legend and lore. Historically its uses have been both practical and symbolic: alder wood was fashioned into shields and clogs by Irish Celts and used by Celtic diviners to construct "wishing rods." Holistic healers used alder bark and fruit as remedies for appendicitis, rheumatism, gout, dropsy, and warts. And the ancient Greeks relied on the alder for protection against a huge range of evils, from witchcraft and demons to headaches and constipation.

The alder is a medium-to-large tree, and a true problem solver. Because alders are legumes, like peas and beans, they can absorb nitrogen from the air; this means they make much of their own fertilizer and improve soil quality while they're at it. This tree will grow where some fussy ones won't, such as in wet soils or even standing water. And it will help hold soil in place on the bank of a stream or swamp. Another incentive to plant an alder is that most species are fast growers—when allowed to grow without pruning, they can create a multistemmed sound barrier screen in just a few years.

While some alders are native to the United States, the most popular landscape species are from Europe. Of these, the European alder (*Alnus glutinosa*) is the one seen most in American home landscapes. But Italian alders are worth considering as well. Alders can serve as a specimen in the landscape, or be grouped in a fast-growing windbreak or visual screen. You can spot alders easily in the winter when their nut-like fruits hold on tightly to the branches. Check them out again in the spring and summer and you'll be impressed with their form and appearance. The easy-to-plant, easy-to-maintain alder surely deserves popularity in America.

European Alder
(Alnus glutinosa)

Also called common alder and black alder, the European alder grows in zones 3 to 7. It is fast-growing, gaining about two to four feet each year. Mature trees can have a 12- to 18-inch-thick trunk. When young, the tree has a pyramidal shape that becomes more oval or oblong as it matures. A full-grown tree is 40 to 60 feet tall, with a spread of 20 to 40 feet.

This alder is deciduous with dark green leaves that are two to four inches long and three to four inches wide. Those who have trouble bidding summer good-bye will appreciate that alder leaves remain bright green late into the fall, contrasting beautifully with the traditional yellows and reds of the season.

Flowers in early spring are yellowish brown pendulous catkins, later turning into large one-inch-long, egg-shaped fruits that resemble small pinecones. These "cones" will stay on the tree throughout the fall and most of the winter, providing some winter adornment while its neighbors remain bare.

EUROPEAN ALDER CHOICES

Imperialis is a small, graceful tree with delicately cut leaves, creating a soft effect in the landscape. An excellent screening tree, **Pyramidalis** is distinctly columnar, reaching 50 feet in height and 25 feet in width.

Italian Alder (Alnus cordata)

The Italian alder is unhappy in extreme cold, preferring zones 5 to 7. A pyramid-shaped tree with a rounded top, it's a bit shorter than its "European" cousin, reaching a mature height of 30 to 50 feet, with a 20- to 40-foot spread. Its dense, glossy, heart-shaped green leaves are two to four inches long, and its yellowish brown pendulous catkins appear in early spring. The Italian alder is similar to the European alder, but while the European shifts from a pyramidal form into a more oval shape as it matures, the Italian variety remains pyramidal throughout its life. The tree's skeleton is handsome in the winter after the leaves have dropped.

Requirements of Your Alder

Alders prefer to be planted in full sun, though they will tolerate partial shade. They're not too picky about soil, accepting clay, sand, or loam, and also tolerate a fairly broad pH range, from fairly acidic to slightly alkaline. They can survive in flooded soil for a short period of time, but prefer to spend most of their time in well-drained soil. They have moderate drought tolerance but require frequent watering if they are living in a dry spot.

Common Symptom	Likely Cause
Webbed nests in tree branches, chewed leaves	Tent caterpillars

Species	Scale at Maturity	Basic Requirements
European Alder (*Alnus glutinosa*)	Height: 40'–60' Width: 20'–40' Shape: Oval	Zones 3 through 7 Full sun/part shade Moist, well-drained soil
Italian Alder (*Alnus cordata*)	Height: 30'–50' Width: 20'–40' Shape: Pyramidal	Zones 5 through 7 Full sun/part shade Moist, well-drained soil

Planting Your Alder

The more care you take when you put your tree in the ground, the better it will do during its long life. Follow the complete planting directions provided in chapter 3.

Caring for Your Alder

Follow the instructions on seasonal care for young and mature trees—watering, mulching, fertilizing, staking, and pruning—described in chapter 3.

A special note: If you want a single trunk, you'll need to allow one stem to grow while pruning out the other leaders that might sprout up during the first few years. Prune your alder in the winter or early spring.

Special Situations for the Alder

True to its reputation as a problem solver, the alder is remarkably resistant to the diseases and infestations that plague other trees.

ASH (*Fraxinus sp.*)

Top Reasons to Plant

~ Fall color
~ Cold tolerance
~ Tolerance for poorly drained or high-alkaline soils

Years ago, I collected seeds from the green ash tree that towers over the humble white clapboard house in Denison, Texas, where Dwight Eisenhower was born. On Memorial Day 2001, members of nearly 5,000 VFW posts planted a quarter of a million new Eisenhower green ashes from those seeds as living memorials to veterans of World War II. The veterans developed "tree fever" as they participated in what was perhaps the largest one-day tree-planting event of all time.

Ash trees, which provide wood for about one million major league baseball bats every year, are rapid-growing large shade trees native to the United States. White ash (*Fraxinus americana*) and green ash (*Fraxinus pennsylvanica lanceolata*) are the most widely grown ash trees in North America. There are other species, such as black ash (*Fraxinus nigra*), blue ash (*Fraxinus quadrangulata*), and Oregon ash (*Fraxinus latifolia*), but none is as common as the white and green ash. Because of their large size, white and green ash are most effective as shade trees in large yards. Showcase them as specimens in an open lawn and enjoy their lavish color and generous shade.

White Ash (Fraxinus americana)

White ash develops a strong central leader and has abundant fall color. White ash is

the tallest in the ash family, reaching 50 to 80 feet at maturity, with a spread of similar dimension. It adds about 18 inches of height a year. Almost pyramidal when young, the white ash gradually slows down in its growth and develops a more spreading rounded or oval shape. It will do well in zones 3 through 9. The white ash also enjoys a longer life span than other ashes, reaching 150 to 200 years old.

Ash trees are deciduous, losing their leaves in the fall. Narrow and lancelike, the leaves are two to six inches long and grow along small stems in groups of five to seven. They are dull on the surface and pale and smooth underneath. On first appearance in early May, they are light green, which deepens to a medium green in summer. Their fall display is a golden yellow, sometimes with purple mottling. The bark is grayish brown, with a weblike texture.

In spring, ash trees produce clusters of deep purple blooms just before the leaves emerge, which by summer yield to drooping clusters of winged seeds. These inch-long pale brown seeds hang on the trees until late winter. When they fall, they're more popular with the squirrels, chipmunks, and songbirds that eat them than with gardeners who want a tidy yard. Many folks opt to plant male cultivars, which produce no seed. Male trees flower every year and female trees every other year. Along with the seeds, the ash family produces lots of pollen, but allergy sufferers need not panic: the pollen problem is usually minor because ash trees aren't highly allergenic.

WHITE ASH CHOICES

While ash trees are a highly adaptable native species, the **Autumn Applause** is a true improvement over the traditional tree, perfect for smaller yards and having exceptional fall color. This dense, oval-shaped, seedless cultivar grows in zones 4 through 8. It is a compact tree, reaching 40 feet tall but spreading only 25 feet wide, and provides distinctive purple color in the fall. **Autumn Purple,** the standard white ash in nursery production, displays gorgeous fall color in various purple-red hues. The color is better in New England than in the South. It grows in zones 4 through 8, reaching a height of 45 feet and an almost equal spread. **Champaign County** is a vigorous grower with a thick trunk and improved branching habit, but it can be sensitive to drought. With a spreading crown, **Rosehill** displays vivid fall color and a balanced arrangement of branches. The **Skyline** white ash may be somewhat difficult to find outside the southern United States, where this moderate grower requires little maintenance and displays symmetrical form.

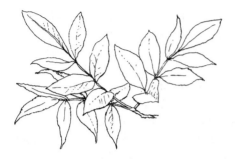

Green Ash (Fraxinus pennsylvanica lanceolata)

Also known as the swamp or river ash, the green ash is happy in zones 3 through 9, and it grows to between 50 and 60 feet tall with a spread about two-thirds its height. The shape can be irregular, more or less pyramidal in its youth, rounded with age. Some of the cultivars, like **Marshall's Seedless,** are shaped more neatly. Green ash trees may grow as fast as two and a half to three feet a year in the North. The green ash is hardy in zones 3 through 9; young trees in zones 8 and 9 may grow six to ten feet in just one year when they are well watered. Like some other rapidly growing trees, its developing surface roots can lift curbs and sidewalks and become your lawn mower's worst nightmare. Planting only in well-drained, uncompacted soil may help keep surface rooting in check.

Each leaf is made up of leaflets, two to five inches long, which turn yellow in the fall. Male and female flowers bloom on separate trees, before the leaves appear.

Because it has been grown successfully in urban areas where air pollution, poor drainage, compacted soil, and/or drought are common, the green ash has been over-planted in some communities, creating the potential for disease and insect problems. You may wish to check with your local arborist to be sure that green ash is a good selection for your neighborhood.

GREEN ASH CHOICES

Marshall Seedless has proven itself to be a tough, adaptable tree, with dark green, glossy foliage. It's a male cultivar, as are the other two listed next, with yellow leaves in the fall. It has been somewhat replaced by **Summit,** a well-shaped tree with a strong central leader, and **Patmore,** an excellent street tree with superior branch structure and better tolerance for cold than other ashes. These cultivars reach heights of 45 to 60 feet; **Summit** has a tall, trim profile, but the others are nearly as wide as they are tall. All do well in zones 3 through 9.

Requirements of Your Ash

Ash trees grow best in full sun, but most types will tolerate light shade. They prefer

a well-drained soil that is acid to neutral (pH 6.1 to 7.5) but will grow in almost any soil as long as it is kept slightly moist. Ash trees have shallow, fibrous roots that spread widely and can disturb sidewalks and driveways, so plant them at least 30 feet from the house and other areas that could be affected.

Planting Your Ash

The more care you take when you put your tree in the ground, the better it will do during its long life. Follow the complete planting directions provided in chapter 3.

Caring for Your Ash

Follow the instructions on seasonal care for young and mature trees—watering, mulching, fertilizing, staking, and pruning—described in chapter 3.

Special Situations for the Ash

A strange phenomenon called ash yellows and various borer problems are common to ash trees and can be deadly, so inspect your ash regularly for early signs of trouble. There is no cure for ash yellows, which is caused by a microbe smaller than bacteria. Its only reliable diagnostic symptom is the presence of witches'-brooms on the trunk and major limbs. "Witches'-broom" refers to a proliferation of small branches that originate at a single point; each branch sprouts at the nodes, giving the shoots a bushy appearance. White ash is more susceptible than green ash.

A serious problem has plagued ashes in the Midwest in recent years. An insect called the emerald ash borer arrived from the Far East a few years ago and has already killed hundreds of thousands of healthy ash trees. So far, there is no cure or form of prevention. If you have an ash tree or are

Common Symptom	Likely Cause
Weakened or scarred trunk, knots on limbs, twig drop	Borers
Witches'-brooms on trunk and major limbs	Ash yellows
Galls on flowers	Mites
Small bumps on leaves and branches, stunted growth	Scale insects
Notched leaves	Japanese weevils
Browning leaves	Anthracnose

Species	Scale at Maturity	Basic Requirements
White Ash (*Fraxinus americana*)	Height: 50'–80' Width: 50'–80' Shape: Oval	Zones 3 through 9 Full sun/part shade Moist, well-drained soil
Green Ash (*Fraxinus pennsylvanica lanceolata*)	Height: 50'–60' Width: 30'–40' Shape: Irregular	Zones 3 through 9 Full sun/part shade Moist, well-drained soil

considering buying one, be sure to check on the status of this problem with your county extension service, even if you don't live in the Midwest. You can find the contact information for your local branch in the phone book.

BEECH (*Fagus* sp.)

Top Reasons to Plant

∾ Elegant silvery bark
∾ Large, noble profile
∾ Unusual leaf color
∾ Rustle and flash in a breeze

An ancient and regal beech tree with a clear gray, smooth, and gleaming trunk caught my attention while I was visiting the Hermitage in Nashville, Tennessee. When Andrew Jackson was elected president in 1828, he called the Hermitage home. It was frontier land when he first settled there, and the beech trees had indicated that the soil was a farmer's ideal: rich limestone overlaid by deep, dark loams.

During my visit, I picked up a bunch of spiny, triangular fruits from the ground beside the beech and brought them back to American Forests Historic Tree Nursery, where we cleaned and planted them. I have always felt a connection to Andrew Jackson: I went to school in Nashville and now live in Jacksonville, a city named for him (though he never visited there).

Any ten-year-old knows that a beech tree is the best climbing tree in the neighborhood, with its majestic spreading branches providing easy footholds. But adults also appreciate this large shade tree for its year-round splendor, its elegant bark, and its colorful autumn foliage. Beech trees produce nuts that are dinner for a wide variety of animals, including squirrels and hummingbirds, which favor this tree for nesting. You must be patient while waiting for these nuts to appear. It may take twelve or more years before you see any, and then sometimes the trees produce nuts only every other year. The nuts are ripe and edible when they separate easily from the branches and when the squirrels begin their feast.

This stately beauty needs lots of space to show itself off in the landscape. The two most commonly grown beeches are the European beech (*Fagus sylvatica*) and

American beech (*Fagus grandifolia*). The American beech, native to North America, is a fine ornamental tree best suited for spacious residential yards. The smaller European beech is becoming more popular in the United States. It offers quite a variety of foliage color.

American Beech
(Fagus grandifolia)

Native to most of eastern North America, American beeches are slow growing, often reaching 50 to 70 feet tall and a similar width. This is a powerful-looking tree, with dense foliage and a short, stocky trunk. During their first ten years, American beeches will typically grow 9 to 12 feet, their fastest growth taking place in the first five years. These grand trees may live from one hundred to three hundred years. They do best in zones 4 through 9.

American beeches are deciduous, losing their foliage over the winter. Individual leaves grow alternately along each side of

their stems. Shaped like slightly elongated ovals, they are about two to five inches long and their edges are visibly toothed, giving the leaf surface a coarse appearance and leathery texture; their undersides are shinier. When they rustle in a breeze, the leaves flash and talk to you. New leaves emerge in April and are a glistening light green, becoming a duller blue green in summer and a clear yellow to golden bronze in autumn. They begin to brown in October but often hang on until January. During the winter the thin, smooth, silvery gray bark and the tree's imposing frame are gorgeous.

Drooping, globe-shaped clusters of inconspicuous yellow-green flowers appear on American beeches in late April or early May after the leaves begin to emerge. Pyramidal-shaped nuts soon follow, each measuring one inch long. Between mid-September and late November, all types of wildlife—woodpeckers, blackbirds, ground birds, and small mammals—and humans seek out these nuts.

European Beech
(Fagus sylvatica)

The European beech is a bit more compact than its American counterpart and produces copper-tinted leaves in the fall. It is slow growing when young, often taking three years after planting to begin visibly growing. European beeches are about 10 feet tall and equally as wide at five years, and almost 50 feet tall at twenty years. A mature tree stands 50 to 60 feet tall—occasionally much taller—with a spread of 35 to 45 feet. Stiffly upright when young, European beeches branch increasingly with age and soon acquire a full, rounded top. Some varieties have graceful, drooping branches. All do best in zones 5 through 7.

Like American beeches, the European beech loses its foliage over the winter months, and its leaves grow on either side of its stems. Each leaf has five to nine pairs of veins and partly toothed edges. New leaves are two to four inches long, a shiny bright green with a gray cast; they become a duller dark green in summer and bronze or yellow in autumn, often remaining on the tree until winter sets in. Some types of European beech have variegated foliage or coppery, purple leaves. Others have finer-textured, feathery foliage with more toothed edges.

European beeches produce inconspicuous clusters of yellow-green to green-brown flowers each spring. These give way over the growing season to small, hanging, soft-spined nuts that mature by September or October.

EUROPEAN BEECH CHOICES

The European beech has been bred over the years to produce a large number of interesting cultivars for landscape use, some with unusual leaf shapes and colors. Some are upright, and some grow in a rounded or weeping form. Most prefer zones 5 through 7, or a sheltered spot in zone 4.

Asplenifolia is a large tree at maturity with delicately cut leaves and a full, billowy profile. **Atropunicea** is a general term for any of the purple-leaf forms of the European beech, whose spring foliage ranges from copper purple to a deep maroon; one popular example is **Spaethiana.**

Requirements of Your Beech

Beech trees will grow in full sun to light shade. Give them plenty of above-ground and below-ground rooting space. They're quite adaptable and won't be fussy about soil type, with the exception that they are not especially fond of clay. Beeches have no problem with alkaline soils (pH 6.5 to 7.5) and overall prefer soil that is rich, moist, slightly acid, and well drained.

Planting Your Beech

The more care you take when you put your tree in the ground, the better it will do during its long life. Follow the complete planting directions provided in chapter 3.

Special notes: Bare-root beech trees do not transplant well, so select container-grown or balled-and-burlapped specimens from the nursery. Bringing some soil along from their previous growing location is important. Choose trees that are between three and eight feet tall—five feet is ideal. Though beech trees are planted most successfully in the spring, the fall is also acceptable. And give this tree plenty of space to stretch itself out in the landscape. The roots are fairly shallow and will lift sidewalks if planted too closely.

Caring for Your Beech

Follow the instructions on seasonal care for young and mature trees—watering, mulching, fertilizing, staking, and pruning—described in chapter 3.

Special notes: Beech roots require lots of oxygen and can be susceptible to damage from compacted soil. You should avoid paving or driving across any part of a beech tree's root zone. Even heavy foot traffic can be detrimental, so ask the mailman to take a different path.

Mature beeches shade an enormous area around their trunks. When covered with a maze of shallow, fibrous feeding roots that typically protrude above the ground, the soil under these trees cannot support additional plants, even lawn grass or other ground covers. Mulching is therefore critical for beech trees. The natural beech leaf litter makes a fine mulch and can be left undisturbed. If you prefer, a two- to three-inch layer of organic mulch over this area looks attractive and protects the roots while enhancing oxygen supply.

While beech trees do not require routine pruning other than removal of the occasional broken or diseased branch, they tolerate considerable cutting back and can be trained into a variety of shapes. The best time to prune is during winter when they are dormant. Multiple leaders, or trunks, are a common cause of limb splitting in older trees, so select one main leader when trees are young and prune back the others. As they become older, remove the lowest branches to reveal the handsome trunk, or leave them if you prefer the imposing effect as they sweep to the ground. American beeches tend to develop suckers from the base of the trunk that need to be pruned off periodically.

Common Symptom	Likely Cause
Curled or distorted leaves	Aphids
Tiny holes in bark, girdled branches	Borers
Small bumps on leaves and branches	Scale insects
Leaves with holes chewed at the edges or completely devoured	Caterpillars
Leaves covered with white powder late in the season	Powdery mildew

Species	Scale at Maturity	Basic Requirements
American Beech (*Fagus grandifolia*)	Height: 50'–70' Width: 50'–70' Shape: Round	Zones 4 through 9 Full sun/part shade Moist, well-drained soil
European Beech (*Fagus sylvatica*)	Height: 50'–60' Width: 35'–45' Shape: Pyramidal, rounded crown	Zones 5 through 7 Full sun/part shade Moist, well-drained soil

Special Situations for the Beech

Beeches are susceptible to the common insect problems, though it's easy to identify the problem so that you can repair it.

BIRCH (*Betula* sp.)

Top Reasons to Plant

- Moderate size
- Colorful peeling bark
- Wide growing range

Some of my fondest memories of adolescence are of hiking trips to the coast of Newfoundland, site of the oldest natural rock formations on the North American continent. Native to that area are river birches with distinctive peeling bark. In the tradition of the original natives, we would gather birch bark to make a fire, then boil some water for tea. I was responsible for gathering the bark. Resting from our hike, we would lean back against the rocks with our tea and watch the seals play below.

The distinguishing feature of most birches is their peeling, curling bark and delicate foliage. Birch bark resembles a smooth, thin sheet of paper. So it's not surprising that the name "birch" has roots in the ancient Sanskrit word *bhurga,* which signifies "a tree whose bark is used for writing upon."

Birches are popular ornamental landscape trees in the northern United States and Canada because of their graceful habit and peeling, textured bark. Canoe or paper birches (*Betula papyrifera*) are most easily recognized by their white bark. Because the bark is impervious to water, early Native Americans used it to cover canoes and wigwams. Paper birches grow best in northern climates; in warmer regions they are more susceptible to borers. River birches (*Betula nigra*) are a good substitute if you live in the South or on the West Coast, but the bark is cinnamon colored, not white. While most birches are capable of living fifty years or more in rural areas, the environmental stresses of an urban setting can shorten their life spans.

The fraying, chalky-white bark of paper,

river, and Japanese birches is an eye-catching accent, especially near a group of contrasting evergreens. Trees with multiple trunks can be especially attractive, lending a more natural feeling to the landscape. The bark of many types of birches turns a darker red, yellow, or brown shade toward maturity.

Often used as specimen trees, the birch's small leaves and open canopy provide light shade that allows perennials, annuals, bulbs, and various types of ground cover to flourish beneath. Birch trees are also attractive when grown in groups near water, either in man-made or natural contexts. Due to their unusually large and extensive root system, they do require quite a bit of room to grow, so they're not the best choice for yards or gardens with limited space.

Some homeowners choose to prune off the lower branches to give the white bark a better showing in the landscape. Others create a multiple-stemmed tree by cutting back the original leader to nearly soil level when it is only a year or two old to stimulate new stem growth. The clump tree that results may be a bit shorter than a typical single-stemmed one.

Birch leaves are two to four inches long. They have toothed edges and, depending on the type of birch, are either somewhat wedge-shaped or more oval with pointed tips. Light yellow-green on top and paler underneath when they emerge in May, they turn a clear yellow to golden yellow before they fall in October, leaving the bare white branches behind.

All birches bear both male and female catkins. Male catkins form in late summer and do not open until the following spring. Female catkins appear in early spring before the leaves unfold. Both are two to three inches long and shaped like miniature

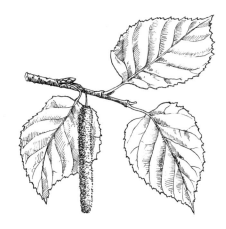

cigars. The male flowers hang down, while the females stand upright. Flowers are pale green to yellow-green in the spring but become light brown over the summer and early fall. The seeds they produce attract all kinds of wildlife, including grouse, squirrels, deer, songbirds such as chickadees and titmice, and several types of woodpecker.

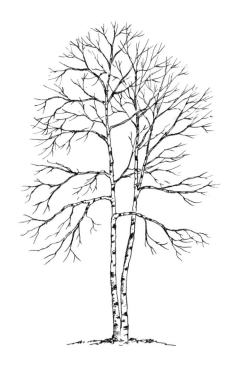

Paper Birch (Betula papyrifer)

Also known as canoe birch or white birch, this popular native tree has brown bark when young and develops creamy white bark that peels off in papery layers as it matures, exposing cinnamon-colored bark beneath. It begins with a pyramidal shape, rounding as it ages. A full-grown tree is 50 to 70 feet tall and spreads from half to two-thirds of its height. Paper birches grow about 18 to 24 inches a year over a period of twenty years and mature in sixty to seventy years. This tree is native to cooler North American climates; it prefers moist soil and dislikes hot, sunny weather. It is classified as a zone 2 through zone 6 tree.

River Birch (Betula nigra)

Also known as black birch, this native tree will thrive best in zones 6 and higher; it's happiest in zones 4 through 9. Its bark is shaggy, cinnamon brown, not black. It flakes off in sheets when the tree is young but thickens and becomes ridged as it ages. Its mature bark is light gray with dark red-brown plates, making it quite attractive in the home landscape. River birches are fast-growing under preferred conditions—up to 5 feet the first year, 30 to 40 feet in twenty years, and 40 to 70 feet at maturity. Pyramidal when young, their shape becomes more rounded as they age; a full-grown tree is 40 to 60 feet wide. River birches can thrive in wet soils but also grow well in drier soils. While paper birches can tolerate somewhat alkaline soils, river birches are unhappy with a pH greater than 6.5. Their toothed leaves are two to three inches long and dark green, with tiny hairs on the midrib beneath. They do not change

color in the fall. River birches are naturally resistant to the bronze birch borer, which can be a lethal pest to other birches.

RIVER BIRCH CHOICES

Because the **Heritage** river birch has fairly pale bark, it resembles the classic white-barked birches of New England or Europe. This cultivar is among the top ten trees for American landscapes and gardens because it is so adaptable to clay soils and intense summer heat. Happy in zones 4 through 9, this sturdy tree has slightly pendulous branches and large leaves. **Heritage** river birches are quite beautiful as specimen trees or planted along stream banks or in groves.

Japanese White Birch (Betula platyphylla japonica)

The Japanese (or Asian) white birch is quite resistant to the bronze birch borer and moderately susceptible to leaf miners. The leaves are two to three inches long and dark green. Marked by black triangles, its snow-white bark does not peel as much as that of other white birches. Some trees may be five to eight years old before the bark begins to whiten. Asian birches can reach 40 to 50 feet at maturity, with a spread of 20 to 30 feet and a pyramidal outline. At home in zones 4 through 7, they withstand heat considerably better than other white-barked birches. But similar to other birches, the farther south the tree is planted, the more susceptible it becomes to borers.

JAPANESE WHITE BIRCH CHOICES

In the 1950s, in a test performed at the National Arboretum, a number of Japanese white birch seeds were collected from the wild in Japan and grown in the United States. Only one tree in the test proved resistant to borers. This single tree, grown at the University of Wisconsin, is the source of all the clones known by the name **Whitespire.** It is a beautiful cultivar with dark green, three-inch-long leaves and a pyramidal shape. Be sure to purchase **Whitespires** produced from cuttings from the original Wisconsin tree; seed-grown versions are not guaranteed to have the same traits. If the plants are not clearly labeled with this information, ask your supplier to confirm the plant's origin.

Requirements of Your Birch

Birches grow well in full sun in their northern ranges but prefer partial or light shade in their southern ranges. In general, birches tolerate a wide range of soil types, but consider planting your birch on the north or east side of your house, as cool and moist soil is ideal. The river birch prefers waterlogged sites with acid soil (pH 5.0 to 6.5). Paper birches, on the other hand, can handle soils slightly drier and more alkaline than normal (pH 5.0 to 8.0).

Planting Your Birch

The more care you take when you put your tree in the ground, the better it will do during its long life. Follow the complete planting directions provided in chapter 3.

Special notes: Fall is the best time to plant, but spring is okay if you are careful to water the area regularly. A note before you plant: birches can be vulnerable to infestation by aphids, which may secrete sticky honeydew that drips off the leaves. Avoid planting your birch where drips can fall onto parked cars, patios, or decks. Also, the tree's high pollen production may contribute to seasonal allergies, but the problem usually dissipates by April.

Caring for Your Birch

Follow the instructions for seasonal care for young and mature trees—watering, mulching, fertilizing, staking, and pruning—described in chapter 3. Heat and dry soil put significant stress on birch trees. Mulching and watering will help reduce the stress, but if the summers in your region are long and hot, consider planting the river birch rather than one of the other types.

Prune your birch in late summer or in winter, because cuts made in the spring tend to "bleed" sap. Remove dead or diseased wood and branches, using a pruning saw for branches not easily cut with lopping or pruning shears. To ensure the tree's best recovery from pruning, use only sharp tools.

Special Situations for the Birch

Birches require special attention in order to catch problems early on, specifically infestation by leaf miners and the bronze birch

Common Symptom	Likely Cause
Tips of leaves turn brown	Birch leaf miners
Top of tree wilts and dies, bark is bumpy and ridged, many holes form in trunk and branches, sawdust gathers at the holes, smaller limbs are girdled	Bronze birch borer
Leaves become curled, yellowed, and distorted, spots on leaves are paler yellow, sticky honeydew substance drips from leaves	Aphids
Leaves become skeletonized; whitish "tents" are filled with caterpillars and their excrement	Tent caterpillars

Species	Scale at Maturity	Basic Requirements
Paper Birch (*Betula papyrifera*)	Height: 50'–70' Width: 25'–40' Shape: Pyramidal, rounded crown	Zones 2 through 6 Full sun/part shade Moist, well-drained soil
River Birch (*Betula nigra*)	Height: 40'–70' Width: 40'–60' Shape: Rounded	Zones 4 through 9 Full sun/part shade Wet to moist soil
Japanese White Birch (*Betula platyphylla japonica*)	Height: 40'–50' Width: 20'–30' Shape: Pyramidal	Zones 4 through 7 Full sun/part shade Moist, well-drained soil

borer. Leaf miners don't kill birches, but they can leave the foliage looking charred and dead and increase the tree's vulnerability to the bronze birch borer, a worm that bores holes in the inner bark and sapwood, ultimately killing the tree. Aphids are also quite fond of birch trees, sucking their sap and secreting a sticky honeydew that may drip off the leaves.

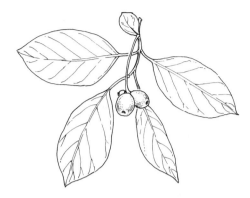

BLACK GUM
(*Nyssa sylvatica*)

Top Reasons to Plant

- ∾ Brilliant fall color
- ∾ Attracts birds and small animals
- ∾ Tolerates dry or moist soil
- ∾ Easy to maintain

In my twenties and thirties, I haunted the deep swamps of the Apalachicola National Forest near my parents' vacation home in Florida. I could always spot the tupelo, or black gum, trees, especially in the fall when their deep purple foliage—unique among autumn colors—presented itself. The bees liked those particular trees too, and for us tupelo honey was always a special treat over ice cream or in tea on cold winter mornings.

This is a midsize tree with a whole lineup of colorful nicknames: bowl gum, gum, pepperidge, plain black gum, quartered black gum, sour gum, stinkwood, swamp black gum, swamp tupelo, tupelo gum, black tupelo, yellow gum, yellow gum tree, and wild pear tree. There is, however, a good explanation for the appearance of "black" in these names: the bark is a dark, almost midnight gray.

Despite all these references to "gum," the black gum has no distinctive sap and no relationship to any kind of chewing gum.

Black gum trees grow relatively low to the ground and resist high winds, so they can live for centuries. Some specimens found in the United States date back to the late 1300s. But age doesn't make them enormous—there's a seven-hundred-year-old champ in Dismal Swamp, Virginia,

that's only about 60 feet tall with a 30-inch trunk, smaller than a typical hundred-year-old white pine.

Living in zones 4 to 9, the black gum is native from east Texas to the East Coast and up to central Michigan and Maine. It can grow along streams or in the uplands but grows best on well-drained, light-textured soils that are moist but not wet. The black gum's unusual root system, consisting of multiple taproots, helps explain why the tree does well in deep, moist soils.

Black gum trees usually grow to a height of 30 to 50 feet—although in rare situations they can reach almost 150 feet—and are most often 20 to 30 feet across. The black gum has a single, straight trunk with branches that emerge at right angles like those of pine trees. Young trees are often pyramidal, while older trees may be more columnar or roundheaded. The ends of the branches often droop, giving the tree a distinctive winter silhouette, and its black bark has deep rectangular fissures that look like building blocks.

The simple three- to four-inch-long leaves are shiny green on their tops and paler and hairy underneath. One of the outstanding attributes of the black gum is its glossy, brilliant red/purple leaf color in the early fall. The leaves are oval shaped and thin enough to let light shine through, so the tree appears to glow red as if lit up. The black gum is generally the first tree to turn autumn's traditional purple to red but does so slowly over a six-week period beginning in early fall. By early October, the tree is a landscape standout.

From April to June, the black gum produces small greenish white flowers borne singly or in clusters high in the branches. The white flowers may be perfect (meaning they contain both sexes), or trees may contain either all male or all female flowers. While the female trees show their flowers, the male trees produce pollen in large quantities. Bees relish the pollen from black gum trees.

The fall brings out edible blue-black berries about the size of a peanut. If you eat one, you'll quickly learn why it is sometimes called a sour gum. But the berries are quite popular with many birds and mammals.

The black gum is an excellent native tree to plant in the home landscape for both fall color and year-round ornamental effect. Several black gums can be grouped for a really dramatic show. Its compact form also renders it ideal for small landscapes, where it can be planted as a single specimen.

Out in the country and suburbs, this tree is a wonderful source of food and shelter for various creatures. Its trunk cavities make it a favorite den tree species for squirrels, owls, and other wildlife. And the wild turkey, yellow-shafted flicker, robin, brown thrasher, wood thrush, pileated woodpecker, gray squirrel, fox, raccoon, opossum, and chipmunk all enjoy the black gum's sweet fruit.

Requirements of Your Black Gum

It prefers a sunny location but can do reasonably well in partial shade. The black gum tree is naturally tolerant of different moisture conditions—it grows wild in both dry and moist soil, though it prefers an acid soil.

Planting Your Black Gum

The more care you take when you put your tree in the ground, the better it will do during its long life. Follow the complete planting directions provided in chapter 3.

A special note: The nursery industry offers the species form of this tree in containers, as it is difficult to transplant otherwise.

Caring for Your Black Gum

Follow the instructions on seasonal care for young and mature trees—watering, mulching, fertilizing, staking, and pruning—described in chapter 3.

A special note: Lower limbs can droop as the tree grows and need to be pruned in winter if you wish to walk under the tree's canopy. Remove storm-damaged limbs as soon as possible.

Special Situations for the Black Gum

The serious insect and disease problems that plague so many other trees don't bother the black gum much.

Common Symptom	Likely Cause
Spots on foliage	Leaf spot
Tips of leaves turning brown	Leaf miners
Swollen, bleeding lesions on stems and trunk	Cankers
Leaves with holes chewed at the edges or completely devoured	Caterpillars
Small bumps on leaves and branches, stunted growth	Scale insects

Species	Scale at Maturity	Basic Requirements
Black Gum (*Nyssa sylvatica*)	Height: 30'–50' Width: 20'–30' Shape: Columnar or rounded	Zones 4 through 9 Full sun/part shade Moist, well-drained soil

BUCKEYE (*Aesculus* sp.)

Top Reasons to Plant

- ∽ Big, dramatic flowers
- ∽ Shiny brown seeds
- ∽ Graceful rounded shape

William Henry Harrison just might owe his 1840 presidential victory to the buckeye. Early in the campaign, an anti-Whig newspaper railed against Harrison, claiming he was "better fitted to sit in a log cabin and drink hard cider than rule in the White House." His supporters seized the chance to portray their candidate as a man of the people, issuing campaign paraphernalia with images of log cabins and cider barrels made of buckeye. Some voters even carried canes made of buckeye wood to show their support for the candidate who called the Buckeye State—Ohio—home.

Some *Aesculus* species are known as buckeyes, others as horse chestnuts. (For true chestnuts, see the next entry.) Buckeyes and horse chestnuts are medium to large trees, depending on the variety. They all have showy blossoms in the spring, as if hundreds of beautiful candles were nestled in the tree's foliage. At the end of the season, most produce chestnut look-alikes that are not edible. The leaves of the various species are quite similar: dark green, three to six inches long, and bunched together in the form of an outstretched hand. Some members of the family have a hint of fall color, while others do not.

The larger members of the family, the horse chestnut (*Aesculus hippocastanum*) and the yellow buckeye (*Aesculus octandra*),

require big open spaces. Their large leaves and spreading branches limit growth underneath, and a 60-foot tree would shade out much of a modest yard. More practical options for the average-size home landscape include the red buckeye (*A. pavia*) and the red horse chestnut (*A. carnea*). Cultivars of these trees are more easily found in garden centers and local nurseries than their larger relatives.

Ohio Buckeye (Aesculus glabra)

The Ohio buckeye's once-popular nickname—fetid or stinking buckeye—is fairly self-explanatory: the flowers, bruised bark, and broken twigs can give off a disagreeable odor. (Some cultivars are available with fragrance-free flowers.) Despite this drawback, the buckeye is the state tree of Ohio, and the term "Buckeye" became Ohio's official nickname in 1954. I would not call it the "stinking buckeye" if I were visiting someone in Ohio.

In the forest, the native Ohio buckeye grows on fertile, moist soils of bottom-

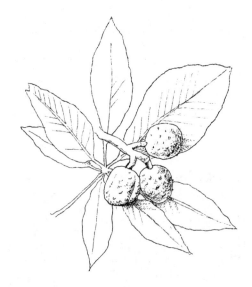

Kentucky, in other words, zones 4 to 8. More in scale with the size of most yards than the Ohio buckeye, it grows to a height of 15 to 20 feet, sometimes even to 30 feet, with a roughly equal width. The leaves emerge in the first days of spring, sometimes as early as February. Unlike the other buckeyes, the red buckeye will flower well in dense shade, but it takes on its best form when grown in full sun with some afternoon shade. The knockout flowers—six-inch panicles of salmon to medium red—come in April and May. Even young trees just three feet tall will produce flowers. When in bloom, this tree attracts hummingbirds and bees, and the eyes of passersby. But even in the winter this is a good-looking tree, when the coarse, open structure of the limbs and the light brown, flaky bark are easy to appreciate.

Prime locations for planting include the edge of a woodland garden, near a patio, or as the focal point at the curve of a path. The red buckeye is especially pretty when underplanted with early spring wildflowers. For the yard, the lower branches can be removed so that you can walk underneath, but the tree looks best planted in the open with the branches dipping naturally toward the ground.

lands and riverbanks. It generally has a short trunk and low branching structure. A slow-growing, roundheaded tree, the buckeye grows to be 20 to 40 feet tall, with an equal spread. Living in zones 3 to 7, it will grow in full sun or partial shade but should not be exposed to extended drought or excessive heat. The late spring flowers are quite ornate, with erect yellow-green six-inch-high panicles decorating the branches. The Ohio buckeye is one of the first trees to shed its leaves in autumn, but it puts on a vivid display of bright orange and yellow before the leaves fall. The nuts have thick husks and prickly spines. Each fruit usually produces a single rounded, shiny brown seed. Its fresh seeds and those of the red buckeye are poisonous to humans but not squirrels.

Red Buckeye (Aesculus pavia)

Also known as the scarlet buckeye, the red buckeye is a small, shrublike tree native to the southeastern United States, from North Carolina south to Florida, west to Texas, and north to southern Illinois and northern

Yellow Buckeye
(Aesculus octandra)

A native of North America, the yellow buckeye grows in zones 4 to 8, from Pennsylvania to Illinois and reaching south to Tennessee and northern Georgia. This large tree has an upright to oval shape with a slightly spreading crown. It will grow to a height of 60 to 75 feet with a width of 30 to 50 feet. Small yellow-green flowers appear in dense six- to seven-inch-long terminal panicles in early spring. The tree displays yellow-orange fall foliage and fruit with smooth husks. Inside each fruit is a rounded, leathery, dark chocolate to chestnut brown smooth and shiny nut, with a light-colored "eye." Seeds ripen and fall in September and October, and squirrels take care of the fallen nuts.

Horse Chestnut
(Aesculus hippocastanum)

Sometimes called the European horse chestnut, this tall tree is indigenous to the Balkans; it was brought from Constantinople and introduced to France in 1615. Its name stems from the Turks' practice of feeding chestnuts to their horses.

The horse chestnut is a beautiful, round-headed tree suited for use in good-size yards in zones 3 through 7. A slow grower, it eventually reaches 50 to 75 feet tall and

40 to 50 feet wide. It bears bright white flowers in panicles 5 to 12 inches long; the flowers attract hummingbirds and butterflies. The horse chestnut's fruits are made up of a spiny capsule containing one or two large seeds, known affectionately by ten-year-old boys as "ammunition." Besides being excellent missiles, nuts from the horse chestnut tree have long been used as fodder for farm animals.

HORSE CHESTNUT CHOICES

The **Baumannii** cultivar grows to 70 feet tall with an oval shape. It bears double white sterile flowers that produce no fruit or nuts.

Red Horse Chestnut
(Aesculus carnea)

A hybrid of the horse chestnut and the red buckeye, the red horse chestnut is a wonderful medium-size tree for the home landscape. More compact than its parents, it will not grow much taller than 30 to 40 feet, with a similar spread. It is moderately

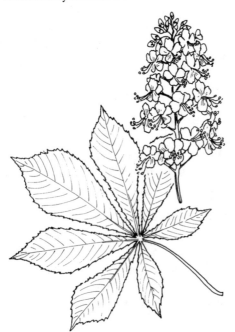

Common Symptom	Likely Cause
Brown leaf margins, dried-up leaves, premature dropping of leaves	Leaf scorch
Defoliation	Fall webworms
Red spots or holes on leaves	Leaf spot
Gray, velvety mold on leaves	Powdery mildew
Browning or curling leaves	Leaf blotch
Skeletonized leaves or flowers	Japanese beetles

Species	Scale at Maturity	Basic Requirements
Ohio Buckeye (*Aesculus glabra*)	Height: 20'–40' Width: 20'–40' Shape: Rounded	Zones 3 through 7 Full sun/part shade Moist, well-drained soil
Red Buckeye (*Aesculus pavia*)	Height: 15'–20' Width: 15'–20' Shape: Rounded, variable	Zones 4 through 8 Full sun/part shade Moist, well-drained soil
Yellow Buckeye (*Aesculus octandra*)	Height: 60'–75' Width: 30'–50' Shape: Upright, oval	Zones 4 through 8 Full sun/part shade Moist, well-drained soil
Horse Chestnut (*Aesculus hippocastanum*)	Height: 50'–75' Width: 40'–50' Shape: Rounded, oval	Zones 3 through 7 Full sun/part shade Moist, well-drained soil
Red Horse Chestnut (*Aesculus carnea*)	Height: 30'–40' Width: 30'–40' Shape: Rounded	Zones 4 through 7 Full sun/part shade Moist, well-drained soil

tolerant of drought, wind, and sleet and can resist the heat of a southern summer. In May it bears attractive pink or red flowers and nearly smooth seed cases. Happy in zones 4 through 7, it develops slowly into a rounded, dense shade tree by five to seven years of age and is an outstanding choice for the home landscape.

RED HORSE CHESTNUT CHOICES

The cultivar **Briotti**'s flowers are a strong red, and larger than some other choices.

Requirements of Your Buckeye

Most buckeyes and horse chestnuts prefer full sun to partial shade. They like moist, well-drained, acidic soil but will handle slightly alkaline soil as well. As a rule, members of the buckeye clan dislike dry soil.

Planting Your Buckeye

The more care you take when you put your tree in the ground, the better it will do during its long life. Follow the complete planting directions provided in chapter 3.

Caring for Your Buckeye

Follow the instructions on seasonal care for young and mature trees—watering, mulching, fertilizing, staking, and pruning—described in chapter 3.

Special Situations for the Buckeye

The buckeye family is fairly problem free. The yellow buckeye is less susceptible to

leaf scorch than other buckeyes. Some homeowners may object to these trees in the summer and fall because the large leaves are slow to decompose; they really have to be raked.

CHESTNUT (*Castanea* sp.)

Top Reasons to Plant

- ∾ Classic shape
- ∾ Good fall color
- ∾ Tasty nuts

Not long ago, the Appalachian mountains looked snowcapped even on warm summer days. The striking cream-colored flowers of American chestnuts created this lovely long-distance illusion. From the earliest days of this country's settlement to the beginning of the twentieth century, chestnut trees produced orchard crops of tasty nuts and fine hardwood lumber from native forest stands. However, the American chestnut (*Castanea dentata*) was devastated by a pernicious fungal disease. Asian blight fungus, introduced into the United States around the turn of the century, killed three and a half billion trees within forty years, making chestnut blight one of the worst ecological disasters in history.

Over the past fifty years, Asian chestnut trees resistant to the disease have gradually replaced the American chestnut, serving primarily in the home landscape. Some Asian types yield good nuts as well, but they have not caught on as an agricultural commodity. Chinese chestnuts (*Castanea mollissima*) and Japanese chestnuts (*Cas-*

tanea crenata) have proven useful and attractive for ornamental and shade use in residential yards, public parks, and along streets.

But we may get our American chestnut back yet. In the past twenty years, much research has been conducted to find both a hybrid that is resistant to the disease and a way to actually eliminate the destructive power of the disease itself. Experts are optimistic that the American chestnut will soon return to common use, once again giving us a harvest of tasty nuts and gracing our landscape with its elegance and beauty.

American Chestnut
(Castanea dentata)

For now, you can buy a hybrid American chestnut that combines the best qualities of Chinese chestnut with the American chestnut, resulting in trees that are quite resistant to the chestnut fungus and, in fact, produce bigger and tastier nuts than either parent.

The American chestnut is native north-

ward to southern Ontario, and from Niagara Falls west to the southern tip of Lake Huron. It ranges south throughout the mountainous areas of the eastern United States to the southern end of the Appalachians. An attractive tree with a low spreading crown, its wood is straight-grained and has excellent resistance to rot. Unlike the leaves of the Chinese chestnut, those of the native chestnut are smooth and narrowly tapered at both ends. They grow to about nine inches in length and turn a golden hue in the fall. The flowers are pale white catkins that appear in early summer after the leaves have come out. And the nuts, which trees will bear when only a few years old, grow inside spiny burs and mature in the fall.

More like a grain than other nuts, these edible chestnuts are low in fat and boast a small amount of high-quality protein. They are high in complex carbohydrates and considered to be the sweetest nut grown in the temperate zones.

Chinese Chestnut (Castanea mollissima)

Think of Chinese chestnuts as medium-sized trees. They are capable of reaching a height of 60 feet, but 40 to 50 feet is more likely in the home landscape and a width of 40 to 60 feet. They have a rounded outline, some with a shrubby habit, growing from multiple trunks at ground level. And they usually branch close to the ground, making them good climbing trees. The bark produces a fine red-brown dye.

Chinese chestnut trees grow hardily in zones 4 through 9. However, in the most northern areas of their range, they may not have a long enough growing season to bring a crop of nuts to maturity. Chinese chestnuts have especially dense foliage. The narrow leaves are a lustrous dark green, with grayish hairs on the reddish veins. They are about six inches long, with 13 to 15 sharp teeth along each edge. The leaves turn a stunning yellow-bronze in the fall before dropping.

Chinese chestnut trees bear both male and female flowers in May and June, but they require at least a couple of other chestnuts nearby for fertilization. The male flowers grow as attractive tassels that add to the ornamental value of the tree in early summer—although their fragrance is considerably less popular! The female flowers give way in the fall to prickly burs about two inches wide. After the frost season, the burs split open, revealing two or three nuts within. When the ripe, edible nuts fall to the ground, you should collect them within a week.

To some, the smell of the male flowers is reason enough not to grow these trees, but my position is that they're handsome, showy trees best observed from a distance—and the flowers don't last that long.

Japanese Chestnut (Castanea crenata)

The Japanese chestnut is smaller than its cousins, growing not much higher than 30 feet with about an equal spread. It is hardy to zone 4, but because it is quite drought tolerant, it prefers to live in areas with hot summers such as zones 8 and 9. The oblong alternate leaves have serrated edges and yellow to bronze fall color. Most important, the Japanese chestnut is resistant to chestnut blight. It flowers in July.

Requirements of Your Chestnut

Chestnuts do best in full sun, although they can tolerate light shade. They prefer a well-drained soil that is acid to neutral (pH 5.0 to 6.5) but will put up with almost any soil so long as it remains slightly moist. Try to avoid soggy soils or standing water for your chestnut.

Planting Your Chestnut

The more care you take when you put your tree in the ground, the better it will do during its long life. Follow the complete planting directions provided in chapter 3.

Special notes: Chestnuts bear male and female flowers on the same tree but usually don't self-pollinate. To guarantee fertilization, plant more than one tree. Fall is the best time to plant.

Caring for Your Chestnut

Follow the instructions on seasonal care for young and mature trees—watering, mulching, fertilizing, staking, and pruning—described in chapter 3.

Special notes: Generally this tree wants to grow with multiple trunks, and that's fine for many gardeners. You can, however, prune the young tree to grow on a single trunk quite easily. Late winter is the best time to do this.

Special Situations for the Chestnut

Insect pests usually spare chestnuts, but these trees are not problem-free. Chinese chestnuts, for instance, may be hit by blight; if you see cankers growing on the branches and then moving into the trunk, seek the advice of a certified arborist immediately. You may also notice some years that growing season has come and gone without nut production, but this is probably caused by a late or early frost.

Common Symptom	Likely Cause
Girdled branches and trunk	Borers
Holes in leaves	Caterpillars
Wormy or deformed nuts	Weevils
Blotches on leaves	Leaf spot

Species	Scale at Maturity	Basic Requirements
American Chestnut (*Castanea dendata*)	Height: 30'–40' Width: 30'–35' Shape: Rounded	Zones 3 through 8 Full sun Moist, well-drained soil
Chinese Chestnut (*Castanea mollissima*)	Height: 40'–60' Width: 40'–60' Shape: Rounded	Zones 4 through 9 Full sun/part shade Moist, well-drained soil
Japanese Chestnut (*Castanea crenata*)	Height: 20'–30' Width: 20'–30' Shape: Rounded	Zones 4 through 9 Full sun/part shade Moist, well-drained soil

ELM (*Ulmus* sp.)

Top Reasons to Plant

∾ Elegant vase shape
∾ Tolerant of city life
∾ Hardy and adaptable

One night in 1765, an unsuspecting American elm in Boston earned the nickname "Liberty Tree" when protesters against the British-imposed Stamp Act hung effigies of detested stamp agents from its branches. The Liberty Tree would serve as a backdrop for hundreds of meetings and rallies calling for colonial autonomy, until ten years later when British soldiers cut it down.

American elms (*Ulmus americana*) remained popular into the early twentieth century, lining the streets of countless communities. Then disaster struck in the 1930s with the arrival of Dutch elm disease (DED), a deadly fungal infection spread by a bark beetle. By the end of the 1960s, more than 100 million elm trees had succumbed. (In fairness to the Dutch, they didn't start the fungus on its way—they were the first to identify it, which is how their name became attached to the disease.) Any original American elms alive today (and there are some) are growing in very isolated conditions, with no other elm trees in the vicinity.

Although DED has been devastating, a fast-growing clone aptly named the liberty elm has reintroduced the classic American elm to the United States. Distributed by the nonprofit Elm Research Institute, in Harrisville, New Hampshire, the liberty elm is not a hybrid but a group of six genetically distinct cultivars. The liberty elm has the same vase shape as the original native species, developing a vigorous upright main trunk in youth, with older branches tending to become more horizontal at maturity. It tolerates urban stresses such as salt injury, soil compaction, and drought damage. Though not entirely immune to DED, it has withstood the disease extremely well for several years. And its genetic diversity helps protect the elm from future diseases.

The Chinese or lacebark elm (*Ulmus parvifolia*) became a prevalent alternative to the American elm when DED began ravaging the species. Chinese elms are broad-crowned shade trees with unusual flaking, multicolored bark and are quite resistant to DED. The Chinese elm remains a valuable landscape tree, but we can happily report that the American elm has returned from what seemed like possible extinction.

American Elm (Ulmus americana)

Both Massachusetts and North Dakota claim the American elm as their state tree, which is a good reflection of its extensive range; it's hardy in nearly every area of the country, from zone 2 to 9. The original American elm displayed a graceful vaselike

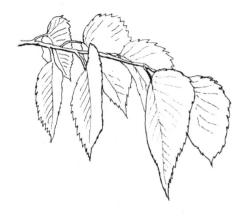

silhouette. Its large size, hardiness, and adaptability to a variety of environments secured its place as a popular street tree. Fortunately, the liberty elm and a number of hybrids offer these advantages as well.

The American or liberty elm (they are virtually interchangeable) is a deciduous tree that reaches a mature height of 60 to 80 feet, with a spread of 30 to 50 feet. The leaves, up to six inches long, are toothed along the edges, have uneven bases, and grow alternately along the stem. American elm foliage turns a rich yellow or gold in fall and doesn't drop until late in the season. The flowers appear in early spring, giving just a tinge of reddish color. Soon after, a heavy crop of papery, disk-winged seeds about one-third of an inch long take their place.

The elm's delicate arching shape has long been a beloved landscape feature. Its natural beauty aside, the elm is unsurpassed as a shade tree. Plantings on the south or west side of your house provide a breezy effect, and elms lining a street or driveway cast a cooling shadow on hot summer pavement. The elm's strongest roots tend to grow downward rather than laterally. Liberty elms are tolerant of salt conditions and soil compaction, making them perfect for urban street planting.

AMERICAN ELM CHOICES

All these trees exhibit excellent resistance to Dutch elm disease—they are not immune, but if attacked, they are able to contain the effects and recover. **Valley Forge**, a variety released by the National Arboretum, has an upright, arching V-shaped branch structure with a dense leaf canopy. **New Harmony** is another variety with a broadly V-shaped crown. Growing best in zones 4 to 7, this cultivar has four-inch-long leaves that turn yellow in the fall. The main trunk divides nearly 30 feet from the ground into a few erect branches.

Chinese Elm (Ulmus parvifolia)

Often called the lacebark elm because of its unique flaking, multicolored bark, this tree is an excellent street or shade tree for residential yards. Sturdy and adaptable, the Chinese elm tolerates a variety of environmental stresses with grace. It can grow a number of trunks naturally or be pruned to develop just one. The tree's strong wood helps it resist wind and ice damage as well as many pests. And it can handle poor soil, compacted soil, restriction of its roots, and drought. It is usually resistant to Dutch elm disease as well as phloem necrosis, another common elm disease.

On average, Chinese elms reach 40 or 50 feet tall at maturity, although some hit 70

feet. The canopy is rounded, but in winter the vaselike shape similar to that of the American elm is more obvious. The mature tree spreads 40 to 50 feet in width from a relatively short trunk. Hardy in zones 5 to 9,

Chinese elms are faster growers in the South, a little slower in northern regions. Their inconspicuous flowers appear in September in green clusters where leaf stems join twigs. A bit later in the fall, these flowers yield a heavy crop of papery, disk-winged seeds in green or maroon about one-third inch long. The leaves measure one to three inches long and about half as wide, with toothed edges. They taper off at the tip, creating a fine, textured look, and grow alternately along the stems. A shiny medium to dark green, they turn yellow or reddish purple in fall and remain on the tree late in the season. But these are deciduous trees, and the leaves fall eventually. The bark peels, exposing orange-brown patches.

CHINESE ELM CHOICES

Cold-hardy **Dynasty** is known for its deep red color in the autumn months and a faster than normal growth rate.

Requirements of Your Elm

Both American and Chinese elms are adaptable to almost any soil, wet or dry, sun or partial shade, and are easy to transplant at any size. Their ideal soil is rich, slightly acid to neutral (6.5 to 7.5), moist, and well drained. American and Chinese elms have surface roots that can raise sidewalks and otherwise be an eyesore. The minimum distance from the street or sidewalk for an elm should be 2 feet; from a house, 15 feet; and from another tree, 30 feet.

Planting Your Elm

The more care you take when you put your tree in the ground, the better it will do during its long life. Follow the complete planting directions provided in chapter 3.

The lower temperatures and abundant rainfall of early spring and early fall create an ideal setting for your young elm to become established. A tree purchased in the fall will be nearly or completely dormant, but once planted its root system will continue growing until the ground freezes.

Unless you want a multistemmed tree, buy a tree with branches spaced along a single trunk. It is not essential that this trunk be straight. Trees that have a trunk less than about two inches in diameter often require staking and early pruning to prevent leaning and blow-over. You should remove the staking within two years.

Caring for Your Elm

Follow the instructions on seasonal care for young and mature trees—watering, mulching, fertilizing, staking, and pruning—described in chapter 3.

Special notes: Pruning an American elm during the first few years of growth is important to develop a strong, well-shaped tree. In the winter, shorten excessively long branches or branches that are out of proportion to the others on the tree.

Avoid pruning American elms from July through September—studies have shown that it makes the trees more disease prone. Remove and destroy diseased American elm wood immediately, as bark beetles that carry DED will breed in dying and broken branches.

Common Symptom	Likely Cause
Leaves skeletonized	Elm leaf beetle
Holes in bark and bud; twig damage	European bark beetle, a principal transmitter of Dutch elm disease
Wilted leaves; dead branches	Dutch elm disease
Bleeding holes in trunk, girdled branches	Borers
Branches encrusted with small bumps	Scale insects
Swollen lesions on stems and trunk	Cankers (caused by at least eight species of fungi)
Curling or withering leaves	Elm phloem necrosis
Leaves that are spotted, turn brown, or drop prematurely	Leaf spot fungi

Species	Scale at Maturity	Basic Requirements
American Elm (*Ulmus Americana*)	Height: 60'–80' Width: 30'–50' Shape: Vaselike	Zones 2 through 9 Full sun/partial shade Moist, well-drained soil
Chinese Elm (*Ulmus parvifolia*)	Height: 40'–50' Width: 40'–50' Shape: Vaselike, rounded	Zones 5 through 9 Full sun/partial shade Moist, well-drained soil

Special Situations for the Elm

Certainly the most dangerous threat to elms is Dutch elm disease. This lethal fungus is spread from tree to tree by bark beetles that burrow under the bark as larvae, by the natural contact of tree roots in the soil, and through wounds and pruning cuts. Older American elms are still susceptible to DED, while more recent cultivars of the American elm and Chinese elm are highly resistant.

Even if you own one of these resistant varieties, it's a good idea to familiarize yourself with the signs of Dutch elm disease. The most obvious symptom is the wilting and yellowing of one or more branches. In a cross section, infected wood shows long brown streaks following the grain of the wood and spots or flecks near the bark.

If disease does hit, act quickly. Trees with more than 5 percent of their crowns infected are probably beyond help and should be removed. If you think your tree is infected, call a professional. Keep surviving elms in vigorous growing condition by carefully feeding and watering them.

GINKGO (*Ginkgo biloba*)

Top Reasons to Plant

- Distinctive fan-shaped leaves
- Resistance to pests and diseases
- Leaves that flutter in breeze

Dinosaurs walked among ginkgo trees. Millions of years ago, ginkgos existed the world over—and they've changed surprisingly little since then, earning them the nickname "living fossils." Although almost all wild ginkgos eventually went the way of the

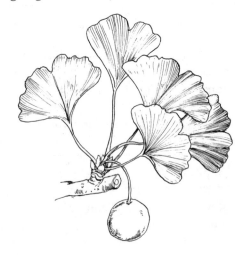

min shops, and on the Internet. Ginkgo is also known for its antioxidant function, and many vitamin and mineral supplements contain the extract in small doses.

The ginkgo can grow as tall as 100 feet, but it usually reaches 50 to 80 feet tall and 30 to 40 feet wide. Its shape can vary from broad to columnar, depending on the variety. Related to conifers, ginkgos have distinctive fan-shaped leaves whose resemblance to those of the maidenhair fern earns it the nickname "maidenhair tree." These unique leaves flutter beautifully in the slightest breeze and in the autumn months turn from green to vivid yellow or golden, though the show doesn't last too long. Ginkgos are deciduous and can lose those fluttering leaves in just one windy night.

Male and female ginkgo flowers are carried on separate trees. The females produce a foul-smelling nut in the fall, so the male trees are preferable. Ginkgos do not flower until they are at least twenty years old. Then they produce inconspicuous green flowers in the spring. When the nuts come in the fall, the leaves turn yellow.

Especially when they're young, ginkgos have widely spaced foliage and limbs, which limits their effectiveness as shade trees. However, their shading value increases with age as they fill out. Slow-growing, tough, and tolerant of urban stresses such as drought and heat reflected from streets and the sidewalk, the male ginkgo makes an excellent street tree. Furthermore, its fibrous root system does not cause damage to sidewalks and driveways.

GINKGO CHOICES

Autumn Gold, true to its name, puts on a gorgeous show in the fall. This nonfruiting

dinosaurs, some were preserved in the temples of China, Japan, and Korea. These survivors are the source of today's ginkgo trees. "Ginkgo" is derived from the Japanese word *ginkyo,* meaning "silver apricot," which refers to ginkgo fruit, which is popular in Japan. The ginkgo can have a long life span, reaching 1,000 years or more. Amazingly China is home to a 3,500-year-old ginkgo tree! The oldest ginkgo in the United States that I know of—aged at approximately 200 years—lives in Historic Bartram's Garden in Philadelphia.

Over the years, the leaves of the ginkgo have become a major source of herbal potions and medications. American consumers hoping to improve their memory and mental clarity purchase ginkgo biloba pills in drugstores, supermarkets, and vita-

Species	Scale at Maturity	Basic Requirements
Ginkgo (*Ginkgo biloba*)	Height: 50'–80' Width: 30'–40' Shape: Variable	Zones 4 through 9 Full sun Moist, well-drained soil

tree starts out upright, then spreads, reaching 45 feet tall and 35 feet wide.

Requirements of Your Ginkgo

The ginkgo is a sun worshipper, suited for coastal regions on both the East and West coasts in zones 4 to 9. It prefers moist, well-drained soil rich in organic material but is amazingly tolerant of a wide range of soil conditions. It can handle clay or sand and a range of pH levels.

Planting Your Ginkgo

The more care you take when you put your tree in the ground, the better it will do during its long life. Follow the complete planting directions provided in chapter 3.

Special note: Spring is the ideal planting time for ginkgos, although young trees in containers transplant well throughout the growing season.

Caring for Your Ginkgo

Follow the instructions on seasonal care for young and mature trees—watering, mulching, fertilizing, staking, and pruning—described in chapter 3.

Special Situations for the Ginkgo

Ginkgos are extremely resistant to pests—even Japanese beetles—and rarely succumb to diseases. However, their branches are somewhat brittle and may suffer storm damage.

HAWTHORN (*Crataegus* sp.)

Top Reasons to Plant

- ∾ Small stature
- ∾ Spring flowers
- ∾ Colorful fall fruit

Don't disturb a hawthorn tree—you might be interrupting a meeting of supernatural beings. Early Englishmen were advised to keep their distance from the tree, as it was thought to provide a route into the underground fairy world. Jesus' crown of thorns is said to have been made of hawthorn branches, perhaps fueling the belief that if hawthorn flowers were brought into a home, death would follow. More recently, folklorists have identified about 150 fairy zones in Ireland—usually centered on hawthorn trees—and have argued successfully that highways be constructed around these areas so as not to disturb the fairies. But don't shy away from hawthorns just yet—the history of these beauties isn't all otherworldly. The Pilgrims named their boat the *Mayflower* after one of the tree's common names, and in colonial America hawthorn berries and flowers were regarded as cures for sore throats.

The hawthorn family is huge in the United States, with nearly two hundred species of trees and another one hundred of shrubs. As with any family, members share some general characteristics. Hawthorns generally live between fifty and one hundred years. They have white blossoms that range in smell from pleasant to not so pleasant. In late fall and early winter, they bear juicy red or yellow fruit as big as crab apples. The trees are small and tend to have short, stout trunks and rather crooked, spreading branches. Perhaps the most distinctive feature of the hawthorn is the long, sharp thorns that adorn its branches. Some homeowners avoid the hawthorn for this reason, but remember that this tree adds richness to the landscape all year long—with its gorgeous spring blossoms, bright green summer foliage, and a golden yellow fall display. Delicately enveloped in snow during winter, these trees attract a number of birds and mammals with their fruit once spring arrives. When they have made your yard look this terrific, you couldn't care less about the thorns.

In the home landscape, single-stemmed hawthorns are somewhat more popular than those with multiple trunks, but the latter make for a better screen if you want to block out sight or sound. Left alone, the single-stemmed trees will develop lower branches reaching down to the ground. Pruning away these lower branches helps keep the thorns at a safe distance from children.

Hawthorn blossoms can bloom indoors in the early spring, and in late fall or early winter, bare branches filled with red or orange berries are often used in flower arrangements. The hawthorn is an attractive ornamental tree that not only adds landscape value but also attracts songbirds. The thorny, thick growths provide for excellent cover and nesting, and the birds eat the thorn apples all winter long. More than thirty-five species eat hawthorn fruit, including mockingbirds, robins, fox sparrows, and purple finches, and chickadees feed on the insects that dwell on its trunk and branches. Hawthorns serve as overwintering sites for admiral butterfly larvae and moths. Not only is this tree beautiful, it is also a valuable tool for keeping your yard's ecosystem healthy.

Good local nurseries and garden centers are apt to carry six to fifteen choices of hawthorn trees. Here's a generous sampling of the cultivars you might want to consider for your home landscape.

Washington Hawthorn (Crataegus phaenopyrum)

Native to the United States, the Washington hawthorn is the most common and the most popular of the several hawthorn choices. The fruit is a brilliant red, and long-lasting. The thorns are dense, and one to three inches long! And though this tree grows quickly in the early years, its growth rate slows with age. At maturity it will be 25 to 30 feet tall, and equally wide. It's more tolerant of warm weather than other hawthorn choices, so it's often grown in the South. The zone preferences are 4 to 8.

Washington hawthorn foliage emerges in late May. Individual leaves are roughly triangular in shape and measure up to two and a half inches long and wide. They have three to five lobes, double-toothed edges, and shiny surfaces with pale undersides. A

lustrous light green at first, the leaves turn dark green in summer, then orange to scarlet red in the fall. A deciduous tree, the Washington hawthorn loses its leaves in early November. Even in full leaf, this tree casts light, rather than dense, shade.

Washington hawthorns bloom a bit later than other members of the family, usually in the late spring once the leaves have developed. Individual white flowers about half an inch wide appear in flat-topped clusters that measure two to three inches across. They have a mildly musty fragrance

that attracts bees. Later in the season the flowers bear the classic orange-red fruits, which continue to grow into the winter until severe cold turns them black or birds eat them.

Winter King (Green) Hawthorn (Crataegus viridis)

The green hawthorn is a native to North America. Winter King is the dominant cultivar, with which the name green hawthorn is virtually interchangeable. Winner of the 1992 gold medal given by the Pennsylvania Horticultural Society, Winter King slowly reaches 20 to 25 feet in height and spread. It derives its name from the persistent color of the red-orange fruits into the winter season.

Happy in zones 4 through 7, Winter King can be pruned to grow with a single trunk or left alone to develop multiple trunks; you can maintain a rounded vase-like shape by removing the lower branches. This tree bears clusters of delicate white flowers each spring whose musty scent attracts pollinating insects. After a show of bronze, red, and gold fall foliage, the green hawthorn reveals silvery bark with orange-brown patches and develops orange-red fruits that resemble rose hips. The fruits persist through winter and are of interest to migrating birds such as cedar waxwings. This tree is a terrific choice for the home landscape because it's highly resistant to disease and, for the thorn wary, its sparse thorns are smaller than those lining the branches of other hawthorn varieties.

Lavalle Hawthorn
(Crataegus lavallei)

The Lavalle hawthorn grows 15 to 30 feet tall, though asymmetrically, and spreads 10 to 25 feet. It has shiny foliage and fewer thorns than some other hawthorns. The large white flowers emerge in the springtime; its fruit are borne in bright orangered clusters marked with brown. In fall, its foliage has a bronze-red hue. The Lavalle is best in zones 4 through 8.

May Hawthorn
(Crataegus aestivalis)

The May hawthorn is a slow-growing tree native to North America that reaches a height of 20 to 30 feet with a rounded canopy that spreads to 35 feet or more. The dark green, deciduous leaves are often three-lobed with reddish brown undersides. This tree isn't known for its fall color, but the white springtime flowers are quite showy, appearing before the new leaves unfurl. Large, red-dotted fruits follow in the fall. Living in zones 6 through 11, this tree is best suited for planting in a large, open area because of its low branching habit. It can be situated closer to a walkway if you're able to prune its drooping branches

on a regular basis. The May hawthorn is thought to be one of the best hawthorns for the South due to its superior disease resistance. I have a fifty-tree May hawthorn orchard that flowers beautifully in spring. The fruit ripens in May and makes a fine jelly, one of my favorites.

English Hawthorn
(Crataegus laevigata)

The English hawthorn reaches 15 to 20 feet tall and grows rapidly in pyramidal form. As it ages, the crown expands into a more oval-like shape with a spread equal to its height. Preferring zones 4 to 7, the tree tolerates most soils and grows well in clay but prefers heavy, dry loam. Its chief ornamental feature is its springtime yield of white, lavender, or pink flowers; some varieties of this hawthorn produce scarlet fruits in the fall.

Because this tree casts a heavy shade, grass cannot easily be grown underneath. When left unpruned, the tree's lower branches are aesthetically pleasing, but you can remove them if you prefer. Remember, though, the branches will be thorny.

ENGLISH HAWTHORN CHOICES

Resistant to leaf blight, **Crimson Cloud** is known for its white and red flowers borne in spring that give the tree a deep pink hue.

Cockspur Hawthorn
(Crataegus crusgalli)

Known also as the haw, red haw, thorn, and thorn apple, the cockspur hawthorn produces bright red, yellow, or black spherical fruit. It usually grows to 20 to 30 feet tall, and 20 to 35 feet wide. The cockspur hawthorn is used in clipped hedges and less formally controlled hedgerows, where the cockspur's density and thorns help keep out animal pests. Because it bears white flowers that emit a slightly disagreeable odor for about a week, you may wish to avoid planting next to the main entry of your home. The bark is an interesting combination of brown and gray, often peeling slightly on older trees to expose an orange-red to rust-colored underbark. Hardy in zones 3 to 7, the cockspur hawthorn is highly tolerant of hot, dry sites, generally maintenance free, and has few pest problems. The **Inermis** variety is thornless.

Requirements of Your Hawthorn

Hawthorns are tolerant of urban conditions, drought, wind, and heat, and grow

Common Symptoms	Likely Cause
Distorted growth, honeydew on leaves, sooty mold growing on honeydew	Aphids
Brown blotches on leaves	Leaf miners
Small, shiny spots on undersides of leaves, foliage that becomes stippled and bleached	Lace bugs
Branch tips that turn brown	Fire blight
Orange or rust-colored spots on leaves (eventually developing horns), early defoliation	Cedar hawthorn rust
Dieback on branches	San Jose scale
Angular red-brown spots on leaves that eventually merge	Hawthorn leaf blight

well in a variety of soils. They grow best in full sun, will tolerate light shade, but don't like heavy shade or poor drainage. They prefer a soil with a pH range of 6.0 to 7.0 but will grow in almost any soil as long as it's kept slightly moist.

Planting Your Hawthorn

The more care you take when you put your tree in the ground, the better it will do during its long life. Follow the complete planting directions provided in chapter 3.

Special notes: The ideal planting time for hawthorns is fall. With the exception of Washington, Lavalle, and cockspur varieties, hawthorns are susceptible to a rust disease hosted by eastern redcedars. Either buy one of the resistant varieties or make sure there are no redcedars in your landscape.

Caring for Your Hawthorn

Follow the instructions on seasonal care for young and mature trees—watering, mulching, fertilizing, staking, and pruning—described in chapter 3.

Species	Scale at Maturity	Basic Requirements
Washington Hawthorn (*Crataegus phaenopyrum*)	Height: 25'–30' Width: 25'–30' Shape: Oval to rounded	Zones 4 through 8 Full sun/part shade Moist, well-drained soil
Winter King Hawthorn (*Crataegus viridis*)	Height: 20'–25' Width: 20'–25' Shape: Variable	Zones 4 through 7 Full sun/part shade Moist, well-drained soil
Lavalle Hawthorn (*Crataegus lavallei*)	Height: 15'–30' Width: 20'–25' Shape: Oval to rounded	Zones 4 through 8 Full sun/part shade Moist, well-drained soil
May Hawthorn (*Crataegus aestivalis*)	Height: 20'–30' Width: 35' or more Shape: Rounded	Zones 6 through 11 Full sun/part shade Moist, well-drained soil
English Hawthorn (*Crataegus laevigata*)	Height: 15'–20' Width: 15'–20' Shape: Oval	Zones 4 through 7 Full sun/part shade Moist, well-drained soil
Cockspur Hawthorn (*Crataegus crusgalli*)	Height: 20'–30' Width 20'–35' Shape: Oval	Zones 3 through 7 Full sun/part shade Moist, well-drained soil

Special notes: Small hawthorn trees may need temporary staking in sites exposed to the wind.

The Winter King is grafted onto rootstock of the Washington hawthorn, and occasionally suckers will develop from below the graft. You should prune them away promptly. For the first two to three years, you may wish to remove the tree's lower branches to avoid walking into sharp thorns. Controlling your tree's early growth is important in the shaping of the mature tree. Some homeowners choose to shear young trees into hedges. Any pruning should be done in late winter.

Special Situations for the Hawthorn

Hawthorns tend to be vulnerable to insect pests and fungal disease problems every few years. All hawthorns are susceptible to hawthorn leaf blight, which appears in early spring as small, angular, reddish brown spots on the leaf surface. Over time, the spots merge and the leaves drop. The English hawthorn is especially vulnerable to this disease. Though the tree may fight off a mild version, for a serious attack seek help from a certified arborist.

If you notice red or brown spots ringed with yellow on the leaves, your hawthorn may have a case of cedar hawthorn rust. If it does, these leaves will eventually develop horns that protrude from the underside, ultimately popping and releasing spores. This disease attacks hawthorn leaves, fruits, and twigs, although Washington, Lavalle, and cockspur hawthorns are somewhat resistant. If you have to treat for cedar hawthorn rust, spray with the appropriate fungicide four to five times at 7- to 10-day intervals.

You should also watch for chlorosis, which is an iron deficiency that appears as yellow areas on the upper leaf surfaces; the undersides may be covered with small brown, sticky flecks. Spray with the appropriate sulfur solution four or five times at 7- to 10-day intervals. Rake up and remove dropped leaves to avoid reinfestation.

HICKORY (*Carya* sp.)

Top Reasons to Plant

∾ Large size
∾ Dense shade
∾ Tolerance of hot summers
∾ Fall color

I grew up in the Amana colonies, an area in eastern Iowa settled in 1854 by the Inspirationists, a group of German Lutherans with social customs similar to those of the Amish. The Amana Society (*amana* means "to remain faithful") considered ornamental and shade trees frivolous, believing they were meant only to please the eye. They believed trees should produce edible fruits or nuts, so if you walk around these quaint towns today, you'll see many hickory trees dotting the landscape in the spirit of this tradition.

Hickories are some of the finest native trees in our country. Common to the central and eastern United States, they have traditionally provided valuable close-grained wood for furniture and tool handles as well as superb firewood for smoking meat. The hickory varieties discussed in this chapter—shagbark, shellbark, pignut, and mockernut—make up a group called true hickories.

True hickories are large, sturdy, handsome candidates for the home landscape. It's important to know that for the first twenty years of its life, a hickory tree bears no flowers or fruit. Each mature tree is self-pollinating and produces both male and female flowers, which bloom in April or May just after leaves emerge.

With their upright, pyramidal form, attractive bark, and rich fall color, hickories are an asset to any property. They can shade a south wall from hot summer sun and are a beautiful addition to a driveway when planted in a row. Most do well in zones 4 to 9, but they're best suited to hot summer areas, so be sure to check on your tree after a snowstorm—its branches can snap under heavy snow or ice loads.

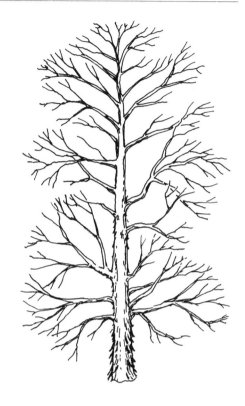

Shagbark Hickory (Carya ovata)

This tree's name comes from the unusual gray bark that hangs loosely in wide strips up to a foot long. In the wild, individual shagbark specimens can live 250 years and

grow to well over 100 feet, spreading usually to half their height. In the home landscape they are more likely to reach 60 to 80 feet tall, and 30 to 40 feet wide. The shagbark's canopy is pyramidal, with a rounded top. These trees are slow growers, adding less than one and one-half inches in trunk diameter over a ten-year period.

Shagbarks are among our hardiest native nut trees, growing from the Canadian border south through the central and eastern states to Texas and Florida (zones 4 to 9). They will tolerate cold winter temperatures as low as −10°F. Shagbark leaves emerge in spring from red or yellow fringed-leaf bud scales. These new yellow-green leaves with pale undersides have slightly fuzzy, shiny surfaces. They are also four to six inches long and made up of a long leaf stalk along which four individual leaflets are arranged, with a fifth one at the tip on its own short stalk. The foliage turns golden brown in the fall and then falls to the ground.

The shagbark's male flowers hang down from the young twigs in groups of three yellowish green scaly spikes, or catkins, each three to five inches long. The female flowers are scentless and much smaller than the male. They appear at the growing tips of twigs, each emerging from a tiny cup; after pollination, the female flowers of a mature tree give way to nuts that develop in smooth green husks about one and a half inches in diameter. They ripen by September, turning nearly black. Once ripe, the husks split along four seams to release the tan-colored nuts. These nuts are favorites of songbirds, squirrels, and, of course, humans. Their flavor is reminiscent of maple syrup and is an exquisite addition to homemade cakes and cookies.

Shellbark Hickory (Carya laciniosa)

The shellbark hickory grows to 80 to 90 feet or more, with a high branching habit and an oval profile. Its bark plates are smaller and less curved than those of the shagbark hickory. Hardy in zones 5 through 8, this species is neither as cold- nor as heat-tolerant as the others mentioned here. It does, however, contain the kingnut, the largest and tastiest of the true hickory nuts. Some consider this hickory the most desirable in the home landscape. If you have space for a very large tree, and you want a hickory, this is the one to choose. The nuts are great to eat and the bark plates are dramatic in winter.

Pignut Hickory (Carya glabra)

A North American native, the pignut hickory usually reaches 50 to 60 feet in height with a 30- to 40-foot spread, so its profile is somewhat narrow. The tree is also called

the smoothbark hickory because the bark is light gray, mostly smooth, and doesn't peel. The three- to six-inch-long leaves create a coarse, oval canopy, and the strong but irregularly spaced branches resist breakage in storms. In fall, the foliage turns a golden yellow. The green fruits of the pignut hickory are too bitter for the human palate, but various forms of wildlife keep coming back for more. Pignuts do well in zones 4 to 9.

Mockernut
(Carya tomentosa)

Common names for the mockernut are white hickory, whiteheart hickory, and bignut hickory. It's a tall, short-limbed tree averaging 60 to 70 feet high and 25 to 35 feet across. The hard, dark-gray bark is closely and deeply furrowed and is often cross-furrowed or netted. The winter buds are large, round or broadly egg-shaped, and are covered with downy, hard scales; recent shoots are short, stout, and also covered with a downy growth. Mockernut hickory leaves are innately compound, which means that between seven and nine little leaflets surround a single stem. The whole leaf reaches 20 inches long, while each leaflet grows up to 8 inches long. They turn a striking yellow in the autumn months.

Like other hickories, the mockernut bears both male and female flowers on the same tree. Its fruit is oval, nearly round, or slightly pear-shaped with a thick, strong-scented husk that splits nearly to the base when ripe. The nut can appear in various forms, but its thick shell is commonly light brown and ridged, enveloping the sweet kernel inside. Between the thickness of the shell and the smallness of the nut, harvesting isn't worth the effort.

Milled mockernut wood is heavy, hard, and tough. It is white in color save for its small, dark brown heart, hence its other name, white hickory. Living mockernut specimens are even more valuable for wildlife. They provide cavities that animals such as woodpeckers, raccoons, and chickadees call home. The thick foliage also creates good nesting sites for birds. The mockernut is hardy from zones 4 through 9.

Requirements of Your Hickory

Hickories grow best in full sun. They prefer a well-drained, fertile soil that is slightly acidic (pH 6.0 to 6.5).

Planting Your Hickory

The more care you take when you put your tree in the ground, the better it will do during its long life. Follow the complete planting directions provided in chapter 3.

Special notes: Spring is the ideal planting time. Select young trees whose roots and soil ball are wrapped in burlap. Because of their long taproots—a year-old tree will likely have a foot-long taproot—they can be difficult to transplant successfully. Once established, however, this taproot ensures that the tree will be stable. Plant two or more trees near each other to ensure efficient pollination and a generous crop of nuts.

Caring for Your Hickory

Follow the instructions on seasonal care for young and mature trees—watering, mulching, fertilizing, staking, and pruning—described in chapter 3.

Common Symptom	Likely Cause
Galls on leaves, stems, and twigs	Gall aphids
Holes in bark and trunk, girdled branches	Borers
Holes in bark, wilted twigs	Bark beetles
Defoliation	Gypsy moths
Browned or blotched leaves	Anthracnose
Spotted or blotched leaves	Leaf spot

Species	Scale at Maturity	Basic Requirements
Shagbark Hickory (*Carya ovata*)	Height: 60'–80' Width: 30'–40' Shape: Pyramidal, rounded	Zones 4 through 9 Full sun Moist, well-drained soil
Shellbark Hickory (*Carya laciniosa*)	Height: 80'–90' Width: 60'–75' Shape: Upright, oval	Zones 5 through 8 Full sun Moist, well-drained soil
Pignut Hickory (*Carya glabra*)	Height: 50'–60' Width: 30'–40' Shape: Upright, oval	Zones 4 through 9 Full sun Moist, well-drained soil
Mockernut Hickory (*Carya tomentosa*)	Height: 60'–70' Width: 25'–35' Shape: Upright, oval	Zones 4 through 9 Full sun Moist, well-drained soil

A special note: Hickories should be pruned while dormant in the late winter or early spring. Prune young trees to a strong central shoot and in a pyramidal shape, and remove all branches three feet to the ground or lower. Established trees need pruning only to maintain their shape and to remove dead wood.

Special Situations for the Hickory

Hickories can fall victim to the usual suspects of aphids, borers, and moths as well as fungal diseases such as anthracnose and leaf spot. Keep an eye out for the symptoms of these potential problems to keep their effects at bay.

HONEY LOCUST
(*Gleditsia* sp.)

Top Reasons to Plant

- ∾ Lovely fernlike foliage
- ∾ Dappled shade
- ∾ Adapts well and needs little maintenance

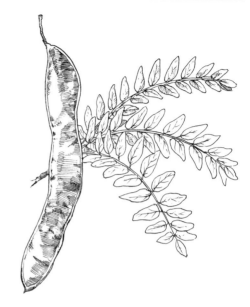

At the Historic Tree Nursery, we grow the offspring of a honey locust that I wish could speak. This tree at Gettysburg National Military Park in Pennsylvania is the last living witness to the stirring words of Abraham Lincoln's Gettysburg Address, delivered in 1863. The president spoke that day for less than two minutes—the photographers were still setting up when he finished and sat down—but his words have been etched into our nation's heritage. The honey locust tree provided little shelter for those who gathered on that chilly November day, but its gnarled branches made a fitting backdrop for the dedication of a new cemetery for those who had fallen on the battlefields at Gettysburg.

Honey locust is native to the United States and is also known as the sweet locust,

thorn tree, three-thorned acacia, and honey shucks. All the native species have substantial thorns on their roots, trunk, and branches, earning them the dubious distinction of being the spiniest trees in our north temperate zone—these thorns can penetrate a farm tractor tire! All females produce fruit in the form of long seedpods some 10 to 15 inches long, depending on the species. These pods happen to be good cattle fodder, but in the home landscape they call for a little tidying.

While most types of honey locusts are not considered ornamental plants, the common honey locust (*Gleditsia triacanthos*) is a terrific asset in the yard. And the good news is that one variety (*Gleditsia triacanthos* f. inermis) is thornless, and some other cultivars do not even produce seedpods. This honey locust is easy to care for, resistant to most insects and diseases, has lovely, lacy foliage, and flourishes in a wide range of soil types.

Medium to fast growers, honey locusts grow up to 2 feet a year during their first twenty years. They reach maturity at 100 to 125 years, when they can be 100 feet tall. But in a residential landscape they are typically only about 40 to 60 feet tall, and equally wide. Their horizontally growing branches give them a tiered, somewhat flat-topped profile. They are vase-shaped at maturity.

The honey locust's foliage emerges in the spring as small, egg-shaped leaflets ranging along eight-inch stems. There may be as many as twenty to thirty leaflets on a stem, and some trees have double leaves. New leaves are light green, turning yellow-green during the summer. By autumn they are a pale or brilliant yellow. Because their foliage is so lacy and light, honey locusts provide a pleasant, dappled shade.

Male and female honey locust flowers are borne on the same tree; they both bloom in early summer, emerging in separate clusters. Male catkins are the most obvious. They are up to 2 inches long and yellow-green. In midsummer these give way to flat, beanlike pods that hang down 12 inches or more from the tree. These purplish brown pods persist until midwinter, when they finally drop. The honey locust is hardy in zones 4 through 9.

Adaptable to urban conditions, honey locusts have been widely planted as replacements for American elms. They are fairly resistant to salt, drought, soil compaction, heat, and disease. It is probably best to use them as specimen trees in the yard and garden. They provide only light shade, so growing grass under this tree is no problem. Honey locusts can also be used as a screen along property lines or as a windbreak at the edges of fields. Some gardeners use the honey locust's seedpods in dried arrangements. The fact that they rattle in the winter wind gives them extra appeal. I've seen them spray-painted gold and festively arranged on a Christmas tree.

HONEY LOCUST CHOICES

Thorn free and typically fruitless, **Imperial** has a symmetrical, broad crown. This cultivar can be vulnerable to insect infestation. One of the earliest cultivars, **Moraine** has ascending upper branches and deep green foliage that turns yellow in the fall. A favorite of municipal arborists, this cultivar has some resistance to insect infestation. **Shademaster** is a vigorous grower with a vase shape. Virtually podless, it has ascending branches. **Sunburst** is a more compact tree, displaying bright yellow foliage in the spring that turns green by the summer.

Requirements of Your Honey Locust

Honey locusts grow best in full sun but will tolerate light shade. Their natural habitats include rocky hillsides and open or wooded pastures. They prefer well-drained soil, either fine, sandy clay or heavy loam that is slightly acid to neutral (pH 6.1 to 7.5), but they grow in almost any soil as long as it's not too wet or acidic.

Planting Your Honey Locust

The more care you take when you put your tree in the ground, the better it will do during its long life. Follow the complete planting directions provided in chapter 3.

Caring for Your Honey Locust

Follow the instructions on seasonal care for young and mature trees—watering, mulching, fertilizing, staking, and pruning—described in chapter 3.

Special Situations for the Honey Locust

The most serious threat to honey locusts, especially the thornless varieties, is the mimosa webworm. Most common in the Midwest, these pests are quickly spreading to wherever honey locusts grow. You can recognize a visit from the mimosa webworm if your tree has webbed tents, browned or scorched leaves, or, most obviously, worms hanging from threads of silk.

The adult mimosa moth is silvery gray, with black dots all over its wings. It overwinters in the bark on the trunk of the honey locust or in debris under the tree. In

Common Symptom	Likely Cause
Small bumps on leaves and twigs; discoloration of leaves; leaf drop; reduced growth; stunted plants	Scale insects
Cankers on trunk and branches, wilting and dieback; bark that turns orange-brown or pale yellow-orange	Canker disease

Species	Scale at Maturity	Zones
Common Honey Locust (*Gleditsia triacanthos*)	Height: 40'–60' Width: 40'–60' Shape: Vaselike	Zones 4 through 9 Full sun/part shade Moist, well-drained soil

June, it emerges to lay its eggs on the tree's leaves. Its larvae, or worms, have five white stripes running along their gray or brown bodies. When they hatch, they web leaves together to form protective tents, under which they feed on whatever leaves are left. In southern regions, webworms may produce several broods in one year. **Sunburst,** with its golden foliage, is highly susceptible to attack, while **Moraine** and **Shademaster** are less so. Use a systemic insecticide in the summer before the larvae appear, because once they're colonized, it's nearly impossible to eliminate them completely with spraying.

Another tiny but problematic pest is the gall midge, whose larvae feed on the leaves and live within podlike galls at the ends of new growth on honey locusts. They lay their first eggs in April and leave five or more midge broods throughout the season. It is important to spray with the appropriate insecticide at the first sign of a gall midge in early spring.

JAPANESE MAPLE (*Acer* sp.)

Top Reasons to Plant

- ❧ Delicate beauty
- ❧ Distinctive red leaves
- ❧ Smaller scale shade tree

The abundant, graceful leaves of the Japanese maple create a lacy effect that softens the home landscape, becoming a focal point in your yard's design. While a flowering tree can put on a spectacular display for a few weeks a year, the Japanese maple provides colorful foliage three seasons of the year and structural beauty all winter. This tree is such a standout—and so different from other maples in all aspects—that it deserves special attention. So I'm treating it separately from the other maples, which begin on p. 139.

Three varieties of Japanese maple are really worthy of attention. All are native to Japan and known collectively as Japanese maples. Unfortunately, one of the three varieties is itself called a Japanese maple— a source of some confusion. The following first describes Japanese maples as a group.

Many Japanese maples have delicate red or greenish red leaves during the growing season, and some varieties have variegated or yellow leaves. In most cases, Japanese maples show stunningly brilliant red or yellow fall color. Some have green or red stems that add color to the winter scene. Speaking of winter, Japanese maples are not quite as tolerant of cold as are other maples. Zone 5 is their northern limit, and they're happier farther south.

Depending on the variety, these trees reach heights in the 10- to 30-foot range. They mature in about twenty years. Typically as wide as they are tall, some grow upright while others have drooping branches. Those with this weeping habit are slower growing, and their width may ultimately be two or three times their height; it can take these trees ten years to reach only 4 feet tall.

Japanese maples can serve as small shade trees, screens, or specimen trees with their interesting three-season color. Red-leafed types stand out dramatically against a dark green background of evergreens. Weeping types, which are smaller and finer textured, can integrate easily into a garden bed or border. They'll also grow in containers two to three feet wide by one to one and a half feet deep. These trees are great on a deck or patio.

You can plant small Japanese maples in shrub borders or garden beds with a ground cover that serves as living mulch, such as pachysandra or English ivy. Low-growing junipers also beautifully accent the graceful foliage of the Japanese maple.

You may also wish to use the smaller Japanese maples as a foundation planting along with rhododendrons. They may need a little pruning to keep them to size. Be sure to plant them far enough from the building to have room for their lacey spread.

Because these trees tend to be fairly expensive, you should ask yourself some questions to narrow down your selection. Do you want an upright tree or a small tree with a wide canopy? Will the maple be planted in a container or in the yard? What color foliage harmonizes with existing plants in your landscape? Will the maple be protected from the hottest afternoon sun? Find pictures of the Japanese maple you envision, and you'll make the best choice among the many cultivars available at your garden center or via mail order.

Japanese Maple (Acer palmatum)

Generally when people speak of Japanese maples, they mean this tree. *Acer palmatum* is perhaps the most widely grown Japanese maple in American home landscapes. A mature tree usually reaches 15 to 25 feet tall and wide, but some varieties are 30 feet tall, and many cultivars are much smaller, measuring only 6 to 10 feet. The shape of the tree also varies greatly by cultivar. Many are upright growers and others have a low,

weeping form. (Some weeping selections look best when they are allowed to branch to the ground. You'll have to clear away all turf from beneath the branches of these low-growing types so that the lawn mower doesn't damage the tree.)

In Japanese maples, fall color ranges from bright yellow through orange and red, and is striking even on trees growing in total shade. The leaves of some trees turn a deep purple in the autumn before dropping.

The leaves are two to five inches wide and long, and are palm-shaped with deeply cut lobes. They usually have between five and nine sharply pointed lobes with serrated edges. Japanese maple flowers appear in spring in small, purplish red hanging

clusters. As the season progresses they develop into small winged seeds.

Japanese maples are hardy in zones 5 through 8. There is a good deal of variation among cultivars. Following are some particularly nice ones.

Bloodgood is a vigorous, upright grower tolerant of heat with deep red to nearly black foliage in both spring and summer; its fall color is an intense crimson. One of the tallest Japanese maples, this cultivar reaches a height of 15 feet with blackish red branchlets. **Sango Kaku** has vivid coral-hued stems in youth on a vase-shaped form. Its light green leaves are yellow tinged with red by autumn. **Moonfire** is another good choice for hot areas; it holds on to its striking purple-red leaves through the steamiest summers.

Threadleaf Maple
(Acer palmatum dissectum)

Also known as the laceleaf or cutleaf Japanese maple, these threadleaf forms of Japanese maple have the most finely divided leaves in the family. They resemble long, slim fingers. The trees have a wide-spreading, roundheaded form with a weeping tendency, and their dark, twisted branches are especially dramatic in the winter. The trees in this group seldom grow taller than 6 feet, their width ranging between 4 and 6 feet. One of the best ways to showcase this plant is to grow it in a raised container. It is hardy in zones 5 through 8.

Requirements of Your Japanese Maple

Japanese maples will grow in full sun, but light shade enhances their red color. They can tolerate direct sun better in their northern ranges. Because they are vulnerable to sunscorch in summer and frost in late winter—especially the light-colored and variegated narrow-leafed types—these trees need a protected site and plenty of moisture. They prefer a well-drained soil that is acid to neutral (pH 5.5 to 7.0) but will tolerate almost any soil as long as it's kept slightly moist and is not extremely clayey or sandy.

Planting Your Japanese Maple

The more care you take when you put your tree in the ground, the better it will do during its long life. Follow the complete planting directions provided in chapter 3.

Special notes: Japanese maples tend to burst into new growth in the spring. Try to situate them where they will be somewhat sheltered from occasional late frosts, yet where they will feel the early morning sun.

Although they can be planted almost any time of the year when the ground is not frozen, the best planting time for young Japanese maples is either early spring or

fall. Choose young trees from 15 inches to six feet tall, depending on the size of the mature tree. It's a good idea to play it safe and plant Japanese maples a little high in the planting hole. They do not do well if they're set too deep. Like all maples, these are vulnerable to a toxin secreted by the roots of black walnut trees. Your maple should be no closer than 50 feet to a walnut.

Caring for Your Japanese Maple

Follow the instructions on seasonal care for young and mature trees—watering, mulching, fertilizing, staking, and pruning—described in chapter 3.

Special notes: The shallow, fibrous roots of all maples prefer moist soil. If grown in soil that is rich in organic material and holds water well, Japanese maples will need special watering only for a period of several weeks when they're first planted and in late fall before the ground freezes for the winter. With normal rainfall, established trees should do fine.

Occasionally a young tree will develop two main trunks. You can cut off one of these to establish a single strong trunk. This

Common Symptom	Likely Cause
Poor growth, weakened branches	Girdled roots
Surface roots, suckers	Compacted soil
Stunted growth, wilting branches or leaves	Black walnut tree too near
Wrinkled leaves, stunted growth, defoliation	Aphids
Girdled branches, premature dropping of leaves, scarred trunk	Borers
Small bumps on leaves and branches	Scale insects
Sunken spots on leaves	Anthracnose
Swollen, bleeding lesions on stems and trunk	Cankers
Mushrooms sprouting at base of tree	Shoestring root rot
Foliage turning yellow or brown, collapsing	Verticillium wilt

Species	Scale at Maturity	Basic Requirements
Japanese Maple (*Acer palmatum*)	Height: 15'–25' Width: 15'–25' Shape: Rounded	Zones 5 through 8 Part shade/full sun Moist, well-drained soil
Threadleaf Maple (*Acer palmatum dissectum*)	Height: 4'–6' Width: 4'–6' Shape: Rounded	Zones 5 through 8 Part shade/full sun Moist, well-drained soil

job is best done in the winter or early spring when the tree is dormant. You may also cut out the dense inside branches of upright trees to open up the foliage canopy to air and light so that the other branches can develop fully. Japanese maples will eventually shed any branches that do not get enough light.

Weeping forms sometimes need pruning to avoid awkward asymmetrical growth. Snip off the young suckers that sprout along the main stems inside the tree, and prune other suckers that may appear low on the trunk, or from aboveground roots. Also cut out any branches with leaves of atypical size or color.

Special Situations for the Japanese Maple

The usual suspects—borers, aphids, and scale insects—can affect Japanese maples. These trees can also suffer from girdled roots or compacted soil.

If you notice a decline in the vigor of your tree, along with a yellowing, dwarfing, or wilting of foliage, as well as telltale golden-brown mushrooms at the base of the trunk, it may be suffering from shoe-string root rot. This nasty fungus feeds on buried roots and stumps, and takes advantage of trees, especially maples and oaks, that have been stressed by drought or other environmental factors. The fungus grows between the bark and the wood at the place where the mushrooms appear (usually during a rainy autumn), infects the roots, and sends the tree into decline. There is no real control of this disease, save removing infected trees, stumps, and large roots, and being careful not to plant new trees in woodland areas where the fungus may have grown. Tending to your tree's overall health on an ongoing basis will also lower the chances for infection.

KATSURA TREE (*Cercidiphyllum japonicum*)

Top Reasons to Plant

∾ Dense shade
∾ Unusual spring and fall color
∾ Handsome winter profile

A beautiful landscape tree, the katsura tree has a spreading habit and full, dense

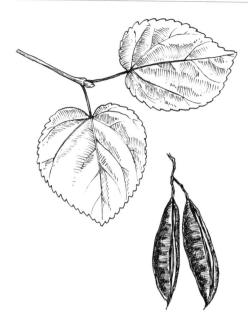

40 to 60 feet tall and wide. It does well in zones 4 through 8.

The flowers of the katsura tree are not as distinctive as some of its other features. They are an inconspicuous green, open from late March to early April. But this tree's foliage color is second to none. In the spring, the leaves emerge a beautiful reddish purple. As the season progresses they turn dark bluish green. The fall color varies from an intense yellow to a striking apricot orange. To add to the tree's appeal, as the leaves drop in the fall they give off a slight, spicy fragrance. But the performance is not over. In the winter, the handsome gray bark peels slightly, and the tree's striking, rounded architecture is on full display.

KATSURA TREE CHOICES

Pendula has a weeping habit, reaching a height of 10 feet and a spread of 5 feet. **Pendulum** is a similar weeping cultivar, reaching up to 20 feet tall and 10 feet wide.

Requirements of Your Katsura Tree

This tree grows best in a sunny exposure, tolerating some shade, and in moist soil. It is drought-tolerant once established but not when first planted. The katsura tree is not suited for compacted soil because its shallow roots can be a nuisance for lawn and sidewalk maintenance.

foliage that casts excellent shade. Katsura trees are pyramidal in youth, but their shape varies with maturity, ranging from pyramidal to rounded and wide-spreading. They have a shallow root system; some roots grow on the surface of the soil and may be six inches in diameter or thicker. They are part of the tree's beauty, along with the trunk, which normally flares out gracefully at the base. The mature tree is

Planting Your Katsura Tree

The more care you take when you put your tree in the ground, the better it will do during its long life. Follow the complete planting directions provided in chapter 3.

Species	Scale at Maturity	Basic Requirements
Katsura Tree (*Cercidiphyllum japonicum*)	Height: 40'–60' Width: 40'–60' Shape: Rounded, spreading	Zones 4 through 8 Full sun Moist, well-drained soil

Special notes: Katsura trees need a site protected from wind, which is too drying for young trees.

The tree has a shallow root system and may be hard to transplant later, so choose its site carefully. Spring planting is best.

Caring for Your Katsura Tree

Follow the instruction on seasonal care for young and mature trees—watering, mulching, fertilizing, staking, and pruning—described in chapter 3.

Special notes: Young katsura trees are intolerant of drought, which can cause the leaves to drop in mid to late summer. Provide supplemental watering during the first two to three years or whenever rainfall is scarce, and remember to keep a good layer of mulch over the roots.

Sometimes the bark will split in winter, usually on the lower portion of the southwest side of the trunk. Wrapping the tree with tree wrap each winter can reduce the occurrence of this problem.

Special Situations for the Katsura Tree

The katsura tree is fairly pest and disease free.

LINDEN (*Tilia* sp.)

Top Reasons to Plant

- ∾ Unique heart-shaped leaves
- ∾ Fragrant flowers
- ∾ Attractive to honeybees

Plant a linden tree and you just might invite a bit of divine luck into your backyard. From the thirteenth century to the early sixteenth, in many European countries, linden wood was used to make altarpieces and other sacred works of art. Healers believed that the linden had a special curative power and used it to treat a variety of ailments, from boils, sores, and cuts to indigestion, epilepsy, and fever. What's more, the honey-producing capacity of this "bee tree" was valued so highly in many areas that local governments passed laws protecting lindens, and cutting them down became associated with bad luck. Not the superstitious type? At the very least, you'll bring splendor and value to your yard by planting a linden.

The first tree I ever planted was a linden. I was five years old, so my dad probably did most of the work, but let me call it "mine." Anyway, the linden always reminds me of my roots in Amana, Iowa. My uncle Buddy took me tree planting every year, my grand-mother put shovels in my hands instead of toys, and my parents always took us on trips to spots where nature was the main attraction.

Large trees with attractive foliage and winter trunks, lindens are superb shade trees. They can be incorporated into a residential landscape in a variety of ways. Of course, they make lovely individual specimen trees on large and moderate-size properties. Clipped as hedges, they can be trained to adapt to smaller spaces. One caveat: it'll take frequent pruning to maintain these hedges.

The linden's small yellow flowers appear in June and attract a large following of honeybees. Lindens are so big and dense that the bees and other insects can't manage to pollinate every flower, so a good deal of airborne pollen is given off. If you or a member of your family is allergic to bee stings or hypersensitive to springtime allergens, the linden may not be the best choice for your yard. However, the problem usually exists just under and around the immediate area of the tree, so if you have a large landscape to work with, the linden remains a possibility. (And if you keep bees, they will be more attracted to lindens than to other trees.)

Varieties include the littleleaf linden (*Tilia cordata*), native to Europe, which is commonly sheared into tall hedges for formal gardens. The silvery underside of the leaves and the rich green glossiness of their tops make the silver linden (*Tilia tomentosa*) a unique and beautiful tree. It is native to Europe and Asia. The American linden (*Tilia americana*) is larger-leafed and coarser in appearance than its imported cousins. You can find the American lin-

den under a variety of names, including basswood, whitewood, bass tree, black lime tree, American lin, American lime, bee tree, daddynut, monkeynut, whistlewood, white lind, red basswood, yellow basswood, and last but not least, wickup.

American Linden
(Tilia americana)

The American linden is native to New England and the upper Midwest. However, it is hardy in zones 2 to 8, growing from New Brunswick and Manitoba to Georgia and Texas. Its favorite haunts are rich, moist bottomlands and hillsides. A handsome shade tree, the American linden transplants easily and grows rapidly. Though it doesn't tolerate urban pollution as ably as the littleleaf linden, it does just fine in the suburbs and country settings. It is also a valuable wildlife tree, with hollows that serve as homes to many creatures.

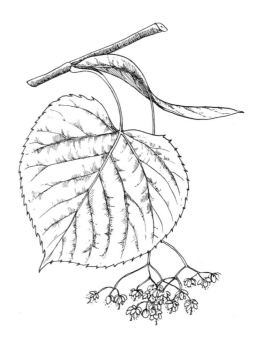

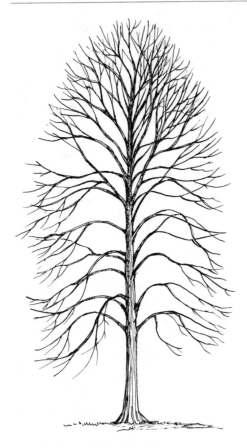

adorning the American linden are larger than other lindens, measuring four to eight inches long. They have toothed edges and grow alternately along the branches and twigs, emerging in late April or early May. In the spring they are lime green, turning medium green in the summer and finally golden yellow, then brown in the fall before they drop at the beginning of October. Their undersides are a bit paler than their tops.

American lindens produce abundant clusters of drooping, pale yellow flowers in late June or early July, after the leaves have developed fully. Made up of five or ten smaller blossoms, these two- to three-inch flower clusters are quite fragrant, warranting devotion from honeybees. Over the season, these flowers give way to small, woody, pea-sized brown fruit that hang like ornaments from the branches through the fall.

Littleleaf Linden (Tilia cordata)

Sometimes called small-leafed linden, this European introduction has a rather formal, round-shaped head, and is often planted in parks, streets, and lawns for ornamental purposes. It's one of the best large ornamental trees on the market, tolerating both urban pollution and drought. It can handle winters as far north as New England and the Great Lakes (Zone 3), with temperatures as low as –20°F, and will grow south into zone 7.

Littleleaf lindens in nature can grow to 90 feet, but more typically they reach 60 to 70 feet. Young trees are pyramidal, spreading to about half their height as they mature, and rounding out a bit. As their name suggests, they have smaller leaves

American lindens commonly grow anywhere from 60 to 80 feet in height but can reach 100 to 150 feet at maturity. Their spread is typically about one-third to one-half their height. Their large, dense canopies make them commanding shade trees. Medium to fast growers, they should reach 30 feet in ten years. Young trees are pyramidal but become more rounded as they age. Their long-lived root systems support these trees for a life span of 100 to 150 years. In 1993 workmen at the Lincoln Home National Historic Site discovered that two lindens thought to be 50 years old in fact dated back to the Civil War!

Lindens are deciduous, shedding their foliage every fall. The oval-shaped leaves

than others in the family. Individual leaves are round with pointed tips and measure only three inches across, giving the tree a fine-textured appearance. Fully mature, they are medium to dark green with paler undersides and toothed edges. The leaves remain green longer than those of the American linden and then turn yellow in fall before browning and dropping in October. The flowers appear in June and are quite similar to those of the American linden.

LITTLELEAF LINDEN CHOICES

Glenleven is a vigorous grower with an open, informal form. The straight trunk, uniform branching, and dense canopy make **Greenspire** the standard of comparison among lindens; this tree is also tolerant of urban conditions.

Silver Linden (Tilia tomentosa)

The silver linden, named for the silvery underside of its leaves, has a broad, pyramidal habit and often grows as a multi-stemmed tree. The species name *tomentosa* refers to the tiny, densely matted hairs under the leaves that give the tree its silvery hue; the tops of the leaves are glossy green. Vigorous and symmetrical, this tree grows to 50 to 70 feet tall and spreads 25 to 45 feet. The last of the lindens to flower each year, this species bears small, fragrant flowers in the summer. The leaves are up to five inches long and so dense that few other plants will grow beneath its branches. The leaves' silvery undersides catch the light when the wind blows, and the bark is initially gray and smooth, later becoming gray-brown and furrowed. This tree tolerates heat, drought, and pollution better than other lindens, and grows well in zones 4 to 7.

SILVER LINDEN CHOICES

Green Mountain grows rapidly and has a dense form and a good branching habit.

Common Symptom	Likely Cause
Curled, wilted, or puckering leaves	Aphids
Defoliation, brown egg masses on trunk	Gypsy moth
Damaged shoots and leaves, visible sawdust	Borers
Skeletonized leaves	Japanese beetles
Mined or blotched leaves	Basswood leaf miner
Brown leaf edges, shoots that have frostbitten appearance	Anthracnose
Reddish brown spots on bark	Canker
White coating on leaves	Powdery mildew
Circular brown spots on leaves	Leaf blight
Brown spots along veins (on European linden)	Leaf blotch

Species	Scale at Maturity	Basic Requirements
American Linden (*Tilia americana*)	Height: 60'–80' Width: 20'–40' Shape: Oval to rounded	Zones 2 through 8 Full sun/part shade Moist, well-drained soil
Littleleaf Linden (*Tilia cordata*)	Height: 60'–70' Width: 30'–45' Shape: Pyramidal, rounded	Zones 3 through 7 Full sun/part shade Moist, well-drained soil
Silver Linden (*Tilia tomentosa*)	Height: 50'–70' Width: 25'–45' Shape: Pyramidal	Zones 4 through 7 Full sun/part shade Moist, well-drained soil

Requirements of Your Linden

Lindens grow best in full sun but can tolerate shade. They prefer well-drained, neutral soil (pH 6.5 to 7.5) but will grow in almost any type of soil so long as it's slightly moist. Lindens survive better in clay soil than do most trees.

Planting Your Linden

The more care you take when you put your tree in the ground, the better it will do during its long life. Follow the complete planting directions provided in chapter 3.

Special notes: Lindens should be planted in the spring. Choose bare-root trees between five and a half and ten feet tall. Or buy a growing potted plant at a nursery, where you likely can find specimens as tall as five feet. Lindens have coarse roots that grow deeply but laterally, so they usually transplant successfully.

Winter is the best time to prune your linden. These trees can handle fairly severe pruning—lindens that have gone ten or more years unpruned can still have their main branches cut back almost to the trunk. They'll rejuvenate over the next five to ten years.

Special Situations for the Linden

A number of pest and disease problems can plague the linden tree, so watch for the symptoms outlined in the table opposite.

MAPLE (*Acer* sp.)

Top Reasons to Plant

- ∾ Spectacular autumn color
- ∾ Wide array of choices
- ∾ Breathtaking shade tree

Inspired by the natural subtlety of Walden Woods, Henry David Thoreau described Walden Pond as "the earth's eye" and the trees on the shore as "the slender eyelashes which fringe it." This early conservationist was especially struck by the red maple, whose flaming leaves, he wrote, are "too fair to be believed."

There are more than a dozen species and hundreds of cultivars of maple trees in this family of well-known yet breathtaking shade trees. While they may vary in rate of growth, size, and leaf character, maples represent some of the best shade trees available for residential yards and gardens. Smaller varieties include Amur, paperbark, and hedge maples. Norway and red maples are medium-size trees, while silver and sugar maples can reach substantial heights.

Maple flowers are small, measuring about one-fifth to one-half an inch long, each with five tiny petals. In some maple varieties, male and female flowers are borne on the same tree; in others, only one sex appears. Some maples have bright red female flowers and yellowish to silver male flowers, while others feature a pale yellow-green color on both males and females. Maple flowers give way to clusters of greenish to bright red winged seeds between three-quarters and one and a quarter inches long. They turn light brown over the summer, while seeds of the sugar maple turn brown in September.

During the spring and summer, maple leaves are fairly ordinary—lobed, untoothed, and green. The show comes in the fall, and it's a sight to behold. Some maples turn a brilliant red, others a spectacular yellow; still others don red, orange, and yellow on the same tree. There are Web sites that track the foliage color as the peak moves south in the fall, so people can make a trip and know they'll see the show, guaranteed.

With such a broad range of characteristics, the maple family offers a variety of options for the home landscape. Most large maples take up significant space, so when you're planting, keep in mind how large they'll eventually get. A practical location is the south or southwest corner of the house (at least 30 to 40 feet away), where you'll eventually have a wonderful shade tree that cools your home in the summer and, after the leaves drop, allows the winter sunlight to reach your house. You can use these tall maples for shade, as screens, or along property lines. Plant them singly as specimens in spacious lawns or in groups to showcase their striking autumn foliage. Sugar maples offer an especially picturesque landmark as they near maturity. They cast an elegant soft shade as well as having a lovely form and beautiful bark. Use fast-growing silver maples to block out an unsightly view until slower-growing shrubs and trees reach the desired height. All maples have sturdy branches that provide shelter for nesting songbirds and squirrels, and their winged seeds are favorites among squirrels, ground birds, songbirds, and deer. Don't be intimidated by the range of options. In the section that follows, I've outlined some of the best choices. (I've given the Japanese maple its own entry. Though it's a member of the same family as the ones mentioned here, it deserves to stand alone. See p. 128.)

Red Maple (Acer rubrum)

Also known as the swamp or scarlet maple, Thoreau's favorite tree consistently tops landscapers' lists of the most hardy, attractive, and easy-to-maintain trees. Growing to 40 to 60 feet tall and half as wide, this beauty stands upright with a slightly rounded shape. It's a relatively fast-growing tree, adding between 18 and 25 feet in a ten-year period.

Red maples prefer wet conditions but will tolerate normal summer dryness with

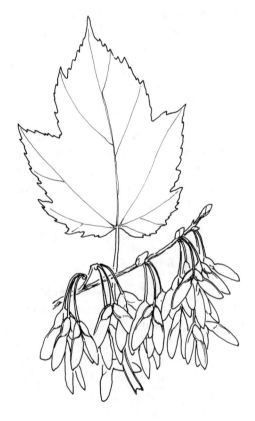

RED MAPLE CHOICES

Autumn Flame grows more slowly than other red maples and reaches 35 feet tall, making it a bit shorter than other varieties. A round-shaped tree with small leaves, this cultivar has good fall color and turns early in the season. **October Glory** is an excellent cultivar that retains its leaves late into the season. Its fall color is crimson red to orange. Broadly oval to rounded in shape, this cultivar reaches 40 feet tall. **Red Sunset,** hardier in the South than many maples, displays classic orange to red fall colors. It has an oval shape and a narrow canopy, measuring 45 feet tall.

Amur Maple (Acer ginnala)

This Asian native gets a head start on spring, producing one- to three-inch leaves while other trees are still bare. It is an excellent low-growing tree for moderate-size yards or problematic soil. Growing to a height of 15 to 18 feet, and an equal width, the Amur maple can be grown as a multistemmed tree, a shrub, or a small tree with a single trunk; it can even be pruned to grow in a container. The tree's rounded, finely branched growth habit creates dense shade under its crown. The late spring flowers are fragrant, and the fall foliage is a brilliant red. The tree is hardy from zones 3 through 8.

Paperbark Maple (Acer griseum)

The papery bark, upright vase shape, and scarlet foliage of the paperbark maple make it a favorite among arborists and home landscapers alike. Its vibrant red fall foliage is especially beautiful when illumi-

grace. Their flowers are small—only one-fifth to two-fifths of an inch long—with short spiderlike filaments. The bright red clusters of flowers—male and female on the same tree—appear in late March or early April just before the leaves emerge. In late spring, they give way to bunches of bright red winged seeds at the tips of branches, which turn reddish brown before they drop early in the summer. These seeds are quite popular with squirrels and birds, not to mention schoolchildren, who spin them about in the air.

Red maple leaves are serrated and range in length between two and five inches. Depending on the species, some are three-lobed, others five; some have light green undersides, while others are silvery white. Red maples are gorgeous specimen trees especially in the fall, when the reds, oranges, and yellows last several weeks. The red maple is often one of the first trees to turn those familiar fall hues. This North American native is hardy in zones 3 to 9.

The red maple's attractive bark is dark and smooth. It's also thin, so be careful when using mechanical yard tools.

nated from below by landscape lights. Most specimens have multiple trunks that branch close to the ground, but it can be trained into a single trunk if you prefer.

Native to China, this slow-growing tree eventually reaches 20 to 30 feet tall and wide. It has trifoliate leaves and unique orange to bronze bark that peels once the tree reaches two or three years old. The bark of the bare tree is gorgeous in the winter. This tree does well in zones 4 to 8.

Sugar Maple (Acer saccharum)

The appropriately named sugar maple is the primary source of the sap used to make maple syrup and sugar. Some nicknames refer to the tree's popularity among woodworkers, such as hard maple, rock maple, curly maple, and bird's eye maple.

Sugar maples predominate in the deciduous forests of the northeast and can be found as far west as the Mississippi River in the northern Midwest. They commonly grow to between 60 and 75 feet with a spread of 40 to 50 feet. Slow growers, sugar maples may take a century to reach 60 feet. The dense, upright, oval to rounded crown and broad spread make the sugar maple an excellent shade tree. It's native to America and Canada, and grows in zones 3 to 8.

The sugar maple's leaves are palm-shaped with five deeply indented lobes, or points. They are relatively large, measuring from three to six inches across. The margins between the lobes are shallow and smooth, distinguishing them from leaves of the similar-looking red maple, which have serrated lobe margins. Another clue to distinguishing between these two very similar trees: sugar maple leaves have U-shaped connections between lobes, while the red maple's are V-shaped. During growing season, the leaves are a dull, light green on top and paler underneath. In the fall, the sugar maple takes center stage

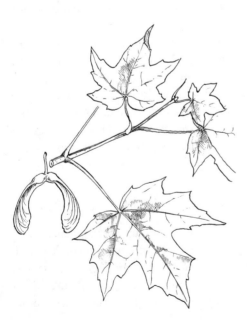

when its leaves display vibrant shades of yellow, golden orange, and orange-red through mid-October.

A pale yellow-green, flowers are small—only one-fifth to half an inch long—with five tiny petals. They appear in clusters before the leaves emerge in April or May.

Avoid planting your sugar maple too near streets and roadways because it's sensitive to the salt used on roads in winter. Because the roots of a healthy, mature sugar maple can exceed twice the diameter of the crown, and because it's not happy in compacted soil, the tree should be located at least 50 feet away from the street, ideally 100 feet. Before you choose this tree, be sure you have good drainage and access to irrigation, because the sugar maple won't tolerate drought.

SUGAR MAPLE CHOICES

Bonfire is a rapid grower with beautiful red fall foliage. This cultivar requires ample space to spread out. Characterized by its dense branches and quick growth, **Commemoration** is a good choice for suburban settings. **Green Mountain** is a good choice for dry, confined areas and has leathery, dark green leaves. Also colorful in the fall, **Legacy** is drought tolerant and can withstand heat and wind.

Hedge Maple (Acer campestre)

The hedge maple is so named because in Europe, where it is native, it's often used as a hedge rather than a shade tree. Some maple hedges have been maintained for more than a hundred years. The hedge maple tolerates severe pruning, but it makes a dense, tall screen whether pruned or not.

At maturity, a hedge maple is 25 to 35 feet tall and equally wide, with a low-branched, rounded form. But there is considerable variability from one tree to the next. If you decide to grow the hedge maple as a tree, the lower branches can be removed to create clearance beneath the crown.

While the hedge maple doesn't thrive in highly compacted soil, it tolerates dry, alkaline soil quite well. Its leaves, which turn yellow in the fall, are two to four inches long and wide, with three to five lobes on each. The hedge maple is a slow grower, averaging about two feet per year when young. It's a desirable option for a patio or yard not only because it stays small and creates dense shade but also because it's relatively insect and disease free. It will do well in zones 4 to 8.

Silver Maple (Acer saccharinum)

The silver maple is known for the sweeping pattern of its branches, whose upturned ends give this tree its own classic character. It's also a favorite because it has a wonderful vase shape for such a large tree, and it's the fastest-growing of the maples, adding between 24 and 36 inches in height each year or about 25 to 35 feet in a ten-year period. Ultimately, the silver maple will reach a height of 50 to 70 feet, with a spread of 30 to 45 feet. Not surprisingly, the silver maple has been a popular shade tree for decades. But because it's so common throughout the United States, it can be vulnerable to insect and disease problems that spread easily from one nearby tree to another. Ecological diversity is key to the health of the landscape.

The silver maple is native to the United States and grows in a large area, from zones 3 to 9. It can do well in acidic, moist areas where other trees suffer, even thriving in standing water for several weeks at a time. It also transplants easily and can grow where few others can, such as in dry, alkaline soil.

The first hint of the silver maple's red flower clusters signals that spring has arrived. The fruit, when it comes, is less than an inch long. The leaves are three to six inches long, opposite, deeply incised, and whitened underneath, giving the tree a silvery appearance as the leaves flutter in the wind. In fall this color gives way to stunning yellow.

Avoid planting the silver maple close to your house because its wood is weak, and the branches are prone to breakage in high winds. Also, the roots often grow aggressively on the surface, entering uninvited into septic tank drainage fields and into broken water and sewer pipes.

SILVER MAPLE CHOICES

Silver Queen has bright green leaves whose undersides have a silvery tint. It has the advantage of being fruitless and therefore neater in the yard.

Norway Maple (Acer platanoides)

There are so many wonderful choices in the maple family, and this is another: a fast grower that produces a profusion of yellow flowers before leaves appear, and an eye-popping display of yellow or deep red foliage in the fall.

As the name suggests, the Norway maple is native to Europe. It adapts to a wide variety of soils, including alkaline, and grows successfully in urban areas where air pollution, poor drainage, compacted soil, and drought are common. It is happy either in part shade or full sun. This tree is quite accommodating to urban and suburban environments and has been planted in large numbers.

The crown of the Norway maple is rounded, and the profile is rounded to oval. The leaves measure four to seven inches across and have five pointed lobes with

slightly toothed edges. Growing well in zones 3 to 7, the Norway maple reaches a height of 40 to 50 feet, with a roughly equal spread. Its yellow flowers come early, then the leaves.

Like many maples, the Norway has a shallow, aggressive root system. Competing with lawn grass for water may cause it to develop surface roots, so be sure to plant your tree four to six feet from any sidewalk or driveway. The tree's most serious problem is that its seeds germinate quite easily and may compete with native plants in the surrounding area.

NORWAY MAPLE CHOICES

Crimson King is oval-shaped, reaching 45 feet tall. Its purple summer foliage gives way to paler maroon or reddish bronze leaves in the autumn. A rapid grower, **Emerald Queen** has a straight trunk and ascending branches. Beside a narrow street is a prime location for an **Olmsted** Norway maple because of the tree's upright growth habit. This tree tolerates a variety of environmental stresses and transplants easily. The **Parkway** cultivar also thrives in somewhat limited space, and is a rapid grower with a strong central leader. A dense shade tree, the **Summershade** cultivar is heat-

Common Symptom	Likely Cause
Poor growth, weak branches	Girdled roots
Surface roots, suckers	Compacted soil
Wrinkled leaves, stunted growth, defoliation	Aphids
Girdled branches, scarred trunk, premature shedding of leaves	Borers
Small bumps on leaves and branches	Scale insects
Sunken spots on leaves	Anthracnose
Swollen, bleeding lesions on stems and trunk	Canker
Mushrooms sprouting at base of tree	Shoestring root rot
Foliage turning yellow or brown, collapsing	Verticillium wilt

Species	Scale at Maturity	Basic Requirements
Red Maple (*Acer rubrum*)	Height: 40'–60' Width: 20'–30' Shape: Rounded	Zones 3 through 9 Full sun/part shade Moist, well-drained soil
Amur Maple (*Acer ginnala*)	Height: 15'–18' Width: 15'–18' Shape: Rounded	Zones 3 through 8 Full sun/part shade Moist, well-drained soil
Paperbark Maple (*Acer griseum*)	Height: 20'–30' Width: 20'–30' Shape: Vaselike, rounded canopy	Zones 4 through 8 Full sun/part shade Moist, well-drained soil
Sugar Maple (*Acer saccharum*)	Height: 60'–75' Width: 40'–50' Shape: Upright, oval to rounded	Zones 3 through 8 Full sun/part shade Moist, well-drained soil
Hedge Maple (*Acer campestre*)	Height: 25'–35' Width: 25'–35' Shape: Rounded	Zones 4 through 8 Full sun/part shade Moist, well-drained soil
Silver Maple (*Acer saccharinum*)	Height: 50'–70' Width: 30'–45' Shape: Vaselike	Zones 3 through 9 Full sun/part shade Moist, well-drained soil
Norway Maple (*Acer platanoides*)	Height: 40'–50' Width: 40'–50' Shape: Rounded to oval	Zones 3 through 7 Full sun/part shade Moist, well-drained soil

resistant, but its surface roots may pose problems. The **Superform** cultivar is so named for its straight trunk and even growth, though in youth it grows slowly.

Requirements of Your Maple

Maples prefer full sun but tolerate light shade. They like a well-drained soil that is acid to neutral (pH 5.5 to 7.0) but accept almost any soil so long as it is kept slightly moist. Sugar maples are more demanding of moist soil than silver maples, which will tolerate dry soil to an extent. Keep in mind that maple roots often grow aboveground and can interfere with existing structures and plants, so be sure your maple has lots of breathing room.

Planting Your Maple

The more care you take when you put your tree in the ground, the better it will do during its long life. Follow the complete planting directions provided in chapter 3.

Special notes: Many maples produce their best color only in their preferred zone range, so ask the nurseryman which maple will be most dazzling in your local area.

Do not plant your maple in the vicinity of a black walnut tree, because a substance secreted by the walnut's roots is poisonous to the maple family. The combination of maple and walnut works well only in ice cream, so plant your maple at least 50 feet away from a black walnut.

Caring for Your Maple

Follow the instructions on seasonal care for young and mature trees—watering, mulching, fertilizing, staking, and pruning—described in chapter 3.

Special Situations for the Maple

Maples can suffer from the usual problems that plague other trees, such as aphid infestation or compacted soil. But they are especially vulnerable to the toxic substance secreted by the roots of the black walnut tree. This substance is poisonous to several types of plants, including the maple, and can stunt, wilt, or even kill plants within a radius of one and a half times the distance from the walnut tree's trunk to its drip line. If your maple's growth is stunted or its leaves become lifeless, move the tree far away from the black walnut tree to restore its health.

OAK FAMILY (*Quercus* sp.)

Top Reasons to Plant

- Majestic scale
- Fall color
- Long life

The poet John Keats described oaks as "those green-robed senators of mighty woods." From their majestic scale to their fabled longevity, oaks are perhaps the standard-bearers for all trees, the trees' tree, if you will.

Generally large, long-living trees, oaks are valued highly for both their timber and stately beauty. Most members of the large oak family are deciduous, losing their leaves in early winter, though some southern and southwestern oaks are evergreen. Northern oaks display gorgeous fall color and produce the familiar acorn. Many oaks are native to the United States, and many specimens are listed as historic trees because of their longevity.

After their fall display of brilliant color, mature, large oaks continue to draw attention as they stand regally in the winter landscape, their wide branches spreading outward and their rough bark presenting an interesting texture. They are among the best specimen or shade trees if you can give them the space they need. Position your oak out in the open, away from buildings, where it will have room to grow to its full size.

Oaks also attract a variety of wildlife with their annual or biannual acorn production. Songbirds, deer, squirrels, and even wild turkeys are just a few of the acorn lovers you may see admiring your oak.

These large trees also provide shelter for many animals.

Oaks are organized into three main groups: red oaks, white oaks, and live oaks. These categories are based on leaf shape, but the groups have other distinguishing traits as well.

White Oak Family

In this family, the leaves have rounded lobes. The bark is whitish, and the acorns mature in one year. This group includes species native to Europe and Asia as well as North America.

White Oak
(Quercus alba)

The definitive trees in the family, white oaks grow into massive trees. At maturity, they can reach 75 to 100 feet in nature (50 to 80 feet in the home landscape), their canopy typically spreading as wide as their height or wider. Though they grow slowly, eventually trunks of mature trees measure three to four feet in diameter. White oaks commonly live 350 to 400 years, some even reaching the ripe old age of 500.

Common in the eastern part of the country, white oaks have rough, scaly bark and rounded leaf canopies with sturdy horizontal branches. They are resistant to a variety of urban ills such as drought, heat, road salt, and pollution. They're also a good investment—according to Gary Moll of the Urban Forestry Center, a healthy white oak in a residential yard can add an estimated $1,500 to $3,000 to the value of your property.

White oaks range farther north than most other oaks. They are cold-hardy up to

the Great Lakes and into southern New England (zone 4) and grow as far south as east Texas and the Gulf states (zone 8).

White oak leaves emerge in May as bright red or pink, turning quickly to silver-gray. Somewhat dull on the surface and pale underneath, they turn medium green by midsummer and then a rich reddish burgundy color in fall. Typically five to nine inches long and two to four inches wide, the leaves have seven to nine deeply cut lobes with rounded tips. They fall in late autumn, although some interior leaves hold on until January. Deer love white oak acorns like candy.

White oaks produce drooping catkins just after the leaves emerge in the spring. They are yellow-green, one to two inches long. By September or early October, the catkins give way to three-quarter-inch light green acorns that turn brown as they ripen. Sometimes acorns grow singly on a twig, other times in pairs.

Chinquapin Oak (Quercus muehlenbergii)

An American native known by a variety of names, including yellow oak and yellow chestnut oak, the Chinquapin (or Chinkapin) oak has light gray or silvery white bark similar to that of the white oak. Hardy in zones 4 to 7, its growth habit is sometimes upright, oval, and symmetrical, but is more often wide-spreading. It grows to 40 to 50 feet tall by 50 to 60 feet wide, and the lower branches are of great diameter. Chinquapin leaves are almost lance-shaped, with their crenations pointing forward, resembling somewhat the flint arrows of Native Americans. Their fall color is chartreuse to yellow-brown, and leaf drop is completed by late autumn. The chinquapin oak's pollen-bearing catkins appear in midspring and fertilize the inconspicuous female flowers on the same tree. Like the acorns of other members of the white oak group, Chinquapin acorns take only a single season to develop. They are relatively small and reportedly sweeter than those of other oaks, but only your squirrels know for sure.

English Oak (Quercus robur)

Native to Europe, northern Africa, and western Asia, the English oak is similar in leaf appearance to the white oak, but its spread and fall color aren't quite as majestic. In urban environments, the English oak will reach 40 to 60 feet tall and wide, spreading out as it ages. Some cultivars, however, are tall and columnar. English oaks grow at a slow to moderate rate, adding 12 to 18 inches a year. They tolerate drought, pollution, restricted root space, and a wide pH range. They are hardy in zones 3 through 7.

The English oak has alternating, somewhat egg-shaped leaves with three- to five-inch-long lobes. The leaf shape is variable and is often confused with that of white oak leaves. Rounded and dark green in color, the lobes have pale undersides that turn brown in the fall. The English oak is monoecious, meaning it has male and female organs on a single tree. It produces catkins in midspring that fertilize female flowers on the same or nearby trees, eventually resulting in long acorns that take a single season to mature. Acorns measure one to two inches long and grow on stalks; crops are heavy at two- to four-year intervals.

Bur Oak (Quercus macrocarpa)

In deepest winter, the structure and furrowed branches of the bur oak make this tree a showstopper. Named for the bristly husks, or caps, of its acorns, the bur oak is also called prairie, blue, scrub, or mossycup oak. Capable of surviving from two hundred to four hundred years, it's found in the wild in deep rich bottomlands, where it reaches a large size, and on dry ridges and western slopes, where it is small and gnarled. The bur oak is the most "western" of the eastern oaks. Its native range extends all the way from the East Coast to the foothills of the Rockies, where it typically grows as a shrub, and from Montana south to western Texas.

The bur oak is often the only tree on hill-sides in the western part of Iowa; in most of the rest of its range, it is found with a variety of other species, including hickory, white ash, white elm, basswood, and aspen. In these settings, the bur oak has earned the name "wolf tree," because as adjoining trees die, it stretches its branches to gobble up the newly voided space.

Bur oaks need room to spread out—one specimen in Paris, Kentucky, measures an astounding 96 feet tall and 103 feet wide. But you can relax—your bur oak probably won't exceed 70 to 80 feet tall, and it will develop an impressive leaf canopy of equal width. The bark is dark gray, thick, and so deeply furrowed that it breaks into distinct ridges. Though the bur oak is a slow to moderate grower, early regular fertilizing can help move things along.

Ten to twelve inches long and half as wide, bur oak leaves are large with rounded lobes, growing alternately along the stems. Some people think the leaf shape is reminiscent of a bass fiddle. Deep sinuses form on the leaves' lower half, while their upper half has very shallow lobes. The top portion of the leaf is wavy rather than lobed. A dark shiny green above, leaves are lighter green to gray underneath. Their fall color is yellow-green to brown.

Bur oak flowers occur as spikes of many florets. They appear on old or new wood, often just as the leaves unfold, but they're not at all showy. The acorns, however, are the largest produced by our native oaks, measuring a whopping two inches across. (The biggest bur oak acorn I ever saw was from the Sam Houston Kissing Bur in San Marcos, Texas, so named because Houston, while campaigning for governor, kissed a group of women there who had presented him with a flag. The Sam Houston bur oak acorn was more than three inches in diameter; everything is bigger in Texas, of course!) Almost round with a bur or mosslike, fringed cup covering half or more of its form, it can be thought of as an acorn with a bad hair day. It usually takes seven to ten years before a bur oak produces its first acorns, and then the acorns come only every three to five years. But in nature, a mature bur oak could produce 5,000 acorns in a single season. Of these, only 25 to 50 will sprout and send down a taproot four feet deep just in the first year. As for all those other acorns, the birds get their share, squirrels and other acorn lovers hoard what they need, and the rest are left for the weevils.

The bur oak tolerates poor soils, wide soil pH ranges, and—because of its extensive root system—serious drought conditions. It does not like continuously wet soil. The bur oak does well in zones 2 through 8.

Red Oak Family

Leaves in the Red Oak family are bristle-tipped and have five to eleven lobes. The bark is dark, and the acorns require two years to mature. Red oaks are native to the Western Hemisphere. The "red" refers to the color of leaves in the fall.

Northern Red Oak
(Quercus rubra)

Red oaks are common trees in residential yards and along streets, and for good reason. They're easy to grow, resist urban ills such as salt and pollution, and tolerate heat and drought fairly well. They also support a variety of wildlife.

Red oaks grow to between 60 and 75 feet tall at maturity. Their large canopy typically measures an equal spread, especially if they have lots of space in which to grow. Their growth rate is medium, about two to three feet a year over their first ten years, then one and a half to two feet a year. Red oaks can live up to three hundred years.

Hardy up to the Canadian border (zone 4), red oaks grow successfully farther north than most other oaks. They can withstand

frigid winter temperatures as low as –30°F. But some varieties of red oaks also thrive in the South, dotting landscapes throughout Texas and the Gulf states (zone 7).

Fuzzy, reddish pink foliage emerges in May, turning light green, then darker green as the summer progresses. The leaves turn a golden shade in the fall before dropping in mid-November. Red oak leaves are four to eight inches long and two to four inches wide. They have from seven to eleven deeply cut lobes with pointed, almost spiny tips (distinguishing them from white oak leaves, which have fewer lobes and rounded tips). The leaves are somewhat dull on the surface and pale yellowish green beneath.

In the spring, red oaks produce male catkins just after the leaves emerge. These yellow-green hanging clusters are three to four inches long. Inconspicuous female flowers grow where the leaf stems join the twigs. By September or early October, the flowers give way to dark brown woolly acorns between three-quarters and one and a quarter inches long with saucerlike caps. They grow individually or in pairs. Birds and mammals from songbirds to deer covet the nuts concealed inside.

Scarlet Oak
(Quercus coccinea)

The scarlet oak is aptly named. Its red foliage in the early spring matches the color of the inner bark, and the leaves turn a bright scarlet red in the first weeks of autumn. This tree has a somewhat more open growth habit than do red oaks. It reaches 70 to 80 feet tall with a spread of 45 to 50 feet as part of a residential landscape, adding one to two feet to its height each year. The crown is rounded and open at maturity, the tree upright and oval. It is hardy in zones 4 through 8.

Scarlet oak leaves are four to seven inches long with five to nine narrow, bristle-tipped lobes separated by deep sinuses. In the summer, the leaves are a deep green with whitish undersides, and the tree bears acorns singly or in pairs. The acorns are about one inch long with deep, bowl-like, scaly cups. Concentric rings are often noticeable around an acorn's tip. Chipmunks, mice, and blue jays relish these tasty nuts.

The scarlet oak tree is more tolerant of dry conditions than are other oaks. Its trunk flares out at the base, so be sure not to plant it too close to sidewalks.

Pin Oak (Quercus palustris)

Its handsome pyramidal shape and dense, somewhat drooping branches have made the pin oak a common sight in city parks and lining suburban streets. Also growing in the wild in the eastern and central United States, the pin oak is notable for its deep red fall color and its leaves that hang on until late winter.

By maturity, around 125 to 175 years, pin oaks are typically 60 to 70 feet tall. Their width is usually about 25 to 40 feet. They thrive in zones 4 through 7. Older trees are high crowned, having shed many of their lower branches over the years. Pin oaks have a smaller canopy than some of their massive oak relatives, but they are one of the fastest growing, reaching 30 feet in only twelve years. For this reason, this tree has been overplanted as a street tree in many communities. Unfortunately, lack of diversity of plantings also means limited diversity of beneficial insects and songbirds. As a result, the trees in overplanted areas become increasingly vulnerable to disease and pest insects.

Pin oaks produce leaves that are three to five inches long and two to five inches wide; the leaves' five deep lobes are toothed and pointed. Male catkins appear in the spring after the leaves have emerged; they are yellow-green and measure two to three inches long. By September or early October, the catkins give way to short, flattened, reddish brown acorns. These ripen only every other year, but waterbirds, songbirds, and a variety of mammals agree that it's well worth the wait. Although the pin oak is deciduous, its leaves are reluctant to fall at the end of the season; some can remain on the tree well into February.

Live Oak Family

To call these "live" is not to imply that other oaks are dead! The word refers to the tree's evergreen foliage. This tree's leaves, which are not lobed, are long ovals with rounded tips. This is a family with a single member, also called the live oak.

Live Oak
(Quercus virginiana)

The majestic live oak is grown widely throughout the South in large residential yards, in parks as specimen trees, and along streets. Spanish moss often drapes its thick branches, giving this already powerful tree a beautiful, haunting look. This is my favorite oak.

"Massive" is the invariable descriptor for live oaks, and it hardly does them justice. Their height is in the fairly modest 40- to 60-foot range, but their trunk is short

and broad, reaching a diameter of 3 to 4 feet. Their large canopy typically spreads 60 to 80 feet, and the horizontally growing limbs of mature trees are often heavy enough to sweep the ground. The live oaks' growth rate is moderate: they typically add two to two and a half feet to their height each year while they are young, slowing a bit as they mature.

Individual leaves are one and a quarter to three inches long and up to one inch wide. Narrow and elongated with rounded tips,

they have smooth edges and a yellowish vein down the center. The texture is leathery, the edges slightly curled. New yellowish green leaves emerge in midspring, turning shiny dark green on their upper surface and grayish green on their hairy undersides.

The live oak's male catkins bloom in hanging clusters. Female flowers appear singly or in clusters of one to five where the leaves join the twigs. They give way over the growing season to narrow, dark brown—almost black—acorns with caps covering about one-third their length. The acorns grow either alone or in groups of three to five on the twigs.

Live oaks grow most successfully in the mild climate of the Deep South (zone 10). While they survive as far north as the Carolinas, and along the coast into Virginia (zone 7), they are semideciduous in these areas, and their thick, spreading limbs are vulnerable to injury from ice storms.

Live oaks tolerate some shade but are most at home in full sun. They do well in sandy soil and will thrive even in compacted soil so long as it is moist. Ideally the soil should be on the acid side (pH 4.0 to 6.5).

The life span of the live oak is measured in centuries. This ultimate southern shade tree is grown widely as an avenue tree, with each set apart about 90 feet. And because live oaks can handle car exhaust, they are often planted along the sides of roadways, forming stately canopies over roads in the South.

Requirements of Your Oak

Most oaks grow best in full sun but can tolerate light shade. Red oaks are the most shade-tolerant of all the oaks, while the bur oak requires full sun to thrive. Oak trees prefer well-drained, moist soil but can manage somewhat dry soil for short periods. They are most comfortable in soils on the acid side (pH 6.1 to 7.0). In alkaline soils (pH 7.0 and above), most oaks develop chlorosis, a mineral-deficiency disease that causes the green leaves to turn pale or even yellow. (Bur oaks are an exception and can handle somewhat alkaline soil.) If you are unsure about your soil, consider testing its acidity level. Use a pH meter for a quick check or, for a more thorough analysis, get a soil test kit from your local county extension service.

Planting Your Oak

The more care you take when you put your tree in the ground, the better it will do during its long life. Follow the complete planting directions provided in chapter 3.

Special notes: Because they have a deep taproot, white oaks can be difficult to transplant. Nurseries sell young trees to increase the chances of successful transplanting. Oaks may not do well in yards with an ecology different from their native horticultural zones, so be sure to select a locally grown tree.

Choose trees that have been dug in the spring and whose roots and soil ball are wrapped in burlap or come in a container. You should also check for the presence of 6 to 12 inches of new growth from the tree's one or two seasonal growth spurts; each year's growth is visible on the bark of the main stem. Steer clear of trees that don't have evidence of new growth. If you buy an oak with a trunk larger than two and a half inches in diameter, hire a professional to plant it.

Stake newly planted oaks only if they

are at risk of being blown over or uprooted before getting established. Where heavy winds are a problem, stake new trees for up to a year. Staked longer, trees may not develop sufficient stabilizing roots on their own.

Caring for Your Oak

Follow the instructions on seasonal care for young and mature trees—watering, mulching, fertilizing, staking, and pruning—described in chapter 3.

A special note: Mature oaks do not require routine pruning. In the case of an injured or broken branch, cut it off cleanly and promptly with a sharp pruning saw, or use loppers for branches an inch or less in diameter. This will promote healing and prevent the invasion of insects or rot into tree tissues. You may also want to prune off lower branches of large trees to allow more light into your yard or to create more walking space. For pruning jobs on large trees, hire a certified arborist. Never prune between April and July—these are prime invasion times for oak wilt.

Special Situations for the Oak

Oaks are vulnerable to the usual pests such as gall insects and especially the gypsy moth, but they can also suffer from an attack by oak mites. These pests are only one-fiftieth of an inch long, but they pack a lot of power from their compact bodies.

Common Symptom	Likely Cause
Defoliation, brown egg cases appearing on trunk	Gypsy moth larvae
Irregular tan or brown spots on leaves at veins, sunken spots on leaves	Anthracnose
Swellings and growths on twigs and leaves	Gall insects
Leaves stippled, yellowing, drying out, galls on leaves	Oak mites
Leaves turning bronze, wilting, dropping	Oak wilt
Leaves coated with white powder	Powdery mildew
Green leaves turning pale or yellow with green veins	Chlorosis (caused by alkaline soil)

Species	Scale at Maturity	Basic Requirements
WHITE OAK FAMILY		
White Oak (*Quercus alba*)	Height: 50'–80' Width: 50'–80' Shape: Oval to rounded	Zones 3 through 8 Full sun/partial shade Moist, well-drained acidic soil
Bur Oak (*Quercus macrocarpa*)	Height: 70'–80' Width: 70'–80' Shape: Rounded	Zones 2 through 8 Full sun Moist, well-drained soil, some tolerance for alkalinity
Chinquapin Oak (*Quercus muehlenbergii*)	Height: 40'–50' Width: 50'–60' Shape: Rounded	Zones 4 through 7 Full sun/part shade Moist, well-drained acidic soil
English Oak (*Quercus robur*)	Height: 40'–60' Width: 40'–60' Shape: Rounded	Zones 3 through 7 Full sun/part shade Moist, well-drained acidic soil
RED OAK FAMILY		
Northern Red Oak (*Quercus rubra*)	Height: 60'–75' Width: 60'–75' Shape: Rounded	Zones 4 through 7 Full sun/part shade Moist, well-drained acidic soils
Scarlet Oak (*Quercus coccinea*)	Height: 70'–80' Width: 45'–50' Shape: Upright, oval	Zones 4 through 8 Full sun/part shade Moist, well-drained acidic soil
Pin Oak (*Quercus palustris*)	Height: 60'–70' Width: 25'–40' Shape: Pyramidal	Zones 4 through 7 Full sun/part shade Moist, well-drained acidic soil

Species	Scale at Maturity	Basic Requirements
LIVE OAK FAMILY		
Live Oak (*Quercus virginiana*)	Height: 40'–60' Width: 60'–80' Shape: Rounded	Zones 7 through 10 Full sun/part shade Moist, well-drained acidic soil

Resembling tiny spiders, oak mites have four pairs of legs and piercing-sucking mouths. They range in color from yellow or green to red or brown. If the top surfaces of the lower leaves of your oak are stippled with small yellow dots or red spots, mites are the likely culprit. You should also look for fine webbing on the leaves, stalks, and adjacent stems.

Fungi also attack oak trees, resulting in oak wilt. This disease hits red oaks the hardest, but all oaks are susceptible, especially in the north-central, mid-Atlantic, and midwestern United States. Small insects such as beetles and borers spread the disease, but so can humans (by inadvertently transporting the bugs on their tools or clothes) and even squirrels. The fungus enters the tree through wounds in the bark, especially during the early spring growth period, when trees are developing new wood. It causes the leaves to turn a sickly bronze color before wilting and eventually falling off.

As a precaution, prune healthy trees only in the winter when they are dormant or well after their vulnerable spring growth spurt (roughly April through July). Also avoid bringing firewood into the yard, because it may be infested with fungus-carrying insects.

OSAGE ORANGE
(*Maclura pomifera*)

Top Reasons to Plant

- Strong form and texture
- Interesting bark
- Orangelike fruit

Whenever I think of the Osage orange, a particular specimen always comes to mind. It's growing on Red Hill Plantation, the Virginia home of the distinguished eighteenth-century statesman Patrick Henry. This tree remains one of the two largest Osage oranges in the United States, measuring in at 54 feet tall and 90 feet wide.

The Osage orange tree was unknown in the East until Lewis and Clark discovered it growing abundantly in a small area of eastern Oklahoma and portions of Missouri, Texas, and Arkansas. Despite this limited early range, the Osage orange has been planted in greater numbers throughout the United States than perhaps any other species in North America. It can be found south of the Great Lakes and north of Florida (zone 9A), stretching across the

whole of eastern North America into the Great Plains states and almost to the Rocky Mountains. Used extensively as a living fence by settlers during the pioneer period, Osage orange trees can be found along western settlement trails and old fort locations even in the Pacific Northwest. (The thorns acted like barbed wire.) It is hardy in zones 4 through 9.

The name "Osage" pays tribute to the Native American tribe that used the tree's flexible wood for bows and arrows, and "orange" refers to the orangelike aroma of the tree's ripened fruit. Also known as

hedge, hedge apple, bowwood, and bodark (from the French *bois d'arc*, meaning "wood of the bow"), these trees are easily recognized by their glossy, lance-shaped leaves and their short, stout one-inch thorns, which increase the tree's value as fence material on farms and ranches.

The Osage orange can function as a shrub or a tree depending on its surroundings. Left standing alone in full sun, it will become a multistemmed shrub. If it has neighboring competition for space from either side, or if it's pruned, it can become a single-stemmed tree. Young trees are fast growers and develop an upright, pyramidal habit. They reach average heights of 30 to 35 feet, spreads of 20 to 25 feet, and have trunk diameters of one and a half feet.

Osage orange bark is light gray-brown tinged with orange; on large trees it separates into shaggy strips. The thick and shiny leaves alternate along twigs, measuring about three to six inches long and two to three inches wide. They have a long, tapering, pointed tip and a rounded leaf base. Dark green on top with paler green undersides, these leaves turn bright yellow in the fall before they drop.

Osage orange trees are either male or female—only the females bear fruit, often called hedge apples. The fruit is a bulky, green-yellow wrinkled ball up to six inches in diameter. Inside is a core surrounded by up to 200 small seeds. When warmed by the sun's rays, its skin smells like an orange rind. The fruit ripens in the fall and often hangs on the tree after all the leaves have fallen off. If you're standing underneath an Osage orange, watch out—you could get beaned by one of these heavy fruits!

Osage orange enthusiasts describe the tree as "picturesque" rather than beautiful. It possesses strong form, texture, and character, and as it matures, it develops a thick, gnarled appearance that some might imagine to have been borrowed from the pages of an Edgar Allan Poe story. There are now several thornless male varieties on the market.

Requirements of Your Osage Orange

The Osage orange prefers open, sunny areas and can grow in a variety of soils.

Planting Your Osage Orange

The more care you take when you put your tree in the ground, the better it will do during its long life. Follow the complete planting directions provided in chapter 3.

Care for Your Osage Orange

Follow the instructions on seasonal care for young and mature trees—watering, mulching, fertilizing, staking, and pruning—described in chapter 3.

A special note: Winter is the best time to remove damaged or diseased Osage orange limbs. Be sure to wear gloves to avoid thorns and the milky sap of Osage orange stems and fruit, which may cause skin irritation. Also remember that this tree has dense wood, so keep your pruning saw sharp.

Common Symptom	Likely Cause
New green, leafy plants appearing in the foliage of the tree	Leafy mistletoe
Foliage turning yellow or brown, collapsing	Verticilium wilt
Weakened or scarred trunk, knots on limbs, twig drop	Stem borers
Branches encrusted with small bumps	Scale insects
Bark at the base of the tree that has been chewed	Rodents

Species	Scale at Maturity	Basic Requirements
Osage orange (*Maclura pomifera*)	Height: 30'–35' Width: 20'–25' Shape: Pyramidal	Zones 4 through 9 Full sun Moist, well-drained soil

Special Situations
for the Osage Orange

The Osage orange's extensive, tough root system can be difficult to control. You may need to remove sprouts two years in a row to be effective in reining it in.

Osage oranges usually live trouble-free lives in the home landscape, but they may sometimes host a variety of invasive insects.

POPLAR (*Populus* sp.)

Top Reasons to Plant

- ∾ Tolerance of hot summers and cold winters
- ∾ Fast growth
- ∾ Fluttering leaves

George Washington loved the outdoors and spent his boyhood afternoons eagerly learning agricultural and farming techniques from his half-brother, Lawrence, owner of an 8,000-acre estate in the Virginia countryside. After Lawrence's death, Washington assumed ownership of the expansive property, Mount Vernon, and added 15,000 acres when he married Martha Dandridge Custis. He relished his role as landscape architect, planting long rows of trees along winding paths. These plantings provided the backdrop for countless hours of entertaining and philosophizing with Mount Vernon's many guests.

Washington especially admired the tulip poplar and in 1785 planted several that still thrive at Mount Vernon today. These national treasures partly inspired my own Famous and Historic Trees project—I realized how lovely it would be to plant descendants of Washington's tulip poplars! We gathered the seeds and planted them several times over a few years, but nothing grew. Dr. Frank Santamour, the late tree geneticist of the National Arboretum, realized that because the trees had grown so tall—between 80 and 100 feet high—bees were unable to reach high enough to pollinate them. When we tried pollinating the seeds by hand, we were finally rewarded with direct descendants of Washington's own tulip poplars.

The poplar family has many members. Also called aspen and cottonwood, the poplar is generally a fast-growing tree—you can have an effective screen in less than five years. But because they are quite sensitive to air pollution, artificial lighting, compacted soil, salt, drought, and heat, they're best in far suburbs and rural areas, where they can grace open fields or riverbanks.

Because poplars grow so rapidly, they are useful as visual screens and for wind protection or shade. These lanky trees are best grown in clumps or groups, space permitting. Because Lombardy poplars grow quickly and have a narrow, erect habit, they are useful planted in rows as privacy screens, to line borders, and for wind protection. They are often used to line rural drives.

Eastern Poplar
(Populus deltoides)

The eastern poplar can add up to four or five feet to its height each year. It reaches

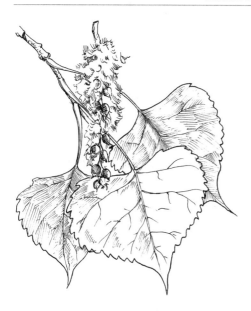

between 40 and 70 feet at maturity, about sixty to seventy-five years old. As the tree grows, its large canopy spreads nearly as wide as the tree is tall. But once it reaches maturity, the poplar can decline rapidly, its brittle branches often falling victim to weather or disease. This tree grows well

from zones 2 to 9. In the Great Plains, the eastern poplar, also known as cottonwood, is highly valued as one of the few large trees that can thrive in such a harsh, dry climate.

Eastern poplar leaves emerge in early May. Between three and six inches long and three and four inches wide, they have a triangular shape and coarsely toothed edges. Light green in the spring, they darken as they mature. Like the leaves of all poplars, eastern poplar leaves have distinctive flattened stems, causing them to twist in the breeze and display their glossy lighter green undersides. Early in the fall, usually September, poplar foliage turns bright yellow before dropping.

Poplars bear male and female flowers on separate trees. The three-inch-long drooping red male catkins emerge in mid to late April before the leaves appear. As spring progresses, catkins on female poplars develop drooping clusters of small, yellow-green flower capsules. These capsules dry and split, releasing silvery white tufted seeds that blow in the wind, accounting for the tree's nickname "cottonwood." These seeds are a favorite snack for songbirds and animals such as chipmunks and squirrels, waterfowl, and deer.

EASTERN POPLAR CHOICES

Male poplars are not messy in the landscape because they don't produce the characteristic tufted seeds. They're called "cottonless cottonwoods" for this reason. Two such cultivars are **Siouxland** and **Noreaster,** with dark green leaves and nice structure.

Quaking Aspen
(Populus tremuloides)

Named for the way its leaves tremble in even the slightest breeze, the quaking aspen is the most widely distributed tree in North America. Also known as the aspen poplar, trembling aspen, golden aspen, and mountain aspen, this poplar has delicate foliage whose flattened stems offer little or no resistance to the wind. The famous quaking leaves have slightly pointed tips with small rounded teeth along the edges. Averaging one to three inches in diameter, they display a light, glossy green that turns a brighter green on top and paler below as they approach maturity. They turn a gorgeous gold before dropping in September or October.

Quaking aspens grow in a tall, columnar form to 35 to 50 feet at maturity—fifty or sixty years. They add three or four feet of growth in the first few years. The spread of their narrow canopy is usually 20 to 30 feet, forming an attractive, open, pyramidal profile. They are cool-weather trees, unhappy in the heat, and their zone range is 1 through 6.

Lombardy Poplar
(Populus nigra italica)

Sometimes called the Italian poplar, the Lombardy poplar offers rapid growth, increasing four or five feet per year, and an attractive narrow columnar habit appropriate for screens and windbreaks. It will reach a height of 70 to 90 feet with a spread of only 10 to 15 feet. It grows from zones 3 to 9.

Lombardy poplar leaves emerge in early May. Up to three inches long, they have a triangular shape and toothed edges. In spring they display a light green that turns gray-green as the weeks pass. Like the leaves of all poplars, Lombardy poplar leaves have distinctive flattened stems that allow twisting in the breeze, showing off their pale undersides. Early in the fall, usually September, Lombardy poplar foliage turns bright yellow before dropping.

Unfortunately, canker disease can infect this tree by the time it is ten to fifteen years old, so trees larger than 30 feet tall and 5 feet wide are rare. There is little to be done to treat this disease if it happens.

Requirements of Your Poplar

Poplars want full sun and have low tolerance for shade. They accept a wide range of soil types including coarse, granular soil, but they prefer fine sandy loam or silt. And while they do best in moist soil, they don't tolerate flooding. If poplars have moisture a good part of the year, they can handle the dry periods typical of the Midwest and Great Plains. Their ideal soil is neutral.

Planting Your Poplar

The more care you take when you put your tree in the ground, the better it will do during its long life. Follow the complete planting directions provided in chapter 3.

Special notes: If you want to avoid pods of the fluffy cottonlike material that accompanies poplar seeds, choose a male tree. All poplars, male and female, can drop leaves, flowers, and twigs around your landscape, so don't plant them in or near garden beds or other trees and shrubs. Also, plant them 60 to 70 feet from buildings, septic tanks, and sidewalks so that their aggressive root systems will do no harm. Poplars can be planted any time in the growing season.

Caring for Your Poplar

Follow the instructions on seasonal care for young and mature trees—watering, mulching, fertilizing, staking, and pruning—described in chapter 3.

A special note: Train young poplars to develop a single trunk, or central leader, by pruning lower, secondary large stems. While it's not necessary to prune poplars routinely, you should remove dead and bro-

Common Symptom	Likely Cause
Swollen, sunken lesions on limbs and trunk	Canker
Brown, spotted leaves, premature dropping of leaves	Leaf spot
White coating on both sides of leaves	Powdery mildew

Species	Scale at Maturity	Basic Requirements
Eastern Poplar (*Populus deltoides*)	Height: 40'–70' Width: 40'–70' Shape: Irregular	Zones 2 through 9 Full sun Moist, well-drained soil
Quaking Aspen (*Populus tremuloides*)	Height: 35'–50' Width: 20'–30' Shape: Pyramidal	Zones 1 through 6 Full sun Moist, well-drained soil
Lombardy Poplar (*Populus nigra italica*)	Height: 70'–90' Width: 10'–15' Shape: Columnar	Zones 3 through 9 Full sun Moist, well-drained soil

ken branches from time to time, especially as the tree ages. You'll also need to prune off the pesky root suckers that will grow into full trees if left unchecked. Prune when the tree is dormant, no later than February, because pruning wounds will bleed if sap is rising.

Special Situations for the Poplar

Poplar is a good tree and easy to grow, but be familiar with the signs of some common poplar problems.

SASSAFRAS (*Sassafras albidum*)

Top Reasons to Plant

∾ Vivid autumn color
∾ Aromatic, edible leaves
∾ Unique angular branches

The short, zigzagging branches of the sassafras tree aren't its only unique characteristic—its leaves are aromatic, smelling like root beer. In fact, "genuine" root beer was made not from artificial flavorings but from the root oil of the sassafras tree.

Sassafras is native to North America and grows well from zones 4 to 8. It's a medium to large tree with a distinctive look, thanks partly to those angular branches. When young, it has a pyramidal shape that becomes more rounded as it matures. Sassafras saplings have smooth orange-brown bark, but the trunk becomes deeply furrowed in larger trees. This tree grows fast

even in poor soil. In a good, sunny spot, the sassafras tree can grow 4 feet in its first year, reaching 15 feet in four years. Mature heights range from 30 to 60 feet, with a canopy measuring 25 to 40 feet across.

The aromatic leaves may have two or three lobes or none. Sassafras trees have four different leaf shapes: three-lobed, elliptical, two lobed/right side, and two lobed/left side. The two-lobed leaves look like mittens, with the smaller lobe as the thumb. The deciduous leaves can grow up to six inches by four inches. Come fall, the leaves turn a striking orange-pink, yellow-red, or even scarlet-purple. This is a spectacular tree for fall color. Trees grown in full sun in the northern part of the growing region have the richest fall display.

The sassafras can begin flowering at only ten years old. Sometime in late March or early April before the leaves appear, fragrant yellow male and female flowers, one- to two-inch-long panicles, are borne on separate plants. Later on, the females bear attractive pea-sized dark blue fruit on bright red stems, ripening in August or September.

Sassafras flowers are popular with honeybees and other beneficial insects that spread pollen and kill pests. In the fall, songbirds devour the fruits as fast as they ripen. Sassafras (along with other members of the laurel family) is a host plant for the spicebush swallowtail butterfly. Human beings also make more practical use of this tree than they do most.

Young sassafras leaves are a great addition to a salad, and both young and old leaves can be used in soups. Ground-up root bark makes a delightful tea. And a powder called *filé*, made by grinding up dried sassafras leaves, is a popular ingredient in Cajun recipes. You can make your own *filé* by drying young leaves, then grinding them in a coffee or spice mill.

In the home landscape, sassafras trees can be used as specimens in a woodland garden or near ponds or streams. They are attractive in naturalized plantings, especially when allowed to grow with multiple stems.

Requirements of Your Sassafras

Sassafras trees grow well in full sun or part shade, but the more sun, the better the fall color. The tree likes a moist, well-drained acid soil but will tolerate drier or rocky sites.

Planting Your Sassafras

The more care you take when you put your tree in the ground, the better it will do during its long life. Follow the complete planting directions provided in chapter 3.

A special note: The sassafras tree develops a deep taproot, so it's best planted when young and should remain in its original site. Plant delicate-limbed sassafras trees on your property's borders, where potential limb breakage will do the least damage to buildings or your garden. Sassafras can be planted any time during the season.

Caring for Your Sassafras

Follow the instructions on seasonal care for young and mature trees—watering, mulching, fertilizing, staking, and pruning—described in chapter 3.

A special note: If you prefer a single-stemmed specimen, remove the suckers while they are small.

Common Symptom	Likely Cause
Defoliation, brown egg cases appearing on trunk	Gypsy moth larvae
Blotched or spotted leaves	Fungal leaf spots
White coating on leaves	Powdery mildew
Holes in leaves, buds eaten, brown blotches at leaf tips	Weevils

Species	Scale at Maturity	Basic Requirements
Sassafras (*Sassafras albidum*)	Height: 30'–60' Width: 25'–40' Shape: Rounded	Zones 4 through 8 Full sun/part shade Moist, well-drained soil

Special Situations for the Sassafras

Sassafras does not fall victim to any unique problems, but several common pests and diseases may affect it.

SWEET GUM
(Liquidambar styraciflua)

Top Reasons to Plant

∾ Excellent fall color, even for warm climates
∾ Good in moist soil
∾ Unusual spiny fruit

Its tall trunk and shapely canopy secures the sweet gum tree, native to the southeastern United States, a mighty reputation. Both the Latin name (translating to "liquid amber") and common name refer to the aromatic gum, or resin, that exudes from the tree's bruised stems. Familiarly known as gum ball tree, red gum, star-leafed gum, alligator wood, and gum tree, the sweet gum produces prickly gum balls that many a creative gardener has struggled to find a use for. One of the more imaginative ideas is to use them as mulch, and hope they keep slugs and other unwanted crawlers at bay. However, there are no guarantees on this idea's effectiveness!

Sweet gums' hard wood makes them resistant to wind damage and commercially useful for furniture. While past uses included soaps, adhesives, and a variety of pharmaceuticals, sweet gum wood remains valuable today as lumber and veneer. Chipmunks and twenty-five species of birds appreciate the sweet gum for its nesting sites and fruit.

Growing at a slow to medium rate, sweet gums add between one and four feet to their height per year when they are young. Their youthful leafy canopy is conical, becoming more pyramidal as the trees age. Sweet gums typically live between 150 and 300 years. Mature trees are 60 to 75 feet tall, and 40 to 50 feet wide.

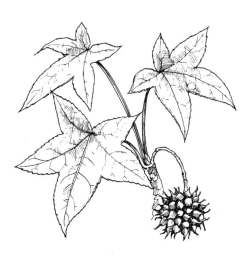

Glossy sweet gum leaves resemble those of maples, but a closer look reveals a more lustrous, smooth surface, and lobes resembling a five-pointed star. Usually four to seven inches across and growing alternately along the tree stems, these leaves emerge in late spring on branches ridged with corky bark. Before they drop, the leaves turn a handsome red, purple, or bright orange. It's notable that the sweet gum's fall colors aren't temperature dependent as, for example, those of sugar maples are. So even in warmer regions of the country, the sweet gum displays a fine mix of vivid color. It is hardy from zones 5 to 9.

Now for the gum balls: I always like an unusual shape or texture to a tree's fruit, although the sweet gum fruit isn't everyone's favorite. The somewhat inconspicuous flowers bloom in the spring, giving way in midsummer to those woody balls covered with curved spines and containing one or two winged seeds. About one inch in diameter, they hang on long stems. They're green at first and turn tannish brown as the season progresses, often persisting through January but usually falling in late fall. Sweet gums younger than fifteen to twenty years old don't usually produce flowers or gum balls.

SWEET GUM CHOICES

Moraine is a cold-hardy sweet gum with fast growth and glossy, dark green leaves that turn wine red in the fall. **Burgundy** has a more pyramidal shape with glossy green and deep purple leaves. The fruitless **Rotundiloba** cultivar has rounded tips on the lobes of its foliage, providing an elegant effect.

Requirements of Your Sweet Gum

Plant sweet gums in full sun and any type of soil that is slightly acidic, rich in organic matter, and well drained. Sweet gums can be pollution sensitive, so while they don't thrive in city environments, they can handle the compacted soil in the average suburban yard, especially where builders have stripped away topsoil.

Planting Your Sweet Gum

The more care you take when you put your tree in the ground, the better it will do during its long life. Follow the complete planting directions provided in chapter 3.

Special notes: Plant a sweet gum at least 15 feet from your home, driveway, flower beds, and sidewalks to ensure that the tree's wide, shallow root system won't damage these areas.

Be sure your tree is grown from seed that comes from the same planting zone as that of your home to ensure that it will thrive. For example, if you live in the northeast, don't buy a sweet gum propagated in the South. Sweet gums do not take well to transplanting; once in the ground, they want to stay put. Be sure you choose your site with care.

Because sweet gum trees grow over a wide area of the United States, they have had to adapt to both warmer southern and cooler northern climates. Only seeds produced by southern sweet gums will grow successfully in the South, because they are genetically programmed to handle the heat there. By contrast, seeds produced by northern sweet gums can handle the limited daylight and cold of northern winters.

Caring for Your Sweet Gum

Follow the instructions on seasonal care for young and mature trees—watering, mulching, fertilizing, staking, and pruning—described in chapter 3.

Special notes: A layer of mulch can obscure the prickly balls when they fall from the sweet gum's branches. Another trick to help you manage the sweet gum's surface roots and accumulating gum balls is to grow ground covers under the tree out to the drip line. If you're still bothered by the spiny gum balls falling from the tree, just sweep them up periodically and throw them away.

Sweet gums tolerate heat and drought well, but because they're native to riverbanks and swampy bottomlands, make sure you water them during a dry spell.

Sweet gums sometimes spontaneously produce suckers from their root system. This is normal for the tree, and some do it more than others. If you cut off the sprouts below the surface of the soil, they often reappear. Wait until the tree has gone dormant in late November or early December and then prune the sprouts below the surface of the soil to prevent them from coming back the following year.

SYCAMORE (*Platanus* sp.)

Top Reasons to Plant

- ❧ Light-catching pale bark
- ❧ Massive, rounded structure
- ❧ High value as solitary specimen

The late Stuart Roosa, who was a friend of mine in the forest service, managed to hitch a ride for some sycamore tree seeds on *Apollo 14* in 1971. Upon their return from the moon, those seeds were planted and thrived, becoming the mighty moon

Common Symptom	Likely Cause
Yellowing leaves, green veins	Chlorosis (from growing in alkaline soil)
Ends of branches turning black	Frost damage
Holes in leaves	Caterpillars

Species	Scale at Maturity	Basic Requirements
Sweet Gum (*Liquidambar styraciflua*)	Height: 60'–75' Width: 40'–50' Shape: Pyramidal	Zones 5 through 9 Full sun Moist, well-drained soil

sycamores planted during the U.S. bicentennial as a tribute to the human spirit and the adventures of the final frontier. I love the sycamore for its resilience and dependability—and for how much it gives of itself to nature.

Sycamores are splendid, large shade trees grown widely both here and in Europe. Two types are available—the American sycamore and a hybrid called the London plane tree. Both are deciduous trees recognizable by their multicolored, patchwork bark and the fuzzy, ball-like fruits hanging on their branches. Both grow in zones 4 to 9.

The wood of the sycamores is heavy, hard, tough, and coarse, and anyone who's tried splitting sycamore slabs for firewood knows that a wedge or maul just won't do it. Cutting sycamore wood is best left to hydraulic splitting machines. This toughness makes sycamore wood ideal for use in butcher blocks, flooring, and fine furniture. For the landscape, a notable feature of the wood is the diameter of the trunk; two to four feet is normal, but many are much larger. Most notable, however, is the bark.

Sycamores support a variety of wildlife. Birds nest and raise families in their generous branches year after year. Cerulean warblers, threatened by loss of habitat, depend on old sycamores as mating territory. As sycamores get larger and older, they develop deep cavities in areas where large limbs have been pruned or have dropped off. These cozy holes shelter generations of squirrels, bats, and the occasional wild honeybee hive.

The sycamore's size can limit its uses in the home landscape somewhat. When full grown, these trees can dwarf small houses and yards and therefore are most appropriate as specimen trees in spacious areas. They are also striking when planted in a row along property lines or drives.

Although sycamores aren't known for their fall color, their bark is quite distinctive. Smooth and marbled, combining pale and dark brown hues, it becomes most obvious after the leaves fall and winter sets in, providing a striking feature in otherwise bare, harsh winter landscapes.

American Sycamore
(Platanus occidentalis)

The American sycamore is native to the eastern United States. It's a rapid grower, sometimes reaching 70 feet in the first twenty years and 100 feet at maturity. The spread of its huge, gnarled branches can equal or surpass its height.

Sycamores have large, coarse leaves that emerge in late spring. Shaped like huge maple leaves, they have three to five sharply pointed lobes and can measure up

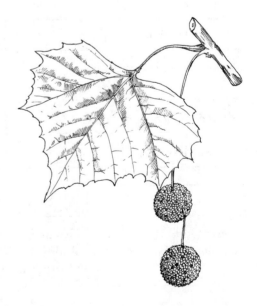

to 10 or 12 inches long and 6 or 8 inches across, and are sometimes broader than they are long. They have smooth, dull medium green surfaces and paler undersides with hairy veins. Most leaves drop by November, although a few may persist until late winter.

Sycamore flowers, small and yellowish green, emerge in late May or early June about the same time that leaves appear. The blooms are formed in round clusters about one inch in diameter, which over the season develop into pale brown, fuzzy seed balls on single stalks. Green at first, they turn brown as the enclosed seeds mature, ultimately hanging on the tree through the fall and much of the winter. If you're allergic, the wind-borne hairs released when these seeds break apart may irritate your ears, eyes, nose, and throat.

After a decade, these trees begin to shed their bark in large patches, creating mot-

tled trunks of cream, tan, and olive green, a sort of calico bark. The fallen bark and large leaf litter may be toxic to turf grass in the area, so clean it up promptly, though chopped-up bark litter and leaves work as a safe mulch for gardens.

London Plane Tree
(Platanus acerifolia)

A hybrid of the American sycamore and Oriental plane tree, the London plane tree has a narrower profile than the American sycamore. Though it grows more slowly, it reaches similar heights. This tree is particularly well adapted to city conditions.

These expansive trees typically grow from 70 to 100 feet tall and spread 65 to 80 feet at maturity. In their first twenty years, they will reach 35 feet tall. Their pyramidal shape in youth gives way to huge, spreading branches as they age. Like the American sycamore, they shed their bark in large patches as they approach maturity.

The large leaves of plane trees are often broader than they are long, measuring six to eight inches long and eight to ten inches across. First emerging in late spring, they drop by December, though a few hang on until late winter.

The flowers of the plane tree emerge with the leaves in late May or early June, developing seed clusters similar to those of the American sycamore. While the American sycamore has one cluster to a stalk, the plane tree has two or three.

LONDON PLANE TREE CHOICES

One of the most common cultivars, **Bloodgood** is resistant to anthracnose, as are **Columbia** and **Liberty**.

Requirements of Your Sycamore

American sycamores grow from northern Florida into North Dakota and Minnesota, up to the Great Lakes and northern New York state. Along the Atlantic coast, where winter temperatures are more moderate, they survive into Canada and can handle winter temperatures as low as −20°F. They're hardy in zones 4 through 9.

Sycamores will tolerate a variety of soil types, as long as the soil is moist and reasonably well drained. They are not particularly drought tolerant and in nature are often found in bottomlands and along rivers and streams. They do fine in neutral or even somewhat alkaline soil (pH 6.6 to 8.0). So long as the roots have enough moisture, sycamores can manage dry air, pollution, compacted soil, and wind fairly well, making them popular city trees. They prefer full sun but will accept light shade.

Planting Your Sycamore

The more care you take when you put your tree in the ground, the better it will do during its long life. Follow the complete planting directions provided in chapter 3.

Special notes: If you seek the thrill of growing a tree from seed, the sycamore is one to cut your teeth on. Sycamore seeds can be planted in a pot of soil as soon as the seed balls turn brown. They sprout easily, and less than three months after you plant the little seedlings, you will find young plants over three feet tall. It's amazing how long sycamores live considering how easy they are to grow.

Because sycamores have relatively shallow, fibrous root systems, they transplant easily. Choose young trees from six to ten feet tall that are either in containers or have roots and soil wrapped in burlap. Plant a sycamore in either spring or fall.

Caring for Your Sycamore

Follow the instructions on seasonal care for young and mature trees—watering, mulching, fertilizing, staking, and pruning—described in chapter 3.

Special notes: Mature sycamores generally present sturdy resistance to winter winds and ice. However, in the Midwest there are problems with frost cracking sycamore trunks. So in winter, it's a good idea to shelter newly planted trees in exposed sites behind a screen of burlap or agricultural fabric.

When they are young sycamores occasionally need pruning to maintain a single central stem. They also benefit from periodic trimming in their formative years, responding so well to even hard pruning that they are often groomed as hedges or shaped to arch over broad walkways. In residential yards, you may sometimes need to trim injured branches or branches growing so low on the trunk that they block a pathway. Judicious trimming of smaller, secondary branches will also encourage maximum development of main branches as the tree ages. Use a sharp pruning saw or loppers, and wear a protective dust mask to avoid irritation from the fuzz that forms on sycamore leaves, fruits, and young twigs.

Special Situations for the Sycamore

American sycamores are more susceptible to anthracnose than is the London plane tree. But the plane tree varieties are plagued especially by canker stain, a fungal problem that causes swollen sores to form on the trunk and major limbs. Tissue around the canker eventually swells to form a callus, or hard bump, while the exposed bark becomes stained with bluish or blackish streaks. The staining penetrates inward to the healthy wood tissue and generates brown, raylike streaks. The foliage of affected trees becomes noticeably thinner until the tree dies within a year or two. As with most other fungal diseases, pruning and leaf collection will help you manage these problems.

Common Symptom	Likely Cause
Sunken spots with raised edges on leaves, browning, early leaf death	Anthracnose
Leaves that turn pale, mottled, drop early	Lace bug
Scarred and weakened trunks and limbs, twig drop	Borers
Fewer, smaller leaves, blue or black stains on bark, swollen sores on limbs or trunk	Canker stain

Species	Scale at Maturity	Basic Requirements
American Sycamore (*Platanus occidentalis*)	Height: 70'–100' Width: 70'–100' Shape: Rounded, irregular	Zones 4 through 9 Full sun/part shade Moist, well-drained soil
London Plane Tree (*Platanus acerifolia*)	Height: 70'–100' Width: 65'–80' Shape: Pyramidal, irregular	Zones 4 through 9 Full sun/part shade Moist, well-drained soil

WALNUT (*Juglans* sp.)

Top Reasons to Plant

- ∽ Edible nuts
- ∽ Stately, rounded profile
- ∽ Good specimen tree

Famous Wild West lawman Wyatt Earp grew up in Monmouth, Illinois, in a simple clapboard house shaded by a black walnut tree that still produces walnuts as big as tennis balls. Black walnut trees also mark the beginning of my own journey with trees. A towering black walnut stood in the yard of our home, planted by my great-uncle four decades before we moved in. Because the walnut is a slow-growing tree, I later realized that my uncle had planted it not for himself but for later generations of our family.

The black walnut is an American native that grows throughout the United States. The English walnut is an import from Europe and China. Of the two, the black walnut is used more often as an ornamental tree. Both grow in zones 4 to 9, have handsome rounded profiles, and produce edible nuts. The walnuts sold commercially come from English walnut orchards in California and Oregon.

Walnuts are best planted in naturalized or wooded areas on property where they have lots of light and space. They also look good in rows along property lines and as individual specimen trees in spacious yards. The English walnut is perhaps the more popular walnut for the home landscape.

Black Walnut (Juglans nigra)

The most familiar of the walnuts, the native black walnut tree grows to between 50 and 75 feet at maturity, its large canopy typically spreading as wide as the tree is tall. Trunks of mature black walnut trees measure two to four feet in diameter, sometimes even six feet. They grow straight and branchless to nearly two-thirds the distance from the ground. Black walnuts mature in about 150 years and can live to be 250 years old.

Black walnut trees are deciduous. Their coarse leaves are composed of rows of pointed, fragrant leaflets growing opposite one another along both sides of a 12- to 24-inch-long stem. On each stem are about 13 to 23 leaflets, each three to five inches long and one and a half inches wide. They are yellowish green when they unfurl in late spring, turning a dull yellow in the fall. They have fuzzy undersides.

As with every type of walnut, male and female flowers grow on the same tree. The females are small, whereas the yellow-green

The English walnut bears clusters of small flowers called catkins, which may be cross- or self-pollinated. After flowering, the tree produces walnuts that have thin shells and develop in clusters of three to nine. Walnuts from the English walnut tree are milder and sweeter than those of the black walnut.

If you live in the northern part of the United States and want to plant an English walnut, be sure to purchase one that comes from European rather than Californian seed. California walnut trees do well in the southern warmth but won't be happy in northern climates.

male flowers are four-inch-long drooping spikes that appear in late spring when the leaves emerge. By late summer, hard-shelled nuts measuring about two inches in diameter form within protective husks. Initially green, the husks turn black as they mature. Upon breaking open, they release the hard, ridged nut that small mammals in the wild love to feast on—more so than do humans.

English Walnut (Juglans regia)

The English walnut, also known as the Persian or Carpathian walnut, is the walnut tree most commonly grown for commercial nut production. It's also a perfectly shaped shade tree, seldom exceeding 60 feet in any dimension in the home landscape. This large, spreading tree can be a fast grower if taken care of properly. It has gray bark, large leaflets, and softer wood than the black walnut. Its leaves are compound, with five to nine leaflets, occasionally up to thirteen, arranged opposite each other along the leafstalk.

Requirements of Your Walnut

All walnuts prefer moist, well-drained soil that is neutral or slightly alkaline (pH 6.6 to 8.0). They don't do well in the light soil typical of urban environments. Like most trees, they prefer full sun but can tolerate light shade.

Planting Your Walnut

The more care you take when you put your tree in the ground, the better it will do during its long life. Follow the complete planting directions provided in chapter 3.

Special notes: Walnut trees usually take between five and eight years to start producing nuts, and if planted alone, a tree will bear only a few nuts. Planting several walnut trees within 30 to 50 feet of one another promotes cross-pollination and therefore more abundant nut production.

It is important to note that black walnut trees pose a problem for some yards. They have a toxic effect on certain plants, such as maples, azaleas, apple trees, sweet gums, blueberries, pines, hemlocks, hawthorn, American elm, beech, locust, tulip tree, white oak, redcedar, gray dogwood, and common daylily, to name just a handful of the plants at risk. These plants should not be within 50 feet of a black walnut. The English walnut tree produces a similar poisonous chemical, in lesser quantities but still dangerous to nearby plants.

Because they have long taproots, walnut trees transplant best when they're young. Look for trees between five and ten feet tall, and keep the roots moist until planting time. Spring is the best time to plant.

Caring for Your Walnut

Follow the instructions on seasonal care for young and mature trees—watering, mulching, fertilizing, staking, and pruning—described in chapter 3.

A special note: Walnuts should be harvested in fall or early winter, either from the ground or by flailing the branches. The husks will be brownish black when ripe, and you should wear impermeable gloves to handle them. They are the source of walnut wood stain, and it would take days of washing to get the stain off your hands. Remove the husks while they're still soft, by hand or

Common Symptom	Likely Cause
Yellowing and curling leaves	Zinc deficiency
Leaves eaten, defoliation	Caterpillars
Bark attacked, leaves curled and distorted	Aphids
Yellow gall on undersides of leaves	Mites
Sunken sores on trunks, branches	Canker
Irregular dark spots on leaves	Brown leaf spot

Species	Scale at Maturity	Basic Requirements
Black Walnut (*Juglans nigra*)	Height: 50'–75' Width: 50'–75' Shape: Rounded	Zones 4 through 9 Full sun/part shade Moist, well-drained soil
English Walnut (*Juglans regia*)	Height: 40'–60' Width: 40'–60' Shape: Rounded	Zones 4 through 9 Full sun/part shade Moist, well-drained soil

with a corn sheller. Then float the nuts in water; those that sink have fruits inside, those that float are empty.

Special Situations for the Walnut

Rapidly growing young black walnut trees draw deeply on soil nutrients and occasionally deplete certain trace minerals. If the foliage on an otherwise healthy tree begins to turn yellow in midseason, and the leaf stems curl upward, there may be inadequate zinc in the soil. Adding zinc sulfate, available at your local garden center, can correct this deficiency.

WILLOW (*Salix* sp.)

Top Reasons to Plant

- Trademark graceful form
- Flutter of leaves in the wind
- Love of wet conditions

There are more than a hundred species of water-loving willow trees growing in the United States along streams and lakes. Willows have contributed more to America than their beauty. Their leaves are bitter from salicylic acid, the same ingredient that gives aspirin its taste. Native Americans were the first to recognize the willow tree's medicinal value, using its extract to alleviate pain, arthritis, and fever. Also, the dried and powdered bark is a natural astringent and detergent, and crushed young leaves can stop severe bleeding.

Willows grace the landscape with flexible branches that have been celebrated in songs and poems because they bend rather than break. They are a large and varied group of plants that grow as trees, shrubs, or ground covers. The trees are composed of two subgroups: weepers, with long, pendulous branches, and contorted willows, whose crooked and angled limbs spruce up flower arrangements. Both willows and contorted willows offer early spring foliage and the familiar fuzzy fruits, and both are deciduous trees. While these beautiful trees can last only about ten to twenty years, they grow and mature rapidly.

Willows trees are either male or female. Their catkins are a light gray-green and turn yellow as they ripen, appearing early in the spring, in late February or early March, before leaves emerge. By mid-April, they turn a greenish yellow and form seeds with tufted hairs. These seeds are released into the wind to the delight of songbirds and small mammals.

Willows love moisture, and thrive along stream banks and lakes. Planted alone, weeping willows are spectacular as specimens for the yard. Contorted willows can be used as specimens or for an accent at the end of a flower bed.

Because willows have a relatively short life span, you might choose to interplant them with other longer-living trees that grow more slowly but will take over the space when the willows eventually die.

The image of the weeping willow is classic—growing gracefully along riverbanks, dipping toward the water, coming to green before winter has completely closed up shop. There is hardly a region of this country that doesn't host a weeping willow, but the Babylon species does best in the South.

Babylon Weeping Willow
(Salix babylonica)

The Babylon weeping willow is hardy in the South into zone 8 and unhappy north of zone 6. It is a short-trunked tree with an open, broad-spreading crown. Babylon weeping willows typically grow to between 30 and 40 feet tall, with long, drooping branches that form a broad canopy as wide as the tree is tall. The yellow shoots herald the early approach of spring, then turn olive brown by winter. Their distinctive bark is dark gray and deeply furrowed. This willow is quite adaptable and will thrive in most soil types except those that are fast draining and dry. It needs moisture and thrives in wet conditions. A sun worshipper, it will grow scraggly in too much shade.

Golden Weeping Willow
(Salix alba "Tristis")

For northern regions, the golden weeping willow is a great choice, surviving well into zone 4 and south to zone 9. It forms a gracefully rounded crown from 50 to 70 feet in height with an equal spread. Characterized by its golden bark and spreading growth habit, the golden weeping willow develops a sturdy, upright, broad crown with long, bright yellow pendulous branches that often touch the ground. The leaves are long and narrow, wider at the base than at the tip, and measuring from two to six inches long and half an inch wide. They are light green with finely toothed edges. The golden weeping willow is a rapid grower that does well in both wet and ordinary garden soils.

Corkscrew Hanklow Willow
(Salix matsudana "Tortuosa")

Growing from zones 5 to 8, this shrubby novelty reaches 30 to 40 feet tall and 15 to 20 feet wide. It's a fast-growing, deciduous tree, with typically long, thin willow leaves that offer bright gold fall color. The corkscrew willow's unique contorted branches are its distinguishing feature, cre-

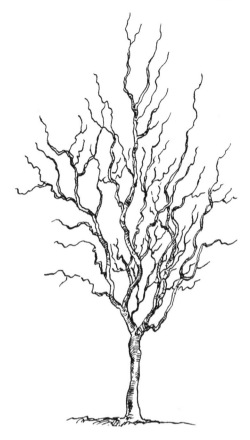

ating a compelling silhouette during the winter months.

Requirements of Your Willow

Weeping willows grow best in full sun but can take a bit of light shade. They are adaptable, tolerating coarse soil with sand or gravel or fine soil with silt. Comfortable in wet, boggy areas, these trees don't demand good drainage. They prefer moist, even wet, soil all the time. Acid to neutral soil (pH 6.6 to 7.5) is fine.

Planting Your Willow

The more care you take when you put your tree in the ground, the better it will do during its long life. Follow the complete planting directions provided in chapter 3.

A special note: Willow wood is often weak and brittle and can split easily in storms or under the weight of ice or snow. The best means of avoiding this problem is by situating willows in areas somewhat sheltered from the wind.

Remember to plant a weeping willow well away (200 to 300 feet) from any septic or sewage pipes. Instead, put it near a stream or a pond so that it drinks from a natural source and the roots don't seek out your home's water supply! You can plant willows in any season, as they are easily transplanted—their shallow, fibrous roots establish themselves quickly. Make sure to water the tree thoroughly after planting.

Common Symptom	Likely Cause
Bark attacked, curled and distorted leaves	Aphids
Leaves consumed, conspicuous tawny egg masses present	Gypsy moth
Damaged undersides of leaves	Imported willow leaf beetle
Wilted or discolored leaves, cankered branches, dieback	Bacterial blight
Tumorlike swellings on roots, trunk, or branches	Crown gall
White powder on leaves	Powdery mildew
Yellow spots and dark pustules on leaf undersides	Rust

Species	Scale at Maturity	Basic Requirements
Babylon Weeping Willow (*Salix babylonica*)	Height: 30'–40' Width: 30'–40' Shape: Rounded	Zones 6 through 8 Full sun Moist soil
Golden Weeping Willow (*Salix alba* "Tristis")	Height: 50'–70' Width: 50'–70' Shape: Rounded	Zone 4 through 9 Full sun Moist soil
Corkscrew Hanklow Willow (*Salix matsudana* "Tortuosa")	Height: 30'–40' Width: 15'–20' Shape: Upright oval, rounded	Zones 5 through 8 Full sun Moist soil

Caring for Your Willow

Follow the instructions on seasonal care for young and mature trees—watering, mulching, fertilizing, staking, and pruning—described in chapter 3.

Special notes: Be especially attentive to willows during summer dry spells, during which you should soak the tree once or even twice a week.

Because they grow so rapidly, willows are heavy feeders, so supplemental fertilization will help them flourish. If you live in a northern region with a short growing season, apply fertilizer only in the spring—if the willows are fed in the fall, their new growth won't harden completely before frost and may suffer winter injury. In the South, apply an all-purpose fertilizer in the fall and spring.

Special Situations for the Willow

Because willows grow so rapidly, they can be vulnerable to many insect and disease problems. Especially in the Northeast, the imported willow leaf beetle causes real damage by feeding on the undersides of willow foliage, leaving only a network of veins behind. These metallic blue beetles are only an eighth of an inch long and spend the winter under the bark scales and in the shrubbery around willow trees. In early June when they emerge, they lay eggs, which develop and then produce a brood of wormlike grubs in August. Use an appropriate insecticide on the adult beetles, or use Bt (*Bacillus thuringiensis*) on the larvae.

Bacterial blight is another common willow problem. It causes willow leaves to turn brown and wilt, and dieback in affected branches. These symptoms are easily confused with frost injury. The bacteria spend the winter in sores on the willow tree and infect young leaves as soon as they emerge, sometimes resulting in complete defoliation. Unfortunately there is no effective treatment for blight.

ZELKOVA
(*Zelkova serrata*)

Top Reasons to Plant

- Superior shade tree
- Fall color
- Heat and drought resistant

The zelkova first gained public attention in the United States when it was recognized as a good alternative to the American elm. But now the zelkova, also known as the Japanese zelkova or Japanese hornbeam, has earned a reputation of its own as a versatile, attractive shade tree.

Zelkova trees grow rapidly, doubling their height in four to six years and reaching 30 feet tall in the first ten years. The mature tree stands 50 to 80 feet tall and wide. Its flowers and fruits are small, and its foliage is bright green, toothed, and oval-shaped, resembling the elm's. Come fall, the leaves turn an array of vivid hues such as yellow, orange, dark red, reddish brown, and even bronze. The interesting patchy bark is quite handsome. Perhaps most important, though related to the elm family, zelkovas are highly resistant to Dutch elm disease. Hardy in zones 5 to 8, they especially thrive in suburban and coastal environments. Their distinctly upright, ascending vase shape and wide-spreading canopy make them a good choice for patios and decks, where low-branched trees might obscure the view.

ZELKOVA CHOICES

The rapid-growing **Green Vase** cultivar comes from Korean seeds and features excellent form and color, holds up well against drought and pollution, and can adapt to clay soil. **Village Green** maintains a vase-shaped form and has rusty, red fall foliage and a broad crown. Highly disease resistant, this cultivar is also fairly immune to Japanese beetle infestation. **Halka** is faster growing and looks more elmlike than other varieties.

Requirements of Your Zelkova

Zelkovas need full sun but are agreeable to almost any type of well-drained soil. They tolerate a broad pH range, compacted soil, pollution, and even drought.

Planting Your Zelkova

The more care you take when you put your tree in the ground, the better it will do during its long life. Follow the complete planting directions provided in chapter 3.

Special notes: When you're purchasing a zelkova, be wary of trees with branches that are clumped together at a single point. Buy a tree with branches that spread out along the trunk so that they can develop a secure hold to the stem.

Zelkovas transplant well but are most successful if planted in the spring, not fall. You can plant container-grown stock any time during the growing season.

While zelkovas are highly resistant to Dutch elm disease, avoid planting them near where a diseased elm once grew—it's not worth the risk. Newly planted zelkovas are susceptible to wind and may need temporary staking their first year.

early years makes for a more even and attractive tree shape.

Caring for Your Zelkova

Follow the instructions on seasonal care for young and mature trees—watering, mulching, fertilizing, staking, and pruning—described in chapter 3.

A special note: Annual pruning in the

Special Situations for the Zelkova

One of the zelkova's greatest attractions is that it's virtually disease free. Occasionally, however, you may notice some beetle activity, which is easy to control if you act quickly.

Common Symptom	Likely Cause
Skeletonized leaves	Japanese beetles
Skeletonized leaves, defoliation	Elm leaf beetles

Species	Size	Basic Requirements
Zelkova (*Zelkova serrata*)	Height: 50'–80' Width: 50'–80' Shape: Upright, vaselike	Zones 5 through 8 Full sun Moist, well-drained soil

Evergreens and Conifers

Evergreens are true mainstays in the home landscape, providing year-round color, effective screening, and distinctive shapes that accent the yard. There are two primary groups of evergreens, distinguished by their leaves: broad-leafed evergreens, which have leaves, not needles (holly, for example), and coniferous evergreens, which bear cones and have the needlelike leaves you see on pines or the scaly leaves on junipers. Conifers represent a grand array of shapes and colors. Just one, properly placed in a small yard, can be perfect punctuation for the landscape. A row of them can form a screen to give you privacy and provide a welcome noise or visual barrier. A sweep of them along a driveway or lining the edge of your property can make an architectural statement. Evergreens certainly give the home landscape more dependable impact per inch and dollar than any other plant in the yard.

ARBORVITAE (*Thuja* sp.)

Top Reasons to Plant

- Rich green seasonal color
- Excellent for a hedge, windbreak, sound screen
- Durable and adaptable

Where did the name "arborvitae" come from? In the 1500s, Jacques Cartier was sailing up the St. Lawrence River in search of the Northwest Passage when his crew took sick. Among those stricken were two Native American boys, whom Cartier left off at their villages, thinking they would probably die. Returning a few days later, he saw the boys alive and well, and asked how they had recovered. One of them told Cartier to boil the leaves and bark of a local tree, and give the tea to the crewmen. It worked. The disease was scurvy, the curative was vitamin C. Cartier returned to Paris with the story and the tree (or cuttings of it), and French botanists gave it the name "arborvitae": "tree of life." It was the first American tree to be grown in Europe, and it provided the treatment for scurvy until citrus fruits were found to work as well—and taste better.

As a group, arborvitae are all coniferous evergreens without needles; their leaves look flattened, as if they'd been pressed in a book. The cones are small and prized by birds, who nest in the dense foliage. Rabbits, deer, and moose also favor the cones; the deer, especially, can be a nuisance.

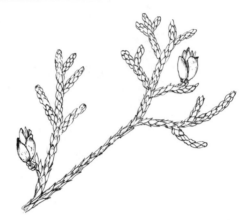

The trees' shapes are pyramidal. The American arborvitae (*Thuja occidentalis*) is the most familiar and the longest-lived; in the wild, specimens can live two or three hundred years. The Oriental arborvitae (formerly *Thuja orientalis*, now *Platycladus orientalis*) is a small tree—or a big bush. Though probably native to China, it has been growing throughout the American South for many years now. The western redcedar (*Thuja plicata*) is confined to the Northwest and used mainly for building materials, but it's a large handsome tree with much to offer to landscapes east or west of the Rockies.

Small to medium-size arborvitae are excellent choices for hedges, windbreaks, screens, or as a background for other plants. The larger trees can be allowed to stand majestically on their own. Not only are arborvitae useful for foundation plantings near buildings, but they are also lovely when clustered in groves. Smaller varieties grow well in containers that are at least two feet deep.

American Arborvitae
(Thuja occidentalis)

This is the tree that saved Cartier's crew. Also called the northern white cedar or the eastern arborvitae, it grows in the northeastern United States and southeast-ern Canada. Typically it has a single trunk, though if a tree is damaged as it grows, multiple trunks can develop and make the plant susceptible to the weight of ice and snow. The tree's mature height is 40 to 60 feet, its width is 10 to 15 feet, and its shape is pyramidal. American arborvitae are hardy in zones 2 through 7.

Leaves of American arborvitae are soft and arranged in horizontal sprays. Their

foliage is dense from top to bottom and is aromatic when bruised. The foliage is medium to dark green on top and lighter underneath, but in some varieties it is gold-tipped or yellow-green.

What appear to be flowers on the ends of branchlets in April or May are actually tiny one-eighth-inch greenish cones. Male and female cones are borne on the same plant. By early August the female cones have 8 to 12 scales and begin to weather to a more visible silvery color. They remain until February or so, unless eaten by birds or squirrels.

AMERICAN ARBORVITAE CHOICES

In the wild, arborvitae species can reach heights of 70 feet, but cultivars available for gardens are shorter. **Emerald** (also known, less pronounceably, as **Smaragd**) has green foliage true to its name, and the color remains vivid throughout the seasons. Highly heat tolerant, this cultivar grows 10 to 15 feet tall and 3 to 5 feet wide. The dark green foliage of **Nigra** adorns the 20- to 30-foot-tall tree all year round. Slow grower **Techny** is a pyramidal 10- to 15-foot tree, with beautiful deep-hued foliage.

Oriental Arborvitae (Platycladus orientalis)

This Asian native now grows throughout the South, where it has a reputation for toughness. Although it is not quite as hardy as our native American arborvitae species, which lives in a harsher northern climate, it tolerates heat, drought, and alkaline soil well. The Oriental arborvitae has a compact, conical, or columnar habit when young. As the tree ages, its branches become more loose and open but its form

remains pyramidal. The mature height of the Oriental arborvitae is 18 to 25 feet, the width 10 to 15 feet. It often has multiple stems. Unlike the American arborvitae and the western redcedar, the foliage on this tree is held vertically, not horizontally. It appears bright green on the top surface and yellow-green beneath, with soft, scale-like leaves. Some shrub varieties have gold-tipped, yellow-green, or even bluish foliage. Oriental arborvitae do best in zones 6 to 10. Because they grow in milder climates, the foliage retains its color year-round.

ORIENTAL ARBORVITAE CHOICES

The most common cultivar is **Aurea Nana.** Choices with green foliage include **Blue Cone** and **Baker.**

Western Redcedar (Thuja plicata)

In its home territory in the Northwest, this tree will grow to a towering height, but in most landscapes it will top out at 50 to 75

feet, with a spread of 15 to 25 feet. Its shape is narrow and pyramidal, and the foliage is glossy green. Though usually a fairly slow grower, in the South it can clip along at two to four feet a year. It does well in zones 5 to 7 and, as a bonus, it resists deer grazing much better than other arborvitae species.

WESTERN REDCEDAR CHOICES

With its glossy, richly colored green foliage, **Atrovirens** is an excellent large cultivar that will grow to 50 or 60 feet. **Zebrina** has yellow-striped leaves tinted with gold. This 30-foot-tall beauty may be difficult to find in garden centers, but catalog nurseries should have it.

Requirements of Your Arborvitae

Arborvitae generally prefer full sun. While partial shade is desirable in regions where very intense summer sun might scorch them, arborvitae tend to become ragged if grown in too much, prolonged shade. Varieties with yellow foliage require daylong sun to maintain their stunning color. Though they tolerate either acid or alkaline soil, they prefer deep, moist, well-drained soil rich in organic matter and on the acidic side (pH 5.5 to 6.5).

Planting Your Arborvitae

The more care you take when you put your tree in the ground, the better it will do during its long life. Follow the complete planting directions provided in chapter 3.

Special notes: These trees root easily and grow quickly. Buy two- to three-foot-tall nursery stock. If the roots are in a soil ball wrapped with burlap, plant in spring to early summer. Container-grown trees can be planted any time from spring through early fall.

The arborvitae's dense foliage and relatively small root-balls make it vulnerable to wind in exposed sites when newly planted, so staking is necessary. Do not put strong tension on your staking cables, as the young arborvitae stem needs leeway for movement so that it will grow strong. Check often to make sure the cables are not binding or injuring the trunk. Remove staking in about six months, by which point the roots should be securely anchored.

Caring for Your Arborvitae

Follow the instructions on seasonal care for young and mature trees—watering, mulching, fertilizing, staking, and pruning—described in chapter 3.

Special notes: For arborvitae on sites

Common Symptom	Likely Cause
Brown foliage in winter or summer, brown leaf tips	Spider mites
Twigs, leaves turning brown during drought	Sunscald or sunscorch
Foliage that browns, trunk that splits near soil	Freeze injury
Foliage chewed, stripped from twigs	Deer, moose, or rabbits
Small silken bags hanging from twigs	Bagworms
Leaves webbed over, turning gray or brown	Spider mites
Leaves curled and distorted, turning yellow or brown; growth retarded	Aphids
Sawdust at base of shrub, poor growth	Cedar tree borers
Leaves and branches encrusted with small bumps; discolored upper-leaf surfaces; leaf drop; reduced and stunted growth	Scale insects
Leaf margins notched	Arborvitae weevils
Twig tips/leaves that turn brown or yellow, dieback	Leaf blight
Leaves straw-yellow or brown and thickly dotted with small, black spots	Leaf spot
Foliage burned	Dog urine

Species	Scale at Maturity	Basic Requirements
American Arborvitae (*Thuja occidentalis*)	Height: 40'–60' Width: 10'–15' Shape: Pyramidal	Zones 2 through 7 Full sun Moist, well-drained soil
Oriental Arborvitae (*Platycladus orientalis*)	Height: 18'–25' Width: 10'–15' Shape: Pyramidal	Zones 6 through 10 Full sun Moist, well-drained soil
Western Redcedar (*Thuja plicata*)	Height: 50'–75' Width: 15'–25' Shape: Pyramidal	Zones 5 through 7 Full sun Moist, well-drained soil

exposed to the cold winter wind, rig a protective barrier of burlap to shield them. Do not use plastic, as it does not allow essential air circulation.

Ideally arborvitae will be planted in areas that accommodate their natural size and shape, so that they need no pruning. Often, however, arborvitae threaten to outgrow their allotted space and need routine pruning to control their size. Although they can be trimmed sparsely at any time if necessary, it is best to prune them before new growth starts in the spring.

Special Situations for the Arborvitae

In general, arborvitae exhibit few serious insect and disease problems. One common problem, however, is simply old age. The plant may lose its shape because harsh weather damages its branches or trunk, resulting in unsightly gaps in the shrub. If pruning does not improve the shrub, the time may have come to replace it.

Although arborvitae trees are evergreens, they do drop some of their foliage every year, usually in the fall. Often some brown, dead needles are visible at the same time that deciduous trees and shrubs are showing their fall color. Normal leaf drop may occur annually or every second or third year. Healthy plants will rejuvenate in the spring.

BALD CYPRESS
(*Taxodium distichum*)

Top Reasons to Plant

∾ Deciduous needles
∾ Peeling bark
∾ Tolerance of moist and dry soil

The association between bald cypresses and the swamps where they often grow is so great that people call these trees "swamp cypresses" and assume they are at home

nowhere else. This is reinforced by the fact that swamp-grown trees develop upright projections near the base, growing up from underwater roots. These projections are called "knees," but they look like stalagmites on the floor of a cave, or a science-fiction skyline. Thought to help swamp-grown trees breathe, they are absent from bald cypresses grown in dry conditions. These trees do well in swamps and on dry land. They're found naturally in the southeastern United States but grow well as far north as southern New England and the Great Lakes. They're hardy in zones 4 to 9 and tolerate winter temperatures as low as –10°F.

These stunning, shapely, large trees bear cones and needle leaves. However, they are deciduous, losing their foliage every fall—hence "bald." They grow at a moderate rate of about two feet a year during their first fifty years. Columnar in shape when young, they acquire a broader pyramidal shape as they mature. A full-grown tree is 50 to 70 feet tall and 20 to 30 feet across at its widest. The straight, single trunks are covered in handsome reddish brown to silvery bark that sheds in vertical peels. Bald cypress trees can live four hundred to six hundred years.

Bald cypress foliage is similar to that of the hemlock. The fine-textured needles appear late in spring. Soft and fernlike, these flat, pointy needles grow opposite one another around each delicate twig. They are bright yellow-green in spring, becoming soft medium green over the summer. As fall arrives, the leaves turn orange to rusty brown before falling. During severe drought, bald cypresses will lose their leaves prematurely and look dead, but they are resilient and are rarely damaged permanently.

On the same tree bald cypresses bear both male and female flowers. The male catkins develop in the autumn and shed pollen the following April, pollinating the female flowers. Before the leaves emerge, the female flowers develop into cones that appear at the ends of the branches; the cones are small, drooping, purplish, and thick-scaled. They contain seeds and resinous glands that are messy when crushed. From October to early December, cones ripen, turn brown, and eventually disintegrate, releasing winged seeds.

Bald cypresses are particularly attractive when planted in groves. And because they thrive in boggy soil, they are excellent near ponds, in low or floodplain areas, or near water features on your property. A single bald cypress planted in the middle of a large lawn is a commanding specimen. For the adventurous, the bald cypress can be clipped into a formal hedge, creating a wonderful screen.

BALD CYPRESS CHOICES

Shawnee Brave is a small, narrow form suited for small yards and streets. **Monarch of Illinois** is a wide-spreading cultivar.

Requirements of Your Bald Cypress

Bald cypresses do best in full sun but will tolerate shade. They are adaptable to a wide range of soil types (pH 6.1 to 6.5, even to 7.5). Because they are accustomed to wet soil, they can tolerate boggy soil and even flooding, but they will also do perfectly well in normally dry soil. They can also handle compacted soil.

Planting Your Bald Cypress

The more care you take when you put your tree in the ground, the better it will do during its long life. Follow the complete planting directions provided in chapter 3.

A special note: Bald cypress trees transplant easily because they have shallow, fibrous roots. They can be planted any time during the growing season.

Caring for Your Bald Cypress

Follow the instructions on seasonal care for young and mature trees—watering, mulching, fertilizing, staking, and pruning—described in chapter 3.

Special notes: Bald cypress trees need generous moisture—from the skies or, in late spring when their leaves appear, a soaker hose.

Routine pruning is not required, as bald cypress trees have a lovely natural growth habit. If a young tree develops two main stems, it is advisable to cleanly cut one away so that the maturing tree will have one strong trunk.

Special Situations for the Bald Cypress

Bald cypress trees are considered to be generally free from disease and insect pests. If needles turn brown and drop in season, the tree may simply be thirsty. Soak the soil well weekly, and the foliage will probably recover. Bald cypresses can, of course, fall victim to other problems, but these seldom occur in the home landscape.

Common Symptom	Likely Cause
Needles turn yellow, stunted appearance	Chlorosis (caused by alkaline soil)
Needles marked with lines, webbed together	Cypress moth
Needles yellowed, fine webbing around needles and stems	Webbed mites
Spots on needles, cones, bark; twigs have dieback in wet seasons	Twig blight

Species	Scale at Maturity	Basic Requirements
Bald Cypress (*Taxodium distichum*)	Height: 50'–70' Width: 20'–30' Shape: Pyramidal	Zones 4 through 9 Full sun/part shade Moist to wet soil

CEDAR (*Cedrus* sp.)

Top Reasons to Plant

- Unique fall bloom period
- Long life
- Standout specimen trees

One of the most fascinating aspects of my work is tracing the history of the world's grandest trees. This is how I came to the blue atlas cedars that stand like sentries on either side of the Normal Arch at the entrance to the Bishop's Garden at the Washington National Cathedral. The first bishop of Washington, Rev. Henry Yates Satterlee, brought them to the cathedral in 1900, when the trees were only 12 inches high. Today these statuesque beauties measure almost 60 feet tall.

Identifying real cedars can be a bit confusing. Some trees have "cedar" in their name but are not true cedars: the western redcedar is really an arborvitae and the eastern redcedar is actually a juniper. True cedars are the only conifers that bloom in the fall. They are always an elegant, dominating feature in the home landscape.

Throughout history, cedar wood and such by-products as cedar oil have proven to be worth far more money than the living trees themselves. Huge forests of cedars were cut down to build ships or supply firewood for trains up until the early twentieth century. Very few natural cedar stands exist today because, throughout centuries of harvesting, few efforts were made to replant.

Plant cedars as single trees to showcase their open, angular growth habit and shapely form. They need lots of space and are ideal as specimen trees out in a wide lawn area.

Deodar Cedar (Cedrus deodara)

The deodar is the most graceful of the true cedars, with gently weeping branches and long cones. It is commonly used for ornamental purposes, especially in the West and Southwest. Most deodar cedars reach a mature height of 40 to 70 feet, and the spread can reach 30 to 40 feet, giving the tree a stately pyramidal shape. In their native Himalayan Mountains, they grow much bigger than in the United States.

Deodar cedars grow rapidly, with dense, wide-spreading branches that droop at the tips when the trees are young. As they grow, their branches stiffen and the tree's shape flattens somewhat, giving it a more asymmetrical profile. They reach mature

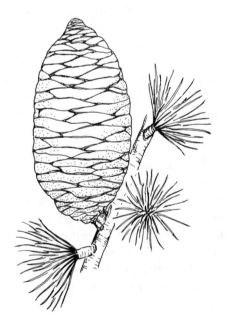

size in thirty to forty years but can survive three hundred to four hundred years.

Like all true cedars, deodar cedars have tufted clusters of stiff needles that develop on spurs that jut from the growing stems. Sometimes more than 30 needles are bunched together, but on fast-growing branches, needles often grow individually. Depending on the variety, the needles may be grayish green, blue, or even silvery, and they remain on the tree through the winter. They are one and a half to two inches long.

Male and female flowers grow on the same tree. The male flowers appear as tiny, upright cones in tight clusters in late summer. Two or three inches long and about one-half-inch wide, they shed their pollen in the fall, then drop. The larger female flowers appear near the top of the tree, developing into compact, upright purplish cones three to five inches long and two inches wide. They have a smoother surface than familiar pinecones, ripening after two years and staying on the tree once they've released their seeds.

This is a warm-climate tree, most comfortable in zones 6 through 8.

The hardiest cedar variety, **Shalimar,** has blue-green needles. **Kashmir** is a good cold-hardy cultivar.

Atlas Cedar
(Cedrus atlantica)

The Atlas cedar (*Cedrus atlantica*), whose name refers to its native Atlas Mountains of Morocco, Algeria, and Tunisia, is one of the most popular of the cedars. It has an elegant pyramidal shape that makes it particularly suitable for residential yards.

Male and female cones are borne on the same tree. The males are two to three inches long, appearing in September. The females are a bit larger and appear only on older trees. Like the deodar, the Atlas cedar grows in zones 6 through 8, but it does better in hot weather. It does not, however, do well in wind. Its leaves are bluish green with occasional glints of other shades, from light green to silvery blue. In youth these trees are pyramidal in shape and rather sparse. But the mature specimens are filled in and dramatic, with an unusual flat top. They reach heights of 40 to 60 feet and widths of 30 to 40 feet. Fast growing in youth, Atlas cedars slow as they age and may live for three hundred years or more.

Glauca Pendula is a blue cedar with weeping branches that require supportive stakes. It can be espaliered on a wall to great effect.

Cedar of Lebanon
(Cedrus libani)

The cedar of Lebanon is a tree not used often enough in American landscapes. Native to Asia Minor, it has been cultivated since ancient times, with historic stands in the Middle East. The Bible notes that this tree was used in the temple built by Solomon. The Egyptians used its resin to mummify their dead and thus called this substance the "life of death."

The cedar of Lebanon reminds me of

American sequoias; both trees have very tall trunks with foliage that grows toward the top of the tree. The foliage of this tree in youth is narrowly conical in shape and becomes wider as the tree ages. Older trees have horizontal branches and a flat-topped crown. The bark is gray-brown and eventually develops a pebblelike appearance. It exudes a gum of balsam that is quite fragrant. The tree's mature height is 40 to 60 feet, with widths of 30 to 50 feet.

Needles are arranged in bundles numbering 30 to 40. Each needle is three-fourths to one and a half inches long and lustrous dark green in color. Cones are barrel-shaped, three to five inches long by two to two and a half inches wide, and require three years to mature. They are purple-brown in the second year and a rich brown in the third, when they scatter their small seeds.

The cedar of Lebanon is more resilient than other *Cedrus* species. Tolerant of zones 5 to 7.

CEDAR OF LEBANON CHOICES

Stiff and rigid, **Stenocoma** is an extremely cold-hardy choice with a pyramidal-columnar habit.

Common Symptom	Likely Cause
Foliage discolored, drops early	Salt damage
Dead branch tips and twigs	Deodar weevils
Needles discolored in summer	Spider mites

Species	Scale at Maturity	Basic Requirements
Deodar Cedar (*Cedrus deodar*)	Height: 40'–70' Width: 30'–40' Shape: Pyramidal	Zones 6 through 8 Full sun Moist, well-drained soil
Atlas Cedar (*Cedrus atlantica*)	Height: 40'–60' Width: 30'–40' Shape: Pyramidal, flat-topped	Zones 6 through 8 Full sun Moist, well-drained soil
Cedar of Lebanon (*Cedrus libani*)	Height: 40'–60' Width: 30'–50' Shape: Broad, conical	Zones 5 through 7 Full sun Moist, well-drained soil

Requirements of Your Cedar

Cedars are sun lovers. Too much shade causes them to grow spindly. They prefer a well-drained, loamy soil that is acid to neutral (pH 5.5 to 7.0), but they will also accept soil that is less fertile, sandy, and more alkaline.

Planting Your Cedar

The more care you take when you put your tree in the ground, the better it will do during its long life. Follow the complete planting directions provided in chapter 3.

A special note: Cedars do not like to be transplanted, so choose young trees in containers. They may look a bit spindly, but they will fill out quickly. The best time to plant cedars is in the fall.

Caring for Your Cedar

Follow the instructions on seasonal care for young and mature trees—watering, mulching, fertilizing, staking, and pruning—described in chapter 3.

A special note: Occasionally in winter, rodents nest in and around young cedars and gnaw at their tender bark. Wrap cedar stems with hardware cloth or commercial tree guards. Wait until the ground freezes hard, then spread a thick winter mulch around the tree to deny these pests a nesting spot.

Special Situations for the Cedar

Dead foliage is often the result of normal aging. Cedars stay green all year round, yet each year some needles turn brown and drop, usually in the fall when deciduous trees are showing color. Normal leaf drop may occur annually or every second or third year.

CYPRESS (*Cupressus*)

Top Reasons to Plant

- Dense, columnar shape
- Good year-round color
- Thrives in warm climates

The cypress is a cone-shaped tree whose many varieties can be found all over the world. My favorite is the Leyland cypress (*Cupressocyparis leylandii*). This handsome, hardy tree is a sterile hybrid of Monterey cypress (*Cupressus macrocarpa*) and Alaskan cedar (*Chamaecyparis nootkatensis*) that originated naturally. In 1888 C. J. Leyland found six seedlings growing on the grounds of Leighton Hall, fabled estate in the south of Wales. The two different parent trees were growing on the estate and crossbred purely by accident. This is remarkable because in the plant world

fairly severe pruning. Group cypresses or plant them individually for a formal accent in large residential yards.

The Leyland cypress is a cone-bearing evergreen that maintains good color in both summer and winter. Hardy in zones 6 through 9, this tree grows in a columnar shape with a single trunk that reaches 60 to 70 feet or more. A rapid grower, it can shoot up three feet or more per year when young. Typically the spread is 6 to 12 feet.

Leyland cypress leaves are needled, evergreen, flat, and round-tipped, covering the pointed branchlets like scales. The foliage resembles arborvitae at first glance, except that it has a finer, almost feathery texture. Young needles are a pale green, turning bluish green with maturity. Leyland cypress foliage gives off a pleasant odor when crushed. When the flowers appear in the spring, they are inconspicuous. The cones that develop later are rounded, about a half inch in diameter and feature eight-pointed scales. About five seeds are contained within each scale.

LEYLAND CYPRESS CHOICES

Cultivars of Leyland cypress offer foliage of a large array of colors, sizes, and shapes. **Castlewellan** has yellow foliage, whereas **Green Spire** is more columnar and dense with bright green foliage. **Haggerston Grey** has a more open habit, a pale gray cast to its foliage and a rougher branching pattern. **Naylor's Blue** has grayish green foliage, whereas **Silver Dust** has white variegations on bluish foliage and a wider habit. The **Leighton Green** cultivar is most commonly used for Christmas trees, as its foliage is dark forest green. Heavy and stout, it has a

intergeneric crossbreeding is rare, particularly between conifers.

Use cypresses in rows to screen out street noise, wind, neighbors' yards, or unattractive buildings and fences. While they are young it is possible to prune them as hedges, but they eventually outgrow even somewhat coarser appearance compared to the other Leyland cultivars.

Requirements of Your Leyland Cypress

The Leyland cypress is known for its adaptability. It grows in Florida yet is hardy enough to withstand winters as far north as the Ohio Valley, southeastern Pennsylvania, and along the Atlantic coast into New England. It will tolerate poor soil as long as it is not boggy, and it will grow in soil that is either slightly acidic or alkaline. This cypress prefers sun but will also accept considerable shade, much more so than junipers. And it is ideal for the seashore, since salt spray does not bother it.

Planting Your Leyland Cypress

The more care you take when you put your tree in the ground, the better it will do during its long life. Follow the complete planting directions provided in chapter 3.

Caring for Your Leyland Cypress

Follow the instructions on seasonal care for young and mature trees—watering, mulching, fertilizing, staking, and pruning—described in chapter 3.

A special note: Leyland cypress trees are already fast growers, so do not overdo the fertilizing. Feed an established tree annually, but modestly.

Because they grow so quickly, Leyland cypresses require some pruning early on before the growth gets out of hand. In the first year, at the beginning of the growing season in spring, cut back side shoots, and late in July trim the sides lightly. In the next few years, trim the sides to encourage denser growth. Once the tree has reached the desired height, trim six inches off the top to encourage dense growth at the top. Thereafter trim the sides and top up to three times during the growing season to maintain desired shape and height.

Common Symptom	Likely Cause
Small silken bags hanging from twigs	Bagworms
Leaves turning yellow and wilt; tree lists	Root rot

Species	Scale at Maturity	Basic Requirements
Leyland Cypress (*Cupressocyparis leylandii*)	Height: 60'–70' Width: 6'–12' Shape: Columnar	Zones 6 through 9 Full sun/part shade Moist, well-drained soil

DAWN REDWOOD
(*Metasequoia glyptostroboides*)

Top Reasons to Plant

∾ Deciduous needles
∾ Fall color
∾ Peeling bark
∾ Fast growth

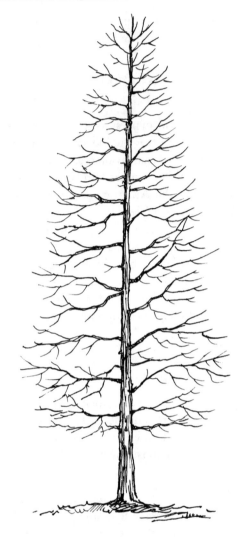

There's an old dawn redwood I love at the Arnold Arboretum, a beautiful tree-filled oasis right in the middle of Boston. This species has a unique history; it has been around for 50 million years but was thought as recently as last century to be extinct. The first discoveries of the dawn redwood's existence were fossils collected in Japan about sixty years ago. Shortly thereafter, a number of live specimens were found in rural China. Because of this history, the dawn redwood is sometimes called a "living fossil." Also known as the water larch, this tree was introduced to the United States and Europe

around 1945 and since then has become a very popular landscape tree. In the United States, it is planted in areas as remote from each other as Maine, Alabama, and California.

The dawn redwood has a feathery, pyramidal shape. Its branches grow straight out from a very straight trunk. Its reddish bark is finer and less rough than that of the sequoia, and as it matures, the bark becomes darker and peels in long, narrow strips. A mature tree will stand 70 to 100 feet tall and 20 to 25 feet wide. This is a fast-growing tree that can add several feet a year.

Like the larch and bald cypress, the dawn redwood is a deciduous tree. Its soft needles are arranged opposite one another on two- to three-inch stems and are about half an inch long. The upper surfaces are bright green and the lower surfaces a lighter green, turning a copper to brown color in the fall. The tree is hardy in zones 5 through 8.

The dawn redwood bears both male and female flowers on the same tree. Whereas the male flowers are clusters at the end of branches, the female flower is solitary. The flower eventually becomes a cone about one inch long, containing five to nine winged seeds. These cones hang in groups at the ends of branches, ripening in early December and shedding their seeds shortly thereafter.

The dawn redwood is usually used as a specimen because of its uniform conical habit and very straight trunk.

Requirements of Your Dawn Redwood

The dawn redwood requires full sun to thrive. It does best in moist, deep, well-drained, slightly acidic soils and does not adapt well to alkaline soils.

Planting Your Dawn Redwood

The more care you take when you put your tree in the ground, the better it will do during its long life. Follow the complete planting directions provided in chapter 3.

Caring for Your Dawn Redwood

Follow the instructions on seasonal care for young and mature trees—watering, mulching, fertilizing, staking, and pruning—described in chapter 3.

A special note: The dawn redwood seldom requires pruning thanks to its neat, uniform, conical habit.

Common Symptom	Likely Cause
Needles discolored, webbed over	Spider mites
Holes in needles	Japanese beetles

Species	Scale at Maturity	Basic Requirements
Dawn Redwood (*Metasequoia glyptostroboides*)	Height: 70'–100' Width: 20'–25' Shape: Pyramidal	Zones 5 through 8 Full sun Moist, well-drained, acidic soil

Special Situations for the Dawn Redwood

The dawn redwood is free of most disease and pest insect problems. However, if planted in dry soils, it may be vulnerable to spider mites. In years when Japanese beetles are rampant, these insects will feed on the dawn redwood.

DOUGLAS FIR
(*Pseudotsuga menziesii*)

Top Reasons to Plant

- ∾ Uniform, spirelike shape
- ∾ Cold-hardiness
- ∾ Good specimen tree

My visit to the old-growth forests of the Pacific Northwest was one of the most powerful experiences I have ever had. Oregon's H. J. Andrews Experimental Forest is a living laboratory for the study of old-growth ecosystems. There I found incredible Douglas firs (named for David Douglas, a nineteenth-century Scottish botanist) that stretch to the horizon, each over two hundred years old—most are three times that old. The trees create a microclimate of moisture and drifting sunlight. I left envying the people who get to walk through that forest—and get paid for it!

In nature, Douglas firs establish themselves primarily after fires clear an area of other trees. They can live for a thousand years, largely due to a very thick bark that allows them to survive moderate fires and spread in the fire's aftermath. Thus, the presence of large Douglas firs in old-growth forests means that fires occurred there many centuries ago.

Although this tree is called a fir, it does not actually belong to the same genus, *Abies,* as true firs. Nevertheless, they share many characteristics.

The Douglas fir is an excellent ornamental evergreen for use in residential yards. Ornamental types feature a stately pyramidal form that becomes more conical with age. They have attractive color and needles that hold on to the stem even in dry conditions. That's why they're often used as Christmas trees. As an added bonus, this tree is relatively tolerant of common air pollutants.

Douglas firs are best displayed individually as specimen trees in a spacious yard. But planted in rows along borders, they make an effective screen. They are not suited for windbreaks, however, as they are susceptible to damage from high winds.

Douglas firs reach 100 feet at maturity, although in a residential landscape they

round tips about one inch long. They grow individually, spiraling around the length of the stems. Dark green or bluish green on top, they are paler underneath with two white lines running the length of their undersides. The leaves have a distinctive camphorlike odor when crushed.

Male and female flowers grow on the same tree. They appear near the top of the tree in late April or early May as bright red cylinder-shaped cones on year-old wood. Three or four inches long, the flowers are distinguished by the whiskerlike extended tips on each of the cone's scales. Unlike the cones on other firs, Douglas fir cones hang downward. They turn brown toward August as they mature. Many remain on the tree through the winter, while others fall to the ground and are relished by small animals such as squirrels and chipmunks, and even by deer.

Requirements of Your Douglas Fir

These trees do best in full sun but will tolerate light shade. An ideal location will give them moist air and moist, well-drained soil—they do not do well in clayey or soggy soil—that is slightly acid (pH 6.0 to 6.5).

Planting Your Douglas Fir

tend to be 40 to 80 feet tall and 12 to 20 feet wide. When young, they grow 1 to 2 feet a year, reaching about 15 feet after ten years, but as they age, their growth slows. The horizontal branches of young Douglas firs are dense, but they open up with age.

Douglas fir foliage is green throughout the winter. The leaves are flat needles with

The more care you take when you put your tree in the ground, the better it will do during its long life. Follow the complete planting directions provided in chapter 3.

Special notes: The cold-hardiness of Douglas firs depends on the variety. So check with a local nursery for types appropriate to your area. Seedlings from the

Pacific coast can be a bit less hardy than those from the Rocky Mountains.

Because Douglas firs are commonly used as Christmas trees, nurseries usually have stock available that is either balled and burlapped or planted in containers.

If cared for properly, container-grown trees will live for several years. Choose the smallest tree available, one growing in a container that has at least a two- or three-gallon capacity. Feed the tree periodically, keep it moist, and leave it outside except for a few days at Christmastime. Each spring, gently pinch off half of its new growth on each branch to shape the tree and slow its growth. Eventually it will become too heavy and unwieldy to bring indoors at holiday time. Plant it outdoors as described in chapter 3 and enjoy it for many more years.

Whether you're planting a newly purchased balled-and-burlapped tree or a tree you've nursed along in a container for several years, choose an outdoor site that gives Douglas firs plenty of room to grow but is not exposed to high winds. They have a shallow root system, which means they transplant easily but are susceptible to winds. Douglas firs do best if they're sheltered from the elements; good sites are to the north or east of a building.

Common Symptom	Likely Cause
Needles that turn yellow	Chlorosis (caused by alkaline soil)
Twigs and roots damaged	Weevils
Leaves chewed, tree defoliated	Caterpillars
Yellow spots on needles near fall; needles appearing reddish brown in spring	Needle cast
Orange, brown, or yellow powdery masses on needles	Rust

Species	Scale at Maturity	Basic Requirements
Douglas Fir (*Pseudotsuga menziesii*)	Height: 40'–80' Width: 12'–20' Shape: Conical	Zones 4 through 6 Full sun/part shade Moist, well-drained, acidic soil

Caring for Your Douglas Fir

Follow the instructions on seasonal care for young and mature trees—watering, mulching, fertilizing, staking, and pruning—described in chapter 3.

Special Situations for the Douglas Fir

If the needles of your Douglas fir turn yellow, it may be suffering from a deficiency of iron, zinc, or manganese, a condition known as chlorosis. Have your needles and soil analyzed before treating the tree with micronutrient supplements, because applying supplements when the problem is *not* chlorosis can make the situation worse.

are bluish in color and appear on the tips of foliage shoots in April, when the male flowers shed pollen. Small cones eventually develop, one-third- to one-half-inch long, that will ripen even in the tree's first year.

False cypress trees vary in color, size, and shape, but many types make useful ornamental plants for residential yards and gardens in the United States, especially the

FALSE CYPRESS (*Chamaecyparis* sp.)

Top Reasons to Plant

- Ability to thrive in cool, humid areas
- Attractive drooping form
- Feathery or pendulous branches

False cypresses are so called because they are very much like cypresses but are not in the same genus. These are large, pyramidal, sometimes columnar evergreens with branches that droop at the tips. False cypress foliage is ferny, like that of the arborvitae. The needles are dark above and silvery underneath. Male and female flowers are borne on the same tree. Female flowers

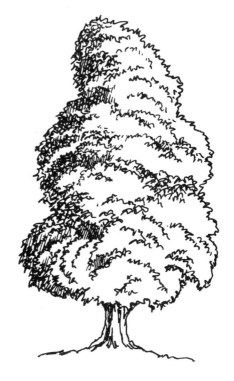

Japanese hinoki false cypress (*Chamaecyparis obtusa*). In Japan it can hit a towering 120 feet tall at maturity, but in North America specimens are typically 50 to 75 feet tall and 10 to 20 feet wide, with a pyramidal shape. The false cypress is hardy in zones 4 through 8.

HINOKI FALSE CYPRESS CHOICES

Nana Gracilis has uniquely clustered dark green foliage and reaches a height of about six feet. The smaller cultivar **Filicoides** has long branches spotted with deep green leaves.

Requirements of Your False Cypress

This tree is native to cool, humid climates and does well in zones 4 through 8. It is best suited to locations with full sun or part shade. Varieties with yellow foliage especially need sun to maintain their color. Their soil should be moist and well drained, and very acid to neutral (pH 4.0 to 7.5).

Planting Your False Cypress

The more care you take when you put your tree in the ground, the better it will do during its long life. Follow the complete planting directions provided in chapter 3.

Be forewarned that the false cypress, unless it's a dwarf variety, may gradually grow into a very tall tree. While they are young and shrubby, false cypresses are ideal for foundation plantings, but even these slow growers do not stay small and compact, and need to be removed eventually. These trees work well in groups as screens along boundaries. As mature trees they are stunning individual specimens in a lawn.

Common Symptom	Likely Cause
Needles that turn yellow; weak, dying branches	Weevils
Yellow needles	Scale
Webbed, sticky needles	Spider mites
Branch tips browned, dieback	Twig blight

Species	Scale at Maturity	Basic Requirements
Hinoki False Cypress (*Chamaecyparis obtusa*)	Height: 50'–75' Width: 10'–20' Shape: Pyramidal	Zones 4 through 8 Full sun/part shade Moist, acidic soil

Dwarf varieties can be kept pruned as a hedge.

Caring for Your False Cypress

Follow the instructions on seasonal care for young and mature trees—watering, mulching, fertilizing, staking, and pruning—described in chapter 3.

A special note: Spraying the foliage with an antidesiccant in the fall will help prevent its evergreen foliage from drying out in harsh winter sun and wind. Nondwarf types must be pruned over the years if their growth is to be restrained.

Reduced moisture during hot summer months sometimes causes false cypress foliage to turn brown and twigs to drop. Check soil moisture under the mulch every two or three weeks if rainfall is sparse. If necessary, soak the soil to a depth of two feet by watering slowly and deeply.

FIR (*Abies* sp.)

Top Reasons to Plant

- ∾ Attractiveness as a formal element in the landscape
- ∾ Rich green needles
- ∾ Handsome spirelike figure

With their narrow pyramids of dark green foliage outlined against the sky, fir trees are one of the enduring symbols of the high-mountain country of the northern and western United States. The fine, textured needles and dense growth of these trees provide shelter and nesting sites for many birds, such as wrens, finches, and robins, and the seeds from the cones are quite popular with squirrels, chipmunks, and deer. The fir tree's resinous wood has enjoyed an abundance of practical uses throughout history, from torches to chewing gum. Firs are also popular Christmas trees.

Though most of the many types of firs do best in the moist coolness of their native mountains, some are suitable for use as ornamental plantings at lower elevations.

Firs can be planted in groups along borders or singly as specimens to display their spectacular shape.

White Fir (Abies concolor)

The white fir, also commonly called concolor fir, is native to the western United States. Because the rings within its trunk are often clearly defined and concentric, tree-ring dating is easy; ecologists are also able to examine the tree rings to learn about changes in climate over time. In the wild, these great firs may reach 350 years of age and stretch over 100 feet tall, but in the landscape the typical height is 30 to 50 feet, with a spread of 15 to 20 feet. The trees are conical and narrow, with a straight trunk. On older white firs, the lower one-half to one-third of the crown often loses its branches.

Hardy from zones 3 through 7, the white fir is considered the best fir to grow in the midwestern and eastern climates. It grows slowly, about 12 to 18 inches a year, producing a whorl of branches that contributes to its conical shape. The needles are flat, one to two inches long, and grow in clusters along the top sides of the twigs. They are silvery gray in the spring and more blue-green in the summer, and their bluntly rounded tips yellow a bit in the winter. Each leaf stays on the tree for four to five years before dropping.

The flowers of both sexes of white firs are cones and appear in May on the same tree. Male cones are small, about an inch long, borne in bunches that shed pollen in the spring. The seed-bearing female cones are rosy red, three to five inches long, and grow mostly near the top of the tree. They become olive green, then purple-brown as the season progresses from July to October. Unlike those of many other evergreen species, fir cones are erect, standing upright on the branches. The cones break apart easily in the late fall, releasing seeds relished by wildlife.

Balsam Fir (Abies balsamea)

This makes a nice landscape tree when young but can lose its shape as it matures, especially if planted in a warm, dry setting. Hardy in zones 3 through 5, this native tree tolerates cold well but is not suited for urban conditions. The balsam fir has several desirable properties, including a dark green color, long-lasting needles, and an attractive overall form. Its crown is dense and pyramidal, and it has a slender spirelike tip. It also retains its pleasing fragrance. (All of which helps explain its popularity as a Christmas tree, and as a landscape specimen.)

Individual needles are somewhat flat and may be blunt or notched at the end. Needles have a broad circular base and are usually dark green on the upper surface, lighter on the lower surface. The cones are two to four inches long and gray-brown. Young cones have a purplish tint.

Balsam fir bark is thin, ash gray, and smooth except for the numerous blisters that appear on young trees. Because of these blisters, which contain a sticky, fragrant, liquid resin, the species is sometimes referred to as "blister pine." Upon maturity, the tree's bark breaks into thin scales and turns a red-brown color, reaching up to one-half inch in thickness. Its annual growth rate is less than 12 inches, but typically it reaches heights of 45 to 75 feet and widths of 20 to 25 feet.

Fraser Fir (Abies fraseri)

The Fraser and balsam firs are quite similar, but the Fraser will grow in slightly warmer climates. Hardy in zones 4 through 7, it is a pyramidal tree with stiff, horizontal branches and very resinous, gray or pale yellow-brown stems. It has shiny dark green needles that are banded with white underneath.

The Fraser fir reaches a maximum

Common Symptom	Likely Cause
Twigs curled and distorted	Aphids
Needles discolored, webbed over, stippled with yellow or red dots	Spider mites
Needles and buds eaten out, defoliation	Spruce budworms
Small bumps on leaves and stems, brown or yellow needles	Scale insects
Trees defoliated, sawdust-colored egg masses on trunks, branches	Gypsy moth
Branches hung with tiny fringed bags	Bagworms
Needles and twigs that look scorched, stunted	Twig blight
Needles that are yellow, shriveled, drop prematurely, have black spots on undersides	Needle cast
Girdling lesions on trunk and branches; long, oval, sunken areas on the trunk with raised edges	Canker

Species	Scale at Maturity	Basic Requirements
White Fir (*Abies concolor*)	Height: 30'–50' or more Width: 15'–20' Shape: Conical	Zones 3 through 7 Full sun/light shade Moist, well-drained soil
Balsam Fir (*Abies balsamea*)	Height: 45'–75' Width: 20'–25' Shape: Pyramidal	Zones 3 through 5 Full sun/light shade Moist, well-drained soil
Fraser Fir (*Abies fraseri*)	Height: 30'–40' Width: 20'–25' Shape: Pyramidal	Zones 4 through 7 Full sun/light shade Moist, well-drained soil

height of about 30 to 40 feet and a width of 20 to 25 feet. Its strong branches are turned slightly upward, creating a compact pyramidal appearance.

The needles of the Fraser fir are flat, dark green, and one-half to one inch long, with two broad silvery white bands on the lower surface. On lower branches, needles grow in two opposite rows on the stem. On upper twigs, leaves tend to curl upward in a more U-shaped form.

Requirements of Your Fir

Firs grow best in full sun but tolerate light shade. They adapt to most soils, from coarse and gravelly to sandy, as long as the soil drains well and is on the acidic side (pH 4.0 to 6.5). They do not like clay, which holds water too long near their roots.

Planting Your Fir

The more care you take when you put your tree in the ground, the better it will do during its long life. Follow the complete planting directions provided in chapter 3.

A special note: Spring is the best time to plant firs.

Caring for Your Fir

Follow the instructions on seasonal care for young and mature trees—watering, mulching, fertilizing, staking, and pruning—described in chapter 3.

A special note: Firs do not normally need pruning, as they naturally maintain their distinctive shape very well. Prune branches from firs only if it is necessary to control a pest problem or disease. Because these trees do not replace lost lower limbs, pruning them risks marring the overall shape of the tree.

HEMLOCK (*Tsuga* sp.)

Top Reasons to Plant

∾ Soft form
∾ Versatility in the landscape
∾ Many choices available

Pay a visit to the Nantahala National Forest in North Carolina and you will see some of the largest hemlock trees in the nation. Within this 14,000-acre tract, there are the most incredible hemlocks you'll ever see—immense trees well over three hundred years old.

A handsome evergreen valued for its deep green color and graceful habit, the hemlock is distinctive for its dark, pyramidal form accented with drooping branches. Several varieties are native to North America. The western hemlock (*Tsuga heterophylla*) and mountain hemlock (*Tsuga mertensiana*) prefer the mountain slopes of the Pacific coast region. The Canadian hemlock (*Tsuga canadiensis*) and Carolina hemlock (*Tsuga caroliniana*) are common in eastern forests and are quite long-lived trees.

The hemlock's dense foliage and bushy growth habit provide valuable cover for nesting birds. And its cones attract many seed-eating songbirds, such as chickadees, robins, goldfinches, and sparrows. Deer and small rodents are attracted to hemlock foliage, as the lower branches are at, or close to, ground level.

Hemlocks are versatile trees: they can be used as individual specimen trees or in groups, as foundation plantings, screens, and even as hedges if kept well pruned. Because hemlocks come in so many sizes and shapes, any landscape design can accommodate at least one variation of hemlock.

Hemlocks are functionally and aesthetically beneficial to residential yards. They support wildlife, and their lovely soft-textured evergreen foliage is beautiful in both summer and winter. The pendulous types add a sculptural element to the yard, which is especially noticeable in winter once deciduous trees lose their leaves. Dwarf varieties are excellent in rock gardens and containers.

Canadian Hemlock (Tsuga canadiensis)

The Canadian hemlock, or eastern hemlock, grows 12 to 18 inches a year, often developing more than one trunk. The mature tree is 40 to 70 feet tall and 25 to 35 feet wide. When the tree is young, the redbrown bark is scaly, and it becomes deeply ridged with age. The Canadian hemlock keeps its lower branches for many years.

The hemlock has fine-textured needles that are arranged along the twigs on a flat plane, like the wings of an airplane. Only about a half inch long, they are flat with rounded or slightly indented tips. They remain dark green throughout the year and have two whitish bands on their undersides. Each needle lasts for three to five years and is replaced after it drops.

The Canadian hemlock bears cones in May through early June. They are one-half-inch long and hang at branch tips, causing them to dip gently. Borne on the same tree, male cones are light yellow, and female cones are light green. In the fall they turn brown, bearing seeds from September through January. The tree is hardy in zones 3 through 7.

CANADIAN HEMLOCK CHOICES

An extraordinary number of Canadian hemlock cultivars are available on the market. One of the most common is **Sargentii,** which is exquisite alongside a streambed or as a single specimen in a yard. This broad, weeping cultivar reaches 10 to 15 feet tall and about 25 feet wide.

Carolina Hemlock
(Tsuga caroliniana)

The Carolina hemlock resembles the Canadian hemlock, but the needles point in all directions around the twig, giving it a sprucelike appearance. It is able to handle city conditions better than Canadian hemlock. But it is not quite so cold tolerant as the Canadian and is hardy in zone 4 to zone 7. At full size, the tree will be 45 to 60 feet tall and 20 to 25 feet wide.

Western Hemlock
(Tsuga heterophylla)

The western hemlock is also known as the Pacific or West Coast hemlock. It is the tallest of the hemlocks; even in the landscape it will reach 75 feet. The trunk is straight with down-swept branches and an open, pyramidal crown. The western hemlock requires a habitat with a moisture-laden atmosphere and cool summer temperatures; hardy from zones 2 to 8, it does especially well in the northwest United States. The tree's shallow rooting system makes it particularly susceptible to damage from wind or fire. Its needles are short but grow in distinctly different sizes on the same twig. They are yellow-green on top and have two white bands on their undersides. The cones are egg-shaped and about one inch long. The tree's annual growth rate is 12 to 18 inches.

Mountain Hemlock
(Tsuga mertensiana)

The mountain hemlock prefers cool, moist mountain conditions as are found in zones

5 and 6. Its gray-green foliage is displayed on branches that droop at the tips. Appearing in clusters that often have a starlike appearance, needles are uniform in size and arrangement. Cones are cylindrical and are one to three inches long. Because this tree starts out as a slow grower, gaining less than 12 inches a year, it's good for containers and rock gardens and can even be trained as a bonsai. This tree will reach 60 feet high and 30 feet wide, and growth will quicken with age.

Requirements of Your Hemlock

Hemlocks appreciate sun but are also tolerant of shade. They grow in moderately coarse, sandy, or gravelly soil as well as in clay or soil with silt. While well-drained soil is always desirable for hemlocks, they are not particularly fussy. They do, however, require moist soil that is fairly acidic (pH 4.6 to 6.5).

Planting Your Hemlock

The more care you take when you put your tree in the ground, the better it will do during its long life. Follow the complete planting directions provided in chapter 3.

A special note: As they grow, hemlock branches will turn brown and drop off if they do not have enough sunlight. Hemlocks do best if planted in an open spot with full sun; otherwise you may need to prune the branches of neighboring trees later to allow sunlight to reach the hemlock.

Stake newly planted hemlocks only if they are at risk of being blown over or uprooted before they get established.

Where prevailing winds are a potential problem, stake newly planted trees for up to a year. If trees are staked for longer periods, they may not develop sufficient stabilizing roots on their own. In addition, the ties used for staking may cause damage to the growing tree.

Caring for Your Hemlock

Follow the instructions on seasonal care for young and mature trees—watering, mulching, fertilizing, staking, and pruning—described in chapter 3.

Special notes: Both Canadian and Carolina hemlocks respond well to shearing and pruning. They can be maintained at a height of three or four feet to make a hedge. Clipped closely, the hedge looks rather formal. If permitted to grow a year or so between prunings, it will acquire a soft, more free-form look. Removing individual shoots every year, rather than shearing the entire plant, creates a more natural effect. Prune in early spring using sharp, clean hand pruners or loppers.

When pruning diseased or broken branches, cut them off cleanly at the side, where the branch joins another and where the wood is healthy.

Hemlocks are highly intolerant of wet soil. They are likewise more sensitive to drought than most other narrow-leaf evergreens, especially when sited in southern regions. Their fibrous roots are shallow and dry out easily. Water newly planted young trees regularly until they are well established. Mature trees need supplemental watering just before the winter freeze sets in and when rain is scarce. Water them slowly to avoid flooding the soil.

Special Situations for the Hemlock

The woolly adelgid, an aphidlike insect, is by far the most significant pest for Canadian and Carolina hemlocks. Infestations are easily identifiable by the deposits of white, cottonlike masses on the undersides of hemlock needles, which turn gray, then yellow, then drop off. See specific advice for treating woolly adelgids on your hemlock in chapter 4.

An occasional problem for hemlocks is the browning and shedding of the lower branches. One possible environmental factor is insufficient sunlight caused by nearby plants that shade the hemlock's lower

Common Symptom	Likely Cause
Lower branches and needles eaten	Deer
Needles discolored, covered with fine webbing	Mites
Small bumps on needles, discoloration of needles, needle drop, loss of tree vigor	Scale insects
Spiny bags dangling from branches	Bagworms

Species	Scale at Maturity	Basic Requirements
Canadian Hemlock (*Tsuga canadiensis*)	Height: 40'–70' Width: 25'–35' Shape: Pyramidal	Zones 3 through 7 Full sun/part shade Moist, well-drained soil
Carolina Hemlock (*Tsuga caroliniana*)	Height: 45'–60' Width: 20'–25' Shape: Pyramidal	Zones 4 through 7 Full sun/part shade Moist, well-drained, acidic soil
Western Hemlock (*Tsuga heterophylla*)	Height: 50'–75' Width: 12'–17' Shape: Pyramidal	Zones 2 through 8 Full sun/part shade Moist, well-drained soil
Mountain Hemlock (*Tsuga mertensiana*)	Height: 50'–60' Width: 20'–30' Shape: Pyramidal	Zones 5 through 6 Full sun/part shade Moist, well-drained soil

branches; these plants need to be pruned or removed. Another is competition from grass or other plants, depriving hemlocks of their share of nutrients and moisture. Mulching under the hemlock will address this problem. It is important to fix these problems because trees under stress from chronic light, water, and nutrient deprivation are more vulnerable to pests.

HOLLY (*Ilex* sp.)

Top Reasons to Plant

- Red or yellow berries
- Glossy, spiny leaves
- Winter color

The American holly (*Ilex opaca*) has long been a part of this country's culture. Before European settlers arrived, Native Americans used extracts from its wood for medicinal purposes. American holly twigs were boiled with pine tops to produce a tea taken to relieve coughs. When the Pilgrims landed in Massachusetts only one week before Christmas in 1620, the evergreen leaves and bright red berries of the American holly greeted them in the nearby forest. They must have been reminded of the English holly (*Ilex aquifolium*) they had left at home, a symbol of Christmas for centuries in England and continental Europe.

Although holly lumber is not a major commercial item, it is sometimes used in the building of fine furniture: holly veneer makes a lovely finish. In the past it was also valued for wood-block engravings, handles of umbrellas, and the backs of hairbrushes. When stained black, holly resembles ebony, so it's often used for the black keys on pianos and organs and for the pegs and fingerboards on violins.

There are now hundreds of known kinds of holly shrubs and trees, many of which make handsome evergreen landscape plants in lawns and gardens. Here are a few of my favorites.

American Holly
(Ilex opaca)

Also called dune holly, white holly, and Christmas holly, the American holly is densely pyramidal in youth with branches growing to the ground. As it gets older, its shape becomes more open and irregular—some homeowners remove the lower branches to make it look more like a typical tree with an exposed trunk. A mature tree will be 40 to 50 feet tall and 18 to 40 feet wide.

American holly leaves are evergreen, stiff, and glossy, and colored either medium to olive green or variegated cream and

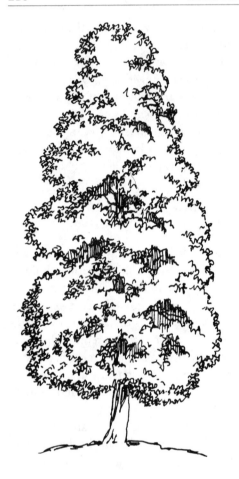

those of the male flowers. Both appear in late spring or early summer. Stunning red berries, or yellow berries in some varieties, about one-fourth inch in diameter, appear within leaf clusters on the female trees in midautumn on the current year's growth. The berries remain until early spring. Like all holly berries, although a favorite of birds, they are poisonous to humans.

The American holly is hardy from zones 5 through 9.

AMERICAN HOLLY CHOICES

There are hundreds of cultivars of American holly to choose from, but since these trees are sensitive to regional differences, it is important to select a cultivar appropriate to your area. Look for plants that bear fruit every year, have large and brightly colored berries, and display a dense habit. **Miss Helen,** which produces red berries, is a fine choice for northern landscapes, as are **Croonenburg** and **Jersey Princess.**

Chinese Holly
(Ilex cornuta)

Chinese hollies are beautiful, densely branched small trees or shrubs. These evergreens are hardy in zones 7 through 9 and are especially popular in the South because they withstand heat well. They are the first hollies to bloom in the spring.

Bushy, dense, and rounded, Chinese hollies grow from 5 to 20 feet tall, although typically they are about 9 feet tall. They will spread from 5 to 20 feet, depending on the variety and whether they're pruned.

Chinese holly leaves are stiff, glossy, dark green on top, and lighter beneath. In

green. They are lighter on their undersides. The leaves' broadly indented margins show the distinctive spines typical of most, but not all, evergreen hollies. Measuring two to four inches long and one to one and a half inches wide, depending on the variety, the leaves are arranged alternately along the holly stems. They remain attached for three years and then shed in the spring.

Male and female flowers are borne on separate plants. They are creamy white and small with four tiny petals. Male flowers grow in small clusters where the leaves join the stems, whereas female flowers grow either alone or in clusters smaller than most varieties they are squarish with four spines, one at each corner, and from one and a half to five inches long. A few varieties have more oval leaves with a single spine at their tips.

Chinese holly flowers are fragrant, yellowish green, and small, with four tiny petals. They appear in the early spring and last about four days. But the berries are the real prize—the largest of all the holly berries—at up to one-half inch across. They grow in large clusters on the previous year's growth, appearing as tiny green dots after the female flowers fade in April, turning red, or in some varieties yellow, by midautumn. They will last until early spring if birds do not get them. Like other holly species, the sexes grow on separate plants, but Chinese hollies are unique because female shrubs do not require pollen from a male shrub to set fruit. Berries are likely to be more abundant, though, if a male plant is nearby.

English Holly
(Ilex aquifolium)

English hollies come to us from Europe and Asia. Hundreds of varieties of this holly are now grown in this country, primarily for Christmas decorations. They are slow-growing evergreen shrubs that mature from a compact, pyramidal shape into handsome trees.

As young plants, English hollies are 3 to 4 feet tall. In maturity they grow 30 to 50 feet tall and 15 to 30 feet wide, but they can be kept to a manageable size with pruning. English hollies have a somewhat limited range. They do not tolerate extreme cold or hot, dry summers. Though they grow in zones 6 and 7, they do best in the coastal regions of these zones, where the air is humid.

English holly leaves are evergreen and more or less oval with a pleasant glossy sheen. But otherwise they vary greatly according to the variety. They may be from one and a half to four inches long and one to two inches wide. Some varieties have smooth edges; others have the spiny edges more characteristic of hollies. Leaves on older trees tend to lose their spines.

The English holly's flowers are small and greenish yellow with four tiny petals, appearing in late spring or early summer on separate male and female plants. Female trees bear pea-sized bright red berries in midautumn on the previous year's growth. Unless devoured by birds, the berries persist into January or later, depending on the variety.

Holly is a versatile plant and can be used in various ways in your yard. Hollies planted singly make excellent specimen trees. Grouped, they screen the yard from neighbors or traffic noise or serve as handsome background plantings. The distinctive berries are a particularly attractive asset especially in winter. Put your hollies where they can be seen from indoors so that you can enjoy this winter gift.

Requirements of Your Holly

Holly grows best in full sun. While it will tolerate some shade, this may result in a tree that is less compact and produces fewer berries. It is also vulnerable to leaf spot diseases if planted in shady, humid locations. A well-drained, loamy soil that is fairly light, sandy, and acidic to neutral (pH 5.8 to 7.0) is ideal for most hollies. Soils with a higher pH (alkaline) cause

Common Symptom	Likely Cause
Foliage damaged in winter	Windburn
Browning leaves	Holly bud moth
Mined and rolled leaves	Leaf miner
Discolored or deformed leaves	Mites
Leaves and branches encrusted with small bumps	Scale insects
Moist, sunken spots with fruiting bodies on leaves; pustules containing pinkish spores	Anthracnose
Leaves covered with white powder	Powdery mildew

Species	Scale at Maturity	Basic Requirements
American Holly (*Ilex opaca*)	Height: 40'–50' Width: 18'–40' Shape: Pyramidal or irregular	Zones 5 through 9 Full sun/part shade Moist, well-drained, acidic soil
Chinese Holly (*Ilex cornuta*)	Height: 5'–20' Width: 5'–20' Shape: Rounded	Zones 7 through 9 Full sun/part shade Moist, well-drained, acidic soil
English Holly (*Ilex aquifolium*)	Height: 30'–50' Width: 15'–30' Shape: Conical	Zones 6 through 7 Full sun/part shade Moist, well-drained, acidic soil

poor growth and can induce chlorosis, a loss of green leaf color.

Planting Your Holly

The more care you take when you put your tree in the ground, the better it will do during its long life. Follow the complete planting directions provided in chapter 3.

A special note: Plant male and female hollies within 300 feet of one another, in a ratio of one male to three female plants. This will ensure a good crop of berries.

Caring for Your Holly

Follow the instructions on seasonal care for young and mature trees—watering, mulching, fertilizing, staking, and pruning—described in chapter 3.

Special notes: Hollies are sensitive to both too much and too little nourishment. Fertilize annually in the fall to combat mineral deficiency, indicated by yellow or white leaves. Do not feed otherwise.

If they are planted in an area exposed to wind, erect a wind barrier of burlap to protect holly trees from winter winds.

Chinese hollies do not require pruning because of their naturally compact pyramidal or mounded shape. American hollies, however, do need shaping if you want to maintain a tight form as the tree ages.

Prune American and English hollies in the winter, when they are dormant. The American holly can be pruned lightly almost any time of the year, but if the plants are pruned heavily after flowering, or during the summer months, berry production may fall off. Never "top" a holly tree by cutting off its central stem to reduce its height; it will never recover its shape.

Special Situations for the Holly

If a holly doesn't produce berries, there may be several explanations. Neither male plants nor young females will produce berries. With the exception of the Chinese holly, these trees need pollination; if no male is nearby, a female will not produce berries. If a male is in close proximity and there are still no berries, the pollination may have been obstructed by rainy weather. Berry-producing flowers may also have been injured by late spring frosts or cold.

Yellow or white leaves signal mineral deficiency. This may occur in the spring when new growth starts and again in the late summer after berries have formed. Fertilize your holly in the fall to avoid this deficiency.

JUNIPER (*Juniperus* sp.)

Top Reasons to Plant

∾ Versatility
∾ Tolerance of city living
∾ Sturdy and long-lived
∾ Good in hot, dry weather

In Dutch, the juniper is called *geniver,* from which "gin" is derived. In the nineteenth century, Scottish Highland juniper berries were collected by the bagful and taken to the Inverness and Aberdeen markets to be exported to Dutch gin distillers. The berries have also been used to flavor other alcoholic beverages such as a Swedish health beer and a French beerlike drink called "genevrette" made from equal amounts of juniper berries and barley. But juniper is not only good for making martinis. Its "berries"—which are actually not berries at all, but a portion of the cone—were used by the Zuni Native Americans to assist in childbirth and by British herbalists to treat congestive heart failure. Native Americans, including the Blackfoot, Cheyenne, Crow, and Ojibwa, made tea from the creeping juniper's berrylike fruits and used it to treat kidney diseases, colds, and sore throats. They also burned creeping juniper as incense in ceremonies.

These coniferous evergreens are popular because they have numerous uses in the landscape, are long-lived, and can withstand urban conditions. Junipers make excellent screens, groupings, or specimens. Narrow, columnar juniper trees make a nice substitute for elegant Italian cypresses, which do not grow well in cold climates. Because they can handle dry, relatively poor soil, junipers are also useful for filling in bare spots where nothing else grows. They mix well with barberry shrubs, which accept the same conditions. Some junipers are large, spreading trees or low-growing shrubs, while others are creeping ground covers, but I'll focus on the trees.

Eastern Redcedar
(Juniperus virginiana)

The eastern redcedar is not a cedar at all. It's the most hardy and popular of the juniper trees. It is also the most widely distributed conifer in the East and grows in all states east of the Great Plains; it is at home, in fact, in more than three-quarters of the country, zones 2 to 9. The eastern redcedar is often an early colonizer of old abandoned farm fields. You can also spot

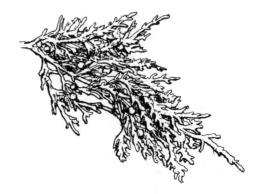

them along interstate highways in the medians and on the hills abutting the road. Before the advent of plantation-grown Christmas trees, southerners used wild eastern redcedars, which they chose for their natural conical shape and ready supply. Because their wood has aromatic oils that repel moths, redcedar is also used to construct storage closets and chests for clothing and blankets.

Eastern redcedar trees typically reach 40 to 50 feet. They are slow growers, reaching only about 20 feet tall after twenty-five or thirty years. Capable of living for as long as three hundred years, eastern redcedars have a dense, relatively small canopy, and their width is normally 10 to 20 feet. They are columnar in shape, and their thin, fibrous reddish brown bark sheds in long vertical strips.

Eastern redcedars have fine-textured evergreen needles. New growth is prickly, becoming flatter and scalelike over time. In spring they appear as a dull blue-green. Then, over the summer, they turn a dark olive green, which gives way in fall to a maroon-green or brownish green. Redcedar foliage is pleasantly aromatic.

Typical of all junipers, sexes are carried in the form of cones on separate trees. The small, spiky cones appear in May. Male

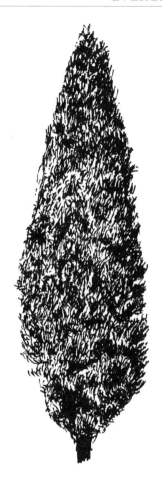

to broad pyramidal form and gray foliage that turns purplish in winter. **Canaertii,** a common cultivar in the Midwest, grows 15 to 20 feet tall and has a compact pyramidal form that opens up with age. Its dark green foliage and copious small cones with a whitish bloom create a picturesque appearance.

Chinese Juniper (Juniperus chinensis)

Like all junipers, the Chinese juniper tolerates hot, dry weather very well. It also adapts well to different soil and climate conditions and is very easy to grow. It does well in zones 3 through 9. The Chinese juniper comes in many forms, from creeping ground covers to bushy shrubs, but the most common form is a tree; usually about 50 to 60 feet tall, it has an upright conical form and a spread of only 15 to 20 feet. The Chinese juniper has brown bark and fine-textured evergreen needles from one-sixteenth- to one-third-inch long, and while newer growth may be prickly, most is flat, arranged like scales on the stems. The needle color varies according to variety, from green to blue. Some turn purplish or even golden in the winter.

cones are yellowish and female cones are bluish purple. Female trees yield blue berries, which last until the following March and are food for an array of creatures, including deer, small mammals, game birds, and songbirds.

Chinese juniper flowers are small, inconspicuous, cylindrical cones. Male

EASTERN REDCEDAR CHOICES

A silver-gray male form with a wide spread, **Silver Spreader** grows low to the ground. **Grey Owl** is a spreading female cultivar with grayish green leaves, reaching only about three feet tall. A taller choice at about 20 feet is **Burkii,** which has a narrow

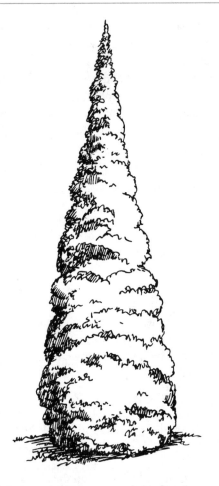

grows to 15 feet with sharply pointed, bright green foliage on dense branches. **Keteleeri** is a common cultivar in the Midwest with its tall, broad shape and frosted cones. It's also a good choice if you want to shape your Chinese juniper into a hedge. **Robusta Green** has an open structure that works within or outside of a container. **Sea Green,** growing four to six feet high and six to eight feet wide, has graceful, arching branches.

Rocky Mountain Juniper (Juniperus scopulorum)

Also known as the Colorado redcedar, this tree is closely related and quite similar to eastern redcedar, and was once believed to be the same species. Along with the pinyon pine, the Rocky Mountain juniper is the predominant tree species in the Southwest, covering millions of acres. It is found at 1,500 to 8,000 feet, in dry, rocky places, along the lower tree line on the mesas, foothills, and plains, in the most arid environments where conifers grow. In nature, the Rocky Mountain juniper is usually bushy and freely branched, growing no higher than about 15 feet, its trunk reaching one foot in diameter. It can survive because its blue-green or green leaves, which it retains all year, have evolved to tiny, waxy scales covering their twigs and small branches; this protects the plant from the snow, ice, and frigid temperatures of its mountainous habitat.

In the landscape, this is a slow-growing evergreen tree with a narrow, pyramidal habit that grows to a mature height of 30 to 40 feet and a width from 3 to 15 feet. The bark consists of many layers of fibrous elongated shreds. Capable of growing with a

flowers are pale brown and the females are yellow-green; they appear in late May or early June. The sexes grow on separate plants. Tiny bluish juniper "berries" appear on the female trees in early August and last until the following April. Only three-eighths of an inch in diameter, the berries are popular with deer and songbirds.

CHINESE JUNIPER CHOICES

A practical choice both in groups and as a singular accent, **Pfitzeriana** is the most popular cultivar of Chinese juniper in residential landscapes. **Hetzii Columnaris** single trunk or multiple trunks, this tree does well in zones 3 through 7.

Rocky Mountain juniper "berries" are actually fleshy cones with scalelike leaves. They are marble-size and reddish brown or bluish with a powdery coating. They contain one or several seeds. When birds and small mammals eat the berries, the indigestible seeds exit in their waste. The process of passing through the animals' digestive systems softens the seed coats, breaking their dormancy and allowing for the seeds' germination.

ROCKY MOUNTAIN JUNIPER CHOICES

Cultivars vary in size, weeping form, and color of foliage. **Skyrocket** forms a narrow 15- to 20-foot-tall column of blue-green foliage. **Tolleson's Weeping** has either

Common Symptom	Likely Cause
Tiny bags hanging on branches	Bagworms
Leaves and twigs webbed together	Webworms
Foliage that curls, turns yellow	Aphids
Small bumps on leaves and twigs, needles that turn yellow	Scale insects
Bright orange galls on leaves or yellow to orange "horns"; branch tips dieback	Cedar apple rust fungus

Species	Scale at Maturity	Basic Requirements
Eastern Redcedar (*Juniperus virginiana*)	Height: 40'–50' Width: 10'–20' Shape: Columnar	Zones 2 through 9 Full sun Moist, well-drained soil
Chinese Juniper (*Juniperus chinensis*)	Height: 50'–60' Width: 15'–20' Shape: Columnar-pyramidal	Zones 3 through 9 Full sun Moist, well-drained soil
Rocky Mountain Juniper (*Juniperus scopulorum*)	Height: 30'–40' Width: 3'–15' Shape: Pyramidal	Zones 3 through 7 Full sun Moist, well-drained soil

green or silvery blue-gray stringlike foliage and develops into a 20-foot-tall tree.

Requirements of Your Juniper

Junipers require full sun for the best growth. In a shady spot they will grow loose and spindly. In nature they appear mostly in sites with open exposure such as prairies, cliffs, dunes, old fields, open hillsides, and rocky ledges, so if you have similarly open areas on your property, consider placing your juniper there. They generally thrive in coarse and sandy soils that drain very well. Their versatility extends to their ability to grow in soil ranging from moderately acidic to alkaline (pH 5.0 to 8.5). However, junipers definitely do not like waterlogged soil such as clay, which makes them prone to disease.

Planting Your Juniper

The more care you take when you put your tree in the ground, the better it will do during its long life. Follow the complete planting directions provided in chapter 3.

Caring for Your Juniper

Follow the instructions on seasonal care for young and mature trees—watering, mulching, fertilizing, staking, and pruning—described in chapter 3.

Special notes: To keep tall-growing types under control, clip half of the new growth on each stem every year. The best time to prune junipers is late winter or early spring.

LARCH (*Larix* sp.)

Top Reasons to Plant

- ᖥ Tolerance for severe cold
- ᖥ Graceful winter skeleton
- ᖥ Breezy, open profile

Larches are among the rare conifers that shed their needles in the fall, leaving a beautiful, haunting skeleton in winter. They're also lovely in the spring as their young needles fill in, creating a loose and open texture that gives off light shade. Soft and flexible, these glossy needles are light green when they emerge in May, turning to a blue-green over the summer and to a vibrant yellow in the fall. They drop in November, leaving behind their small cones. The best yard for a larch is at least a quarter of an acre so that the tree can grow freely—it doesn't like to be tucked in among other trees. Larches can also be used to lead off the corner of a house, helping to frame the house in color. They work well planted behind small- or medium-size flowering shrubs. As a specimen plant in a good-size landscape, the larch is simply breathtaking.

The eastern larch (*Larix laricina*) is native to North America, while the Japanese larch (*Larix kaempferi*) is an import.

Eastern Larch
(Larix laricina)

The eastern larch (also called the American larch or the tamarack) is one of the hardiest, and most northern growing, native trees in North America. It reaches

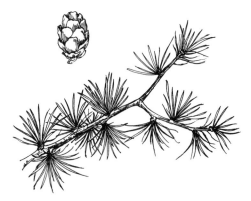

30 to 50 feet tall at maturity; the span of its strongly horizontal branches measures one-half to two-thirds its height, giving the tree a slim profile. This larch is an open, pyramid-shaped tree with branches that droop at the tips. It will grow a speedy one and a half to two feet per year during its early years, slowing after that. After twenty-five to thirty years, the tree is self-pruning, dropping the branches off the lower half of its length. The trees live 150 to 180 years, and do best in zones 1 through 4. They can withstand severe cold, surviving temperatures as low as −50°F.

Eastern larches bear finely textured one-inch-long needles that emerge in clusters spiraling around the branches. Flowers first appear when the tree is about fifteen years old and measure one-half to three-quarters of an inch long. The bright reddish purple female cones and smaller, yellow males appear upright along the twigs in May just before the foliage appears. In the fall, the needles yellow and drop, and the flowers give way to light brown cones about half an inch long. The cones usually remain on the tree for a year or so, then serve as a tasty meal for small animals and songbirds when they finally drop to the ground.

Japanese Larch
(Larix kaempferi)

This Japanese native grows to be 50 to 70 feet tall with a spread of 25 to 40 feet. Hardiest in zones 4 to 7, it prefers a more southern climate than its American counterpart. It is also fuller looking, with a pyramidal shape. The pendulous blue-green branchlets turn golden yellow in the fall. Another distinguishing feature is that the tips of the cone scales are bent outward and then backward.

Requirements of
Your Larch

Larches need a sunny location but not an extremely dry one. These trees don't mind moist soil—they've even been known to enjoy wet feet!—and they are good choices for soggy areas. The Japanese larch will tolerate soil a bit drier than that tolerated by the Eastern larch. It's not too particular about soil type, managing in clay and limestone, so long as it's mildly acid to neutral (pH 6.5 to 7.5).

Planting Your Larch

The more care you take when you put your tree in the ground, the better it will do during its long life. Follow the complete planting directions provided in chapter 3.

Caring for Your Larch

Follow the instructions on seasonal care for young and mature trees—watering, mulching, fertilizing, staking, and pruning—described in chapter 3.

A special note: Though larches are able to handle bitterly cold winters, they're vul-

Common Symptom	Likely Cause
Curled or puckered needles, distorted growth	Aphids
Leaves browned in the spring, holes in needles	Casebearer
Notched or stripped needles	Sawfly
Consumed needles, visible tawny egg masses	Gypsy moth
Girdled branches and stems, visible resin	Canker
Yellowed needles, fungus on undersides of leaves	Rust

Species	Scale at Maturity	Basic Requirements
Eastern Larch (*Larix laricina*)	Height: 30'–50' Width: 15'–30' Shape: Slim, pyramidal	Zones 1 through 4 Full sun Moist, well-drained soil
Japanese Larch (*Larix kaempferi*)	Height: 50'–70' Width: 25'–40' Shape: Slim, pyramidal	Zones 4 through 7 Full sun Moist, well-drained soil

nerable to wind damage for their first three or four years in the ground. Protect young larches with a screen of burlap. See chapter 3 for directions.

Special Situations for the Larch

Aphids, gypsy moths, and other pests are attracted to larches, so be on the lookout for distorted growth and ripped leaves. Eastern larches can also suffer from fungal diseases such as canker, to which Japanese larches are resistant, and rust.

PINE (*Pinus* sp.)

Top Reasons to Plant

- ∾ Versatile in landscape
- ∾ Graceful free-form shapes
- ∾ Toughness, longevity
- ∾ Fragrance

Pine trees grow in temperate climates all over North and South America, from the coasts to the timberline. For centuries, they've been harvested and put to commercial use—for furniture and boxes and floorboards, for the pine tar on the roof and the turpentine that cleans the paintbrushes. But as landscape plants, they come with a long list of first-class traits. They can be used in many different ways—as windbreaks, accent trees, backdrops or screens, or to line driveways or define property lines. They're tough and long-lived. As they age, many pines tend toward graceful, free-form shapes; even the most uniform growers don't have that run-through-a-pencil-

sharpener look. Their color is lovely year-round; their boughs are fragrant. The trees make a wonderful rustling sound when the wind blows through the upper branches. They provide home for finches, woodpeckers, chickadees, warblers, and owls. And squirrels love the cones.

Eastern White Pine (Pinus strobus)

Perhaps my favorite pine is the eastern white pine, a large, soft-wooded, fine-needled pine native to eastern North America. Since the colonial period, the white pine's heartwood (the tree's hardest, oldest interior wood) has provided classic pinewood for homes and furniture.

Eastern white pines have soft, flexible needles that are three to five inches long and grow in bundles of five. These thin, straight needles develop at the ends of twigs rather than uniformly along their length. Drooping gently from their twigs, they seem to me to be more graceful than the stiff needles of most other conifers. The foliage is green or bluish green year-round, though it yellows somewhat in the winter, and the needles have pale stripes on their undersides. They are shed and replaced in cycles, so that pines appear to be evergreen. As the trees age, the foliage density and pyramidal shape evolve to a flat-topped, more asymmetrical growth.

White pines' cones take two years to mature and are actually male and female flowers borne in separate clusters on the same tree. Their scales are green and smooth, overlapping like shingles on a roof. When unripe, female cones are pinkish purple, about two-fifths of an inch long; males are yellowish green. Both sexes bloom in early June until mid-July. They are narrow and five to six inches long when mature, carrying seeds that have a small wing at one end.

Hardy in zones 3 through 8, white pines mature at 50 to 80 feet, with a spread of 20 to 40 feet. They're fairly tolerant of adverse environmental conditions; however, they're susceptible to damage from ice storms, sulfur dioxide, ozone, and salt sea spray.

WHITE PINE CHOICES

An exquisite choice for general landscape use, the white pine has several beautiful cultivars. **Fastigiata** has a rapid-growing columnar form that expands with age. **Pendula,** a weeping type with gracefully arching branches, should be used sparingly as an accent plant. Sometimes these cultivars become too large for the scale of the typical yard. Dwarf versions of white pines have been developed to remedy this problem, such as **Nana, Globosa,** and **Compacta,** which have rounded outlines.

Bristlecone Pine
(Pinus aristata)

In the pine family, this tree is part tough hombre and part wise elder. You can hear both in the name: bristlecone, *aristata.* It is found naturally on dry, harsh sites in mountainous areas in the interior West. To call the bristlecone pine long-lived hardly does it justice. One tree in California lived to be more than 4,800 years old, and the age of others is estimated at 7,000. Ancient bristlecone pine trees found in the wild are always gnarled and broken with a dried-out appearance. They've survived for millennia in harsh environments with desiccating

winds, little rainfall, and very alkaline, sandy soil. Particularly old trees on harsh, windy sites may have only a few strands of bark remaining in crevices where they are protected from sandblasting winds. In fact, these ferocious conditions are their ally, discouraging insects, fungus, and rot from infesting the tree. Bristlecones are further protected from pests, disease, and dry winds alike by their dense, highly resinous wood.

The bristlecone pine reaches only 10 to 20 feet in height and half that in width, so if you want an evergreen that can fit into a small landscape, the bristlecone pine is a good choice. And it won't look like a dried-out, old survivor—just like a young, green tree. It will have the characteristic gnarled and twisted growth, though, and the upright stem tips that look like candles. The dark green needles are about one inch long, displayed in bundles of five and creating a bushy appearance that resembles a fox's tail. Sticky from white resin, the needles remain on the tree for ten to seventeen years. The fruit is a woody cone with a short stalk about three to three and a half inches long. These cones have thick brown scales and are tipped with a long prickly point, which gives the tree its name. Young bark is thin, smooth, and gray, later becoming furrowed and reddish brown. The light red-brown heartwood is fairly soft and not used commercially. This tree grows in zones 4 to 7.

Swiss Stone Pine
(Pinus cembra)

Also called arolla pine, this European native is a slow-growing tree with ultrasoft, dark green needles, two to three inches long in bundles of five. The tree has a narrow, dense pyramid shape when young, becoming more open and round-topped with age, but it is still one of the more compact and symmetrical of the pines. It naturally

branches close to the ground. A mature tree will be 30 to 40 feet tall and 15 to 25 feet wide.

Swiss stone pines are hardy in zones 4 to 7. Although they grow in heavy clays, they do equally well in sandy to loamy soil. The Swiss stone is the only pine for the home landscape that produces edible nuts known as pine nuts. The cones take three years to mature, but each year new cones are formed, ensuring a continuous crop of pine nuts once they reach bearing age, which is usually eight to ten years.

Japanese White Pine (Pinus parviflora)

The Japanese white pine is a striking landscape presence, with a dense, conical form when young and a more graceful, irregular shape when mature. It will reach anywhere from 20 to 50 feet in height with a width roughly similar. As it matures, its top flattens—an unusual and distinctive feature.

The Japanese white pine's needles are one to two and a half inches long, stiff, and twisted, and they are held in bundles of five. They form blue-green tufts of foliage at the branch tips, giving an overall fine texture to the tree's silhouette. The brownish red cones are one to four inches long and remain on the tree for six to seven years. The tree is hardy in zones 4 to 7.

Red Pine (Pinus resinosa)

Over the years, the red pine has been used extensively as a reforestation pine tree, and for its lumber and pulpwood. At the same time, this tree makes a fine specimen because it has the ability to withstand cold winters, mild summers, and low rainfall. Native to North America, it is also known as Norway pine because the early settlers of New England mistook it for the Norway spruce.

The red pine's shape is upright and oval in youth, spreading without becoming too irregular with age. Its common name comes from the fact that its young, scaly bark is a distinct orange-red while its mature, plated bark is more red-brown. A medium-fast grower, the mature tree is 50 to 80 feet tall, but widths vary considerably.

The red pine has medium green to dark green needles that grow in pairs. They are about five inches long and last for up to four years on the tree's twigs and branchlets. The two-inch-long cones are green in the beginning, tan by the end of the first growing season, and brown as mature two-year-olds.

Hardy in zones 2 to 5, red pines thrive on exposed, dry, acid, sandy, or gravelly soils and require full sun. They will grow poorly or die if planted in wet clay but are less susceptible to insects and diseases than most other species of pines.

Himalayan Pine (Pinus wallichiana)

The Himalayan pine is an elegant, upright tree with a loosely broad pyramidal form when it is young. Though it spreads as it ages, and the branches become pendulous, it retains a somewhat pyramidal form. A mature tree is 30 to 50 feet tall and a similar width.

Also called the Bhutan pine, the Himalayan pine has soft, blue-green needles that are five to eight inches long and grouped in bundles of five. Their upper surfaces are green and their lower surfaces are blue-white, creating a silvery blue cast. And whereas the young needles are erect, older needles tend to droop. This tree's cones are cylindrical, six to twelve inches long, and turn brown with age. In some instances the winter winds can cause some discoloration. This tree tolerates air pollution well and thus is a good choice for urban settings. It is hardy from zones 5 to 7.

Scotch Pine
(Pinus sylvestris)

The Scotch or Scot pine is a lovely pine used widely throughout North America as a landscape tree. Notable for its beautiful bluish green or yellowish green foliage, it is an extremely hardy species that can be grown successfully even in poor soils. The zone range is 2 through 7.

This pine has a crooked or twisted trunk that may split into several widely divergent branches at maturity, thus forming a picturesque frame of gnarled branches. It can reach 30 to 60 feet tall and 30 to 40 feet wide. More or less upright and pyramidal when young, it quickly becomes irregular and contorted, as if twisted by the wind. With age, it tends to lean.

The Scotch pine's upper trunk and the wood of its branches are an attractive coppery orange. The needles are variable in length, from slightly more than one inch for some varieties to nearly three inches for others. Ranging in color from bluish green to medium green to yellow-green, and occurring in bundles of two, these needles are most distinguished by their twisted

shape. Needles generally remain on the tree for two to four years. Unlike those of most pines, the small cones, which mature in their second year, do not have prickles on their scales.

SCOTCH PINE CHOICES

Sentinel (Fastigiata) has an obvious columnar habit, reaching 25 feet or taller, but can suffer from snow and ice damage. Slow-growing **Watereri** has steel-blue needles, and its bark has a hint of orange. Densely pyramidal to flat-topped, it reaches about 10 feet in height.

Austrian Pine (Pinus nigra)

The Austrian pine, also known as black pine, is rapidly becoming widespread in American landscapes. Its striking dark green foliage, stout, whorled branches, distinctive bark, and flaring, pyramidal shape make this pine a good tree for specimen planting, either alone or in groups. Hardy from zones 4 to 7, it grows well in sand, loam, or clay soils. It makes an excellent windbreak that can withstand wind as well as heavy snow, ice storms, and salt injury.

In its youth, the Austrian pine's limbs and foliage drape completely to the ground, but at maturity its lower limbs are usually absent, and its trunk is exposed. Over time, the pine's crown becomes spreading and open. The tree has deep cinnamon-colored bark with coarse, irregular plates and distinctive, deep fissures—one of the handsomest barks in the pine family. In an open landscape with minimal competition, the Austrian pine will reach 50 to 60 feet tall and 20 to 40 feet wide.

The Austrian pine has dark green needles that grow in pairs. The needles tend to form tufts on the ends of the branches, making the branches somewhat sparse in the spaces closer to the trunk. These three- to six-inch-long, thick, stiff needles last between four and eight years. The brown cones mature to about three inches long and have small prickles on the back side of their scales, which spread to release their seeds; cones remain on the tree for several years.

Requirements of Your Pine

Most pines grow best in full sun, but the soft-wooded varieties tolerate light shade better than hard pines do. While all pines prefer soil that drains well, many can handle poorer soil, though not usually clay. Ideally soil should be fairly acidic (pH 4.5 to 6.5).

Planting Your Pine

The more care you take when you put your tree in the ground, the better it will do during its long life. Follow the complete planting directions provided in chapter 3.

Special notes: Plant pines at least 50 feet away from the street or sidewalk to avoid salt damage in the winter. Avoid planting them wherever the soil becomes waterlogged after rain or snow, since they do not tolerate flooding. They won't do well in a lawn, either, because they are susceptible to the growth-inhibiting substances released into the soil by the roots of lawn grass. Consider using ground cover plants such as pachysandra or ivy instead of grass under pine trees. Southern exposure with no protection from late-winter sun browns the needles, as do dry winter winds. Research suggests that the health of many pines varies with climatic conditions in various regions, so it is best to buy nursery stock that you are sure is adapted to the local climate.

Caring for Your Pine

Follow the instructions on seasonal care for young and mature trees—watering, mulching, fertilizing, staking, and pruning—described in chapter 3.

Special notes: Pines and other conifers bleed, or leak sap, when they are pruned. You can minimize this bleeding by pruning only one-third of their new growth each year. Prune early in the season, just after the soft new growth shoots, or "candles," develop at the branch tips and before they sprout long needles. Cut back the center candle quite close to its starting point to enable it to produce new buds on the remaining short sections. Repeat this annually if you wish to contain the tree's growth and make it denser.

Do not prune your pine during the summer, especially a hot, dry summer. This can invite an unwelcome attack of bark beetles, a potentially fatal problem.

In late winter, prune broken or diseased branches from your pine promptly to forestall disease and insect invasions. Cut them off cleanly at the point where they join another branch and where the wood is healthy. If you cut way back to older, bare wood no new shoots will develop. Try to keep lower branches lengthier than upper ones so that they receive sufficient light. This way trees stay dense and bushy all the way to their base.

Special Situations for the Pine

In addition to having some common tree problems, pines are uniquely susceptible to a number of diseases and pests.

A major concern for pines is pine wilt disease, caused by the pinewood nematode, a microscopic worm that works its way into the tree from the soil. Once infected, a tree dies within a few weeks to a month, with needle color usually changing from dark green to grayish green, then finally to brown branch by branch or over the whole tree. Austrian, red, and Scotch pines are most susceptible to this problem (though the Austrian pine may first show symptoms of leaf color change on the branch tips rather than on whole branches), while the white pine is not particularly vulnerable. If you are doing a multiple planting, be sure to include a variety of pines, spruces, and firs to help avoid major problems with insects or disease.

In the Midwest white pines can suffer or

Common Symptom	Likely Cause
Flecked needles, red-brown appearance, needle drop	Spider mites
Encrusted needles and branches, stunted growth, cottony masses on undersides of branches	Scale insects
Yellowish green needles, tunnels in bark	Pine bark beetles
Wilted needles, cankers on trunk, blisters	Rust or blister rust
Discolored or shriveled needles, premature drop	Needle cast
Trunk bark and roots have been gnawed	Rodents
Foliage eaten, bark damaged in flat strips	Deer

Species	Scale at Maturity	Basic Requirements
Eastern White Pine (*Pinus strobus*)	Height: 50'–80' Width: 20'–40' Shape: Irregular	Zones 3 through 8 Full sun/part shade Moist, well-drained, acidic soil
Bristlecone Pine (*Pinus aristata*)	Height: 10'–20' Width: Varying Shape: Irregular	Zones 4 through 7 Part shade Dry soil
Swiss Stone Pine (*Pinus cembra*)	Height: 30'–40' Width: 15'–25' Shape: Columnar	Zones 4 through 7 Full sun Well-drained, slightly acid soil
Japanese White Pine (*Pinus parviflora*)	Height: 20'–50' Width: 20'–50' Shape: Irregular	Zones 4 through 7 Full sun Any soil
Red Pine (*Pinus resinosa*)	Height: 50'–80' Width: Varying Shape: Oval to irregular	Zones 2 through 5 Full sun Dry soil
Himalayan Pine (*Pinus wallichiana*)	Height: 30'–50' Width: 30'–50' Shape: Irregular, pyramidal	Zones 5 through 7 Full sun Moist, well-drained soil
Scotch Pine (*Pinus sylvestris*)	Height: 30'–60' Width: 30'–40' Shape: Irregular, contorted	Zones 2 through 7 Full sun/part shade Any soil
Austrian Pine (*Pinus nigra*)	Height: 50'–60' Width: 20'–40' Shape: Pyramidal	Zones 4 through 7 Full sun Any soil

even die from a relatively new disease called white pine decline, caused by a combination of environmental stresses, including poor location, alkaline soil instead of acid, heavy clay soil, crowding, salt damage, heat, and drought. Identifying and correcting these problems—or avoiding them in the first place—is crucial to the life of your tree. Affected trees sometimes appear healthy for a decade or more before decline symptoms are noticed. Look for shorter-than-normal needles with brown tips that drop prematurely. Their color is also a paler green or yellow than those of healthy trees. Other pine species don't appear to be affected by this disorder.

On white pines, it's easy to mistake white pine decline for annual needle drop. While it is normal for conifers to drop their oldest needles (all pines do this in the fall), in cases of white pine decline, an abnormal needle drop occurs in the spring or summer and affects only one or a few trees, rather than all or most of them.

Injury from salt used for de-icing is a potentially fatal hazard for white pine needles and branches. Traces of salt will appear on the sides of affected trees. Trees closest to the salted road are at greatest risk.

The presence of spittle masses on pine twigs in May and June is indicative of the pine spittlebug nymph. This brown, wedge-shaped pest feeds on Scotch, Austrian, and white pines along with spruces and firs. The nymphs feed on sap juice—a heavy infestation can reduce sap flow—and leave punctures along twigs and branches, resulting in browning tips and even death. Spray with an appropriate insecticide in early July.

Originally discovered in a Christmas tree plantation in Ohio, the pine shoot beetle has spread through the Midwest and into Pennsylvania, New York, and Ontario. Beetles are larvae of reddish brown moths that hibernate in bud tips of pines. Their presence is revealed by masses of a whitish, sticky pine pitch on the infested buds. When the weather warms they emerge to infiltrate healthy buds on the newly developing shoots. These shoots grow only one or two inches before they become distorted and die. Then the adult moths emerge to lay eggs on twig tips, bark, and needle sheaths for the next generation. When these eggs hatch, new beetles bore through the base of the needles, causing them to yellow and die.

There is no reliable treatment for pine shoot beetle infestation other than pruning and burning infested, sticky buds as soon as you spot them in order to prevent the moths from emerging. Hire a certified arborist for larger trees. When you are choosing your pine, buy nursery stock guaranteed to be free of this pest.

SPRUCE (*Picea* sp.)

Top Reasons to Plant

- ∾ Good cold tolerance
- ∾ Tidy growth and shape
- ∾ Fragrance

An evocative tree, the spruce stirs thoughts of Christmases past. My northern friends get living blue spruce trees for the holidays—they last longer and have a much stronger fragrance than other evergreens. Then they plant them outdoors to create living memories of the holidays.

Spruces are needled evergreen trees common in the cold northern parts of the United States. Although they have commercial value as a source of paper pulp, many types of spruces have a valuable ornamental function as well. They also grow well in a number of harsh environments and put up with adverse environmental and soil conditions.

Spruce trees do not blend quietly into the landscape, so they are positioned more appropriately as specimen trees, especially when they are young and have not yet begun to lose their lower branches. In spacious lawns, group them in threes for a striking effect. Rows of spruces along the borders of a property make effective windbreaks or screens. A single tree can punctuate the corner of a property. Because of their tall, slender profile, spruces are not suitable for planting close to low buildings, walls, or fences.

The white spruce variety **Conica**, as well as other dwarf spruce cultivars, is ideal for year-round container growing. Popular as a living Christmas tree, it grows only about one inch a year and boasts fine-textured, dense foliage. If you take it indoors for the holidays, set it where it will receive light but is away from dry heat. Do not keep it inside more than 10 days. Many other small spruces will grow in tubs or large containers that can be placed near decks or on patios. In hot weather, shield them from the hottest sun and dry winds. In very hot weather, hose down the foliage occasionally.

In the winter, the spruce's neat habit and evergreen needles relieves the bleakness of the landscapes they inhabit. Widely planted in the Northwest to block wind, most spruces also trap large amounts of snow; the thick, white frosting is a sea-sonal delight. Their fragrant foliage and large cones make excellent holiday decorations.

Spruces work well in yards designed to attract wildlife. Cones feed wildlife such as squirrels, deer, and songbirds. Their stiff, dense branches provide secure nesting sites for woodpeckers, chickadees, mockingbirds, robins, and many other birds.

Norway Spruce (Picea abies)

The Norway spruce, known also as common spruce, is the most widely used of the spruces in residential landscapes in the northern United States. Among the largest spruces, some Norways will grow to over 100 feet at maturity. More typically they are 40 to 60 feet tall, spreading 25 to 30 feet wide. They are pyramid shaped, and their fairly uniform branches grow stiffly at first, then loosen and droop as they age. The tree has reddish bark, giving it the nickname "red fir."

The Norway spruce's needles are stiff, about one-half to one inch long and sharply pointed. Like most spruce needles,

they are distinctively angular and somewhat square in shape. Usually the needles are dark green and last for about eight years before being replaced by new ones. This species of spruce will display two different forms of branching. "Comb" branches are new, reddish brown shoots that hang in rows from each branch. "Brush" branches grow at the ends of older branches.

The flowers of Norway spruces are soft cones; male cones appear on the lower branches of the tree while female ones appear on the upper branches. Measuring from five to seven inches long, young purple or green cones are visible in late May or early June. As the season progresses they dry and turn brown, and as they mature, they begin to hang downward from the branches. Cones may last for more than a year before they drop. They are valued as food by squirrels, deer, ground birds, and

songbirds. Many birds find nesting sites in the trees as well.

The Norway spruce is hardy in zones 2 through 7

NORWAY SPRUCE CHOICES

There are hundreds of cultivars of Norway spruce, but most nurseries offer only a handful. A notable cultivar is **Nidiformis,** or "bird's nest" spruce, which grows densely to six feet. Requiring little pruning, it has a distinctive depression in its flat top and has horizontal layers of branches with numerous branchlets. Intense summer heat can take its toll on this cultivar.

White Spruce (Picea glauca)

Though native to Canada, the white spruce, also known as Alberta spruce, is familiar in our country as a valued addition to residential landscapes. White spruces are medium-size conifers that grow to 40 to 60 feet at maturity and can live from 250 to 300 years. Slow growers, they may increase in height by 15 feet over 10 years. They are fairly narrow, maintaining a spread of roughly one-fourth to one-third of their height. Their neat habit and spreading branches give white spruces an attractive appearance that is perfect for ornamental use. White spruce bark is silvery gray, sometimes displaying a purplish cast, and develops thin, irregularly shaped scales on its surface. This tree is tolerant of considerable shade. It grows best in moist, acidic, loamy soils and in nature is often found on stream banks, lakeshores, and their adjacent slopes.

White spruce foliage is evergreen, remaining on the tree all year round. It is usually bluish green, but brand-new growth appears to be more silvery. The stiff needles are four-sided or square when cut in cross section. About one-half to three-fourths of an inch long, they lack the spined tip common of the needles of some other types of spruces. Needles grow at an angle and in spirals from the spruce twigs, pointing more forward than straight out. When crushed, needles have a disagreeable odor; thus white spruces are sometimes called by the nicknames "skunk spruce" or "cat spruce."

The flowers of white spruces are soft cones about one to two inches long. The male ones are orange and appear on the lower branches of the tree, and reddish purple female cones grow on the upper regions. Opening in April, the cones are visible by late May or early June. In July the cones, which have rounded scales, begin to dry and turn brown, then silvery gray as they weather. They often continue to hang from the spruce branches through January. White spruce cones are valued as food by many wild animals. Various kinds of birds nest in these spruces as well.

The white spruce is hardy from zones 2 through 5.

WHITE SPRUCE CHOICES

Conica, or **Dwarf Alberta,** is a broad-shaped white spruce cultivar with light green needles arranged around the stem like a bun.

Serbian Spruce
(Picea omorika)

Standing on its slender trunk and feathered branches, the Serbian spruce is considered the best spruce for residential landscapes in the eastern United States. It does well in zones 4 through 7, typically growing slowly to a mature height of 50 or 60 feet, which takes from fifty to sixty years. Columnar in shape, at mature height it will be no wider than 20 to 25 feet.

Whereas most spruce needles are square when cut in cross section, Serbian spruce foliage is flat like that of hemlocks and firs. The needles are from one-half to one inch long, a dark, lustrous green with two white lines on their undersides. They grow densely on the upper surfaces of stiff, up-tilted branches that droop a bit as the tree ages.

The flowers of Serbian spruces are soft cones; the greenish male cones cluster around the ends of the tree's lower branches, and the orange-red female cones congregate higher in the tree. The female cones can be seen standing erect on the branches beginning in late May or early June. As the season progresses they darken to purple and grow large. They then hang down from the branches from July through January. The cones of Serbian spruces are eaten by much of the wildlife that feeds on the cones of Norway and white spruces. Birds also find their branches to be excellent nesting sites.

Colorado Blue Spruce
(Picea pungens)

Colorado blue spruces are most at home in the mountains out west. However, because of the trees' striking silvery blue needles and tolerance of cold, drought, and poor soil, homeowners in the northern United States and Canada have adopted them as ornamental trees for the yard. Their sharp, prickly needles make them resistant to deer

damage. Although blue spruces are tough and grow in almost any type of soil, they are intolerant of air pollution and wet soil. They are hardy in zones 2 through 7.

Blue spruces grow 30 to 60 feet in landscape situations, much shorter than their growth potential in the wild, and may reach 350 years of age. They are slow growers, growing only 5 or 6 feet over the course of ten years. Narrow in habit—only 10 to 20 feet wide—and stiffly erect, they possess a distinctive pyramidal shape. Their rigidly horizontal limbs turn up slightly at the tips, especially when young. Some varieties spread more widely or have weeping branches.

Blue spruce bark is initially thin, becoming moderately thick with age. Its small, flattened scales are pale gray when the tree is young, turning reddish brown and furrowed with age. A deep, penetrating root system makes them resistant to being blown over.

The evergreen needles are stiff, about three-fourths inch to one inch long, and sharply pointed. Spruce needles are four-sided, and they spiral around the twigs and branches, pointing in all directions. The characteristic silvery blue cast is the effect of a powdery patina produced by the tree. For this reason the silver color is most prominent in the spring on new growth and less obvious in the winter when winds thin out much of the coating. Needles growing near the trunk tend to be more green than blue all year. Needles last for four to six years.

Blue spruces bear cones, which are male and female flowers borne in separate clusters on the same tree. Male cones are orange and soft and appear on the lower branches, while female cones are greenish to red-purple and appear on upper branches. Cones appear on older trees in late May or early June. As the season progresses, the male cones fall off and the female cones dry out and turn tan. From two and a half to four inches long, they hang downward, lasting from July through to January.

COLORADO BLUE SPRUCE
CHOICES

A relatively fast grower, **Hoopsii** has silver-green needles and a full, pyramidal shape. **Moerheimii** is a slower-growing cultivar with an open, spreading habit.

Requirements of Your Spruce

Most spruces are noted for their cold-hardiness. They grow best in full sun but tolerate light shade. They prefer well-drained soil that is on the acidic side (pH 4.6 to 6.5) and will grow in almost any soil, from silt to clay loams, as long as it is kept slightly moist and is well drained.

Planting Your Spruce

The more care you take when you put your tree in the ground, the better it will do during its long life. Follow the complete planting directions provided in chapter 3.

A special note: The spruce is not at all tolerant of highway salt, so it is best sited in yards rather than near the street or sidewalk. Spruces can be planted any time in the growing season.

Common Symptom	Likely Cause
Galls on shoots	Aphids
Leaves defoliated, twigs girdled	Bagworms
Wilting, new growth deformed	Budworms
Needles turning yellow	Spider mites
Tree girdled, holes in stems	Borers
Needles webbed together	Spruce needle miner
Tree defoliated	Sawflies
Branch dieback, needle drop, resinous cankers	Canker
Blistered, discolored needles	Rust

Species	Scale at Maturity	Basic Requirements
Norway Spruce (*Picea abies*)	Height: 40'–60' Width: 25'–30' Shape: Pyramidal	Zones 2 through 7 Full sun/part shade Moist, well-drained, acidic soil
White Spruce (*Picea glauca*)	Height: 40'–60' Width: 10'–20' Shape: Pyramidal	Zones 2 through 5 Full sun/part shade Moist, well-drained, acidic soil
Serbian Spruce (*Picea omorika*)	Height: 50'–60' Width: 20'–25' Shape: Columnar	Zones 4 through 7 Full sun/part shade Moist, well-drained, acidic soil
Colorado Blue Spruce (*Picea pungens*)	Height: 30'–60' Width: 10'–20' Shape: Conical-pyramidal	Zones 2 through 7 Full sun/part shade Moist, well-drained, acidic soil

Caring for Your Spruce

Follow the instructions on the seasonal care for young and mature trees—watering, mulching, fertilizing, staking, and pruning—described in chapter 3.

Judicious pruning encourages denser branching in whorl-branching trees like the spruce. Most of these conifers have a period of rapid growth each spring. So late spring to early summer, after the new needles have expanded but before they have stiffened, is the best time to cut back tender new growth.

Special Situations for the Spruce

Some symptoms of distress may simply be the results of old age. But spruces also fall victim to some common parasites and diseases. Be careful not to plant your spruce near a Douglas fir, which is a preferred host of problematic aphid insects.

Spruces do not age well. The lower branches of Norway spruces become ragged and eventually die. And trees planted in groups can begin to crowd one another so that the branches no longer get enough light and space.

YEW (*Taxus* sp.)

Top Reasons to Plant

ఴ Beautiful bark
ఴ Versatility in the landscape
ఴ Naturally elegant, broad habit

Some of the oldest known plants, yews are very popular evergreen shrubs and trees in residential landscapes and are grown throughout the eastern and midwestern United States. It is easy to understand why they are popular: They have a dense, compact appearance, are easy to transplant, require little maintenance, and have few pest or disease problems. Yews also tolerate heavy pruning and many kinds of urban pollution (with the exception of road salt). They are tolerant of both poor soils and dry conditions.

Most yew trees are native to Britain and are particularly common in England and Wales, where they are a familiar sight in churchyards. These multistemmed trees grow very slowly and live for hundreds of years. Some of the most ancient yew trees are believed to be more than two thousand years old.

While some yews are native to the United States, the most common yew trees in the home landscape are the Japanese yew and the English yew. Others, such as the Native American yew and Pacific yew, grow in the wild and are uncommon in residential landscapes.

Yews are excellent for yards designed to attract wildlife. With their dense evergreen foliage, they provide summer nesting sites and winter shelter for many birds. Their colorful red berries are popular with deer as well as birds such as robins and thrushes, though they are poisonous to humans and pets.

Many evergreens, including the yew, are perfect for creating contrast in the winter landscape. Other yard plantings may look dreary and dead this time of year, but this effect can be mitigated by the vibrant dark green textures of yews and other evergreen shrubs. The persistent, colorful berries are an added bonus. Many yews have handsome reddish brown bark as well.

Japanese Yew (Taxus cuspidata)

Japanese yews can reach 40 to 50 feet tall, but there are many, many cultivars sold, with a surprising range of traits. Some are only three feet tall at maturity. Japanese yews are known for their ability to resist dust and air pollution; they are ideal for urban sites and hardy from zones 4 to 7.

JAPANESE YEW CHOICES

Capitata is upright-pyramidal, often growing to reach 20 feet tall by 5 feet wide. Its tight pyramidal form in youth yields to more angled branching and finally

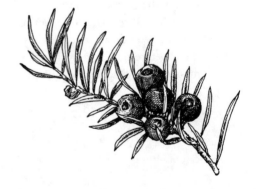

wide, most trees used in landscaping are smaller cultivars. It does best in slightly warmer territory below the Mason-Dixon Line (zones 6 to 7) and is less hardy than the Japanese varieties. This tree can be grown in shade, but it will not become as dense as it will when exposed to full sun. As with all yews, only female plants will produce red fruits.

Requirements of Your Yew

One of the great virtues of yews is that, although they thrive in full sun, they can also handle shade. Few needled evergreens are this adaptable. Yews do well in normal soil, preferring it to be moist and slightly alkaline to slightly acid (pH 6.0 to 6.5). They object to soil that is too acidic and are therefore unhappy among flourishing hollies, rhododendrons, and azaleas. They have little tolerance for soggy soil, which causes their needles to turn brown in protest.

becomes rounded at maturity. This cultivar is a popular screen and hedge in the eastern and midwestern parts of the country.

English Yew
(Taxus baccata)

The English yew can grow into a tree but is often pruned to the form of a shrub. Although the species can be very large, from 30 to 60 feet tall and 15 to 25 feet

Planting Your Yew

The more care you take when you put your tree in the ground, the better it will do during its long life. Follow the complete planting directions provided in chapter 3.

Common Symptom	Likely Cause
Needles that turn yellow; branches that die	Black vine weevils
Cottony tufts on foliage and stems	Mealybugs
Needles that have bumps, are discolored, drop	Scale insects

Species	Scale at Maturity	Basic Requirements
Japanese Yew (*Taxus cuspidata*)	Height: 40'–50' Width: 15'–20' Shape: Pyramidal	Zones 4 through 7 Full sun/part shade Well-drained, nonacidic soil
English Yews (*Taxus baccata*)	Height: 30'–60' Width: 15'–25' Shape: Pyramidal	Zones 6 through 7 Full sun/part shade Well-drained, nonacidic soil

A special note: Yews can be planted any time in the growing season. Stake newly planted yew trees only if they are at risk of being blown over or uprooted before they get established. Where prevailing winds are a potential problem, stake newly planted shrubs for up to a year.

Caring for Your Yew

Follow the instructions on the seasonal care for young and mature trees—watering, mulching, fertilizing, staking, and pruning—described in chapter 3.

Special notes: To keep the soil moist and to control weeds, spread a two- to four-inch layer of organic mulch underneath yews.

Yews lend themselves to routine pruning, responding well to shearing for hedges and topiary. Be aware, however, that repeated severe pruning may result in forlorn-looking shrubs with a fringe of foliage on the perimeters and bare stems on the interior. Furthermore, many types of yews have beautiful natural growth habits and do not need anything more than removal of an occasional broken branch.

To keep tall-growing types under control, clip half the new growth on each stem every year, using hand pruners to ensure a more natural look. Sometimes very old yews that spread too much and lose their shape need a major pruning for rejuvenation. Unlike arborvitae or junipers, yews can be moderately to severely cut back to the bare stems below the evergreen foliage. This will reshape a plant or restrict it if it has grown too large for its space. Yews will often recover slowly and send out sparse new shoots, especially if the pruning is done in very early spring. With a pair of loppers or a pruning saw, cut all the stems back to within 12 inches of the ground to stimulate new dense growth over the next two or three years.

Special Situations for the Yew

Yews are sensitive to their soil conditions, and if they are unhappy, the condition of their needles will let you know.

Flowering and Fruit Trees

We are singularly blessed in the moments when the flowering and fruit trees in our yard share their gifts. There's the splendor of the creamy, velvety cups of the magnolia blooms or the delicate pinks of cherry blossoms in spring and the golden, wisteria-like blooms of the goldenchain tree or camellia-like blossoms on the stewartia in summer. An embarrassment of riches!

Fruit trees—with the added bonus of also being flowering trees—are great fun to plant, though they can take a little effort to nurture through the seasons. And what a payoff! Apple tarts made from your own apples; lemonade from your Meyer lemon tree; peach crumble for which you only have to walk outside to gather the main ingredient. It's undeniably gratifying to harvest and share the bounty of your own backyard.

The period of blooming on flowering trees can be short, so be sure you'll love the shape and habit of your tree without its blooms during the rest of the year. Think about planting a few different flowering trees that bloom in succession so that you're never without a little eye candy in the yard. Or plant a few apple trees and call it your own orchard.

APPLE (*Malus domestica*)

Top Reasons to Plant

- Delicious fruit
- Wide growing range
- Improved disease resistance in new varieties

Ask anyone who the best-known tree planter of all time is, and you'll invariably get one answer: Johnny Appleseed. Many people believe that he's a legend, but John Chapman was a real, living guy who made planting apple trees his life's work. What was his inspiration? The most widely accepted story begins when he was kicked in the head by a mule and lapsed into a coma. After regaining consciousness, he reported visions of the streets of heaven lined with fruit trees, an image he took as a calling from God. In the late 1700s, John Chapman left his Massachusetts home and headed for the cider mills of Pennsylvania, where he collected seeds about to be discarded. He planted these apple seeds as he traveled down the Ohio River and around the surrounding land. These trees became

incredibly important to new settlers in what was then the American West because they were sustainable and tradable, especially as applejack, a brandy distilled from hard cider, which served as frontier currency.

In 1996 I began grafting from the Algeo family's 150-plus-year-old apple tree, in Ashland County, Ohio, the last remaining apple tree planted by Johnny Appleseed. It was a true labor of the heart, to propagate the offspring of this great tree—and to eat the same apples Johnny loved all those years ago.

People don't plant apple trees in their

yard as often as in past generations. Though we can now buy a fair number of apple varieties in the grocery store all year round, homegrown fruits have a better texture and flavor. Millions of Americans plant tomatoes each year for this reason, yet few are aware that two dwarf apple trees will take up about the same area as two tomato plants while requiring about the same amount of care, and producing a similar number of fruits per plant.

Small is in. Whereas the standard apple tree can be 20 feet high and 15 feet wide, the dwarf and semidwarf trees available today grow to be 6 to 8 feet tall and 2 to 3 feet wide. They're easy to care for and the fruit production is much better suited to the home landscape than larger varieties. A mature dwarf tree will give you 60 to 120 apples a year, and a mature semidwarf will produce around 350, essentially the same number of apples as a full-size tree. Apple trees grow in zones 3 to 9.

Apple leaves are two to four inches long and a dull medium green with pale undersides. They are shaped like elongated ovals, coming to a point at their tips, with slightly toothed edges. The blossoms are white, often with a pink blush, and they begin to appear on young trees in their third year, on woody "spurs" that are at least two years old.

There are hundreds of apple varieties to choose from and every one of them is tempting. Before you buy an apple tree, go to your local nursery to investigate which are the best, most disease-resistant varieties you can grow in your area. Also understand that although some apple trees are self-pollinating, many are not, so you need at least two trees that bloom around the same time to ensure an apple crop. A nearby flowering crab apple will also pollinate apple trees. So will a neighbor's tree, if it's within 50 feet. If you are going to plant dwarf trees, two, three, or even four varieties will ensure good pollination and can extend the harvest with different ripening times. Early apples will ripen as soon as August.

APPLE TREE CHOICES

The charmingly named **Adams** apple cultivar bears small pink flowers and juicy red fruit. **Harvest Gold** produces golden apples well into the winter season. Pale pink buds that open into white flowers adorn this cultivar's 25-foot-tall frame. **Indian Summer** is a slightly shorter tree that also bears fruit late into the season. Its globular form is about 18 feet tall and wide. **Narragansett** has a high disease resistance and also thrives in hot temperatures. Its rainbow of white, pink, and red flowers stand out against the tree's deep green foliage. **Prairifire** bears extraordinary fuchsia flowers and reddish purple fruit. This tree has a rounded growth habit and is highly disease resistant. **Red Jade** has a weeping habit with broad branches. It often flowers and fruits in alternate years, producing dark red buds. **Sugar Tyme** is a disease-resistant cultivar with a rounded habit and tiny, cherry-red fruit. **White Angel** bears white flowers from light pink buds. Its glossy red fruit grows on a 20-foot-tall central leader.

Requirements of Your Apple Tree

All apple trees need a period with cool temperatures to bring on dormancy. But "cool" varies widely depending on your apple tree, so there are varieties suitable for any climate except subtropical and low-

desert regions. One variety or another will grow in every zone from 3 to 9.

Apples prefer full sun but can still produce fruit with only five to six hours of sun a day. They will grow in most types of slightly acidic soil (pH 6.0 to 6.5).

Planting Your Apple Tree

The more care you take when you put your tree in the ground, the better it will do during its long life. Follow the complete planting directions provided in chapter 3.

Special notes: In central and northern areas of the United States, plant dormant apple trees in the spring. Where winters are mild, it is better to plant them in the fall—but the tree must be dormant.

Plant dwarf apples 8 to 10 feet apart. These trees will bear fruit in their first year. Plant semidwarfs 18 to 20 feet apart; they will begin to bear fruit in three to six years.

Caring for Your Apple Tree

Follow the instructions on the seasonal care for young and mature trees—watering, mulching, fertilizing, staking, and pruning—described in chapter 3.

Special notes: If you select varieties that have good resistance, and if you are willing to do some preventive spraying, you will be able to protect your trees against many or even most common problems. If necessary, consult your nurseryman regarding a spraying program that is effective for the variety of apple tree you are growing.

Other care for your apple tree is fairly simple.

Many varieties tend to set more apples than they can handle. If you thin out some of the young apples, leaving others spaced

Common Symptom	Likely Cause
Leaves stippled yellow, discolored and distorted, white dots appearing	Mites
Twig dieback, foliage loss	Scale insects
Leaf buds and early bark eaten	Weevils
Defoliation; egg masses appearing on trunk and branches	Gypsy moth caterpillar
Apples that fall, have cuts in skin	Plum circulio beetle
Olive green spots on undersides of leaves; cracked and distorted leaves; apples that develop spots	Scab
Gray, velvety mold; dwarfed twigs; etched apples	Powdery mildew
Small brown spots on fruit, clustered around wound; spots expanding and turning black	Black rot
Tiny yellow spots on leaves; larger orange spots on foliage and fruit	Cedar apple rust

Species	Scale at Maturity	Basic Requirements
Apple Tree (*Malus domestica*)	Height: 6'–8' (dwarf and semidwarf) Width: 2'–3' Shape: Depends on variety	Zones 3 through 9 Full sun/part shade Moist, well-drained soil

six to eight inches apart on the branches, those left will grow to a larger size.

Apples should be picked when they're fully ripe. How do you know? Pick one and taste it! (If you want to store the apples for winter, pick them a little early, as they will continue ripening off the tree.) To harvest, cup the apple in your hand, tilt it upward, and twist to separate the apple's stem from the spur at the point of attachment. Be careful not to damage the spur—next year's apples will appear on it. The point is to take the stem with the apple and to leave the spur on the tree.

Store apples in a cool, humid place with good air circulation. Storage time varies greatly by variety.

Special Situations for the Apple Tree

Watch out for signs of fire blight, a bacterial disease that cannot be prevented by even a rigorous spraying program.

Telltale signs of fire blight include withered and dead blossoms, brown or black shoots, and water-soaked, reddish bark lesions that ooze an orange-brown liquid on warm days. Cut off diseased leaves, stems, or fruit a good 12 inches below damage. Also cut off suckers and water shoots, as these are prone to fire blight. Disinfect your pruning tool after each cut so that you don't spread the blight.

Apple maggots, the larvae of the apple maggot fly, are white worms that sometimes eat the flesh of maturing apples. The best way to control apple maggots is to hang sticky traps (available at your nursery) in targeted fruit trees in late June and remove them after harvest. Keep them clear of sur-rounding branches, and remove all fallen fruit immediately. The sticky traps will also help control codling moth infestations.

CATALPA (*Catalpa* sp.)

Top Reasons to Plant

∾ Spectacular spring blossoms
∾ Distinctive seedpods
∾ Fast growth
∾ Autumn color

The catalpa is one of my favorite flowering trees. Its dazzling blossoms add an elegant, decorative touch to the home landscape. The spring blooms, vivid yellow autumn foliage, and slender foot-long seedpods distinctively punctuate the home landscape. My kids were crazy about those seedpods, which account for this tree being known affectionately as the "cigar tree." It grows swiftly and surely, in just about any kind of soil, and is as agreeable in an urban environment as it is in the Mississippi River Valley, its native home. Along with its blossoms and seedpods, the tree's medium to large size and spreading, horizontal branches give it a striking appearance wherever it is placed.

The catalpa is primarily a specimen tree best used as a background or perimeter planting rather than front and center in your yard. Because it grows agreeably in a variety of soils, it can be planted in hard-to-grow areas such as wet, low-lying locations or dry areas with less than optimum soil.

Northern Catalpa
(Catalpa speciosa)

The northern catalpa is a rugged-looking tree with an irregularly rounded or oval crown, though at a glance somewhat ordinary in its shape and habit. But come springtime, watch out. No other large deciduous tree in North America can match the show put on by the northern catalpa when it's in bloom. Native to the Midwest, it grows easily in cities, along roadways, and in suburbs where it once grew on farms.

The northern catalpa grows into a medium to large, upright tree with horizontal branches and a wide range of crown shapes. At maturity, it will be 40 to 60 feet tall with a spread of 20 to 40 feet. The tree is fast growing, with large, heart-shaped green leaves that form a broad, oval leaf canopy. In the fall, the leaves turn a greenish yellow. This catalpa's reddish brown to grayish brown bark is ridged and furrowed, and its textured quality adds an element of interest to the yard.

All other points aside, the northern catalpa's claim to fame is its spectacular early-summer flowers; each bloom is two inches long, tubular, and white, accented with frilled edges and yellow or purple tinges and spots. They are clustered on four- to eight-inch upright stalks that are visible even from a good distance. The flower's nectar is popular with honeybees, which produce an excellent honey from it. After blooming, the tree develops an abundance of distinctive 8- to 20-inch green seedpods, shaped like skinny cigars or beans, that mature to brown in autumn. The seeds usually drop to the ground in the fall but occasionally remain attached through the winter, which is a nice visual treat in your winter landscape. The tree is hardy in zones 4 through 8.

Southern Catalpa
(Catalpa bignonioides)

The southern catalpa loves hot summers—it's hardy in zones 5 through 9—and is extremely resistant to urban pollution. It is a fast-growing, tough, and durable tree, though smaller than the northern catalpa. A mature tree is 30 to 40 feet tall and has a comparable width. With leaves and flowers similar to those of the northern catalpa, this tree takes two to three years to overcome an adolescent period of inhibited growth, after which it branches more freely and begins to dominate the landscape. Its bean pods will often cling to the branches after the leaves fall in autumn.

SOUTHERN CATALPA CHOICES

Aurea has yellow foliage, which in cooler climates remains on the tree throughout all four seasons.

Chitalpa
(Catalpa X Chilopsis)

This tree is a cross between the southern catalpa and the desert willow (*Chilopsis linearis*). Created in Russia, this hybrid has since become a popular ornamental tree in the United States. The chitalpa is a small tree that grows quickly, capable of reaching 15 feet in just three or four years and an ultimate height of 25 to 30 feet. It may have either multiple stems or a single trunk, with open upright branches that form a nice, broad oval crown. The most attractive feature of this deciduous tree is its long blossom period—from July to September in areas of the eastern United States and from March to September in the West. The delicate, orchidlike flowers are a pale lavender-pink and appear in large clusters at the tips of the branches, as with true catalpas. Rather than falling fresh, the flowers dry on the tree, which explains their staying power. And this tree is sterile, so it doesn't produce the seedpods for which the catalpa is known. It is tolerant of wind and drought and loves a hot, dry, sunny location. The chitalpa grows in zones 6 to 9.

Requirements of Your Catalpa

Catalpas prefer deep, moist, fertile soil, but they can handle wet, dry, or even alkaline soil if they must. Site them in full sun and give them plenty of space.

Planting Your Catalpa

The more care you take when you put your tree in the ground, the better it will do during its long life. Follow the complete planting directions provided in chapter 3.

Special notes: Because northern and southern catalpas drop their pods, you may want to plant them away from patios, walkways, and your house's gutters—or else be prepared to sweep up after them.

These trees can be planted any time during the growing season.

Common Symptom	Likely Cause
Dead areas of leaf developing along main veins	Anthracnose
Red or purple spots that appear on leaves, then become holes	Leaf spot
Gray, velvety mold or powder appearing on leaves	Powdery mildew
Leaves that wilt and turn yellow	Verticillium wilt

Species	Scale at Maturity	Basic Requirements
Northern Catalpa (*Catalpa speciosa*)	Height: 40'–60' Width: 20'–40' Shape: Oval, irregular	Zones 4 through 8 Full sun Moist, well-drained soil
Southern Catalpa (*Catalpa bignonioides*)	Height: 30'–40' Width: 30'–40' Shape: Rounded, irregular	Zones 5 through 9 Full sun Moist, well-drained soil
Chitalpa (*Catalpa* X *Chilopsis*)	Height: 25'–30' Width: 10'–15' Shape: Open, irregular	Zones 6 through 9 Full sun Moist, well-drained soil

Caring for Your Catalpa

Follow the instructions on the seasonal care for young and mature trees—watering, mulching, fertilizing, staking, and pruning—described in chapter 3.

Special Situations for the Catalpa

The catalpa does not require a great deal of seasonal care in order to stay healthy. However, it can sometimes be threatened by pests and diseases, especially the catalpa worm, of which the catalpa tree is the only victim.

Catalpa trees are also the only host for catalpa sphinx moths. In the larval, or caterpillar, stage they feed on catalpa foliage and can actually defoliate a tree. However, defoliated catalpas usually produce new leaves readily. Adult moths first appear in March to April and deposit anywhere from 100 to 1,000 eggs on the underside of the leaves. In five to seven days, eggs hatch and young larvae feed voraciously, skeletonizing leaves until they grow to about three inches long. When at that point they drop to the ground, they look like tomato hornworms—green with black markings. Harvest the worms and go fishing—nothing makes better bait.

CITRUS TREES (*Citrus,* sp.) ORANGE, GRAPEFRUIT, LEMON, LIME

Top Reasons to Plant

- Edible, brightly colored fruit
- Fragrant blossoms
- Shiny foliage

As might happen with many northerners, when I moved to the South, the first things I noticed were "exotic" trees like oranges and grapefruits and limes growing effortlessly in nearly every backyard. Growing citrus trees is a particular kind of hobby—obsession?—in the South that's hard to shake once you've taken it up. Now I myself grow big, sweet grapefruit, three kinds of oranges, key limes, and Meyer lemons almost year-round, right in my own yard. I guess I've gone native.

Whereas apples, pears, and peaches can be grown in most areas of the country, citrus trees are limited to the frost-free sections: southern Florida, Texas, Arizona, and California, or, in terms of zones, primarily 10 and 11. I'm in zone 9 so I have to take special care to protect my trees.

Though there are dozens of types of citrus fruit, homeowners tend to be most interested in the big four: oranges, lemons, limes, and grapefruit. Trees that bear these fruits give us something delicious to eat and add to the landscape with their shiny leaves, fragrant blossoms, and brightly colored fruits.

Citrus trees are actually evergreens; they retain the majority of their leaves year-round and never go completely dormant as do deciduous trees. Their growth does slow down during the winter and again in the hottest part of the summer, picking up in February as the weather warms and then in mid-August through October.

Most varieties of the common citrus fruits come in full-size trees, which grow from 30 to 40 feet tall; semidwarf trees, which reach 12 to 15 feet; and dwarf trees, reaching 7 to 10 feet. All are round in shape. The tree size does not affect the fruit size—dwarf and semidwarf trees produce full-size fruit.

Although lemon and lime trees may flower all year long, the majority of citrus tree flower production occurs in late February through March. Interestingly, though a mature citrus tree can produce hundreds of thousands of blossoms, only 2 percent or fewer of these become edible fruit. This heavy blossom production is nature's way of ensuring that insects, attracted by the tree's fragrance, pollinate the maximum number of flowers possible.

Some experts say that citrus fruits improve in flavor after they are picked. Others say they don't. All agree, however, that fruits should be allowed to ripen on the tree. Each citrus fruit has its own specifications for the color, size, and flavor that indicate full ripeness.

Selecting a cultivar of orange, lemon, lime, or grapefruit based on flavor is largely a matter of personal choice, so investigate the citrus options at your local nursery to see what grows well in your area. A general rule of thumb when buying a citrus tree is to choose a variety that is hardy one zone colder than your own, or one that grows at the northern end of your zone. This way you'll never be disappointed by a citrus tree that fails during a bit of cold weather because it isn't hardy enough.

Orange Tree

Satsuma oranges are my personal favorite because they are fairly cold-hardy, very sweet, and peel like a dream. **Cara Navel Orange** harvests in January into March. A unique navel orange that has deep pink flesh, its fruit is excellent-tasting, sweet and juicy. **Fukumoto Navel Orange** harvests from December into March. It is a nearly navel variety that has attractive deep reddish orange skin with sweet, juicy flesh. **Lane Late Navel Orange,** an excellent late-ripening navel variety, harvests from March into June. **Washington Navel Orange** harvests from December into May. It is the number one commercial navel orange, offering large, juicy, sweet fruit. **Midnight Seedless Valencia** harvests from March into October, bearing large fruit with a high juice content. **Valencia Orange** harvests from March into October and makes the best orange for juice. A vigorous, attractive plant, it produces medium-size sweet fruit that have a high juice content and hold well on the tree. **Tarocco Blood Orange** harvests from January into May. A large blood orange, with a high juice content, its rich, reddish orange flesh has berry-flavored overtones.

Grapefruit Tree

Cocktail Hybrid Grapefruit harvests from January into June. This is a grapefruit crossed with a sweet orange. The pale orange flesh is exceptionally sweet and juicy. **Marsh** harvests from February into September. An excellent-quality white grapefruit, it is a vigorous grower. **Melo Gold** harvests from November into April, yielding a delicious, sweet, seedless, large fruit that weighs several pounds. It is also a vigorous grower. **Oro Blanco** harvests from December into May. This seedless grapefruit is excellent for fresh eating or juice and is a vigorous grower. **Star Ruby** harvests from February into September. The fine-flavored fruit develops a deep red flesh color.

juice and cooking. This is a vigorous tree with beautiful blush-pink flowers.

Lime Tree

Key Lime is an excellent commercial variety with juicy, acidic flesh. **Sweet Lime** is an

Lemon Tree

Lisbon Lemon produces a high-quality, juicy, acidic lemon. It is a vigorous, productive tree and is quite cold-hardy. **Meyer Lemon** is a very juicy, orange-yellow-skinned fruit. **Pink Lemonade** has a unique variegated eureka-type fruit. Its flesh is pale pink when ripe. The tree's foliage is streaked green and ivory. **Pomona Sweet Lemon** is a sweet lemon, excellent for both everbearing tree with medium-size, round fruit that is sweet with a slight acid flavor. The flowers are pure white. **Kaffir Lime** harvests from October into March, producing small, orange, bumpy, very acidic fruit. The tree's unique, double-lobed leaves are used in Middle Eastern and Asian cooking; its flowers make a fine tea.

Requirements of Your Citrus Tree

Citrus trees should be planted in full sun, preferably in a location free from frost, sheltered from wind, and with southern exposure. Sometimes you can develop a friendly microclimate for your citrus tree by planting it where it receives reflected heat from sidewalks, walls, driveways, or other structures. The trees want sandy soil if they can get it. However, they are famous for tolerating a wide variety of soils, including clay. What is most important is good drainage, and some clays can drain very well. Soil pH should be between 5.5 and 6.5.

Planting Your Citrus Tree

The more care you take when you put your tree in the ground, the better it will do during its long life. Follow the complete planting directions provided in chapter 3.

Special notes: Most citrus trees are purchased in containers and can be planted any time of year, but late winter or early spring is best. When you buy a tree, try to select one with little or no fruit, or else harvest the existing fruit immediately after planting the tree. It takes a lot of energy for a young tree to grow fruit, and this detracts from the newly planted tree's ability to produce new roots and leaves. Some gardeners will go ahead and pinch off all fruit and blossoms for the first year or two after a new planting, which encourages stronger root and branch development. It is best to plant two or more citrus trees for fruit production.

Don't crowd your tree; even if it is a dwarf, it will need sufficient room to reach full size. If you want to plant two or more standard-size trees, they should be set at least 20 to 25 feet apart. However, necessary spacing will vary with the specific cultivar and its optimum density. On the whole, grapefruit trees are usually larger than orange trees.

Don't worry if you have some wilting on your newly planted citrus tree. You can expect wilting and as many as one-third of the leaves to drop within the first two weeks after planting.

Caring for Your Citrus Tree

Follow the instructions on the seasonal care for young and mature trees—watering, mulching, fertilizing, staking, and pruning—described in chapter 3.

Special notes: After the first year, fertilize every March, June, and September using a blended citrus food such as 16-8-4 or 16-8-2. Fertilization is essential for the proper growth and development of young citrus trees. After their first five years, citrus trees need less fertilizer.

Light pruning can be done any time of year except winter; major pruning should be done in spring or fall. Citrus trees may be pruned to any shape. Pinching back tips of new growth is the best way to round out the trees without affecting future fruit. You can prune back leggy branches as well as suckers growing from below where it's grafted (all good edible citrus is grafted), which can be seen as a diagonal scar between four and eight inches from the soil. Especially on young trees, suckers are vigorous, and they drain energy from the top of the tree. Some trees may develop erratic juvenile growth above the graft. If so, prune them for shape and balance. Any growth above the graft can eventually bear fruit.

Of all the tasks involved in caring for citrus trees, perhaps the most challenging and most important is protecting the trees from unexpected frost. Frost damages both the fruit and the trees. The tree's susceptibility to frost depends on it's variety and vigor.

Protect the trunk and major branches as well, especially those of trees in the ground only a year or two. The trunk, especially near the graft union, can be protected by a covering sold for this purpose. One type comes in a roll and is made of treated paper; another is a spiral ribbon of white plastic.

If frost is predicted in the immediate future, cover the tree with old bedsheets,

Common Symptom	Likely Cause
Twig dieback, foliage loss	Scale insects
Leaves stippled yellow, white dots appearing	Mites
Foliage that curls, puckers, turns yellow; blooms stunted	Aphids
Cottony tufts on foliage and stems	Mealybugs

Species	Scale at Maturity	Basic Requirements
Citrus Fruit Trees Orange (*citrus sinensis*) Grapefruit (*citrus paradisi*) Lemon (*citrus limonia*) Lime (*citrus aurantifolia*)	All citrus trees are small, no taller than 20', and ranging from 5' tall for dwarf, 15' for semidwarf, and up to 20' for standard sizes. The best source for size information on your particular citrus is the nursery where you buy it.	Zones 10 through 11 Full sun Moist, well-drained soil

painters dropcloths, or clear plastic sheeting, which will give protection but must be rigged so that material does not touch the foliage, which needs to breathe. Even watering the soil may protect the tree, as water retains heat longer than air does. If you have good drainage and can run a soaker hose slowly through the night, it may help to protect your trees. The greater the risk of frost in your area, the shorter you need to keep your trees in order to be able to cover them easily.

Citrus fruits let you know when they are ripe—they will separate from the tree with just a tug. If a tug doesn't do the trick, don't force it, or you'll have a bitter orange or a hard lemon.

Special Situations for Citrus Trees

Sometimes, incomplete pollination and various environmental factors can cause difficulties for citrus trees. Citrus blossoms are produced year-round but often will fail to develop fruit. To ensure the setting of fruit, use a small brush to lift the pollen from the stamen (the male part of the flower) of one blossom and gently dust it onto the pistil (the female part of the flower) in the center of another. Within a few days the pistil should begin to develop a tiny new fruit.

Leaf drop during the winter reflects nothing more than normal aging and replacement of leaves. But if the leaves of your tree yellow and fall during the growing season, you'll have to diagnose to see which of several factors may be at fault. Citrus leaves can remain on the tree for as long as three years depending on tree vigor, but leaf longevity will be significantly reduced

by disease, inadequate or excessive nitrogen fertilizer, excessive salt in the soil, poor irrigation practices, freezing temperatures, and low light levels.

DOGWOOD (*Cornus* sp.)

Top Reasons to Plant

- ∾ Profuse spring flowers
- ∾ Colorful fruit
- ∾ Fall color

One Native American tribe has a legend of a wicked chief who had four beautiful daughters. Many suitors sought to marry the young women, but the chief required his daughters to marry only the men who offered them the richest gifts. Soon the chief's lodge was filled with furs and other treasures. But the gods became angered by his greed and turned him into a gnarled dogwood tree. His four daughters are the four white bracts (on the dogwood, these are often mistaken for flowers), and the flowers (which are greenish yellow) are the gifts borne by the maidens' suitors.

Another legend proclaims the dogwood was once as grand and sturdy as an oak. The tree was so strong, the legend continues, that its wood was chosen for building the cross on which to crucify Jesus Christ. Because the tree was so upset by this use of its timber, Jesus himself swore that the dogwood would never again grow large enough to be used as a cross. It would be slender, bent, and twisted, and its blooms would be in the form of a cross. The outer edge of each petal would be stained with red, and in the center of the flower would be a crown of thorns.

Such a storied past befits the flowering dogwood, one of the most beloved of all our native trees.

Dogwood trees display their spectacular blossoms to best advantage against a background of either needled or broadleaf evergreens such as spruce, pine, or rhododendron. They also stand out well against a brick wall. Their wide, leafy branches soften strong vertical lines of buildings, especially at their corners, so that homes seem larger. Planted at the bottom of a slope or below a second-floor deck, their beautiful blossoms peek up from below. Dogwoods and azaleas are a classic combination reflecting their native association in the eastern woodlands of the United States. Dogwoods also work well in unlandscaped and wooded areas on your property. They grow best planted in groups of two or three; however, standing individually in a yard, they are eye-catching specimens.

Woodland gardens and naturalized areas on your property are ideal places to plant dogwoods to attract and shelter wildlife. Create a miniature grove by planting a few dogwood trees so that their canopies will just barely overlap at maturity; then plant smaller seed-and-fruit-bearing shrubs and ground covers. The red berries that appear on flowering dogwoods attract waterbirds, ground birds, songbirds, large and small mammals, and deer. Their berries usually have been eaten completely before winter sets in. This does not harm the tree or affect its next blooming season.

Though there are dozens of dogwood tree choices, I've selected the three that are most valuable to the home landscape: flowering dogwood, kousa dogwood, and pagoda dogwood. Like all dogwoods, these bear showy flowers, which are actually modified leaves, called bracts. The small true flowers appear at the center of the bracts.

Flowering Dogwood (Cornus florida)

The flowering dogwood is probably my favorite of all the dogwood varieties. This tree has it all: flowers, flower buds, fruit, foliage, fall color, textured bark, and layered branching. Flowering dogwoods bloom in late April or early May, before the leaves appear. Their large creamy white or pink bracts have a distinctive notch at their rounded tips. In early September through mid-November, small, football-shaped berries develop in their place in clusters of four to eight. Favorites of songbirds, waterbirds, and many other animals, these bright red berries will last until December if they aren't eaten first.

Flowering dogwoods can be trained either as single-trunked trees or as multi-stemmed shrub. Their bark is reddish brown to black and broken into small four-sided blocks. The mature tree can reach

30 to 40 feet tall and be equally wide, or wider. As the tree ages, its horizontally growing branches create a tiered and flat-topped profile. This tree is slow growing and may live to one hundred years or more. It is hardy in zones 5 through 9.

The leaves of flowering dogwoods are arranged opposite one another on the branches. They're three to six inches long, egg-shaped, with prominent veins aligned almost parallel to the leaf edges. Before they drop in the fall, they turn brilliant red to purple. Shiny red fruit appears in the fall as well.

FLOWERING DOGWOOD CHOICES

Many cultivars of flowering dogwood are available in the marketplace, with varying floral color, blossom density, and foliage variegation. **Cherokee Chief** has red-pink flowers and foliage that emerges reddish bronze and eventually becomes green. **Cherokee Princess** bears large white flowers in abundance every year, blooming a bit earlier in the spring than do other cultivars. **First Lady** displays variegated greenish yellow foliage and white buds.

Kousa Dogwood
(Cornus kousa)

Also called the Japanese or Chinese dogwood, this native Asian tree grows to 20 to 30 feet tall and wide at maturity, slightly shorter than the flowering dogwood. The young trees are vase-shaped, but as they age they become quite bushy and spread as wide as they are tall in a distinctive, low horizontal branching habit. Kousas can be multitrunked or single-trunked; the light brown-gray trunks are characterized by smooth yellow-beige or dark gray and white blotches that proliferate and make the bark increasingly attractive with age.

Kousa dogwoods bloom in late May or early June. They have a four- to six-week bloom period that begins when the bracts are still small and green. As the bracts grow, they become large and creamy white, appearing on the upper side of the hori-

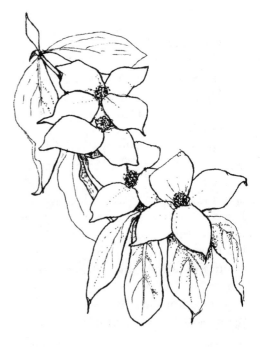

zontal branches. The bracts are one and a half to two inches long, and distinctively pointed. Sometimes spots of pink appear on the white bracts as the bloom fades. In September, bright red fruits shaped like large raspberries dangle from the branches on long stems. They last until December if birds do not get them.

Kousa leaves are arranged opposite one another flatly on the upper sides of the branches. They are egg-shaped, from one and a half to two inches long, with prominent veins aligned almost parallel to the edges. They turn a stunning scarlet red in the fall.

Hardy from zones 5 through 8, these trees are more resistant to dogwood dieback than are other varieties.

KOUSA DOGWOOD CHOICES

Kousa dogwood cultivars of every height and color exist in the marketplace. **Milky Way** is a familiar cultivar with vivid fall color and unique shedding bark. **Samaritan** grows a strong central leader and is quite cold-hardy; its variegated leaves display excellent color in the autumn. **Satomi** is a fine tree with pink flowers but is some-what less tolerant of winter temperatures than are other kousa cultivars.

Pagoda Dogwood
(Cornus alternifolia)

The pagoda dogwood is native to much of the upper Midwest and is hardy in zones 3 through 7. As with many native plants, it has accumulated many common names, including blue pagoda, green osier, pigeon berry, and umbrella dogwood. As it grows from 15 to 25 feet high and nearly as wide, the pagoda dogwood is an excellent small tree that can be grown either as a single- or multitrunked specimen. Its form is oval to rounded, and it has a unique horizontally layered branching structure that accounts for the "pagoda" in its name, as it looks something like a pagoda. Its unique form adds a great deal of interest to the winter landscape. The pagoda dogwood's twigs have smooth, glossy purplish bark, adding an ornamental element in winter.

Unlike those on other dogwoods, the leaves and buds on this tree are arranged in an alternating pattern. Leaves have parallel veins and are two and a half to five inches long. Usually they are crowded at the ends of twigs. In the fall they are deep red to maroon.

Pagoda flowers are white and small, grouped in three- to four-inch flat clusters. They open in May or June, covering the whole tree with a splendid show. The bluish black fruit ripens in August and is readily eaten by birds.

PAGODA DOGWOOD CHOICES

Variegata is a hardy grower with cream-colored divided leaves.

Requirements of Your Dogwood

Because dogwoods in both wild and residential landscapes have been plagued in recent years by a fungal disease, their location in the landscape is critical in order to maintain their health and resistance to disease. Dogwood foliage needs at least six hours of sun a day, yet its roots prefer moist woodland conditions. They prefer well-drained, slightly acidic soil with plenty of organic matter and a protective layer of mulch. Avoid placing dogwoods where they will be vulnerable to salt spray; this will decrease their chances of surviving even their first winter.

To minimize risk of infection in any dogwood variety, locate young dogwoods where they are not stressed by hot summer afternoon sun yet enjoy good air circulation. Plant the root-ball slightly higher

Common Symptom	Likely Cause
Tunnels under bark, branches girdled	Dogwood borers
Small bumps on leaves and branches	Scale insects
Sunken spots on leaves	Spot anthracnose
Leaves stunted and lighter in color than usual, swellings on trunk or roots	Crown canker
Wilting of flowers, leaves, or twigs; cankers on twigs	Blight

Species	Scale at Maturity	Basic Requirements
Flowering Dogwood (*Cornus florida*)	Height: 30'–40' Width: 30'–40' or more Shape: Broad, oval	Zones 5 through 9 Morning sun Moist, well-drained soil
Kousa Dogwood (*Cornus kousa*)	Height: 20'–30' Width: 20'–30' Shape: Rounded to broad	Zones 5 through 8 Morning sun Moist, well-drained soil
Pagoda Dogwood (*Cornus alternifolia*)	Height: 15'–25' Width: 10'–15' Shape: Pagodalike	Zones 3 through 7 Morning sun Moist, well-drained soil

than it was in the nursery container. Water faithfully during dry spells, giving trees at least one inch of water every 10 days. Fertilize in the spring with a product that features slow-acting nitrogen. Clean up organic debris that might shelter disease and insects. Do not prune your tree when leaves or twigs are wet. If you do prune, disinfect equipment between cuts by dipping it in a solution of hot water and household bleach. This will prevent you from spreading any disease that you may not be aware of.

Planting Your Dogwood

The more care you take when you put your tree in the ground, the better it will do during its long life. Follow the complete planting directions provided in chapter 3.

Caring for Your Dogwood

Follow the instructions on the seasonal care for young and mature trees—watering, mulching, fertilizing, staking, and pruning—described in chapter 3.

Special Situations for the Dogwood

Since 1977 a disease called dogwood decline, carried by the fungus *discula* and fueled by damp spring and fall weather, has been spreading steadily throughout the mid-Atlantic states. The first sign that a dogwood might have dogwood decline is that many leaves remain on the tree and do not drop in the fall as they would normally. The following spring, affected dogwoods develop sunken spots on their leaves. Small end twigs suffer dieback and sometimes

trunk cankers develop. Progressive twig dieback in the lower part of the tree signals advanced decline and is often accompanied by borer attacks. If neglected, a tree in advanced stages of decline may die within two seasons. If cared for, with proper watering, feeding, and mulching, it might live four or five more years.

Flowering dogwoods are particularly vulnerable to dieback, and the kousa dogwood is fairly resistant.

FLOWERING ALMOND (Prunus *triloba*)

Top Reasons to Plant

- Rich pink color
- Double flowers
- Small size and delicate build

Almonds, cherries, peaches, apricots, and plums may provide very different sensations to the tongue, but the trees on which they grow are fairly close relatives. Whether they come from orchard trees or ornamentals, they all belong to the diverse family of trees that bear stone fruits (*Prunus*). Flowering almonds are grown in large part for their burst of spring pink. The flowers are doubles (which means twice the number of petals per stem), and they appear in profusion on the bare branches before the leaves open in the spring. A favorite spring tree, the flowering almond is small and delicate, quietly lovely like a ballerina in the corps de ballet.

This tree will reach 12 to 15 feet tall with an equal spread. It has thin, upright,

accent or in a container on the patio. The flowering almond is hardy in zones 3 through 6.

Requirements of Your Flowering Almond

These trees need full sun to partial shade and rich, moist, acidic soil.

Planting Your Flowering Almond

The more care you take when you put your tree in the ground, the better it will do during its long life. Follow the complete planting directions provided in chapter 3.

dark brown stems that become slightly pendulous over time. The leaves have an elongated oval shape and finely toothed edges. About two inches long, they are a medium or gray-green. Some varieties show a bit of autumn color, usually yellow. The blooms measure about one and a half to two inches in diameter, and are followed by insignificant fruits. The tree does well alone in the spotlight, or planted in a row or group border. It can also be grown as an upright vase-shaped tree, either as a garden

Caring for Your Flowering Almond

Follow the instructions on the seasonal care for young and mature trees—watering, mulching, fertilizing, staking, and pruning—described in chapter 3.

Special note: Pruning immediately after flowering encourages fuller blossoms next season. You will also want to prune your flowering almond in order to maintain an upright shape and vaselike crown. They can get straggly otherwise. Cut back each upright stem several inches (about one third of its length) to stimulate increased blooming next season. This also helps forestall mildew attack.

Special Conditions for the Flowering Almond

Almond trees may be affected by blossom blight and dieback.

Common Symptom	Likely Cause
Foliage that curls, puckers, turns yellow	Aphids
Small bumps on leaves and branches	Scale insects
Shoots that turn black and brown, flowers and shoots that wilt in spring, plant appears scorched	Fire blight
Gray, velvety coating on leaves	Powdery mildew
Spots on leaves that run together, ooze	Bacterial leaf spot
Holes in trunk	Flatheaded borer
Blossoms that seem water-soaked, shriveled, and brown	Blossom blight
Dieback	Clearwing borers

Species	Scale at Maturity	Basic Requirements
Flowering Almond (*Prunus triloba*)	Height: 12'–15' Width: 12'–15' Shape: Shaggy, irregular	Zones 3 through 6 Full sun/part shade Moist, well-drained soil

FLOWERING CRAB APPLE
(*Malus* sp.)

Top Reasons to Plant

- ∽ Profusion of blossoms
- ∽ Beautiful buds
- ∽ Fruit for jam or jelly
- ∽ Long life

Flowering crab apple trees are apple trees that bear fruit smaller than two inches across. Because these fruits tend to be sour, they are used primarily in preserves and jellies, for which they are sweetened heavily. The real value of these trees is ornamental. Their wonderful flowers are much showier than those of common apple-tree blossoms.

Flowering crab apple trees, also known as American crab apple, wild crab apple, or sweet crab apple, may be dwarf or full-size trees. Most average less than 20 feet tall, and the dwarf types grow to only six to eight feet in height. Different varieties offer different growth habits, including upright columnar, upright oval, upright rounded, horizontally spreading, and pendulous weeping, with either single or multiple trunks.

The flowers on this tree are beautiful even before they open. Often the buds are pink, but they may be red and white. The flowers themselves are either white or pink, the pink ones eventually fading to white. Most varieties of flowering crab apple have single flowers with five petals, but some have double or semidouble flowers with up to ten petals. Individual flowers are typically one-half to one and a half inches across and fragrant. They bloom in mid-May, lasting anywhere from two days to almost two weeks. When you have a number of different varieties, it is possible to have blooms over the course of up to four weeks.

Flowering crab apple leaves grow in alternate positions along the branches. They have finely toothed edges and are shorter and narrower than regular apple leaves, giving flowering crab apple foliage a finer texture. Most of these trees have green leaves, although some varieties have a subdued red-bronze color in summer. There are even some varieties with purple leaves, but these tend to be more vulnerable to disease. Only a few crab apples have foliage that turns color in the fall, and it often has more to do with climatic conditions than the nature of the tree; trees with a southwestern exposure are most likely to show some color before the leaves drop in the fall.

Although most common apple trees require pollinators such as bees to set fruit, flowering crab apples are self-pollinating. When the tree reaches bearing age, short twigs, or "spurs," develop on its branches. These spurs will bear the fruit and should not be disturbed. Fruits are miniature apples, ranging from pea size to two inches in diameter. They may be red, pink, green or yellow, or any shade in between. The fruits develop any time from August through September and in some varieties persist into the winter. Crab apples provide food for birds such as pheasants, mockingbirds, and finches. Squirrels and deer also enjoy crab apples and conveniently remove those that fall onto the ground. Crab apple trees may bear fruit for thirty years or more.

Though there are hundreds of cultivars of flowering crab apple trees, most available in garden centers are hybrids that have been developed to be more disease resistant than the species. In fact, the American crab apple, native to the United States, is not readily available for sale, nor is it very desirable, because of the diseases it so often develops. Since disease resistance can vary depending on where a particular cultivar is grown, be sure to choose a tree shown to resist to disease in your area.

Flowering crab apples add most to the home landscape when planted individually. Only in spacious yards do they look good planted in lines or small groups.

Crab apple blossoms and fruits also work well in floral arrangements. Budded crab apple branches can be forced to bloom indoors in March or later, enabling you to add a hint of spring to your house in winter. The closer you cut them to their normal bloom time in early spring, the sooner they will bloom indoors. Cut branches with small flower buds early in the morning on a mild day. Slit the woody ends and soak them in two or three inches of warm water for three to four hours so that they can absorb as much moisture as possible. Strip off any leaves below the water level. Then place the container in a cool room out of direct sunlight until the buds swell and begin to show color. This will take about two to three weeks, during which you should change the water periodically. Once you see pink in the buds, arrange the branches in a display vase with fresh water laced with floral conditioner or some citrus-based carbonated soda to help prolong flower bloom. Place the vase in a bright room where the flowers can be appreciated. They will last about one week

if they are not in the sun, one or two days if they are.

Japanese Crab Apple (Malus floribunda)

The Japanese crab apple is one of the best choices in terms of both form and flower, reaching 20 to 25 feet in height and a similar spread that forms a broad, rounded, densely branched canopy. The profusion of fragrant blooms, one to one and a half inches in diameter, begins as beautiful deep pink to red buds, eventually fading to white as they open. The yellow and red fruits appear from August to October.

JAPANESE CRAB APPLE CHOICES

Madonna is a double white-flowered, compact, and upright tree that blooms from early until late in the season. It is disease resistant, though it may sometimes have some problems with scab.

Sargent Crab Apple (Malus sargentii)

The sargent crab apple is a dwarf species, forming a dense, wide-spreading, irregularly rounded silhouette, 6 to 10 feet tall with an equal or greater width. It can be purchased as a single or multitrunked tree and has small, fragrant springtime blossoms that start out as red or pink buds and open to sparkling white flowers. The fruits that result from these dazzling flowers are bronze-green in summer and bright red in autumn, but they turn dark red as they hang on to the tree throughout much of the winter, serving as a food source for wildlife.

Unlike many other crab apples, the sargent crab apple is quite resistant to scab, fire blight, and leaf spot. The tree is hardy from zones 4 through 8.

SARGENT CRAB APPLE CHOICES

Bearing lovely white flowers, **Tina** is a dwarf reaching only five feet tall.

Requirements of Your Crab Apple

Crab apple trees grow best in full sun but will tolerate light shade. They prefer soil that is on the fertile side but are comfortable with most soil conditions, even clay, if drainage is good. Soil should be on the acidic side (pH 6.0 to 6.5).

Planting Your Crab Apple

The more care you take when you put your tree in the ground, the better it will do during its long life. Follow the complete planting directions provided in chapter 3.

Special notes: Avoid planting crab apple trees in a "frost pocket," an area where cold air flowing downhill collects behind large obstructions such as hedges. Also avoid low spots in the ground where the trees will be exposed to poor drainage and excessive wind. This helps prevent winter damage.

Stake a newly planted crab apple if there is any chance it will be blown over or uprooted before it becomes established.

Caring for Your Crab Apple

Follow the instructions on the seasonal care for young and mature trees—watering, mulching, fertilizing, staking, and pruning—described in chapter 3.

Special notes: It is important not to overfertilize crab apples, because this can increase the incidence of disease. After the tree's first season, fertilize annually in the spring at a rate of one-half pound or less fertilizer for each half inch of trunk diameter, measured at its base. After the first four or five years, annual fertilization is not necessary, especially if the tree is mulched.

Crab apple trees require some routine pruning. Start establishing well-spaced branch architecture soon after planting.

Common Symptom	Likely Cause
Powdery orange spots on leaves	Rust
Flowers and leaves that wilt; bark cankered; tree having the appearance of being scorched	Fire blight
Galleries drilled in trunk, girdling	Borers
Small bumps on leaves and branches	Scale insects
Leaves distorted, turning yellow or brown	Aphids
Leaves webbed and deformed	Spider mites
Sunken lesions on stems and trunk	Canker
Leaves covered with white powder, discolored or distorted, dropping prematurely	Powdery mildew
Olive green or light brown spots leading to curled, scorched leaves	Scab

Species	Scale at Maturity	Basic Requirements
Japanese Crab Apple (*Malus floribunda*)	Height: 20'–25' Width: Up to 20' Shape: Broad, rounded	Zones 4 through 8 Full sun/part shade Moist, well-drained soil
Sargent Crab Apple (*Malus sargentii*)	Height: 6'–10' Width: Up to 15' Shape: Rounded, irregular	Zones 4 through 8 Full sun/part shade Moist, well-drained soil

But make sure not to overdo it. With crab apples, overpruning is worse than no pruning at all because it stimulates too much growth, which may cause unattractive water sprouts to develop and crowd the interior of the leaf canopy. Cut off these weak, vertical shoots on an annual basis.

Special Situations for the Crab Apple

Because some crab apple trees bloom on a biennial cycle, many gardeners may become concerned if their tree does not produce a large quantity of blossoms in a given year. It is important to distinguish between this natural occurrence and symptoms that indicate trouble. Native crab apples of the Northeast and Midwest are particularly affected by the fungus condition called rust.

FRINGE TREE (*Chionanthus*)

Top Reasons to Plant

- ∾ Lovely fragrant flowers
- ∾ Easy to grow
- ∾ Versatile in the landscape

The fringe tree is one of the most beautiful flowering trees in North America. Though white fringe trees (*Chionanthus virginicus*) are native to the southeast, they have acclimated very well to the North since they were introduced there in 1736. John Bartram included them in his early plant catalog, and they were among the many trees grown by Thomas Jefferson at Monticello. The Chinese fringe tree (*Chionanthus*

retusus) is similar in many ways to our native variety, but it originates in China and Japan. Some say that the Chinese fringe tree is even prettier in blossom than our American native, a question of personal taste.

Fringe trees vary in shape, some shrubby, others lanky. They are an ideal size for the typical residential yard, compact enough that they won't interfere with utility wires. They offer dazzling blossoms with a wonderful fragrance in the spring, good fall color, and in some cases attractive blue berries. Both the American and Chinese species seem able to handle contemporary urban conditions well. An asset to any home landscape, fringe trees look spectacular when in bloom, especially when accented by a dark background. They are ideal for bordering a patio or a deck or in a container. They also make good understory trees in a wooded landscape as long as they are not in dense shade.

White Fringe Tree (Chionanthus virginicus)

Also known as "old man's beard," the white fringe tree has a native range from Pennsylvania to northern Florida. Today it grows almost anywhere in the United States, zones 4 through 8, with a spreading, open habit and a slow to medium growth rate. At maturity, it will reach 12 to 20 feet tall and wide. The fringe tree is often grown with multiple trunks, but I prefer it as a single-trunk tree.

One of the last plants to produce leaves in the spring, the fringe tree has dark green leaves that are thick and waxy, growing five to nine inches long. Its fall color is yellow in the North and a less interesting brown or black-green in the South. The bark is thin

and can be damaged easily by lawn mowers or string trimmers.

This tree does not produce blossoms for three to five years after planting, but the wait is definitely worth it. Blooms appear on old wood in May through June, and they are honey scented. Like hollies, fringe trees are either male or female and both sexes must be present for pollination to occur. Both males and females produce spectacular long hanging white panicles that create the impression of a tree covered in white cotton balls. Flowers on male trees may be slightly longer and more showy than those on

females. After flowering, female trees produce inconspicuous fruits that attract birds. (Though you don't need two trees for blossoms to occur, you do need two trees, one of each gender, for the female tree to produce berries.) The fruits are oval, three-quarter-inch long, and dark blue to nearly black, with a fleshy pulp that encloses a large stone seed. Fringe tree fruits mature in September to October.

Chinese Fringe Tree (Chionanthus retusus)

The Chinese fringe tree is about the same size as the white fringe tree but has a shrubbier appearance. It does not grow well as far north as its counterpart, preferring zones 4 through 9. Its flowers and fruit look similar to those of the white fringe tree, but they bloom on new wood only. The Chinese fringe tree produces leaves earlier than the white fringe tree does, but it begins flowering about a week later. Leaves are narrow and elliptic to oblong in shape, measuring three to eight inches long and about half as wide. This tree produces a stunning floral display, the fragrant white flowers appearing on the tips of the branches and not at all hidden. Like its American relative, this tree appears to be covered in snowy white cotton during the blossom period. Its fruits are more obvious and ornamental than those of the native variety, and its gray, diamond-patterned bark peels and provides interest to the winter landscape.

Requirements of Your Fringe Tree

Site fringe trees in full sun or partial shade, ideally in full sun in the morning with some afternoon shade. Fringe trees will also do well in filtered shade from larger trees. They accept just about any soil type as long as it is rich in organic matter that holds moisture. Though they like damp soil and are ideal for stream banks, they do just fine in drier spots if watered during droughts.

Planting Your Fringe Tree

The more care you take when you put your tree in the ground, the better it will do during its long life. Follow the complete planting directions provided in chapter 3.

A special note: Fringe trees do not react well to transplanting, so choose a location carefully when you plant a young fringe tree in early spring.

Care for Your Fringe Tree

If left alone, the fringe tree will develop a kind of rounded ball shape with multiple trunks. To keep it tidy, or to produce a single-trunk tree, prune in the spring after it blooms. Clip off suckering stems in order to establish and maintain a single trunk. It is important not to prune in the fall; buds for the next year's flowers are set later in the season and will be lost to fall pruning. As it gets older, the fringe tree tends to spread out and will need some judicious pruning.

Special Situations for the Fringe Tree

Deer are attracted to these plants, which grow low enough for the deer to eat their

Common Symptom	Likely Cause
Yellowed leaves, bumps on twigs	Scale insects
Leaves webbed and deformed	Spider mites
Red spots and holes on leaves	Fungal leaf spot
Leaves covered with white powder	Powdery mildew

Species	Scale at Maturity	Basic Requirements
White Fringe Tree (*Chionanthus virginicus*)	Height: 12'–20' Width: 12'–20' Shape: Rounded	Zones 4 through 8 Full sun/part shade Moist, well-drained soil
Chinese Fringe Tree (*Chionanthus retusus*)	Height: 12'–20' Width: 12'–20' Shape: Rounded	Zones 4 through 9 Full sun/part shade Moist, well-drained soil

lower limbs and do some real damage. If you live in an area with a deer population nearby, you will want to take some precautions, such as using an animal repellent or building a physical barrier.

GOLDENCHAIN
(*Laburnum* X *watereri*)

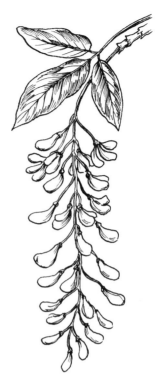

Top Reasons to Plant

- Spectacular yellow flowers
- Fragrance
- Ability to thrive in alkaline soil

The goldenchain is a small, deciduous tree that is rather unremarkable when not in bloom. But for a couple of weeks every spring, it becomes the focal point of the entire yard, a truly stunning sight with an abundance of long, pendulous yellow flowers that give off a pleasant, wisteria-like fragrance.

A vase-shaped tree that grows fairly rapidly, the goldenchain belongs to the pea or legume family. It collects nitrogen in its root system, actually improving the soil within the range of its root mass. The goldenchain tree will grow from 15 to 20 feet, both tall and wide, with an upright, sometimes flat-topped profile. It is often mistaken for the golden rain tree (*Koelreuteria paniculata*), as the two trees have similar names and blossom color, but the goldenchain is smaller and its flowers are pendulous.

The goldenchain's extremely green, alternating leaves look something like those of a three-leaf clover and reach about two

to four inches long. Its drooping golden yellow flowers can grow from 10 to 24 inches long, depending on the variety. Blooms last 10 to 14 days, especially if the weather stays cool, and the flowers produce elongated pods one to three inches long that contain seeds. In the fall the seed-pods will drop, but the small chore of cleaning them up is well worth the benefits of this tree.

The goldenchain tree is versatile. It makes a lovely specimen in small yards, especially if you have a particular area that would benefit from two weeks of bright color in late spring and early summer. The tree's spring explosion of color is amplified when planted in groups of three to five. A good tree for a border or beside a patio or deck, the goldenchain can even be grown in a container and kept pruned to a small

size. It can also be trained to grow on an arbor, pergola, or espalier.

GOLDENCHAIN CHOICES

Vossii is a graceful cultivar with a dense habit and flower clusters.

Requirements of Your Goldenchain

When it comes to climate, it would be fair to call this tree finicky; it will grow from zones 5 through 7 but is happiest in zone 6. It prefers full sun for part of the day, with some light shade during the hottest two or three hours in the afternoon. The soil should be alkaline and well drained; the goldenchain does not tolerate wet soil or soil with a pH below 7.0.

Common Symptom	Likely Cause
Pale or yellow spots on leaves, curled and distorted leaves	Aphids
Cottony tufts on foliage and stems	Mealybugs
Wilting or dying shoot growth on twigs	Twig blight

Species	Scale at Maturity	Basic Requirements
Goldenchain (*Laburnum* X *watereri*)	Height: 15'–20' Width: 15'–20' Shape: Oval	Zones 5 through 7/best in 6 Full sun/part shade Moist, well drained, alkaline soil

Planting Your Goldenchain

The more care you take when you put your tree in the ground, the better it will do during its long life. Follow the complete planting directions provided in chapter 3.

Special notes: It is best to plant the goldenchain in the spring. The tree may need to be staked for a year or two after planting.

Caring for Your Goldenchain

Follow the instructions on the seasonal care for young and mature trees—watering, mulching, fertilizing, staking, and pruning—described in chapter 3.

Special notes: When a goldenchain is young, it needs to be pruned so that there is only one main trunk; otherwise it may generate a number of shoots and turn into a shrub. To keep this tree looking its best, do some modest pruning once a year in the late summer. Take off all shoots coming out from the trunk at the ground. To encourage upward branching, thin out new growth that is pointing toward the center of the tree and any limbs that are almost horizontal. Avoid cutting large branches, as this tree heals slowly.

Special Situations for the Goldenchain

For all its fussiness toward its environment, the goldenchain tree is relatively free of major insect and disease problems.

GOLDEN RAIN TREE
(*Koelreuteria paniculata*)

Top Reasons to Plant

- Summer or fall bloom period
- Profusion of yellow blossoms
- Handsome winter profile
- Relatively trouble-free nature

Most of the flowering trees in this book do their dazzling in the spring, but here is a tree that blooms when other trees have quieted down. In bloom, it is so covered with tiny yellow blossoms that it looks as if it has been coated by a golden rainfall—hence, the name.

This gorgeous tree grows to 30 to 40 feet tall and equally wide in a broad, somewhat irregular globe shape. A fast grower, it gains 10 to 12 feet during its first seven years. This tree has a coarse, open structure garnished with exotic-looking leaves. Composed of up to 15 coarsely toothed leaflets, the leaves decrease in size as the tree grows older, turning orange-yellow in fall; when they drop, they expose the tree's handsome, twisting branches. Golden rain bark is thin and easily damaged by lawn mowers and string trimmers. The wood tends to be brittle, making the tree a bit vulnerable to heavy wind and ice storms.

Bloom time depends on climate and the tree's variety. Some varieties create a spectacular display in May in the Deep South, while blooming in midsummer in Illinois. Other varieties do their showing off as late as September. The golden rain delights gardeners with large 12- to 15-inch panicles of bright yellow flowers that attract honey-

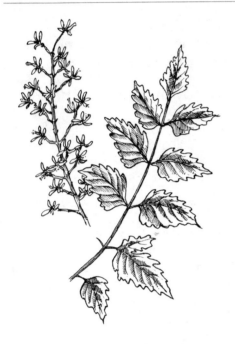

bees. Because they are similar to the gold-enchain tree's (*Laburnum* X *watereri*), many people confuse the two. (Goldenchain flowers are pendulous; golden rain flowers are close to the stem.) The beautiful golden rain flowers develop into green lantern-shaped pods that turn yellow, then brown, and eventually release black seeds the size of peas.

This tree stays relatively small and is suitable as a specimen in the middle of the lawn, as a street tree that will stay clear of utility wires, or nearer to the house to provide a bit of shade. Golden rain trees also work well in smallish yards and near the shore. They will not overpower one-story homes. You can even grow this tree in a large container.

GOLDEN RAIN TREE CHOICES

September lives up to its name by bearing clusters of yellow flowers into September, beautifully accenting its broad, rounded habit. **Fastigiata** is an upright tree with a narrow growth habit that reaches a height of about 30 feet and a width of only 4 to 6 feet.

Requirements of Your Golden Rain Tree

The golden rain tree is not suitable for the more northern parts of the country, preferring zones 5 through 8. It likes full sun and flowers best in the heat. It also appreciates rich soil but is amazingly tolerant of poor soil (including alkaline soils) as well as drought, air pollution, and wind.

Planting Your Golden Rain Tree

The more care you take when you put your tree in the ground, the better it will do during its long life. Follow the complete planting directions provided in chapter 3.

Special notes: These trees plant and transplant easily in the spring but not in the fall. Young trees look a bit gaunt at first but fill out quickly.

Common Symptom	Likely Cause
Small yellow, white, brown, or black bumps/blisterlike outgrowths on tree stems and leaves; yellowish brown branches; gray-green, wilting foliage	Scale insects

Species	Scale at Maturity	Zones
Golden Rain Tree (*Koelreuteria paniculata*)	Height: 30'–40' Width: 30'–40' Shape: Rounded	Zones 5 through 8 Full sun/part shade Moist, well-drained soil

Caring for Your Golden Rain Tree

Follow the instructions on the seasonal care for young and mature trees—watering, mulching, fertilizing, staking, and pruning—described in chapter 3.

Special note: These trees will develop more branches when pruned lightly during their first few years. Prune them during dormancy in late winter.

Special Situations for the Golden Rain Tree

Though this tree has few problems, it does produce a huge number of seeds, which can sprout under and around the tree. The seeds are easily pulled up in the spring.

JAPANESE FLOWERING PLUM (*Prunus cerasifera*)

Top Reasons to Plant

- Deep purple foliage
- Fragrant pink or white flowers
- Fruiting and nonfruiting varieties

This is another member of the huge *Prunus* genus. Like its relatives, it produces an early spring flower show, but it follows up with a display of plum-colored foliage that's as dramatic as the flowers, and longer lasting. It's a great landscape tree and does well in containers too.

Japanese flowering plum trees reach maturity in ten to fifteen years. At that point they are 24 to 26 feet tall and 16 to 20 feet wide. As young trees they have a strongly upright habit that softens and rounds with age as more branches develop.

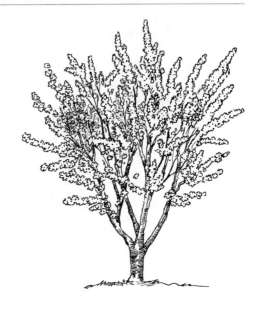

Their blossoms usually appear in mid to late April, before the leaves. Emerging on the branches in clusters of two or three, each single or double fragrant flower is about one inch wide and may be white or pink, depending on the variety. Blooms on flowering plum trees are short-lived, lasting four or five days at best. In the fall, small purplish to black plums develop. They are about an inch in diameter and are edible. However, a few varieties have been bred to produce no fruit, so you can enjoy the flower and leaf color without having to clean up the dropped fruit.

Japanese flowering plum leaves are oval, tapering at the tips, and about two inches long. They are a stunning dark purple, sometimes appearing almost black. Somewhat glossy, these leaves have a softer texture than those of apples, peaches, and most other fruit trees. The foliage drops in the fall, often turning a paler purple or reddish color first.

Atropurpurea, known also as **Pissard Plum,** maintains reddish purple foliage all summer. This heat-tolerant cultivar bears small pink flowers just before the leaves emerge and can grow to 25 feet tall. **Thundercloud** produces pink buds with a light fragrance and displays dark purple color during the summer. **Krauter Vesuvius** is a similar tree with paler-hued flowers, reaching between 25 and 30 feet high. **Newport** measures 15 to 20 feet tall at maturity and bears few or no fruits.

Requirements of Your Japanese Flowering Plum

These trees need about eight full hours of sun a day to be at their best. They can tolerate some shade, though it may cause their foliage to lose its rich, purple color and turn greenish. Flowering plums cannot cope with soggy soil; they need good drainage. Apart from this, they are not terribly fussy about soil, tolerating heavier soils than many other kinds of fruit trees. They prefer soil that is slightly acidic to neutral (pH 6.0 to 7.5) and have a wide growing range, from zones 2 through 8.

Planting Your Japanese Flowering Plum

The more care you take when you put your tree in the ground, the better it will do during its long life. Follow the complete planting directions provided in chapter 3.

Special notes: These trees can be planted any time in the growing season. To avoid damage from late frosts, it is a good idea to site them on a north slope or on the north side of a building. A high spot ensures good air circulation. Make sure not to plant them in or very near a vegetable garden. These trees are vulnerable to the fungal disease verticillium wilt, which is common in many vegetable gardens.

Caring for Your Japanese Flowering Plum

Follow the instructions on the seasonal care for young and mature trees—watering,

Common Symptom	Likely Cause
Foliage that curls, puckers, turns yellow	Aphids
Leaves stippled yellow; fine webbing on leaf stems	Spider mites
Holes in blossoms, tree stunted	Weevils
Gray, velvety mold on leaves	Powdery mildew
Wilted leaves and leaf drop in midsummer or early fall	Verticillium wilt
Holes in trunk surrounded by brown frass; trunk exuding gum	Peach tree borers

Species	Scale at Maturity	Basic Requirements
Japanese Flowering Plum (*Prunus cerasifera*)	Height: 24'–26' Width: 16'–20' Shape: Rounded	Zones 2 through 8 Full sun Moist, well-drained soil

mulching, fertilizing, staking, and pruning—described in chapter 3.

Special notes: Japanese flowering plum trees are branched, even when young, and tend to spread wide. Though they do not require routine pruning, judicious clipping in the late spring after the bloom period will promote vigorous vegetative growth and thick foliage. It is important to thin interior branches once in a while to encourage good light and air circulation inside the body of the tree's branches. It is possible to achieve a very formal, dense shape for a flowering plum tree if you prune it intensely from the time it is first planted. Of course, it is also necessary to remove the occasional damaged or diseased branch. Cut all pruned limbs as short as possible. Stubs that are too long to heal properly invite the entry of bacteria into the heartwood, resulting in heart rot.

On milder winter days, heat from the sun may become quite intense on the tree's dark bark, causing the sap to rise. If nighttime temperatures then drop below freezing, the sap may freeze, causing the bark to split, a condition called sunscald. To prevent sunscald, buy a commercially available tree wrap and put it around the trunks of your trees in the fall. Remove it in spring.

JAPANESE PAGODA TREE (*Sophora japonica*)

Top Reasons to Plant

- Summer flowers
- Good shade
- Large profile
- Relatively trouble-free nature

This tree gives us a spectacular and somewhat unusual combination of traits. It has commanding size and scale, foliage dense enough for good shade, and a summer show of creamy yellow flowers. Though it makes a fine shade tree, with its late summer bloom it also becomes a wonderful specimen when planted where it can show off its flowers. Also known as the Chinese scholar tree, it is native to China, Korea, and Vietnam but, ironically, not Japan.

The Japanese pagoda matures at 50 to 70 feet tall and wide. It has a broad, rounded crown in its youth that spreads more with

times weighing down the thin stems. They ripen in October and November, and while some remain on the tree for the birds to get, others litter the ground and need periodic cleaning up.

JAPANESE PAGODA TREE CHOICES

The **Regent Scholartree** is a popular cultivar selected for its rapid growth rate, relatively straight central leader, earliness to flower (at about five years old), and glossy dark green foliage. The upright branching habit and small size of **Princeton Upright** makes it a suitable street tree. This cultivar is also more resistant to diseases and pest infestation than the species.

Requirements of Your Japanese Pagoda Tree

Japanese pagoda trees, for best performance, should be grown in moist, well-drained loam that is acidic or slightly alkaline. The soil should be deep enough to accommodate the tree's long root systems, though they will tolerate fairly poor soil conditions if they have to. Japanese pagodas flourish in full sun and tolerate urban conditions.

Planting Your Japanese Pagoda Tree

The more care you take when you put your tree in the ground, the better it will do during its long life. Follow the complete planting directions provided in chapter 3.

Special notes: The Japanese pagoda tree is somewhat sensitive to being planted or transplanted in autumn, so do this work in the spring.

age. Young trees grow rapidly, but they slow down as they approach middle age (about fifteen to twenty years). Thus, after thirty years of growth, this tree is still relatively small at 25 to 35 feet tall. Young pagoda trees, especially in the northern areas of the tree's range (zones 4 through 7), may not flower for the first ten years or so of their lives. If you live in the North, you may want to consider the cultivar **Regent,** which flowers anywhere in its zone at a young age.

Japanese pagoda trees cast a light-dappled shade in youth and a much denser shade in maturity. Their leaves have a somewhat fernlike appearance, with 6- to 10-inch compound leaves, each composed of 9 to 13 small leaflets. Japanese pagodas hold their green leaves well into November. Twigs stay green as well, which provides winter color but makes them vulnerable to severe winters or drastic temperature fluctuations.

The large, creamy white to yellowish green pealike flowers hang in long clusters, appearing any time from early August to early September. They blanket the tree during a three-week bloom period. Eventually they become green pods that mature to yellow-green, with large seeds showing as bumps within the otherwise thin pods. The pods hang profusely from the tree, at

Species	Scale at Maturity	Basic Requirements
Japanese Pagoda Tree (*Sophora japonica*)	Height: 50'–70' Width: 50'–70' Shape: Rounded	Zones 4 through 7 Full sun Moist, well-drained soil

Caring for Your Japanese Pagoda Tree

Follow the instructions on the seasonal care for young and mature trees—watering, mulching, fertilizing, staking, and pruning—described in chapter 3.

Special Situations for the Japanese Pagoda Tree

The Japanese pagoda tree may occasionally suffer from insect attack or disease, but it's essentially pest free. It tends, however, to have weak wood and brittle stems, which may result in storm damage with age.

MAGNOLIA (*Magnolia* sp.)

Top Reasons to Plant

- Showy, fragrant flowers
- Many available varieties for cold and warm climates

I know a lot of tree stories, but one of my all-time favorites is about the Andrew Jackson Southern Magnolia. In the winter of 1828, before Jackson left the Hermitage, his Tennessee home, to assume the presidency in Washington, D.C., his wife, Rachel, died of a heart attack. Devastated by the loss, Jackson dug up a southern magnolia by the site of her grave at the Hermitage and planted it at the White House in his wife's honor soon after his inauguration. Every president since Jackson has followed this tradition, leaving behind a legacy of beautifully landscaped trees on the White House lawn.

Magnolias are one of the most popular flowering trees in residential yards. Twenty-two kinds of these lovely trees are available for landscape use, offering a wide variety of size, form, foliage, and bloom. They are relatively tolerant of common air pollutants, so many magnolias do well in urban areas. And while they have a reputation as southern trees, some will actually thrive in the North. There is a variety of magnolia for every zone from 4 to 9. Of course, the queen of the South is the southern magnolia. In the North, two fine choices are the saucer magnolia and the star magnolia.

Use magnolias as individual specimens to create shade in your yard, or in groups for screens or borders. Include them in a mixed garden bed with perennials and annuals. A backdrop of tall evergreens accents magnolia blooms spectacularly. The smaller magnolias can be grown in containers two to three feet wide by one to one and a half feet deep.

Southern Magnolia
(Magnolia grandiflora)

The southern magnolia is a large tree, growing 60 to 80 feet tall, or taller, with a spread of about 30 to 50 feet. The mature trunk diameter is usually more than three feet, and the tree has a medium growth rate with a pyramidal habit. Its branches hang downward off the trunk, and the lower branches may actually touch the ground. It is hardy in zones 7 through 9.

Flowering begins in late May to early June and continues sporadically throughout the summer. The showy, creamy white flowers have a sweet, lemony fragrance and are the largest of any cultivated tree. These plate-size blooms can be 5 to 12 inches in diameter, and have from 9 to 15 petals, but each flower lasts only two to four days. On the first day of bloom the flowers are cup-shaped; after that they become more saucer-shaped.

The only evergreen magnolia, this tree has alternate leaves with dark glossy green on the top sides and a fuzzy-looking rusty or light brown color underneath. The leaves feel thick and stiff, and they are

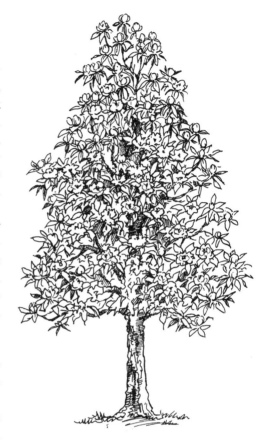

large—from 5 to 10 inches long and 4 to 5 inches wide. Their leathery texture makes them pest resistant.

It is not unusual for southern magnolias to drop a large number of leaves in June. Most trees will, in fact, shed some leaves all season long, with new leaves regularly replacing the fallen ones. The dead leaves that accumulate under the tree take what seems like forever to decompose, which is viewed as a bit of a nuisance by some homeowners. I say the magnolia is such a great tree to have, get out a rake if you don't like the fallen leaves!

The pinkish red fruit is about five inches long, and it splits open in late summer to expose dark red seeds that are a favorite food for wildlife. This tree is a show-off even when it's dropping its seeds. When the seeds ripen, they are expelled from the fruit, but for a few days the seeds are held suspended by short silky strands before falling to the ground. Attractive downy pods decorate the magnolia branches over the winter months and protect the flower buds.

Saucer Magnolia
(Magnolia X soulangiana)

The saucer magnolia is a cross between a Japanese and a Chinese magnolia. Also known as tulip magnolia, it is a reliably cold-hardy tree, helping make it one of the most popular magnolias in the northern United States. It is hardy in zones 5 through 9, and in contrast to its southern cousin, will reach a height of only 10 to 20 feet, with an equal spread. It has an upright and open habit and dark green leaves that are an

elliptical shape with a sharply pointed tip, from three to seven inches long.

Saucer magnolia leaves are medium green in the summer and brown in the fall. The showy flowers appear in early spring before the leaves emerge. The five- to eight-inch-wide, fragrant, saucer-shaped blossoms are usually white with a pink or purplish blush on the undersides of their outer petals. Unfortunately, saucer magnolia flowers will often emerge early and be turned to mush by a frost. To reduce the incidence of this problem, plant saucer magnolias in a place where they are not exposed to early morning sun. This will allow them to thaw more slowly and minimize frost damage. When they avoid the frost they are spectacular!

SAUCER MAGNOLIA CHOICES

Bronzonii bears incredible flowers that spread to ten inches wide when open. A late flowerer, this cultivar grows to 25 feet tall. **Rustica Rubra**'s five-inch-long flowers are rose colored. **Verbanica** has a rounded form and bears copious red and white buds.

Star Magnolia
(Magnolia stellata)

All magnolias have scented flowers, but the star magnolia is most fragrant of all, and as a bonus the flowers are doubles. Eventually reaching 15 to 20 feet tall and 10 to 15 feet wide, the star magnolia is a slow-growing tree with an upright, open habit. Its leaves are medium green in the summer and yellow to bronze in the fall, and it has a more limited range than the saucer magnolia, doing best in zones 4 through 8.

The star magnolia produces beautiful star-shaped flowers in early spring. They are usually white, but some varieties have pink blossoms. Like those of other magnolias, these flowers are vulnerable to frosts. Breeders are now working on cultivars that will flower later and escape the problems of late frost or freeze.

STAR MAGNOLIA CHOICES

Cold-hardy **Centennial** is the most vigorous cultivar, thriving in temperatures as low as 30°F. **Waterlily** has an upright, bushy form, with pink buds and white flowers. **Royal Star** is a slow grower but offers numerous four-inch-wide flowers early in the season.

Requirements of Your Magnolia

Magnolias grow best in full sun and demand at least half a day of sunshine. These trees tend to get leggy, lose their lower branches, and decrease flower production if they get too much shade. Essentially adaptable, magnolias can handle a wide range of soils. They are at home in acidic woodland settings as well as in more alkaline urban sites (pH 5.0 to 7.0). Exceedingly alkaline soils, however, will cause chlorosis, or a yellowing of the leaves. As long as the soil has sufficient organic matter to ensure good moisture retention and drainage, magnolias are happy.

Planting Your Magnolia

The more care you take when you put your tree in the ground, the better it will do during its long life. Follow the complete planting directions provided in chapter 3.

Special notes: To avoid frost damage in the spring, plant a magnolia in a site where it's not exposed to early morning sun and the frozen flowers thaw slowly, reducing tissue damage and browning when there is a surprise early frost. To avoid damage from wind, site big-leafed magnolias in sheltered locations. Do not plant a magnolia anywhere in the vicinity of a black walnut tree, as the walnut roots give off a substance toxic to magnolias. You can plant magnolias any time of the season. Because their roots are slow to establish, stake newly planted trees for the duration of their first year.

Caring for Your Magnolia

Follow the instructions on the seasonal care for young and mature trees—watering, mulching, fertilizing, staking, and pruning—described in chapter 3.

Special notes: Newly planted magnolias require a lot of water. If they dry out during their first year, they may die. Once they are well established, magnolias need supplemental watering only in periods of drought, or if their soil is poor and does not retain moisture.

Magnolias require little winter pruning, except to maintain shapeliness and remove water shoots that spring up along the branches. When pruning a branch, cut it all the way back to the bark collar, which circles the branch at its base (do not actually cut this collar). This will discourage the development of the fast-growing vertical water shoots that spoil the silhouette of the tree. Use clean, sharp hand pruners or loppers to make a smooth cut that will heal well and protect the tree from wood diseases that infect it through jagged open wounds.

Special Situations for the Magnolia

Magnolias can be affected by a few tree-specific problems. One common fungal disease is Nectria canker, which produces rounded, targetlike lesions on magnolia

Common Symptom	Likely Cause
Small bumps on leaves and branches	Scale insects
Leaves spotted, dropping prematurely	Leaf spot
Leaves stippled, covered with webs	Spider mites
Dead leaves matted together	Leaf blight
Leaves that turn brown and collapse	Verticillium wilt
Brown spots on flowers, mushy texture	Frost damage

Species	Scale at Maturity	Basic Requirements
Southern Magnolia (*Magnolia grandiflora*)	Height: 60'–80' Width: 30'–50' Shape: Pyramidal	Zones 7 through 9 Full sun/part shade Moist, well-drained soil
Saucer Magnolia (*Magnolia X soulangiana*)	Height: 10'–20' Width: 10'–20' Shape: Upright, open	Zones 5 through 9 Full sun/part shade Moist, well-drained soil
Star Magnolia (*Magnolia stellata*)	Height: 15'–20' Width: 10'–15' Shape: Upright, open	Zones 4 through 8 Full sun/part shade Moist, well-drained soil

branches and trunks, eventually girdling and killing infected trees. Another disease is heart rot, which causes foliage to thin out and the branches to die back. You can spot the rot by its grayish black to brown color and distinct black lines near the advancing edge of decay on the bark of infected portions of the tree.

The best cure for these problems is good prevention. Keep the tree healthy, well fed, and watered. Avoid bark injuries, and promptly treat any that do occur. Young magnolias especially are damaged easily by lawn mowers and string trimmers. Mulching under the tree—always a good idea to retain water and limit weeds—will keep mowing equipment from coming too close.

Magnolias can also be vulnerable to insect infestation. Whiteflies are tiny, white-winged, mothlike insects that suck plant sap. They secrete a shiny, sticky honeydew that coats the leaves. Infested trees weaken and the leaves turn yellow and die. While these pests won't harm a mature magnolia tree seriously, they can take a toll on a youngster's vigor. Certain caterpillars also attack magnolias. On the West Coast, the omnivorous looper caterpillar is a common culprit, while the saddleback caterpillar is busy in the East.

ORIENTAL CHERRY (*Prunus* sp.)

Top Reasons to Plant

- Dense pink or white flowers
- Upright or weeping branches
- Fall color
- Fragrance

My grandmother had a large sour cherry tree in her yard, and when the season was just right, she would make the most delicious pies you can imagine. But there was a catch: we had to pick the cherries. We'd scrub a large metal bucket and prop a ladder against the tree trunk. In order to use both hands (one to pick, one for balance), we fashioned an S-shaped hook from a clothes hanger. The hook would go over the branch, and the bucket went on the other end of the hook. It was a lot of work, but we figured the faster we picked, the faster the pie made it into the oven.

Cherry trees are part of a diverse genus of trees that bear stone fruits. Cherries, peaches, apricots, plums, and almonds are the most popular members of this clan. While some types of these familiar trees are grown primarily for their fruit, many others, such as the Oriental cherry, are valued for their looks. Many ornamental cherry trees have virtually no fruit—flowers are their chief product—but I've included a couple of trees that will give you the makings of a pie. It's because these varieties come to us from Japan and China that they are often called Oriental cherry trees.

Oriental cherries can be spectacular when in full bloom. Plant them individually in the open as specimen trees in order to get the most out of their natural elegance. Most are also successful when used near the deck or patio for shade, along walkways, or near water. On particularly spacious properties, you can even group them in threes, as a focal point.

Here's a bonus: you can cut cherry blossom branches for indoor display. Choose stems on which the blossoms are not fully opened, and cut them cleanly with sharp pruners where they meet larger branches. Plunge the branches into warm water immediately and allow them to sit for an hour or two, taking up water, before arranging them in a vase. These blossoms will last only two or three days before their petals begin to drop.

Japanese Flowering Cherry (Prunus X serrulata)

For many, these vase-shaped trees are synonymous with Oriental cherries, and Kwanzan is the variety they know best. It's a tree that will be about 12 feet tall and about 8 feet wide at five years. At maturity it usually reaches 20 to 35 feet in height and width. Kwanzan cherry trees are relatively short-lived, their normal life span being

about twenty years. They also have their share of pests, but they're still worth growing—they're just glorious when in flower.

Kwanzan cherry leaves are usually narrowly oval with pointed tips and toothed edges. About three inches long, they have prominent veins and turn reddish copper before they drop in the fall. This is a bonus, but the real story is in those purple-pink flowers that come in early May: drooping clusters of large double flowers (meaning they have two layers of petals). The flower color contrasts beautifully with the bronze of the early spring foliage. Typically flowers last about 10 days. Then you have to wait until next year.

Kwanzan, like other varieties of the Japanese flowering cherry, is hardy in zones 5 through 8.

Yoshino Cherry (Prunus X yedoensis)

This is the cherry tree known for its spectacular show around the Jefferson Memorial and Tidal Basin in Washington, D.C. In early spring, before the leaves develop, the pink flower buds appear, opening into snowy white flowers. The tree is upright, making it ideal for planting along walks

and over patios. Larger specimens take on a weeping habit over a stout trunk. This tree's attractive winter form, yellow fall color, and handsome bark make it a year-round asset to any home landscape. The yoshino cherry grows quickly and can reach 40 to 50 feet at maturity. It's hardy in zones 5 through 8.

YOSHINO CHERRY CHOICES

Shidare Yoshino is a weeping tree that bears white flowers. A vigorous grower,

Akebono has delicate pink flowers and a spreading habit. **Snow Fountains** reaches 6 to 12 feet tall and about equal width, producing white flowers that lend this cultivar its name. Its dark green foliage turns a rainbow of gold and orange in the fall.

Sargent Cherry
(Prunus sargentii)

In my book, Sargent is the best of the flowering cherries. It's beautifully rounded, long lived, and one of the first trees to flower in spring. An ideal shade tree, it spreads as wide as it is tall and casts dense shade below. The Sargent grows at a moderate rate into a 20- to 30-foot tree, upright in youth and then rounding to a width equal to its height.

In late April or early May the one-inch-wide light pink to deep pink single blooms appear. The small, pea-size fruits that follow are red, ripening to a dark purple in June and July. Though inconspicuous because of their size and color, these fruits are found easily by birds, which quickly devour them.

The Sargent cherry's attractive cinnamon-brown bark has a shiny, almost polished surface. Its shiny three- to five-inch-long leaves are red-tinged at first and dark green in midseason. They then take on various shades of orange, bronze, and red in late September, often while other trees are still green. Because these trees are deciduous, the leaves will drop after the fall color show.

Once established, the Sargent cherry requires little maintenance and is quite tolerant of drought and clay soil. It's hardy in zones 4 through 7.

Accolade reaches 25 feet tall and displays a rounded habit with ornate pink flowers.

Higan Cherry
(Prunus subhirtella)

Another long-lived cherry, this tree, like the Sargent, is hardy in zones 4 through 8, but it does better than the Sargent in heat. The pendulous branches extend to ground level all around the trunk; they're amazingly graceful, but they can be pruned back for a more formal look or to permit mowing, other plantings, or maintenance access underneath the tree.

Higan cherries grow at a medium rate. At twenty years they are about 15 feet tall. They usually reach 20 to 40 feet in height and 15 to 30 feet wide by maturity. Older specimens are often wider than they are tall, adding to the beauty of this tree when flowering.

Higan cherry tree leaves are narrowly oval with pointed tips and finely toothed edges. About five inches long, they have prominent veins. They are light green in the spring, turning medium green over the growing season and yellow in the fall before they drop. Each flower cluster contains three to five flowers. These clusters emerge before the leaves in late April or early May and last about 10 days. Additional flowers may appear in autumn if the weather is warm.

Autumnalis is an upright, oval form with a few sporadic flowers in the fall (mostly obscured by the still-persistent foliage) and a heavy floral display of pink flowers in spring. This cultivar matures at 30 feet tall and 20 feet wide. **Pendula** bears pink flowers on its stately form.

Nanking Cherry
(Prunus tomentosa)

The Nanking cherry is native to northern China and is very cold-hardy. Its zone range is 2 through 6. It is a small tree that will stand 6 to 10 feet tall at maturity, with a spread of up to 15 feet. This tree is grown primarily for the showy pink to white flowers that cover the plant in early spring, and for the bright red fruit that follows if cross-pollination has occurred. (Nanking cherries require cross-pollination in order to bear fruit, so you will need to plant two trees). Unlike many other Oriental cherries, the fruits of Nanking trees are edible once they have ripened in early July. They are a little tart for fresh eating, but they make excellent jams and jellies. The pit is also quite large in relation to the fruit size, so you may need to reserve a lot of cherries for use in the kitchen.

Nanking cherry leaves are dark green with fuzzy undersides, creating a beautiful contrast with the light-colored flowers. Although it can be planted in the shade, the Nanking cherry flowers best in sun and partial shade. Rabbits, mice, and deer all love this tree for its fruit, of course.

Amur Chokecherry
(Prunus maackii)

The Amur chokecherry is a small, pleasant tree with delicate, clustered flowers and stunning amber or honey-colored flaky bark that makes for terrific visual appeal, espe-

cially in winter when the leaves have fallen. The young trees are pyramidal, rounding out with age. This is a nice landscaping tree for a small yard because of its size and shape, and the flowers are best appreciated up close. The white flowers appear on the previous season's wood in April or May. A full-grown tree measures 35 to 45 feet tall and wide. The Amur chokecherry can be grown with single or multiple stems, and produces red fruit that turns black in August if the birds don't get it first. The tree does best in a moist, well-drained site. Like the Nanking cherry, it is very cold-hardy, growing in zones 2 through 6. It will show stress in hot, dry sites.

Common Symptom	Likely Cause
Holes in leaves and flowers, leaves skeletonized	Japanese beetle or pear slug
Holes in trunk	Peach borer
Plant parts skeletonized	Asiatic garden beetle
Webbed nests in tree branches	Tent caterpillars
Small bumps on leaves and twigs, leaves turning yellow and covered in sticky honeydew	Scale insects
Red spots on leaves, holes; leaf drop	Leaf spot
Leaves that yellow, then drop	Soil too wet, dry, or too cold
Cracks in trunk and branch crotches	Temperature too cold
Light tan to brownish upper leaf surfaces and chewed appearance	Pear slug

Requirements of Your Cherry Tree

These flowering trees like sun, but they will tolerate some light shade during part of the day. They are not terribly fussy about soil as long as it is reasonably fertile, well drained, and not too acidic (pH 6.5 to 7.5). Drainage is critical. Amur chokecherries will tolerate some salt and can handle clay, but they do not do well with drought, heat, strong wind, or air pollution.

Species	Scale at Maturity	Basic Requirements
Japanese Flowering Cherry (*Prunus* X *serrulata*)	Height: 20'–35' Width: 20'–35' Shape: Vaselike, upright	Zones 5 through 8 Full sun/part shade Moist, well-drained soil
Yoshino Cherry (*Prunus* X *yedoensis*)	Height: 40'–50' Width: 40'–50' Shape: Upright to weeping	Zones 5 through 8 Full sun/part shade Moist, well-drained soil
Sargent Cherry (*Prunus sargentii*)	Height: 20'–30' Width: 20'–30' Shape: Upright to rounded	Zones 4 through 7 Full sun/part shade Moist, well-drained soil
Higan Cherry (*Prunus subhirtella*)	Height: 20'–40' Width: 15'–30' Shape: Upright to rounded	Zones 4 through 8 Full sun/part shade Moist, well-drained soil
Nanking Cherry (*Prunus tomentosa*)	Height: 6'–10' Width: Up to 15' Shape: Upright, semispreading	Zones 2 through 6 Full sun/part shade Moist, well-drained soil
Amur Chokecherry (*Prunus maackii*)	Height: 35'–45' Width: 35'–45' Shape: Pyramidal to rounded	Zones 2 through 6 Full sun/part shade Moist, well-drained soil

Planting Your Oriental Cherry

The more care you take when you put your tree in the ground, the better it will do during its long life. Follow the complete planting directions provided in chapter 3.

Caring for Your Oriental Cherry

Follow the instructions on the seasonal care for young and mature trees—watering, mulching, fertilizing, staking, and pruning—described in chapter 3.

Special Situations for the Oriental Cherry

One common problem for these trees is the pear slug, which targets ornamental cherry trees in particular. Take special note if you have the Kwanzan variety; this tree is especially prone to pests.

are two excellent species. The callery pear tolerates restricted space, poor soil, and wind. The Ussurian pear is even hardier than the callery. (If you want to grow fruit-bearing pear trees, see page 300.)

To showcase the spring flowers and fall foliage of ornamental pears most effectively, plant them as individual specimens in the yard. Or use them to line property frontage or long drives. The narrower vari-

ORNAMENTAL PEAR (*Pyrus* sp.)

Top Reasons to Plant

- Abundant pink or white blossoms
- Fall color
- Trouble-free nature

It's a worthwhile trade-off: give up the pear harvest in favor of beautiful spring flowers, fall color, and ease of care. You don't have to spray ornamental pear trees, of which there

eties, such as **Whitehouse** or **Capitol**, are good for smaller spaces and also make excellent street trees. Ornamental pears also adapt well to espalier training, placed flat against a south-facing wall that protects it from the cold.

Callery Pear
(Pyrus calleryana)

Callery pear trees typically grow from 30 to 50 feet tall, spreading 20 to 35 feet at maturity. They grow at a moderate rate in a pyramidal form, with large limbs stretching upright from narrow crotches where they join the main trunk. The trees spread out a bit with age. Shaped like elongated eggs, the leaves are rounded at their base, with irregularly toothed edges and pointed tips. Measuring from one and a half to three inches long, they are a glossy light green in season, turning a gorgeous deep wine red in October just before they drop. The callery pear is hardy in zones 5 through 8.

Individual pear blossoms are pale white, appearing in delicate clusters in early spring before, or just as, the new leaves emerge. The flowers give way to inconspicuous fruits obscured by the foliage. Only one-half inch or so in diameter, these little knobs are green at first, later turning russet or black. They are appetizing only to birds.

CALLERY PEAR CHOICES

Cultivars of callery pear are handsome small- to medium-size trees. **Bradford** is a classic cultivar that is widely planted because of its tolerance of urban stresses and adaptability to a variety of landscapes. Abundant white flowers and long green leaves adorn this cultivar's conical habit and dense branching. **Chanticleer** has a narrow, pyramidal crown that becomes more oval with age. It is resistant to fire blight and less susceptible to wind breakage than other cultivars. Ideal for narrow spaces in northern landscapes, **Capital** has upward-curving branches and a compact crown, with lovely dark green leaves. This 30-foot cultivar is extremely susceptible to fire blight in southern areas. **Redspire** bears large, orange-yellow flowers on its strong branches. Though also suffering from fire blight in southern climates, it does well in northern regions. **Whitehouse** is a good choice for limited spaces due to its narrow growth habit and ascending branches. Its flower production is somewhat moderate compared to that of other cultivars.

Ussurian Pear
(Pyrus ussuriensis)

The cold-hardiest of all the ornamental pears, the ussurian pear will grow in zones 3 and 4, where the callery will not, and south to zone 6. Maintaining a rounded shape through maturity, this pear tree grows 40 to 50 feet tall with an equal spread. Its leaves are egg-shaped, a glossy green in the summer, and an attractive yellow to purple in the autumn. In April or early May before the leaves emerge, this tree becomes covered in blossoms that start out pink, eventually fading to white. And it does produce some visible fruit that matures in early September, though it is not edible or even particularly ornamental. The fruits will need to be cleaned up from the ground when they drop with the leaves in fall. Solitary trees do not bear fruit, since cross-pollination is required for fruit development.

Requirements of Your Ornamental Pear

Pear trees appreciate full sun. Not terribly demanding about soil type, as long as it is reasonably fertile, they prefer slightly acidic soil (pH 5.5 to 7.5). Ornamental pears are valued in the South because, unlike many plants, they have no difficulty with clay soil.

Planting Your Ornamental Pear

The more care you take when you put your tree in the ground, the better it will do during its long life. Follow the complete planting directions provided in chapter 3.

Caring for Your Ornamental Pear

Follow the instructions on the seasonal care for young and mature trees—watering, mulching, fertilizing, staking, and pruning—described in chapter 3.

Special notes: Feed ornamental pears in the fall, but beware of using too much; excess nitrogen from fertilizer makes pear trees vulnerable to leaf disease problems. When trees are five or six years old, especially if they have been mulched regularly over that time, there is no need for routine annual fertilizing.

Ornamental pears do not need regular pruning and, in fact, may resent it. But when you need to cut away the occasional

Common Symptom	Likely Cause
Withered, dead blossoms; shoots that turn brown or black and seem scorched	Fire blight
Foliage that curls, puckers, turns yellow	Aphids
Tree defoliated	Gypsy moth
Leaves stippled yellow	Spider mites

Species	Scale at Maturity	Basic Requirements
Callery Pear (*Pyrus calleryana*)	Height: 30'–50' Width: 20'–35' Shape: Pyramidal	Zones 5 through 8 Full sun Moist, well-drained soil
Ussurian Pear (*Pyrus ussuriensis*)	Height: 40'–50' Width: 40'–50' Shape: Rounded	Zones 3 through 6 Full sun Moist, well-drained soil

broken or damaged branch, do so in late winter before the tree's flower buds swell.

Special Situations for the Ornamental Pear

Callery pear trees are often susceptible to a splitting of their wood due to the combination of their natural forms and harsh weather. Ornamental pears may also be affected by several common pests and diseases. However, they are nowhere near as problem prone as their cousins, the pear trees that produce substantial amounts of edible fruit.

PEACH TREES
(*Prunus persica*)

Top Reasons to Plant

- ∾ Delicious fruit
- ∾ Attractiveness in hedgerows
- ∾ Suitability for porch or patio in containers

Peach trees belong to the large and varied *Prunus* genus, which includes other stone fruit trees, such as cherries, apricots, and plums. Peach trees grow in zones 5 through 9, so they do well in a large part of the United States, though they are the least hardy of the stone fruits, better in mild climates than cold. The hybrid cultivar **Redhaven** is the most widely planted variety in the world and is very hardy. Most peach trees are grown for their fruit, not their flowers, although the varieties below have very showy blossoms. They are available in several sizes and varieties.

Dwarf peach trees are typically four to six feet tall; larger varieties grafted onto dwarf stock may reach eight to ten feet. Semidwarf trees are seven to nine feet tall, and standard peach trees reach fifteen to twenty-five feet. All peach trees are about as wide as they are tall. They grow rapidly during their first two or three years, adding as much as 15 inches to the length of their branches in the first year. Peach trees have a life expectancy of about twenty years.

Peach trees bloom in midspring before the leaves emerge. Generally their flowers are small, single, and pink, and grow on the previous year's growth. Peach tree foliage emerges after the flowers. Leaves are medium green, two to four inches long, and up to an inch wide. They are lance-shaped,

tapering to a point at their tips, and lightly toothed along their edges. They grow all along the branches, drooping or curling downward slightly.

The fruit is round and characteristically fuzzy. It is yellow, often with a pink blush on the outside, and depending on the variety, its flesh may be white, yellow, or nearly orange. Peaches ripen in mid to late summer, depending on the variety. They are rich in vitamin A (except for the white-fleshed varieties) and vitamin C.

Although peach trees may begin to bear fruit in their second year, it is best to remove the fruits when they appear to encourage maximum development of the branches during that year. By a standard peach tree's third season, it is capable of developing as many as 30 buds along each branch, resulting in a harvest of 75 to 150 peaches (one bushel). Typically it will produce roughly one additional bushel for each year, up to about six bushels in its eighth year. Dwarf trees may bear fruit in their second year, yielding 30 to 60 peaches.

Standard-size peach trees can be planted singly or in a row to define property boundaries or to provide a screen. Semidwarf

trees make nice hedgerows. Cluster several varieties close together to create the effect of multiple kinds of fruit on a single tree. Dwarf trees are especially well suited for growing in containers on porches and patios. In containers they can be easily moved indoors or under shelter when it gets cold.

PEACH TREE CHOICES

A hardy hybrid, **Redhaven** is one of the most popular peach cultivars. The abundant flowers adorning **Rio-oso-gem, Velvet,** and **RedFree** ensure that these cultivars are planted widely year after year. **J. H. Hale, Indian Free,** and **Indian Blood Cling** are non-self-pollinating cultivars. **Dixigem, Loring, Monroe, Summercrest,** and **Sunshine** are resistant to leaf curl. **Carmen Elberta, Greensbore, Orange Cling, Red Bird, Sneed,** and **Sunbeam** are usually not affected by brown rot infection. Check with your local nursery to determine the best cultivars available in your area.

Requirements of Your Peach Tree

Peach trees produce the most fruit where the mean summer temperature is 75°F. Though they require a period of cold for a successful dormancy, they cannot withstand extreme winter cold or late frosts. In winters colder than −10°F, they will lose their fruit buds to frost. The trees themselves die if temperatures dip down to −20°F, especially if milder weather has immediately preceded the drop. Peaches are grown most successfully along the West Coast, on the East Coast from Florida to Massachusetts, south and east of the Great

Lakes, and on the western slopes of the Rocky Mountains. Some varieties bred especially for cold-hardiness will grow farther north, but the fruit lacks flavor. All peach trees like full sun and mildly acidic soil (pH 6.0 to 6.5) that is well drained and somewhat sandy.

Planting Your Peach Tree

The more care you take when you put your tree in the ground, the better it will do during its long life. Follow the complete planting directions provided in chapter 3.

Special notes: Plant one-year-old trees in the spring while they are still dormant. Plant dwarf and semidwarf trees 10 to 12 feet apart, and plant standard trees about 25 feet apart.

After planting, apply a wrapping of burlap or building paper around the trunks to protect the new trees from rabbits, mice, and sunscald. Tie the wrapping loosely so that it does not bind the bark. Stake young trees for the first year or two, but no longer. Until the third season, remove the fruit before it fully ripens to prevent too much weight on young branches. Do not fertilize the tree when it is first planted.

Caring for Your Peach Tree

Follow the instructions on the seasonal care for young and mature trees—watering, mulching, fertilizing, staking, and pruning—described in chapter 3.

Peach trees are shallow-rooted. More than 90 percent of their roots lie within the top 28 inches of soil, so they suffer more quickly from weed competition and drought. Make sure you mulch them and keep them well watered.

Prune peach trees in late winter when they are dormant to ensure, for maximum health and production, that the tree's center is free of branches around the trunk. Prune year-old youngsters back to 30 to 36 inches above the ground. After their first season, cut off any branches that grow upward at an angle too close to the trunk. Cut off any suckers that shoot out from the trunk, especially those that crowd the center, with a sharp knife. If they are ignored, they will grow faster than the main trunk and the tree will soon turn wild. Cut out any limbs that are crossed or out of line.

After the tree's second year, prune to establish a bowl shape, preventing any branch from growing straight up the center. Keep the tree to a height of about 10 feet. By cutting it back when you prune, you'll help the tree grow wide instead of tall, making for easier harvesting.

Many varieties of peach trees tend to set more peaches than the trees can handle. Overbearing weakens peach trees so that they are much more prone to winter injury. Also, fruit size suffers when too much fruit is allowed to mature, and flavor may also suffer. Several weeks after the trees bloom, thin young peaches so that they are six to eight inches apart on the branches. Removing mature peaches by hand ensures the most accurate thinning, but gently hitting each branch two feet from the tip with a broom will also cause many fruits to drop. This is much faster than hand thinning if you happen to have a number of trees to care for.

Begin harvesting when the trees are in their third or fourth year. Look for fully colored, resilient, juicy fruits that come off the tree easily. Peaches usually ripen within a two-week period and when daytime temperatures are above 80°F, usually in July or early August. Warm nights quicken ripening. Once the peaches begin to ripen, pick them every two or three days. If picked just before peak ripeness, when they have good color but are still firm, peaches will hold at room temperature for about three days.

In order to prolong storage life, store fresh peaches in the refrigerator at 40°F for four to five days. The storage life of peaches has been known to be doubled by wrapping them in plastic wrap and holding them at 34°F.

Special Situations for the Peach Tree

Peach trees may be affected by more general problems than almost any tree, as well as more specific problems, such as peach leaf curl and brown rot. Spraying will greatly reduce the pests and plagues. Check with your local nursery for products that are appropriate for your area.

Common Symptom	Likely Cause
Holes low in trunk exuding brown frass and gum	Peach tree borer
Foliage that curls, puckers, turns yellow	Aphids
Defoliated tree	Gypsy moth caterpillar
Skeletonized leaves	Japanese beetle
Dark greenish spots on fruit; yellow-brown spots on twigs and branches; fruit that may crack	Scab
New leaves blistered, curled	Peach leaf curl
Brown spots on fruit	Brown rot

Species	Scale at Maturity	Basic Requirements
Peach Trees (*Prunus persica*)	Height: 4'–10' (dwarf and semidwarf) Width: 4'–10' Shape: Rounded	Zones 5 through 9 Full sun Moist, well-drained soil

PEAR TREE (COMMON)
(*Pyrus communis*)

Top Reasons to Plant

∾ Delicious fruit
∾ Showy spring flowers
∾ Fall color

The essential difference between common pears and ornamental pears (see page 293) is the pear itself. Common pear trees produce delicious fruit—along with a stellar spring flower show and colorful autumn foliage.

Pear trees come in two sizes. Dwarf trees grow 10 to 15 feet tall and 8 to 10 feet wide but can be pruned to remain at only 8 to 10 feet tall. Standard trees reach 20 to 30 feet tall and 15 to 20 feet wide but can also be pruned to stay smaller. Before you choose a pear tree, ask yourself how much fruit you really want to harvest from your backyard. A dwarf tree will begin to yield fruit about three years after planting. After five years it will produce about a bushel of pears a year. Standard trees will not bear much fruit until six to eight years after planting but will then produce a substantial yield of 5 to 10 bushels (350 to 1,500 pears) in an average harvest—more pears than most families would want. Personally, I prefer dwarf pear trees. You can plant more than one variety in the space a standard tree would occupy, and they are much easier to care for.

The common pear is no slouch when it comes to giving you a beautiful display of blooms in early spring. Individual pear blossoms are white, an inch across, and held in clusters that appear before the foliage does. The leaves are shaped like elongated eggs and are a glossy light green in season and a good red in fall. Some types of pear trees have silvery or grayish leaves, and some bare thorns.

The fruits have the distinctive pear shape and are green or red when they first appear on the tree. Most ripen to a yellow, which is often russeted and blushed with red or pink.

Despite its name, the common pear tree is quite attractive, so don't relegate it to the vegetable garden area or some far-off corner. It's a very good specimen tree on its own. Planted in rows, dwarf types can serve as screens. Pear trees are also well adapted to espalier training along a south-facing wall. A good choice for small gardens, they can also be grown in containers.

Requirements of Your Common Pear Tree

Pears trees can usually be grown wherever apple trees are successful, though they are somewhat less resistant to extremes of heat and cold. The common pear is hardy from zones 4 through 8.

Most types of pear trees, especially those with silvery foliage, like full sun. They are not terribly demanding about soil type as long as it is reasonably fertile. And they prefer it to be slightly acidic (pH 6.0 to 6.5).

Planting Your Common Pear Tree

The more care you take when you put your tree in the ground, the better it will do during its long life. Follow the complete planting directions provided in chapter 3.

Special notes: Because frost can damage flowers and reduce yields, locate pears in a spot with good air circulation and drainage, or on the north side of a building to delay flower development. While many pear trees are advertised as self-pollinating, it is best to have at least two trees to ensure the best harvest of fruit.

Plant pear trees in the early spring while they are still dormant. Space dwarf trees from 12 to 15 feet apart. Standard trees should be spaced from 20 to 25 feet apart. If you are planting in a container, use one that is at least 24 inches in diameter and equally deep.

All types of pear trees are weakly rooted, especially when young, so extra care must be taken in preparing the soil at the planting site. Add peat, compost if it is available, or other organic material to the loosened soil in the hole to facilitate root development when the tree is planted.

For a bare-root tree, dig the hole large enough to accommodate the roots when they are spread out. If the tree is grafted, it should sit in its hole so that the graft point, the bulging part of the trunk, is one inch or less above the soil line.

Caring for Your Common Pear Tree

Follow the instructions on the seasonal care for young and mature trees—watering, mulching, fertilizing, staking, and pruning—described in chapter 3.

Special notes: Pear tree care is pretty straightforward. Lawn grass growing over the roots of pear trees suppresses growth, so adding a layer of mulch in the spring is important. Thinning the fruit is another spring job, because many pear varieties set more pears than they can handle. When the fruits begin to form, thin them out so that the remainders are six to eight inches apart on the stem.

A spray of liquid seaweed extract on pear foliage two or three times during the growing season provides boron, which improves their disease and drought resistance. An indicator of a healthy, well-fertilized tree is the length of new growth each year. On a dwarf tree, a season's growth of 8 to 12 inches indicates that the tree is receiving adequate but not excessive nitrogen. On a standard tree, a season's growth of 12 to 18 inches is a good sign.

Drying out is dangerous for pear trees. Make sure you keep them watered through the summer.

The harvest season for pears generally runs from early August through September, depending on the type. Harvest pears about two weeks before they are ripe, and allow them to ripen in a cool room (70° to 75°F) for five to ten days. Tree-ripened pears do not have the quality of flavor and texture of those ripened indoors.

Common Symptom	Likely Cause
Foliage that curls, puckers, turns yellow	Aphids
Defoliated tree	Gypsy moth caterpillar
Leaves stippled yellow	Mites
Leaf buds and early bark eaten	Weevils
Twig dieback, foliage loss	Scale insects
Velvety olive green spots on pears, fruit distorted and drops early	Pear scab
Worms in fruit	Apple maggots
Tunnels in fruit	Codling moths
Leaves that yellow, may drop	Pear psylla
Small, misshapen pears	Cherry fruit fly

Species	Scale at Maturity	Basic Requirements
Common Pear (*Pyrus communis*)	Height: 10'–15' (dwarf) Width: 8'–15' Shape: Rounded	Zones 4 through 8 Full sun Moist, well drained soil

If you want to store your pears for longer, keep them at temperatures just above freezing for a month after picking. Then move them to room temperature to ripen.

When feeding pear trees in the fall, beware of using too much nitrogen. It makes them much more vulnerable to fire blight, the most serious disease to which they fall victim. It is best to use ammonium nitrate at about one-eighth pound per tree.

Special Situations for the Pear Tree

When it comes to pests, pear and apple trees have much in common. Fire blight fungus is the worst of what they share. Very few trees are completely resistant to this fungus, and those that are usually produce poorer fruit than susceptible trees. Spraying doesn't help. But timely fertilization and pruning do.

Shoots infected with fire blight turn brown or black and have a scorched appearance, and the blossoms wither and die. Reddish water-soaked bark lesions appear, and on warm days they ooze an orange-brown liquid. Later they become brown and dry. The best defense against fire blight is diligent pruning. In the winter, look for affected branches with visible cankers, and prune them off 12 inches below the cankers. In the summer, cut off blackened leaves, stems, or fruits 12 inches below the sign of disease. Also snap off suckers thrown up from branches and rootstock; these are especially prone to fire blight. It is critical that you disinfect your pruning tool in a bleach solution (one part household bleach to four parts water) after each cut.

Varieties of pear trees resistant to fire blight are: Asian varieties and **Comice, Dawn, Douglas, Duchess d'Angouleme, El Dorado, Fan-Stil, Harvest Queen, Lincoln, Luscious, Mac, Magness, Maxine, Moonglow, Orient, Seckel, Starking Delicious, Sugar, Sure Crop, Waite,** and **Winter Nelis.** Disease-resistant rootstocks are: **Kieffer, Moonglow, Old Home,** Oriental (*Pyrus bitulafolis*), Oriental (*Pyrus communis*), Oriental harbin pear (*Pyrus ussuriensis*), **Seedling, Stark Honeysweet,** and **Starking Delicious.**

SERVICEBERRY
(*Amelanchier* sp.)

Top Reasons to Plant

∾ Profuse flowers
∾ Delicious berries
∾ Fall color

The serviceberry is a multistemmed shrub or small tree that is native to the United States. It has dazzling flowers, good fall color, and delicious berries in the summertime. Serviceberries are susceptible to very few pest and disease problems, require little care after their first few years, and do not have strict environmental requirements.

For lawns, shrub borders, and woodland margins, the serviceberry is an attractive understory tree. The shrub forms can be grown as tall informal hedges or screens. Particularly attractive against a dark or shaded backdrop, which tends to highlight its attractive flowers, fall color, and overall form, the serviceberry also does well in windbreaks, roadside plantings, and along the banks of streams and ponds. It is resistant to air pollution and suitable for urban planting.

Serviceberries interbreed easily and produce many hybrids, though these are difficult to identify and differentiate because they have very similar characteristics and common names. Following are three varieties I can recommend for the yard. They are quite a bit alike, but some fundamental differences will help you determine which is right for you.

Downy Serviceberry
(Amelanchier arborea)

The downy serviceberry is the most commonly used serviceberry in the home landscape. Its main ornamental features are its flowers and fall color; the fruits are not as ornamental as those of other species. As a shrub, its multiple stems form a dense plant with many thin branches. With early pruning, it can be grown as a small tree, and one-trunk serviceberry trees are often found

in nurseries. The trees grow to be 15 to 25 feet tall, while their spread varies from 15 to 20 feet wide, resulting in an overall rounded shape. Hardy in zones 4 through 9, the downy serviceberry has a moderate growth rate in most soils.

Downy serviceberries will bloom even in their first year. The flowers are plentiful, appearing before the leaves in March and lasting until June; they are pure white and one inch in diameter with numerous stamens and five narrow petals. They cluster in showy groups at the ends of branches and are fragrant, which other varieties are not.

The two- to four-inch leaves of the downy serviceberry grow alternately on short stalks that shoot off the stems. Initially a purplish brown color, they turn bright green in the summer and dazzling orange to red in the fall. The young leaves are covered with scattered silky hairs and are oval to elliptical in shape. One half of the leaf edge is toothed, and the other half is smooth.

Sweet, edible, and resembling dark purple to purple-black blueberries, the fruits appear in early June and last through August. Unfortunately, many birds and other animals will eat them, leaving few for you to munch on. However, you can protect your serviceberry from animals by covering it with netting that you can buy at a garden store. Harvested berries can be used in jams, jellies, and wines.

Allegheny Serviceberry
(Amelanchier laevis)

The Allegheny serviceberry is very similar to the downy serviceberry, but its leaves are hairless and tinged with purple when they're new; also, the berries are sweeter and juicier, but the blossoms are not fragrant. Less happy in hot weather than the downy is, the Allegheny does best in zones 4 through 8. It is native to thickets, open woods, sheltered slopes, and wood margins in eastern North America, where it typically grows 15 to 25 feet tall and wide in an upright shape.

ALLEGHENY SERVICEBERRY CHOICES

Cumulus is a vigorous, upright-growing plant with orange-red fall color.

Apple Serviceberry
(Amelanchier X grandiflora)

A hybrid between the downy and Allegheny serviceberries, the apple serviceberry displays characteristics of both parents. It produces few suckers, is adapted to a wide range of soils, and tolerates drought. But its main feature is its flowers, which are larger than those of other species but not fragrant. Borne in groups in early May, the flowers are at first tinged with pink but later fade to white. The young leaves are purplish, soon turning to green, then a striking yellow to orange in the fall. Hardy

Common Symptom	Likely Cause
Holes in leaves and flowers	Japanese beetles

Species	Scale at Maturity	Basic Requirements
Downy Serviceberry (*Amelanchier arborea*)	Height: 15'–25' Width: 15'–20' Shape: Rounded	Zones 4 through 9 Full sun Moist, well-drained soil
Allegheny Serviceberry (*Amelanchier laevis*)	Height: 15'–25' Width: 15'–25' Shape: Upright	Zones 4 through 8 Full sun Moist, well-drained soil
Apple Serviceberry (*Amelanchier X grandiflora*)	Height: 20'–25' Width: 20'–25' Shape: Irregular oval	Zones 5 through 9 Full sun Moist, well-drained soil

in zones 5 through 9, and 20 to 25 feet tall and wide at maturity, the tree has an irregular oval shape.

Requirements of Your Serviceberry

The serviceberry is happiest in full sun to partial shade. The largest yields, and best-quality fruits, are produced when the plant is grown in a sunny location. In partial shade, the plant will still do well but its harvest will be limited. Serviceberries are grown most easily in medium-wet, well-drained soil with a neutral pH. Nevertheless, they are tolerant of a wide range of soils, even heavy clay. Serviceberries are fairly drought tolerant but do not handle flooding well.

Planting Your Serviceberry

The more care you take when you put your tree in the ground, the better it will do during its long life. Follow the complete planting directions provided in chapter 3.

Caring for Your Serviceberry

Follow the instructions on the seasonal care for young and mature trees—watering, mulching, fertilizing, staking, and pruning—described in chapter 3.

Special note: Root suckers will pop up each spring at the base of the trunk. They should be pruned.

Special Situations for the Serviceberry

The serviceberry has few insect or disease problems.

SMOKE TREE
(*Cotinus* sp.)

Top Reasons to Plant

- Textured, puffy leafstalks
- Fall color
- Tolerance of poor soil
- Trouble-free nature

Some may think that the smoky look of this tree comes from its flowers, but the yellow-green blossoms are in fact quite inconspicuous. The effect comes instead from billowy hairs attached to elongated stalks on the spent flower clusters. These hairs turn a smoky pink to purplish pink for much of the summer, thus covering the tree with fluffy, hazy, smokelike puffs. The smoke tree is truly a unique and beautiful addition to any home landscape.

The most popular and widely available smoke tree variety is the imported common smoke tree (*Cotinus coggygria*), which comes from Europe and Asia. Many landscape designers believe the smoke tree native to the United States (*Cotinus obovatus*) is more attractive, but it is often available only through special mail order. Either variety is breathtaking when grouped together or planted singly. Both can be kept small to grow in a container alongside a deck or patio. The smoke tree is particularly good for growing in poor soils where few other trees will grow. Both varieties are hardy in zones 4 through 8.

American Smoke Tree
(Cotinus obovatus)

Also called chittamwood, the American smoke tree is a small, deciduous, rounded tree or large, upright shrub. The greenish yellow flowers arrive in early spring. The oval four- to eight-inch leaves are a blue to blue-green during the growing season, but they turn dazzling colors in the fall—yellow, orange, amber, or even a fine red-purple. Soft bursts of color, they look more like flowers than leaves. Mature trees are 20 to 30 feet tall with varying spreads and a rounded shape.

Common Smoke Tree
(Cotinus coggygria)

The imported common smoke tree is smaller than the American version, growing 10 to 15 feet tall with a wide-spreading, bushy crown. The leaves are smooth and oval, colored light green to wine depending on the cultivar. As with its American cousin, the common smoke tree has inconspicuous green-yellow flowers that are later replaced by hairs that give the tree its hazy,

smoky appearance. The hairs look like a filmy veil thrown over the shrub.

COMMON SMOKE TREE CHOICES

Cultivars include the aptly named **Royal Purple,** with dark purple leaves. Other reddish purple models are **Velvet Cloak** and **Notcutt's Variety,** which have spectacular fall color. **Daydream** is a smaller cultivar, reaching about 10 feet high and bearing deep green leaves.

Requirements of Your
Smoke Tree

Smoke trees do best in full sun. They are adaptable to a wide range of soils of any pH, including poor rocky soils, as long as they are not wet.

Planting Your Smoke Tree

The more care you take when you put your tree in the ground, the better it will do dur-

Common Symptom	Likely Cause
Red spots on leaves, holes in leaves	Leaf spot
Wilting or drooping foliage in midsummer	Verticillium wilt

Species	Scale at Maturity	Basic Requirements
American Smoke Tree (*Cotinus obovatus*)	Height: 20'–30' Width: Varying Shape: Oval to rounded	Zones 4 through 8 Full sun Moist, well-drained soil
Common Smoke Tree (*Cotinus coggygria*)	Height: 10'–15' Width: Varying Shape: Rounded	Zones 4 through 8 Full sun Moist, well-drained soil

ing its long life. Follow the complete planting directions provided in chapter 3.

Caring for Your Smoke Tree

Follow the instructions on the seasonal care for young and mature trees—watering, mulching, fertilizing, staking, and pruning—described in chapter 3.

Special Situations for Smoke Tree

The smoke tree has no serious insect or disease problems, although stress may make it more vulnerable to common tree problems than usual.

SNOWBELL (*Styrax sp.*)

Top Reasons to Plant

∾ Fragrant white flowers
∾ Attractive bark
∾ Delicate structure

If you want a tree that isn't already growing throughout the neighborhood, here's a good place to start. An underused tree, the snowbell is distinguished most by the aromatic, bell-shaped flowers that give the tree its name—flowers that could never be confused with those of any other tree. Snowbells are graceful, medium-size trees with bark that's especially handsome in the winter; some varieties have interesting fall foliage as well. Snowbells are particularly suitable for a smaller yard, require little special care, and are not especially vulnerable to pests or disease. Both varieties listed here are hardy in zones 5 through 8.

The branches of a snowbell hanging over a patio can be quite effective because the flowers and bark can be viewed up close. Snowbell flowers will attract honeybees in large numbers; however, as long as these bees remain undisturbed they will not pose a problem. Snowbell trees also make a wonderful addition to a mixed shrubbery border. Thanks to their small stature and vaselike shape, they even make nice street trees where overhead space is limited.

Japanese Snowbell
(Styrax japonicus)

The Japanese snowbell is a graceful, upright tree with arching, spreading branches and a delicate look. It reaches 20 to 30 feet high at maturity with an equal spread. The tree's lower branches are usually removed, result-

ing in a vase-shaped patio-size shade tree. The snow white bell-shaped flowers appear in May and last through June. Slightly fragrant, the petite flowers can appear either singly or in clusters. The snowbell's attractive bark has interlacing fissures that will add winter interest, and the heart-shaped leaves turn yellow or sometimes red in the fall.

JAPANESE SNOWBELL CHOICES

Pink Chimes is a pink-flowered willowy form. **Pendula** is a weeping cultivar with uniquely shaped flowers and foliage.

Fragrant Snowbell
(Styrax obassia)

A bit smaller than the Japanese snowbell, the fragrant snowbell has a broad, columnar shape that reaches 20 to 30 feet high and spreads 15 to 25 feet wide. The six- to eight-inch clusters of white flowers are larger and somewhat more fragrant than those of the Japanese species, but the three- to eight-inch long, dark green leaves often obscure the beauty of the flowers, so the Japanese snowbell is often preferred

Species	Scale at Maturity	Basic Requirements
Japanese Snowbell (*Styrax japonicus*)	Height: 20'–30' Width: 20'–30' Shape: Irregular	Zones 5 through 8 Full sun/part shade Moist, well-drained, acidic soil
Fragrant Snowbell (*Styrax obassia*)	Height: 20'–30' Width: 15'–25' Shape: Broad, columnar	Zones 5 through 8 Full sun/part shade Moist, well-drained, acidic soil

between the two species. On the other hand, those big leaves give the flowering tree an unusual textured look that is really appealing.

Requirements of Your Snowbell

Snowbells are a bit picky about light and soil. They do not like clay or wet or compacted soil, preferring well-drained, acidic soil. Though they will grow in full sun in their northern range, in the South they require partial shade. In the North, they will also need protection from winter winds. If you plant them where they have the light and soil they need, they will be low-maintenance trees.

Planting Your Snowbell

The more care you take when you put your tree in the ground, the better it will do during its long life. Follow the complete planting directions provided in chapter 3.

Special note: Snowbells are highly sensitive to wind, especially in their northern range. Select a spot protected somewhat from high winds.

Caring for Your Snowbell

Follow the seasonal care for young and mature trees—watering, mulching, fertilizing, staking, and pruning—described in chapter 3.

Special Situations for the Snowbell

Snowbells have no serious problems in terms of insects or disease.

STEWARTIA (*Stewartia* sp.)

Top Reasons to Plant

- Camellia-like flowers
- Handsome peeling bark
- Glossy green leaves
- Fall color

The stewartia commands attention in all four seasons. In June or early July, its showy white flowers look like their cousins, wild camellias. Leaves are glossy dark green through the summer, turning a spectacular yellow to reddish purple for three or four weeks in the fall. Finally, in the winter, the contrast of newly fallen snow and the stewartia's peeling, reddish brown bark is breathtaking.

Stewartias make a great specimen plant and work well as a focal point in a small landscape. Place your stewartia near a patio, deck, or walkway where it can receive the attention it deserves. On a large property you might consider a grove of a dozen or more to create a stunning effect.

The three species of stewartia that follow are all small to medium trees that can also be grown as multistemmed shrubs.

Japanese Stewartia (Stewartia pseudocamellia)

The Japanese stewartia has a pyramidal shape and the exfoliating reddish brown bark characteristic of all stewartias. The tree's glossy green leaves are oblong-shaped, measuring about three inches in length. In the fall, they turn reddish orange to burgundy.

Neither fragrant nor particularly numerous, the flowers nonetheless are beautifully cup-shaped, with five petals each and a showy orange and yellow center. The mature tree stands 20 to 40 feet tall and wide. It's hardy in zones 5 through 7.

Korean Stewartia (Stewartia koreana)

Although similar to the Japanese stewartia, the Korean stewartia has its own virtues. It grows a bit smaller than the Japanese stewartia, at 20 to 30 feet high and 15 to 20 feet wide. The flowers last a little longer, the fall color is a bit redder, and the bark tends to flake off in irregular puzzle-piece shapes rather than in long strips. The bark color is a mix of steel gray, brown, and orange-brown and has a smooth texture

underneath. This tree is hardy in zones 5 through 7.

Tall Stewartia
(Stewartia monadelpha)

Ironically, the tall stewartia is no taller than the others, reaching 20 to 30 feet in height and width. While it offers the attractions of the other species, the flowers of the tall stewartia are a bit smaller and the center is violet, not orange and yellow. The tall stewartia's main advantage over the others is that it is better heat tolerant and thus more suited to southern gardens. It does well in zones 5 through 8.

Requirements of Your Stewartia

An ideal site has sunlight during the morning and light shade from taller trees during the heat of the day. Stewartias like moist, acidic soil that drains well.

Planting Your Stewartia

The more care you take when you put your tree in the ground, the better it will do during its long life. Follow the complete planting directions provided in chapter 3.

Special note: Stewartias resent transplanting, so choose your plant's permanent site carefully.

Caring for Your Stewartia

Follow the instructions on the seasonal care for young and mature trees—watering, mulching, fertilizing, staking, and pruning—described in chapter 3.

Common Symptom	Likely Cause
Holes in leaves, skeletonized leaves	Japanese beetles

Species	Scale at Maturity	Basic Requirements
Japanese Stewartia (*Stewartia pseudocamellia*)	Height: 20'–40' Width: 20'–40' Shape: Oval	Zones 5 through 7 Full sun/light shade Moist, well-drained soil
Korean Stewartia (*Stewartia koreana*)	Height: 20'–30' Width: 15'–20' Shape: Oval	Zones 5 through 7 Full sun/light shade Moist, well-drained soil
Tall Stewartia (*Stewartia monadelpha*)	Height: 20'–30' Width: 20'–30' Shape: Oval	Zones 5 through 8 Full sun/light shade Moist, well-drained soil

Special Situations for the Stewartia

The stewartia not only needs little seasonal care but also has no serious pest insect or disease problems.

SUMAC (*Rhus* sp.)

Top Reasons to Plant

∾ Bold foliage in all seasons
∾ Good as a specimen tree
∾ Erosion-control ability

Common along highways and in farm fields, fifty-four species of sumac are native to North America. (These do not include the poison sumac.) While many sumacs are undistinguished, three species whose striking fall foliage and clusters of long-lasting red winter berries have made their way into the field of ornamental landscaping. Shining sumac (*Rhus copallina*), staghorn sumac (*Rhus typhina*), and smooth sumac (*Rhus glabra*) are small trees or shrubs with much to offer in the home landscape.

While each of these sumacs can be kept as a single tree, all three have underground runners that if left unmanaged will produce dozens of new trees. Unwanted shoots must be removed every spring, or else you can plant your tree in a container to control the root growth. Sumacs are relatively short-lived trees, lasting only ten to fifteen years. However, the sumac's benefits outweigh its drawbacks. A smooth sumac, for example, is suited for group plantings in small to large yards, and it's especially useful in attracting birds.

Shining Sumac (Rhus copallina)

Also known as winged sumac, the shining sumac is probably the best suited of the three for natural or informal landscapes. It is a small tree and has a short trunk and spreading branches. Typically it reaches 20 to 30 feet high at maturity and spreads the same distance wide. If you are looking for a fairly dense shrubby barrier or screen that attracts birds, this is a good choice. With regular pruning, it also works well alongside a patio or deck.

This plant's winged compound leaves, reminiscent of a giant fern's, are a rich, lustrous green and are so shiny that they sometimes appear to be lacquered. The 12-inch-long leaves are actually 7 to 27 leaflets arranged alternately on a stem. Lance-shaped and hairy underneath, these featherlike leaves turn a brilliant red in the fall, which is when the shining sumac is at its best.

Shining sumac flowers appear in July and August and are greenish yellow. They are small, measuring only one-sixteenth of an inch, and are borne on three- to five-inch-wide pyramid-shaped panicles, where dark red berries later form. The individual berries are only about one-eighth of an inch across and are covered with short, sticky red hairs; but because there are so many berries on the panicles, they make a good show. The berries mature in September to October and, if the birds don't eat them, they will ornament your garden through winter. The shining sumac is hardy in zones 4 to 9.

Smooth Sumac
(Rhus glabra)

Native from the Rockies east to the Atlantic coast, the smooth sumac is most often used as a shrub, with up to 25 stems. It is the smallest of the sumacs featured here, with a mature height of only 10 to 15 feet and a similar spread. The smooth sumac has a short or multistemmed trunk and spreading branches that give the appearance of a hedge if not controlled. However, the plant is an excellent choice for sites with poor soil where many other plants refuse to grow. It is hardy in zones 2 through 9.

The smooth sumac's 12- to 18-inch-long leaves are made up of 11 to 31 alternately placed leaflets. Two to four inches long, these leaflets are lance-shaped, with fine hair underneath. They are a medium green during the growing season; in the fall they turn to a red-orange, scarlet, or even a striking wine red color.

The greenish white flowers are borne on upright panicles that are up to eight inches long, appearing in June to August. Materializing later on the panicles are dark red, round, and hairy fruits, measuring one-eighth inch long. The fruit matures in September to October but remains through the winter.

Staghorn Sumac
(Rhus typhina)

Especially picturesque in the winter, the bare, forked branches and heavy twigs of the staghorn sumac resemble a deer's antlers, giving rise to the common name "staghorn." The staghorn sumac grows rapidly, reaching a mature height of 15 to 25 feet and similar width. It tolerates most exposures and poor soil, and its fall foliage is red, yellow, orange, or scarlet.

Relatively long at 12 to 24 inches, the staghorn sumac's leaves display from 13 to 27 leaflets each. The four- to eight-inch panicles of greenish white flowers appear in summer, becoming velvety bunches of red fruit in the fall. The fruits will last all winter, or until the birds get them. This tree is hardy in zones 3 through 8.

STAGHORN SUMAC CHOICES

The female cultivar **Laciniata** has a cut-leafed form that often attains an unusual fernlike shape and develops orange fall color.

Requirements of Your Sumac

Sumacs want full sun. They will grow in almost any soil but thrive in soil that is moist and well-drained with a pH of 5.0 to 8.0.

Caring for Your Sumac

Follow the instructions on the seasonal care for young and mature trees—watering, mulching, fertilizing, staking, and pruning—described in chapter 3.

Special notes: These plants can become invasive in the home landscape if not supervised. Remove suckers that come up where you don't want them. Be sure to wear gloves when pulling up suckers to avoid having their onionlike odor stay with you.

Special Situations for Sumac

Sumacs generally are free of pest and disease problems. Because they are short-lived, they may eventually attract some pests or a disease simply because they're old and need to be replaced.

Planting Your Sumac

The more care you take when you put your tree in the ground, the better it will do during its long life. Follow the complete planting directions provided in chapter 3.

Species	Scale at Maturity	Basic Requirements
Shining Sumac (*Rhus copallina*)	Height: 20'–30' Width: 20'–30' Shape: Upright	Zones 4 through 9 Full sun Moist, well-drained soil
Smooth Sumac (*Rhus glabra*)	Height: 10'–15' Width: 10'–15' Shape: Upright	Zones 2 through 9 Full sun Moist, well-drained soil
Staghorn Sumac (*Rhus typhina*)	Height: 15'–25' Width: 15'–25' Shape: Upright	Zones 3 through 8 Full sun Moist, well-drained soil

TULIP TREE
(*Liriodendron tulipifera*)

Top Reasons to Plant

- ⤳ Tulip-shaped flowers
- ⤳ Large, deciduous native
- ⤳ Fall color

Tulip trees have a prominent place in this country's history. Daniel Boone used a single tulip tree for his 60-foot canoe. Tulip trees indicated to pioneers the location of the best farming soils. Thomas Jefferson, a great admirer of trees, planted thousands of tulip trees at Monticello, where about half a dozen remain today. One of them has a trunk with a diameter of seven feet! Jefferson affectionately called tulip trees the "Juno of the woods."

Also known as tulip poplars or yellow poplars, tulip trees are the tallest deciduous trees growing in the wild in the eastern United States, some reaching 200 feet in height. Although shorter when grown in a landscape, they still reach 70 to 90 feet tall and 35 to 50 feet wide. They also retain their trademark ramrod-straight trunks, which are branchless two-thirds of the way up. Because the tulip tree is so large, it is a beautiful choice as a specimen tree on a spacious residential lot.

Related to magnolias, tulip trees are one of the first trees to leaf in spring. Their distinctive bluish green leaves make them easy to recognize. As broad as they are long, the leaves' squarish shape suggests a

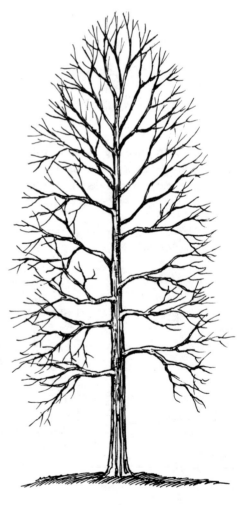

cat's face, the top two lobes resembling its ears. In the fall they give a spectacular show of yellow foliage. The trees are hardy in zones 4 through 9.

This tree's tulip-shaped flowers are greenish yellow with an orange center. Although the flowers are two to three inches wide, the leaves, especially those that are high in the canopy of mature trees, may obscure the flowers. Sometimes the only evidence they have bloomed is dropped petals on the ground. The flowers attract hummingbirds, honeybees, and butterfly larvae.

TULIP TREE CHOICES

Fifty feet tall and 30 feet wide, **Aureo-Marginata** has eye-catching yellow and green variegated foliage. **Arnold (Fastigiatum)** is a narrow cultivar that forms an effective screen when planted in groups.

Requirements of Your Tulip Tree

Tulip trees prefer to be in full sun and deep, rich, moist, well-drained soil. Though they do best in acidic soil, they can withstand slightly alkaline soil at a pH of 7.5.

Common Symptom	Likely Cause
Leaves puckered, wilted, brown, and sticky	Aphids
Yellowed leaves, bumps on twigs	Scale insects
Purplish spots on leaves	Gallfly
Gray coating on foliage	Powdery mildew
Visible rotting on branches, bark	Canker
Leaves that wilt suddenly	Verticillium wilt
Black fungal growth on leaves; shiny, sticky material on leaves	Sooty mold

Species	Scale at Maturity	Basic Requirements
Tulip Tree (*Liriodendron tulipifera*)	Height: 70'–90' Width: 35'–50' Shape: Pyramidal	Zones 4 through 9 Full sun Moist, well-drained soil

These trees are drought sensitive but ideal for floodplains.

Planting Your
Tulip Tree

The more care you take when you put your tree in the ground, the better it will do during its long life. Follow the complete planting directions provided in chapter 3.

Special note: Be sure to plant tour tulip tree away from the house and driveway, because the wood breaks easily and the tree's height can attract lightning.

Caring for Your
Tulip Tree

Follow the instructions on the seasonal care for young and mature trees—watering, mulching, fertilizing, staking, and pruning—described in chapter 3.

Special notes: Considered drought-indicator plants, tulip trees are among the first to exhibit drought-related stress, because they have relatively shallow roots. (In the wild, tulip trees prefer moist areas near rivers or streams.) When water is lacking, their leaves turn yellow and are sometimes sprinkled with brown speckles between the veins. Eventually they turn brown and drop. During dry periods, be sure to provide supplemental watering.

YELLOWWOOD
(*Cladrastis kentukea*)

Top Reasons to Plant

- ❧ Showy white fragrant flowers
- ❧ Beechlike bark
- ❧ Fall color

This tree is called yellowwood because its freshly cut heartwood is a muted to brilliant yellow, and the wood is known to yield a yellow dye. If you don't cut your tree down, you'll never see the yellow. The yellowwood is a native tree, often called the American yellowwood, but it has never multiplied in large numbers in the wild—in fact, it is rel-

ally seven) leaflets along 8- to 12-inch-long stems. Green on their upper surfaces, the leaves are paler below. The yellowwood's fall color is a soft mix of yellow, gold, and orange.

This tree becomes the star of the home landscape in late May or early June, when 8- to 14-inch-long hanging clusters of creamy to white pealike flowers appear in profusion. Resembling the blooms of a wisteria, these flowers are not only beautiful but fragrant as well. As might be expected, when the yellowwood is in bloom its nectar attracts large numbers of honeybees. The truly spectacular floral displays come in cycles of two to five years. The fruits are two- to four-inch-long flat brown pods that ripen in early fall.

atively rare in nature. But it has become a popular landscape tree for its attractive bark and foliage and its fantastic show of white flowers in early summer. One drawback of this tree is that it doesn't flower until it is ten years old—sometimes older—but the flowers are so breathtaking that for many people it is well worth the wait.

The yellowwood grows to 30 to 50 feet tall and 40 to 55 feet wide in zones 4 to 8. If not pruned, the lowest branches can reach almost to the ground. Its broad, rounded crown has delicate branches that are upright and spreading. The bark is smooth and gray, similar to that of a beech; it is also thin, making it vulnerable to damage.

The yellowwood has alternate, pinnate, compound leaves with five to nine (but usu-

YELLOWWOOD CHOICES

Rosea, a cultivar that bears pink flowers, was developed in New England and is becoming more readily available at local nurseries.

Requirements of Your Yellowwood

The American yellowwood prefers well-drained, moist soil and full sun, but it will tolerate partial shade. In the wild it is found in alkaline soils, but it also tolerates slightly acid soils, with a pH no lower than 6.0.

Species	Scale at Maturity	Basic Requirements
Yellowwood (*Cladrastis kentukea*)	Height: 30'–50' Width: 40'–55' Shape: Rounded	Zones 4 through 8 Full sun/part shade Moist, well-drained soil

Planting Your Yellowwood

The more care you take when you put your tree in the ground, the better it will do during its long life. Follow the complete planting directions provided in chapter 3.

Caring for Your Yellowwood

Follow the instructions on the seasonal care for young and mature trees—watering, mulching, fertilizing, staking, and pruning—described in chapter 3.

Special notes: Summer is the time to prune yellowwood trees. Their branches have a tendency to grow at narrow angles, making them subject to damage and breakage in harsh weather. Prune a yellowwood when it is young to develop branches that meet the trunk at a wide angle, forming a U-shaped crotch. Develop seven to ten major lateral limbs spaced along the trunk, not clustered together, which will help them form strong attachments to the trunk. You may also want to remove the lower branches when the tree is young to produce a taller-looking trunk.

The yellowwood will drop its ripe seedpods in the fall and winter. You will want to collect these to avoid a mess.

HOW TO TALK TREE:
A GLOSSARY

Trees, like any area of interest, have their own vocabulary. Though we'll leave the many technical terms for the scientists, here are some common terms and definitions that should help you navigate the world of trees.

Acid—having a pH value less than 7

Alkaline—having a pH value greater than 7

Alternate leaves—leaves arranged on opposite sides of an axis but not exactly across from each other, one leaf per node

Bole—the trunk of a tree from ground level to the first major branch

Branch axil—the angle formed between two branches attached to each other

Branch bark ridge—a ridge of bark that forms in a branch crotch caused by the growth of the stem and branch tissues against each other

Branch collar—the bulge formed at the base of a branch by the annual production of overlapping layers of branch and stem tissues

Callus—bark scab that forms in response to a wound

Catkin—a pendulous spike or flower cluster of a male or unisex tree flower

Compound leaf—a leaf composed of two or more separate leaflets

Cone—the woody seed-bearing fruit of a conifer

Conifer—trees that reproduce through distribution of seeds by cones

Crown—the parts of a tree above the trunk, including leaves, branches, and limbs

Crown reduction pruning—a method of tree cutting used to reduce the height of the tree by cutting branches back to laterals that are at least one-third the diameter of the limb being removed

Crown thinning—a method of pruning used to increase sunlight and air circulation through the crown of the tree by selective removal of branches

Cultivar—a tree variety produced through selective breeding to develop certain desired characteristics

Cutting—a section of a tree that is removed and used for propagation

Deciduous—refers to trees that lose their leaves every year

Dieback—the gradual decay of a tree that begins at its young shoots and works back to established stems and old wood

Dioecious—having male flowers on one tree and female flowers on another

Drip Line—the circular area on the ground corresponding to the outermost edges of the crown of the tree

Evergreen—refers to trees that keep their leaves year-round

Flush cut—a pruning cut that is made inside the branch bark ridge or branch collar, injuring the stem tissues

Frass—debris or excrement produced by insects

Girdled roots—roots that slowly strangle the trunk tissue from below ground due to bad planting, usually eventually killing the tree

Girdling—a ring of bark and underlying tissue cut into the trunk by rope or lawn equipment, causing the tree to be unable to distribute water and nutrients, and eventually killing it

Grafting—a method of propagation involving growing a piece of one tree against another

Habit—the general appearance of a tree, including shape and form

Hardwood—trees that have broad leaves, such as oak, maple, and ash

Heel—the portion of old wood that is left at the base of a cutting after it is removed from the stem

Hybrid—a cross between two trees, usually within a species

Lateral—a side growth

Leader—the tip of the main stem of the tree

Leaflet—a segment of a compound leaf

Loam—soil that has moderate amounts of sand, silt, and clay

Monoecious—having male and female flowers on the same tree

Native—a tree that originates in a particular area

Naturalized—(a tree) having established itself in the wild of an area to which it is not native, and now growing as if a native

Neutral—having a pH value of 7; that is, not acid and not alkaline

Node—the point on a stem where a leaf or a bud grows

Opposite leaves—leaves arranged in pairs at each node (not alternate or whorled)

Petiole—the leaf stalk that connects the leaf blade to the stem

Pinnate—leaflets arranged on either side of a central axis, like a feather

Pollard—to prune a tree's main branches to encourage growth

Serrated—notched edges of a leaf

Skeletonized—characteristic of a leaf that has been eaten by a pest, with just the faint frame of the leaf and no flesh remaining

Softwood—a tree that has needles, such as pine, spruce, or fir

Species—a genetically distinct group of trees

Standard—a tree with a distinct length of bare stem below the first branches

Stub cut—a pruning cut made too far outside the branch bark ridge or branch collar, leaving branch tissue attached to the stem

Sucker—a shoot that grows from the tree stem or from the root at ground level

Taproot—a prominent, often bulky root that extends down below the stem of the tree and has fine lateral roots

Topping—bad tree-maintenance practice used to control the size of trees and that involves pruning from the top of the tree and cutting branches and stems at right angles, leaving long stubs

Variegated—marked with patches of different colors

Variety—genetically different trees within a species

Water shoots—fast-growing branches that grow vertically from other branches

Whip—a young tree that doesn't yet have any lateral branches

Whorl (leaves)—a group of three or more leaves originating at a single node

PROPAGATION PRIMER:
GROWING TREES FROM SEED

Buying either a young or mature tree from the nursery is easy and understandably gratifying because you can go home, plant it, and start watching it grow. But I've always loved growing trees from seed better. It takes a little longer, to be sure, but it's easy and its magic is supremely enjoyable. And you will end up with a little farm of seedlings to plant in your own yard or to give to friends and family.

The process has three simple parts: collecting the seeds, storing the seeds, and planting the seeds.

COLLECTING SEEDS

Timing your seed harvest is key to their successful propagation. Most seeds are ready to be harvested about a week or so before they naturally drop from the tree. A good rule of thumb is to pick seeds from the tree after a few have already dropped to the ground. Handpicking from the branches ensures that your seeds won't have attracted the larvae and fungi that quickly infest dropped seeds.

Look for seeds that appear to be drying, have changed color, or are easily plucked. With pines, the cones should still be closed, indicating that seeds are still inside, but they should also appear to be drying or just beginning to open to disperse their seeds. You can gently flail a tree with a tarp laid beneath to collect the seeds.

STORING SEEDS

All seeds should be cleaned of debris and dirt; and you should discard any seeds that look broken or damaged or could possibly be infested with larvae. Acorns can be dropped in a bucket of water, and those that float should be discarded.

After you collect the seeds, most should be dried for a few days before being packaged up in Ziploc bags for two to three months in a kind of a cold storage (known as stratification) that mimics winter for the seed. Other seeds, such as those for black walnut or Osage orange, are allowed to rot naturally before being planted. Still other seeds have hard outer shells that require soaking or scarifying (small cuts made to the shell) in order to germinate.

PLANTING SEEDS

After whatever stratification is necessary, plant almost all kinds of seeds in trays of potting soil, and allow them to spend three to four months germinating, sprouting, then growing to about three inches tall before planting them in individual pots. When the seedlings have grown to a height of 15 inches and the trunks are pencil thick, they can be planted in the ground just like the seedlings or young trees you buy from the nursery.

Below are step-by-step instructions for growing four different kinds of trees: the maple, with its feathery samara-type seed; the oak, with its acorn seed; the apple; and the walnut.

GROWING A MAPLE FROM SEED

April–May: Gather fruits from the maple. These appear on all maples as a samara, a propeller-shaped fruit that contains the seed. The samaras are green when they first appear, gradually turning red and then a reddish brown as they mature. The actual seed is contained in the swollen tip of the samara. Each samara contains one seed, so to grow 10 to 20 trees you should collect 20 to 40 samaras. Samaras may be collected where they have fallen on the ground, or from the tree if they have already started to turn reddish brown.

The best germination of maples occurs when the freshly collected seed is immediately planted in three- to four-inch-deep planting trays filled with loose potting soil. Place the seeds on the soil surface in rows that are two to three inches apart, then cover with one-quarter inch of soil.

Place trays in an area protected from freezing temperatures, with lots of sunshine and temperatures from 72° to 85°F. Mist the soil to keep it just moist. Once the tiny sprouts emerge, incorporate a liquid

fertilizer, at one-quarter strength for every other watering, and spray weekly with a fungicide to prevent mildew.

June: When the seedlings are two to three inches tall, carefully transplant each to an individual three- or four-quart growing pot with potting soil. After five days, incorporate the liquid fertilizer once a week at recommended strength.

August–September: When seedlings reach a height of 15 inches and the trunks are pencil thick, plant them in the ground.

GROWING AN OAK FROM SEED

October: Gather the fruits, which are acorns, from the tree. The acorns are round in shape, green at first, then turning dark brown as they ripen, and topped with a corky overcap that is scaly in appearance. Acorns can be gathered from the tree, but they must be fully ripe, with no green on the acorn. Or else you can collect them from the ground, but be careful not to choose acorns with tiny weevil holes or that feel hollow. Each fruit contains one seed, so for 10 to 20 trees, gather 20 to 40 acorns.

Place the acorns in an open container in a cool, airy spot, out of the sun, for a few days until they are no longer sweating. Then remove the scaly cap, keeping only the actual acorn and being careful not to puncture the seed coat. Plant acorns immediately in three- to four-inch-deep planting trays in rows that are two to three inches apart, then cover with one half inch of soil.

Place trays in an area protected from freezing temperatures, with lots of sunshine and temperatures from 72° to 85°F. Mist the soil to keep it just moist. Once the tiny sprouts emerge, incorporate a liquid fertilizer, at one-quarter strength for every other watering. Spray weekly with a fungicide to prevent mildew.

March: When the seedlings are two to three inches tall, carefully transplant each seedling to an individual three- or four-quart growing pot with potting soil. After five days, incorporate the liquid fertilizer once a week at recommended strength.

August–September: When seedlings reach a height of 15 inches and the trunks are pencil thick, plant them in the ground.

GROWING AN APPLE TREE FROM SEED

September: Pick 30 desirable apples from trees. Don't be tempted to gather "drops"—apples that have already fallen to the ground—as they tend to have larvae or fungus invasions when on the ground for more than 24 hours. And store-bought apples are often infertile from being kept in cold storage over time, so pick just fresh ones from the tree.

Carefully remove the seeds from the apple cores. With room-temperature water, gently wash off all the pulp from the seeds, being sure not to break or pierce them. Rinse the seeds thoroughly three times.

Place the seeds in a large resealable plastic bag. In a large bowl, mix three cups of coarse-grade Perlite with three cups water so that the mixture is thoroughly moist. With a slotted spoon, add the drained Perlite to the seeds in the bag. Lightly toss to mix the seeds with the Perlite; then mark the date on the bag, seal it, and refrigerate in the vegetable storage bin at a temperature setting of 40° to 44°F. The seeds will need to remain in the refrigerator for 30 to 60 days.

Check the seeds for mold every second week. If it appears, rinse them in a 10 to 1 solution of water to household bleach, mix with a new batch of moist Perlite, and reseal in a new resealable plastic bag, dated with the original date.

March: Prepare a three- to four-inch-deep planting tray with loose potting soil. Remove the seeds from the Perlite and place them on the soil surface in rows that are two to three inches apart, then cover with one-half inch of soil. A thin layer of sawdust or wood shavings applied over the soil surface encourages seed emergence and discourages mildew.

Place the trays in an area where they are protected from freezing, with lots of sunlight and temperatures from 72° to 85°F. Mist the soil to keep it just moist. After the seeds sprout, incorporate a liquid fertilizer at one-fifth strength for every other watering, spraying weekly with a fungicide to prevent mildew.

May: When the seedlings are two to three inches tall, carefully transplant each to individual three- or four-quart growing pots with potting soil. After three days, use liquid houseplant fertilizer at recommended strength and fertilize at every other watering.

August: When the seedlings reach a height of 15 inches and the trunks are pencil thick, plant them in the ground.

GROWING A WALNUT TREE FROM SEED

October: Gather the fruit from the walnut tree, round nuts covered in a thick husk. Green at first, the husk turns dark brown to black as the nut ripens and the husk dries out. The fruit needs to be gathered before it is this ripe and dry, because once dry, the husk is impossible to remove. The best stage for harvesting is when the husk is green, giving somewhat to the touch. The actual seed is protected within the hard nutshell. Each nut contains one seed, so for 10 to 20 trees gather 20 to 40 nuts.

Once you've gathered the nuts, immediately remove their green husks. The best method is to cut through the husk with a sharp knife and peel the husk away from the shell. Then place the seeds in a large resealable plastic bag. In a large bowl, mix three cups of coarse-grade Perlite with three cups of water so that the mixture is thoroughly moist. With a slotted spoon, add the drained Perlite to the seeds in the bag, and lightly toss to thoroughly mix the seeds with the Perlite. Mark the date on the bag, seal it tight, and refrigerate in the vegetable storage bin at a temperature setting of 40° to 44°F. The seeds will need to remain in the refrigerator for 90 to 120 days.

Every second week, check the seeds for mold. If it appears, rinse the seeds in a 10 to 1 solution of water to household bleach; then mix with a new batch of moist Perlite and reseal in a new plastic bag, dated with the original date.

February: By this time, the nuts should have been in refrigeration between 90 and 120 days, and it is time to transfer them to three- to four-inch-deep planting trays, filled with loose potting soil. Remove the seeds from the Perlite and place them on the soil surface in rows that are two to three inches apart, then cover with one-quarter inch of soil.

Place the trays in an area that is protected from freezing temperatures, with lots of sunshine and temperatures from 72° to 85°F. Mist the soil to keep it just moist. The nutshells will eventually rot away from the seeds. Once the tiny sprouts emerge, incorporate a liquid feed fertilizer at one-quarter strength for every other watering, and spray weekly with a fungicide to prevent mildew.

May: When the seedlings are two to three inches tall, carefully transplant each seedling to an individual three- or four-quart growing pot with potting soil. After five days, incorporate the liquid fertilizer once a week at recommended strength.

August: When seedlings reach a height of 15 inches and the trunks are pencil thick, plant them in the ground.

THE TREES AT A GLANCE

The following table lets you see features of the trees highlighted in *The Tree Book* at a glance, including zone range, whether the tree has notable flowers, whether the tree exhibits fall color, whether the tree attracts birds and wildlife, the tree's size at maturity (S = small trees, 15 to 30 feet; M = medium trees, 30 to 50 feet; L = large trees, 50 feet or taller), and how fast they generally grow (S = slow-growing; M = medium-growing; F = fast-growing).

Tree	Zone	Flowers	Fall	Wildlife	Size	Growth
SHADE TREES						
Alder						
European Alder	3–7			Yes	M–L	F
Italian Alder	5–7			Yes	M–L	F
Ash						
Green Ash	3–9	Yes	Yes	Yes	L	F
White Ash	3–9	Yes	Yes	Yes	L	F
Beech						
American Beech	4–9		Yes	Yes	L	S
European Beech	5–7		Yes	Yes	L	S

Tree	Zone	Flowers	Fall	Wildlife	Size	Growth
Birch						
Japanese White Birch	4–7			Yes	M	M
Paper Birch	2–6			Yes	L	M
River Birch	4–9			Yes	M–L	F
Black Gum	4–9		Yes	Yes	M	M
Buckeye						
Ohio Buckeye	3–7	Yes	Yes	Yes	S–M	S
Red Buckeye	4–8	Yes	Yes	Yes	S	S
Yellow Buckeye	4–8		Yes	Yes	L	S
Horse Chestnut	3–7	Yes	Yes	Yes	L	M
Red Horse Chestnut	4–7	Yes	Yes	Yes	M	S
Chestnut						
American Chestnut	3–8		Yes	Yes	M	M
Chinese Chestnut	4–9		Yes	Yes	M	M
Japanese Chestnut	4–9		Yes	Yes	S	M
Elm						
American Elm	2–9		Yes		L	F
Chinese Elm	5–9		Yes		M–L	F
Ginkgo	4–9		Yes		L	S
Hawthorn						
Cockspur Hawthorn	3–7		Yes	Yes	S	M

Tree	Zone	Flowers	Fall	Wildlife	Size	Growth
English Hawthorn	4–7	Yes	Yes	Yes	S	M
Lavalle Hawthorn	4–8	Yes	Yes	Yes	S	F
May Hawthorn	6–11	Yes		Yes	S	S
Washington Hawthorn	4–8	Yes	Yes	Yes	S	F
Winter King Hawthorn	4–7	Yes	Yes	Yes	S	F
Hickory						
Mockernut	4–9		Yes		L	S
Pignut Hickory	4–9		Yes	Yes	L	S
Shagbark Hickory	4–9			Yes	L	S
Shellbark Hickory	5–8		Yes	Yes	L	S
Honey Locust	4–9		Yes		L	F
Japanese Maples						
Japanese Maple	5–8	Yes	Yes		S	M
Threadleaf Japanese Maple	5–8		Yes		S	M
Katsura Tree	4–8		Yes		M–L	M
Linden						
American Linden	2–8	Yes		Yes	L	M–F
Littleleaf Linden	3–7	Yes		Yes	L	M
Silver Linden	4–7	Yes		Yes	L	M

Tree	Zone	Flowers	Fall	Wildlife	Size	Growth
Maple						
Amur Maple	3–8	Yes	Yes	Yes	S	M
Hedge Maple	4–8		Yes		S	S
Norway Maple	3–7	Yes	Yes		M	F
Paperbark Maple	4–8		Yes		S	S
Red Maple	3–9	Yes	Yes	Yes	M–L	M–F
Silver Maple	3–9	Yes	Yes		L	F
Sugar Maple	3–8		Yes		L	S
Oak						
Bur Oak	2–8			Yes	L	S–M
Chinquapin Oak	4–7			Yes	M	S–M
English Oak	3–7			Yes	M–L	
Live Oak	10			Yes	M–L	S–M
Northern Red Oak	4–7		Yes	Yes	L	S
Pin Oak	4–7		Yes	Yes	L	M–F
Scarlet Oak	4–8		Yes	Yes	L	
White Oak	4–8		Yes	Yes	L	S–M
Osage Orange	4–9				M	F
Poplar						
Eastern Poplar	2–9		Yes	Yes	M–L	F

Tree	Zone	Flowers	Fall	Wildlife	Size	Growth
Lombardy Poplar	3–9		Yes	Yes	L	F
Quaking Aspen	1–6		Yes	Yes	M	F
Sassafras	4–8	Yes	Yes	Yes	M–L	F
Sweet Gum	5–9		Yes		L	S–M
Sycamore						
American Sycamore	4–9			Yes	L	F
London Plane Tree	4–9			Yes	L	F–M
Walnut						
Black Walnut	4–9			Yes	L	S
English Walnut	4–9			Yes	M–L	S
Willow						
Babylon Weeping Willow	6–8			Yes	M	F
Corkscrew Hanklow Willow	5–8		Yes		M	F
Golden Weeping Willow	4–9			Yes	L	F
Zelkova	5–8		Yes		L	F
EVERGREENS AND CONIFERS						
Arborvitae						
American Arborvitae	2–7			Yes	M–L	S–M
Oriental Arborvitae	6–10			Yes	S	S–M

Tree	Zone	Flowers	Fall	Wildlife	Size	Growth
Western Redcedar	5–7			Yes	L	S–M
Bald Cypress	4–9			Yes	L	S–M
Cedar						
Atlas Cedar	6–8				M–L	F
Cedar of Lebanon	5–7				M–L	F
Deodar Cedar	6–8				M–L	F
Cypress						
Leyland Cypress	6–9				L	F
Dawn Redwood	5–8			Yes	L	F
Douglas Fir	4–6			Yes	M–L	M
False Cypress						
Hinoki False Cypress	4–8				L	M
Fir						
Balsam Fir	3–5			Yes	L	S
Fraser Fir	4–7			Yes	M	S
White Fir	3–7			Yes	M	S
Hemlock						
Canadian Hemlock	3–7			Yes	M–L	S
Carolina Hemlock	4–7			Yes	M–L	S
Mountain Hemlock	5–6				L	S
Western Hemlock	2–8			Yes	L	S

Tree	Zone	Flowers	Fall	Wildlife	Size	Growth
Holly						
American Holly	5–9			Yes	M	M
Chinese Holly	7–9			Yes	S	M
English Holly	6–7			Yes	M	M
Juniper						
Chinese Juniper	3–9			Yes	L	S
Eastern Redcedar	2–9			Yes	M	S
Rocky Mountain Juniper	3–9			Yes	M	S
Larch						
Eastern Larch	1–4		Yes		M	M–F
Japanese Larch	4–7				L	M
Pine						
Austrian Pine	4–7			Yes	L	S–M
Bristlecone Pine	4–7			Yes	S	S–M
Eastern White Pine	3–8			Yes	L	S–M
Himalayan Pine	5–7			Yes	M	S–M
Japanese White Pine	4–7			Yes	S–M	S–M
Red Pine	2–5			Yes	L	S–M
Scotch Pine	2–7			Yes	M–L	S–M
Swiss Stone Pine	4–7			Yes	M	S–M

Tree	Zone	Flowers	Fall	Wildlife	Size	Growth
Spruce						
Colorado Blue Spruce	2–7			Yes	M–L	S
Norway Spruce	2–7			Yes	M–L	S
Serbian Spruce	2–7			Yes	L	S
White Spruce	2–5			Yes	M–L	S
Yew						
English Yew	6–7			Yes	M	S
Japanese Yew	4–7			Yes	S	S
FLOWERING AND FRUIT TREES						
Apple Trees	3–9	Yes		Yes	S	M
Catalpa						
Chitalpa	6–9	Yes		Yes	S	F
Northern Catalpa	4–8	Yes		Yes	M–L	F
Southern Catalpa	5–9	Yes		Yes	M	F
Citrus Trees						
Grapefruit	10–11	Yes		Yes	S	F
Lemon	10–11	Yes		Yes	S	F
Lime	10–11	Yes		Yes	S	F
Orange	10–11	Yes		Yes	S	F

Tree	Zone	Flowers	Fall	Wildlife	Size	Growth
Dogwood						
Flowering Dogwood	5–9	Yes	Yes	Yes	S–M	F
Kousa Dogwood	5–8	Yes	Yes	Yes	S–M	F
Pagoda Dogwood	3–7	Yes	Yes	Yes	S	F
Flowering Almond	3–6	Yes	Yes	Yes	S	F
Flowering Crab Apple						
Japanese Crab Apple	4–8	Yes		Yes	S	F
Sargent Crab Apple	4–8	Yes		Yes	S	F
Fringe Tree						
Chinese Fringe Tree	5–8	Yes		Yes	S	M
White Fringe Tree	4–9	Yes		Yes	S	M
Goldenchain	5–7	Yes		Yes	S	M
Golden Rain Tree	5–8	Yes	Yes		M	F
Japanese Flowering Plum	5–8	Yes		Yes	S	F
Japanese Pagoda Tree	4–7	Yes		Yes	L	M
Magnolia						
Saucer Magnolia	5–9	Yes		Yes	S–M	M
Southern Magnolia	7–9	Yes		Yes	L	S–M
Star Magnolia	4–8	Yes	Yes	Yes	S	M

Tree	Zone	Flowers	Fall	Wildlife	Size	Growth
Oriental Cherry						
Higan Cherry	4–8	Yes		Yes	S	F
Japanese Flowering Cherry	6–9	Yes		Yes	M	F
Nanking Cherry	2–6	Yes		Yes	S	F
Sargent Cherry	4–7	Yes	Yes	Yes	S	F
Yoshino Cherry	5–8	Yes		Yes	M–L	F
Amur Chokecherry	2–6	Yes		Yes	M	F
Ornamental Pear						
Callery Pear	5–8	Yes	Yes	Yes	S–M	M
Ussurian Pear	3–6	Yes		Yes	M–L	M
Peach Tree	5–9	Yes		Yes	S	F
Pear Tree (Common)	4–8	Yes	Yes	Yes	S	M
Serviceberry						
Allegheny Serviceberry	4–8	Yes	Yes	Yes	S	M
Apple Serviceberry	5–8	Yes	Yes	Yes	S	M
Downy Serviceberry	4–9	Yes	Yes	Yes	S	M
Smoke Tree						
American Smoke Tree	4–8	Yes		Yes	S–M	M
Common Smoke Tree	4–8	Yes		Yes	S	M

Tree	Zone	Flowers	Fall	Wildlife	Size	Growth
Snowbell						
Fragrant Snowbell	5–8	Yes		Yes	S–M	M
Japanese Snowbell	5–8	Yes		Yes	S–M	M
Stewartia						
Japanese Stewartia	5–7	Yes	Yes	Yes	S–M	M
Korean Stewartia	5–7	Yes	Yes	Yes	S–M	M
Tall Stewartia	5–8	Yes	Yes	Yes	S–M	M
Sumac						
Shining Sumac	4–9	Yes	Yes	Yes	S–M	F
Smooth Sumac	2–9	Yes	Yes	Yes	S	F
Staghorn Sumac	3–8	Yes	Yes	Yes	S–M	F
Tulip Tree	4–9	Yes	Yes	Yes	L	M
Yellowwood	4–8	Yes	Yes	Yes	M–L	M

USDA Hardiness Zones

The USDA Hardiness Zone Map of the United States (see page 16) divides the country into 11 zones according to the range of average annual minimum temperatures in each zone.

For Zone 1, the average minimum temperature is –50°F and generally encompasses the core of Alaska.

For Zone 2, the average minimum temperature is –50° to –40°F, encompassing the northern reaches of Alaska, as well as the area surrounding the core.

For Zone 3, the average minimum temperature is –40°F to –30°F, encompassing some of the outer edges of Alaska, and the northern halves of Montana, North Dakota, Minnesota, Wisconsin, and Maine.

For Zone 4, the average minimum temperature is –30°F to –20°F, and encompasses much of the upper Midwest, including the southern halves of Idaho, Montana, North Dakota, Minnesota, Wisconsin, and Maine, as well as most of Wyoming and South Dakota and the northern halves of Nebraska, Iowa, Michigan, New York, and New Hampshire.

For Zone 5, the average minimum temperature is –20°F to –10°F, encompassing a curving band across the Midwest, starting from southern Maine, through New Hampshire, Massachusetts, New York, Pennsylvania, Ohio, Indiana, Illinois, Missouri, Kansas, Nebraska, and Colorado, as well as pockets of Washington, Oregon, Idaho, Nevada, Utah, and New Mexico.

For Zone 6, the average minimum temperature is –10°F to 0°F, encompassing a band across the southern Midwest, including southern Massachusetts, Rhode Island, Connecticut, Pennsylvania, northern Virginia, West Virginia, Kentucky, Tennessee, Missouri,

Kansas, Oklahoma, northern Texas, New Mexico, and pockets of the Southwest and Pacific Northwest.

For Zone 7, the average minimum temperature is 0°F to 10°F, encompassing Virginia, North Carolina, northern parts of South Carolina, Georgia, Alabama, Mississippi, Arkansas, and Texas, the southern half of Oklahoma and New Mexico, and pockets of the Southwest and the Pacific Northwest.

For Zone 8, the average minimum temperature is 10°F to 20°F, encompassing southern South Carolina, Georgia, Alabama, Mississippi, Louisiana, Texas, northern Florida, and pockets of the Southwest and Pacific Northwest.

For Zone 9, the average minimum temperature is 20°F to 30°F, encompassing central Florida, southern Louisiana and Texas, southwestern Arizona, and the western half of California.

For Zone 10, the average minimum temperature is 30°F to 40°F, encompassing southern Florida, small pockets of southern Arizona and California, the western edge of California, and pockets of Hawaii.

For Zone 11, the average minimum temperature is above 40°F, encompassing most of Hawaii and small pockets of southwestern California.

THE TREES BY ZONE

The Tree Book offers viable, practical species for the home landscape primarily in USDA Growing Zones 2 through 9, with a few exceptions on the extreme hot and cold ends of the zone map. Catalogues and other commercial sources are notorious for stretching the promise of zone hardiness on trees, but the consumer (and the trees) never benefit from that approach; the zone assignations in *The Tree Book* are very conservative to ensure the most success when planting your trees. We've chosen to highlight these trees because they're (1) good solid trees that are (2) readily available to the home landscaper at nurseries or through catalogues, and (3) are viable, that is, they can and do grow well in the home landscape in the appropriate zones.

ZONE 1

Eastern Larch
Quaking Aspen (Poplar)

ZONE 2

American Arborvitae
Paper Birch
Nanking Cherry
Amur Chokecherry
American Elm
Eastern Redcedar (Juniper)
Eastern Larch
American Linden
Bur Oak
Red Pine
Scotch Pine

Eastern Poplar (Cottonwood)
Colorado Blue Spruce
Norway Spruce
White Spruce
Smooth Sumac

ZONE 3

European Alder
Flowering Almond
Apple Trees
American Arborvitae
Green Ash
White Ash
Paper Birch
River Birch

Ohio Buckeye
American Chestnut
Horse Chestnut
Black Cherry
Nanking Cherry
Amur Chokecherry
Pagoda Dogwood
American Elm
Balsam Fir
White Fir
Cockspur Hawthorn
Canadian Hemlock
Chinese Juniper
Eastern Redcedar (Juniper)
Rocky Mountain Juniper
American Linden
Littleleaf Linden
Amur Maple
Norway Maple
Red Maple
Silver Maple
Sugar Maple
Bur Oak
English Oak
White Oak
Peach Trees
Ussurian Pear
Eastern White Pine
Red Pine
Scotch Pine
Quaking Aspen (Poplar)
Eastern Poplar (Cottonwood)
Lombardy Poplar
Colorado Blue Spruce
Norway Spruce
White Spruce
Smooth Sumac
Staghorn Sumac

ZONE 4

European Alder
Flowering Almond
Apple Trees
American Arborvitae
Green Ash
White Ash
American Beech
Paper Birch
River Birch
Japanese White Birch
Ohio Buckeye
Red Buckeye
Yellow Buckeye
Northern Catalpa
Black Cherry
Higan Cherry
Nanking Cherry
Sargent Cherry
American Chestnut
Chinese Chestnut
Horse Chestnut
Japanese Chestnut
Amur Chokecherry
Red Horse Chestnut
Japanese Crab Apple
Sargent Crab Apple
Bald Cypress
Hinoki False Cypress
Sawara False Cypress
Pagoda Dogwood
American Elm
Balsam Fir
Douglas Fir
Fraser Fir
White Fir
White Fringe Tree
Ginkgo
Black Gum
Cockspur Hawthorn
English Hawthorn

Lavalle Hawthorn
Washington Hawthorn
Winter King (Green) Hawthorn
Canadian Hemlock
Carolina Hemlock
Mockernut (Hickory)
Pignut Hickory
Shagbark Hickory
Honey Locust
Chinese Juniper
Eastern Redcedar (Juniper)
Rocky Mountain Juniper
Katsura Tree
Eastern Larch
Japanese Larch
American Linden
Littleleaf Linden
Silver Linden
Star Magnolia
Amur Maple
Hedge Maple
Norway Maple
Paperbark Maple
Red Maple
Silver Maple
Sugar Maple
Bur Oak
Chinquapin Oak
English Oak
Northern Red Oak
Pin Oak
Scarlet Oak
White Oak
Osage Orange
Japanese Pagoda Tree
Peach Trees
Common Pear Tree
Ussurian Pear
Austrian Pine
Bristlecone Pine
Eastern White Pine
Japanese White Pine

Red Pine
Scotch Pine
Swiss Stone Pine
London Plane Tree
Quaking Aspen (Poplar)
Eastern Poplar (Cottonwood)
Lombardy Poplar
Common Flowering Quince
Japanese Flowering Quince
Sassafras
Allegheny Serviceberry
Downy Serviceberry
American Smoke Tree
Common Smoke Tree
Colorado Blue Spruce
Norway Spruce
Serbian Spruce
White Spruce
American Sycamore
Shining Sumac
Smooth Sumac
Staghorn Sumac
Sweet Gum
Tulip Tree
Black Walnut
English Walnut
Golden Weeping Willow
American Yellowwood

ZONE 5

European Alder
Italian Alder
Flowering Almond
Apple Trees
American Arborvitae
Western Redcedar (Arborvitae)
Green Ash
White Ash
American Beech
European Beech

Japanese White Birch
Paper Birch
River Birch
Ohio Buckeye
Red Buckeye
Yellow Buckeye
Northern Catalpa
Southern Catalpa
Cedar of Lebanon
Black Cherry
Higan Cherry
Japanese Flowering Cherry
Nanking Cherry
Sargent Cherry
Yoshino Cherry
American Chestnut
Chinese Chestnut
Horse Chestnut
Japanese Chestnut
Red Horse Chestnut
Amur Chokecherry
Japanese Crab Apple
Sargent Crab Apple
Bald Cypress
Hinoki False Cypress
Sawara False Cypress
Flowering Dogwood
Kousa Dogwood
Pagoda Dogwood
American Elm
Chinese Elm
Balsam Fir
Douglas Fir
Fraser Fir
Korean Fir
White Fir
White Fringe Tree
Chinese Fringe Tree
Ginkgo
Goldenchain
Golden Rain Tree
Black Gum

Cockspur Hawthorn
English Hawthorn
Lavalle Hawthorn
Washington Hawthorn
Winter King (Green) Hawthorn
Canadian Hemlock
Carolina Hemlock
Mockernut (Hickory)
Pignut Hickory
Shagbark Hickory
Shellbark Hickory
American Holly
Chinese Juniper
Eastern Redcedar (Juniper)
Rocky Mountain Juniper
Katsura Tree
Japanese Larch
American Linden
Littleleaf Linden
Silver Linden
Honey Locust
Saucer Magnolia
Star Magnolia
Amur Maple
Hedge Maple
Japanese Maple
Norway Maple
Paperbark Maple
Red Maple
Sugar Maple
Silver Maple
Threadleaf Japanese Maple
Chinquapin Oak
Bur Oak
English Oak
Northern Red Oak
Pin Oak
Scarlet Oak
White Oak
Osage Orange
Japanese Pagoda Tree
Peach Trees

Callery Pear
Common Pear Tree
Ussurian Pear
Austrian Pine
Bristlecone Pine
Eastern White Pine
Himalayan Pine
Japanese White Pine
Red Pine
Scotch Pine
Swiss Stone Pine
London Plane Tree
Japanese Flowering Plum
Quaking Aspen (Poplar)
Eastern Poplar (Cottonwood)
Lombardy Poplar
Common Flowering Quince
Japanese Flowering Quince
Dawn Redwood
Sassafras
Allegheny Serviceberry
Apple Serviceberry
Downy Serviceberry
American Smoke Tree
Common Smoke Tree
Fragrant Snowbell
Japanese Snowbell
Colorado Blue Spruce
Norway Spruce
Serbian Spruce
White Spruce
American Sycamore
Japanese Stewartia
Korean Stewartia
Tall Stewartia
Shining Sumac
Smooth Sumac
Staghorn Sumac
Sweet Gum
Tulip Tree
Black Walnut
English Walnut

Corkscrew Hanklow Willow
Golden Weeping Willow
American Yellowwood
Zelkova

ZONE 6

European Alder
Italian Alder
Flowering Almond
Apple Trees
American Arborvitae
Oriental Arborvitae
Western Redcedar (Arborvitae)
Green Ash
White Ash
American Beech
European Beech
Japanese White Birch
Paper Birch
River Birch
Ohio Buckeye
Red Buckeye
Yellow Buckeye
Northern Catalpa
Southern Catalpa
Cedar of Lebanon
Atlas Cedar
Deodar Cedar
Black Cherry
Higan Cherry
Japanese Flowering Cherry
Nanking Cherry
Sargent Cherry
Yoshino Cherry
American Chestnut
Chinese Chestnut
Horse Chestnut
Japanese Chestnut
Red Horse Chestnut
Amur Chokecherry

Citrus Trees
Japanese Crab Apple
Sargent Crab Apple
Bald Cypress
Hinoki False Cypress
Leyland Cypress
Sawara False Cypress
Flowering Dogwood
Kousa Dogwood
Pagoda Dogwood
American Elm
Chinese Elm
Douglas Fir
Fraser Fir
Korean Fir
White Fir
Chinese Fringe Tree
White Fringe Tree
Ginkgo
Goldenchain
Golden Rain Tree
Black Gum
Cockspur Hawthorn
English Hawthorn
Lavalle Hawthorn
May Hawthorn
Washington Hawthorn
Winter King (Green) Hawthorn
Canadian Hemlock
Carolina Hemlock
Mockernut (Hickory)
Pignut Hickory
Shagbark Hickory
Shellbark Hickory
American Holly
Chinese Juniper
Eastern Redcedar (Juniper)
Rocky Mountain Juniper
Katsura Tree
Japanese Larch
American Linden
Littleleaf Linden

Silver Linden
Honey Locust
Saucer Magnolia
Star Magnolia
Amur Maple
Hedge Maple
Japanese Maple
Norway Maple
Paperbark Maple
Red Maple
Silver Maple
Sugar Maple
Threadleaf Japanese Maple
Bur Oak
Chinquapin Oak
English Oak
Northern Red Oak
Pin Oak
Scarlet Oak
White Oak
Osage Orange
Japanese Pagoda Tree
Peach Trees
Callery Pear
Common Pear Tree
Ussurian Pear
Austrian Pine
Bristlecone Pine
Eastern White Pine
Himalayan Pine
Japanese White Pine
Scotch Pine
Swiss Stone Pine
London Plane Tree
Japanese Flowering Plum
Quaking Aspen (Poplar)
Eastern Poplar (Cottonwood)
Lombardy Poplar
Common Flowering Quince
Japanese Flowering Quince
Dawn Redwood
Sassafras

Allegheny Serviceberry
Apple Serviceberry
Downy Serviceberry
American Smoke Tree
Common Smoke Tree
Fragrant Snowbell
Japanese Snowbell
Colorado Blue Spruce
Norway Spruce
Serbian Spruce
Japanese Stewartia
Korean Stewartia
Tall Stewartia
Shining Sumac
Smooth Sumac
Staghorn Sumac
American Sycamore
Sweet Gum
Tulip Tree
Black Walnut
English Walnut
Babylon Weeping Willow
Corkscrew Hanklow Willow
Golden Weeping Willow
American Yellowwood
Zelkova

ZONE 7

European Alder
Italian Alder
Apple Trees
American Arborvitae
Oriental Arborvitae
Western Redcedar (Arborvitae)
Green Ash
White Ash
American Beech
European Beech
River Birch
Japanese White Birch

Ohio Buckeye
Red Buckeye
Yellow Buckeye
Northern Catalpa
Southern Catalpa
Cedar of Lebanon
Atlas Cedar
Deodar Cedar
Black Cherry
Higan Cherry
Japanese Flowering Cherry
Sargent Cherry
Yoshino Cherry
American Chestnut
Chinese Chestnut
Horse Chestnut
Japanese Chestnut
Red Horse Chestnut
Citrus Trees
Japanese Crab Apple
Sargent Crab Apple
Bald Cypress
Hinoki False Cypress
Leyland Cypress
Sawara False Cypress
Flowering Dogwood
Kousa Dogwood
Pagoda Dogwood
American Elm
Chinese Elm
Fraser Fir
White Fir
Chinese Fringe Tree
White Fringe Tree
Honey Locust
Ginkgo
Goldenchain
Golden Rain Tree
Black Gum
Cockspur Hawthorn
English Hawthorn
Lavalle Hawthorn

May Hawthorn
Washington Hawthorn
Winter King (Green) Hawthorn
Canadian Hemlock
Carolina Hemlock
Mockernut (Hickory)
Pignut Hickory
Shagbark Hickory
Shellbark Hickory
American Holly
Chinese Juniper
Eastern Redcedar (Juniper)
Rocky Mountain Juniper
Katsura Tree
Japanese Larch
American Linden
Littleleaf Linden
Silver Linden
Saucer Magnolia
Southern Magnolia
Star Magnolia
Amur Maple
Hedge Maple
Japanese Maple
Norway Maple
Paperbark Maple
Red Maple
Silver Maple
Sugar Maple
Threadleaf Japanese Maple
Bur Oak
English Oak
Chinquapin Oak
Northern Red Oak
Pin Oak
Scarlet Oak
White Oak
Osage Orange
Japanese Pagoda Tree
Peach Trees
Callery Pear
Common Pear Tree

Austrian Pine
Bristlecone Pine
Eastern White Pine
Himalayan Pine
Japanese White Pine
Scotch Pine
Swiss Stone Pine
London Plane Tree
Japanese Flowering Plum
Eastern Poplar (Cottonwood)
Lombardy Poplar
Common Flowering Quince
Japanese Flowering Quince
Dawn Redwood
Sassafras
Allegheny Serviceberry
Apple Serviceberry
Downy Serviceberry
American Smoke Tree
Common Smoke Tree
Fragrant Snowbell
Japanese Snowbell
Colorado Blue Spruce
Norway Spruce
Serbian Spruce
Japanese Stewartia
Korean Stewartia
Tall Stewartia
Shining Sumac
Smooth Sumac
Staghorn Sumac
American Sycamore
Sweet Gum
Tulip Tree
Black Walnut
English Walnut
Babylon Weeping Willow
Corkscrew Hanklow Willow
Golden Weeping Willow
American Yellowwood
Zelkova

ZONE 8

Oriental Aborvitae
Apple Trees
Green Ash
White Ash
American Beech
River Birch
Red Buckeye
Yellow Buckeye
Northern Catalpa
Southern Catalpa
Atlas Cedar
Deodar Cedar
Black Cherry
Higan Cherry
Japanese Flowering Cherry
Yoshino Cherry
American Chestnut
Chinese Chestnut
Japanese Chestnut
Citrus Trees
Japanese Crab Apple
Sargent Crab Apple
Bald Cypress
Hinoki False Cypress
Leyland Cypress
Sawara False Cypress
Flowering Dogwood
Kousa Dogwood
American Elm
Chinese Elm
Chinese Fringe Tree
White Fringe Tree
Ginkgo
Golden Rain Tree
Black Gum
Lavalle Hawthorn
May Hawthorn
Washington Hawthorn
Mockernut (Hickory)
Pignut Hickory

Shagbark Hickory
Shellbark Hickory
American Holly
Chinese Juniper
Eastern Redcedar (Juniper)
Katsura Tree
American Linden
Honey Locust
Southern Magnolia
Saucer Magnolia
Star Magnolia
Amur Maple
Hedge Maple
Japanese Maple
Paperbark Maple
Red Maple
Silver Maple
Sugar Maple
Threadleaf Japanese Maple
Bur Oak
Scarlet Oak
White Oak
Osage Orange
Peach Trees
Callery Pear
Common Pear Tree
Eastern White Pine
London Plane Tree
Japanese Flowering Plum
Eastern Poplar (Cottonwood)
Lombardy Poplar
Common Flowering Quince
Japanese Flowering Quince
Dawn Redwood
Sassafras
Allegheny Serviceberry
Apple Serviceberry
Downy Serviceberry
American Smoke Tree
Common Smoke Tree
Fragrant Snowbell
Japanese Snowbell

Tall Stewartia
Sweet Gum
Shining Sumac
Smooth Sumac
Staghorn Sumac
American Sycamore
Tulip Tree
Black Walnut
English Walnut
Babylon Weeping Willow
Corkscrew Hanklow Willow
Golden Weeping Willow
American Yellowwood
Zelkova

ZONE 9

Oriental Aborvitae
Green Ash
White Ash
American Beech
River Birch
Southern Catalpa
Black Cherry
Chinese Chestnut
Japanese Chestnut
Citrus Trees
Bald Cypress
Leyland Cypress
Flowering Dogwood
American Elm
Chinese Elm
White Fringe Tree
Ginkgo
Black Gum
May Hawthorn
Mockernut (Hickory)
Pignut Hickory
Shagbark Hickory
American Holly
Eastern Redcedar (Juniper)

Chinese Juniper
Honey Locust
Southern Magnolia
Saucer Magnolia
Red Maple
Silver Maple
Osage Orange
Peach Trees
London Plane Tree
Eastern Poplar (Cottonwood)
Lombardy Poplar
Sassafras
Shining Sumac
Smooth Sumac
Sweet Gum
American Sycamore
Tulip Tree
Black Walnut
English Walnut
Golden Weeping Willow

ZONE 10

May Hawthorn
Live Oak
Citrus Trees

ZONE 11

Citrus Trees

RESOURCES

Following are books and Web sites I value, as well as addresses for some seed and catalog nurseries that do good work.

BOOKS

Growing Greener Cities by Gary Moll and Stanley Young (Living Planet Press)

Know It and Grow It by Carl E. Whitcomb, Ph.D. (Lacebark Publications)

The Man Who Planted Trees by Jean Giono (Chelsea Green Publishing)

Woody-Plant Seed Manual by the Forest Service, United States Department of Agriculture (Government Printing Office)

Pirone's Tree Maintenance (seventh edition) by John R. Hartman, Thomas P. Pirone, and Mary Ann Sall (Oxford University Press)

WEB SITES

www.americanforests.org—A great place to keep up with what's happening in the world of trees, forests, and environmental issues.

www.ces.uga.edu—Sponsored by the University of Georgia's College of Agriculture and Environmental Sciences, this site does a great job of helping you conserve water when landscaping.

www.historictrees.org—This site will give you a deep appreciation for the lives of trees and their roles in our nation's collective history.

www.usna.usda.gov—You should visit this site from the U.S. National Arboretum regularly. It has current topics, views of the arboretum, and a great search engine—try "soil" and see recommendations for specific plants. The site is a little technical, perhaps, but it will help you ask the right questions at your nursery or garden center.

CATALOGS AND ORGANIZATIONS

The American Chestnut Foundation
469 Main Street, Suite 1
P.O. Box 4044
Bennington, VT 05201–4044
(802) 447-0110
www.acf.org

Bay Laurel Nursery
2500 El Camino
Atascadero, CA 93422
(805) 466-3449
www.baylaurelnursery.com

Historic Tree Nursery
8701 Old Kings Road
Jacksonville, FL 32210
(800) 320-8733

J. Frank Schmidt & Son Co.
Wholesale Tree Growers
Boring, OR 97009
(800) 825-8202
www.jfschmidt.com

Seed Savers Exchange
3076 North Winn Road
Decorah, IA 52101
(319) 382-5990
www.seedsavers.org

Spring Hill Nurseries
P.O. Box 330
Harrison, OH 45030
(513) 354-1509
www.springhillnursery.com

BOTANICAL GARDENS
AND ARBORETA

A great place to do your window-shopping for the best trees that grow in your area is your local botanical garden or arboretum. The trees you will see there are planted and tended professionally, so they'll be looking their best. You can see them year-round to get a good idea of what they really look like in full leaf or bloom or leafless in winter. And because they're there, and growing well, you can be fairly certain the trees are suitable for your zone and climate. Here are some of this country's best botanical gardens and arboreta.

ALABAMA

Birmingham Botanical Gardens
2612 Lane Park Road
Birmingham, AL 35223
(205) 414-3900
www.bbgardens.org

Dothan Area Botanical Gardens
5130 Headland Avenue
Dothan, AL 36301
(334) 793-3224
www.dabg.com

Huntsville-Madison County Botanical
Garden
4747 Bob Wallace Avenue
Huntsville, AL 35805
(256) 830-4447
www.hsvbg.org

ALASKA

Alaska Botanical Garden
P.O. Box 202202
Anchorage, AK 99520
(907) 770-3692
www.alaskabg.org

ARIZONA

Desert Botanical Garden
1201 North Galvin Parkway
Phoenix, AZ 85008
(480) 941-1225
Recorded info line: (480) 481-8190
www.dbg.org

Tucson Botanical Gardens
2150 North Alvernon Way
Tucson, AZ 85712
(520) 326-9686
www.tucsonbotanical.org

ARKANSAS

South Arkansas Arboretum at South
Arkansas Community College
501 Timberlane
El Dorado, AR 71730
(870) 862-8131
www.arkansasstateparks.com/parks/
park.asp?id=52

CALIFORNIA

Huntington Botanical Gardens
1151 Oxford Road
San Marino, CA 91108
(626) 405-2100
www.huntington.org/BotanicalDiv/
HEHBotanicalHome.html

Mendocino Coast Botanical Gardens
18220 North Highway One
Fort Bragg, CA 95437
(707) 964-4352
www.gardenbythesea.org

Quail Botanical Gardens
230 Quail Gardens Drive
Encinitas, CA 92024
(760) 436-3036
www.qbgardens.com

Rancho Santa Ana Botanic Garden
1500 North College Avenue
Claremont, CA 91711
(909) 625-8767
www.rsabg.org

Santa Barbara Botanic Garden
1212 Mission Canyon Road
Santa Barbara, CA 93105
(805) 682-4726
www.santabarbarabotanicgarden.org

Strybing Arboretum Society
9th Avenue at Lincoln Way
San Francisco, CA 94122
(415) 661-1316
www.strybing.org

University of California Botanical
Garden
200 Centennial Drive #5045
Berkeley, CA 94720
(510) 643-2755
http://botanicalgarden.berkeley.edu

COLORADO

Denver Botanic Gardens
1005 York Street
Denver, CO 80206
(720) 865-3500
www.botanicgardens.org

Denver Botanic Gardens at Chatfield
8500 Deer Creek Canyon Road
Littleton, CO 80128
(303) 973-3705
www.botanicgardens.org/pageinpage/
chatfield.cfm

CONNECTICUT

Connecticut College Arboretum
270 Mohegan Avenue
Box 5201
New London, CT 06320
(860) 439-5020
www.conncoll.edu/ccrec/greennet/
arbo/aboutus.html

DELAWARE

University of Delaware Botanic Gardens
113 Townsend Hall
University of Delaware
Newark, DE 19717
(302) 831-1364
http://ag.udel.edu/udbg

FLORIDA

Flamingo Gardens
3750 S. Flamingo Road
Davie, FL 33330
(954) 473-2955
www.flamingogardens.org

Key West Botanical Garden
P.O. Box 2436
Key West, FL 33045
(305) 296-1504
http://prometheus.cc.emory.edu/kwbs/

Marie Selby Botanical Gardens
811 South Palm Avenue
Sarasota, FL 34236
(941) 366-5731
www.selby.org

Mounts Botanical Garden
531 North Military Trail
West Palm Beach, FL 33415
(561) 233-1757
www.mounts.org

Naples Botanical Garden
4820 Bayshore Drive
Naples, FL 34112
(239) 643-7275
www.naplesbotanicalgarden.org

GEORGIA

Atlanta Botanical Garden
1345 Piedmont Avenue NE
Atlanta, GA 30309
(404) 876-5859
www.atlantabotanicalgarden.org

State Botanical Garden of Georgia
2450 South Milledge Avenue
Athens, GA 30605
(706) 542-1244
www.uga.edu/~botgarden

HAWAII

Lyon Arboretum
University of Hawaii—Manoa
3860 Manoa Road
Honolulu, HI 96822
(808) 988-0456
www.lyonarboretum.com

National Tropical Botanical Garden
3530 Papalina Road
Kalaheo, HI 96741
(808) 332-7324
http://ntbg.org

IDAHO

Idaho Botanical Garden
2355 N. Penitentiary Road
Boise, ID 83712
(208) 343-8649
www.idahobotanicalgarden.org

ILLINOIS

Chicago Botanic Garden
1000 Lake Cook Road
Glencoe, IL 60022
(847) 835-5440
www.chicago-botanic.org

Morton Arboretum
4100 Illinois Route 53
Lisle, IL 60532
(630) 968-0074
www.mortonarb.org

INDIANA

Hayes Arboretum
801 Elks Road
Richmond, IN 47374
(765) 962-3745
www.hayesarboretum.org

Mesker Park Zoo and Botanic Garden
2421 Bement Avenue
Evansville, IN 47720
(812) 428-0715
www.meskerparkzoo.com

Taltree Arboretum and Gardens
71 North 500 West
Valparaiso, Indiana 46385
(219) 462-0025
http://taltree.org

IOWA

Cedar Valley Arboretum and Botanic
Gardens
1927 East Orange Road
Waterloo, IA 50704
(319) 226-4966
www.cedarnet.org/gardens

Iowa Arboretum
1875 Peach Avenue
Madrid, IA 50156
(515) 795-3216
www.iowaarboretum.com

KANSAS

Kansas Landscape Arboretum
488 Utah Road
Wakefield, KS 67487
(785) 461-5901
www.naturalkansas.org/kansas.htm

Overland Park Arboretum and Botanical
Gardens
8500 Santa Fe
Overland Park, KS 66212
(913) 895-6200
www.opprf.org/arb4.htm

KENTUCKY

Bernheim Arboretum and Research Forest
State Highway 245
P.O. Box 130
Clermont, KY 40110
(502) 955-8512
www.bernheim.org

University of Kentucky
Lexington-Fayette
Urban County Government
Arboretum Park
500 Alumni Drive
Lexington, KY 40503
(859) 257-6955
www.uky.edu/Arboretum

Western Kentucky Botanical Garden
P.O. Box 1411
Owensboro, KY 42303
(270) 993-1234
www.wkbg.org

LOUISIANA

Louisiana State Arboretum
4213 Chicot Park Road
Ville Platte, LA 70586
(337) 363-6289 / (888) 677-6100
www.lastateparks.com/arbor/Arbor2.htm

New Orleans Botanical Garden
Victory Avenue
New Orleans, LA 70124
(504) 288-6444
www.neworleanscitypark.com/nobg.php

MAINE

Coastal Maine Botanical Gardens
P.O. Box 234
Barters Island Road
Boothbay, ME 04537
(207) 633-4333
www.mainegardens.org

Maine State Gare Farm
Route 26
Gray, ME
(207) 657-4977

MARYLAND

Adkins Arboretum
12610 Eveland Road
P.O. Box 100
Ridgely, MD 21660
(410) 634-2847
www.adkinsarboretum.org

Cylburn Arboretum Association
4915 Greenspring Avenue
Baltimore, MD 21209
(410) 367-2217
www.cylburnassociation.org

MASSACHUSETTS

Arnold Arboretum of Harvard University
125 Arborway
Jamaica Plain, MA 02130
(617) 524-1718
www.arboretum.harvard.edu

Berkshire Botanical Garden
P.O. Box 826
(Intersection Routes 102 & 183)
Stockbridge, MA 01262
(413) 298-3926
www.berkshirebotanical.org

Tower Hill Botanic Garden
11 French Drive
P.O. Box 598
Boylston, MA 01505
(508) 869-6111
www.towerhillbg.org

MICHIGAN

Matthaei Botanical Gardens
University of Michigan
1800 North Dixboro Road
Ann Arbor, MI 48105
(734) 998-7061
www.lsa.umich.edu/mbg

Leila Arboretum
928 West Michigan Avenue
Battle Creek, MI 49017
(269) 969-0722
www.leilaarboretumsociety.org

Nichols Arboretum
University of Michigan
1610 Washington Heights
Ann Arbor, MI 48104
(734) 998-9540
www.umich.edu/~wwwarb

W. J. Beal Botanical Garden
Michigan State University
 412 Olds Hall
East Lansing, MI 48824
(517) 355-9582
www.cpp.msu.edu/beal

MINNESOTA

Minnesota Landscape Arboretum
University of Minnesota
3675 Arboretum Boulevard
Chaska, MN 55318
(952) 443-1400
www.arboretum.umn.edu

MISSISSIPPI

Crosby Arboretum
Mississippi State University
370 Ridge Road
P.O. Box 1639
Picayune, MS 39466
(601) 799-2311
www.msstate.edu/dept/crec/camain.html

MISSOURI

Missouri Botanical Garden
P.O. Box 299
St. Louis, MO 63166
(314) 577-9400 / 800-642-8842
www.mobot.org

Missouri State Arboretum
Northwest Missouri State University
800 University Drive
Maryville, MO 64468
(660) 562-1329
www.nwmissouri.edu/arboretum

MONTANA

ZooMontana
2100 South Shiloh Road
Billings, MT 59106
(406) 652-8100
www.zoomontana.org

NEBRASKA

Lauritzen Gardens
100 Bancroft Street
Omaha, NE 68108
(402) 346-4002
www.omahabotanicalgardens.org

Nebraska Statewide Arboretum
University of Nebraska—Lincoln
P.O. Box 830715
Lincoln, NE 68583–0715
(402) 472-2971
http://arboretum.unl.edu

NEVADA

Wilbur D. May Arboretum and
Botanical Garden
1502 Washington Street
Reno, NV 89503
(775) 785-4153
www.museumsusa.org/data/museums/
NV/136716.htm

Southern Nevada Zoological-Botanical
Park
1775 North Rancho Drive
Las Vegas, NV 89106
(702) 647-4685
www.lasvegaszoo.org

NEW HAMPSHIRE

Horatio Colony House Museum and
Nature Preserve
199 Main Street
Keene, NH 03431
(603) 352-0460
www.horatiocolonymuseum.org

NEW JERSEY

Holmdel Arboretum
P.O. Box 1255
17 Lafayette Place
Freehold, NJ 07728–1255
(732) 431-7903
www.fieldtrip.com/nj/84317903.htm

New Jersey Botanical Garden at Skylands
P.O. Box 302
Ringwood, NJ 07456
(973) 962-7527 / (973) 962-9534
www.njbg.org

NEW MEXICO

Albuquerque Biological Park
Rio Grande Botanic Garden
903 Tenth Street SW
Albuquerque, NM 87102
(505) 764-6200
www.cabq.gov/biopark

NEW YORK

Brooklyn Botanic Garden
1000 Washington Avenue
Brooklyn, NY 11225
(718) 623-7200
www.bbg.org

Buffalo and Erie County Botanical
Gardens
2655 South Park Avenue (Route 62)
Buffalo, NY 14218
(716) 827-1584
www.buffalogardens.com

Cornell University Plantations
1 Plantations Road
Ithaca, NY 14850
(607) 255-2400
www.plantations.cornell.edu

New York Botanical Garden
Bronx River Parkway at Fordham Road
Bronx, NY 10458
(718) 817-8700
www.nybg.org

Staten Island Botanical Garden
1000 Richmond Terrace
Staten Island, NY 10301
(718) 273-8200
www.sibg.org

NORTH CAROLINA

Daniel Stowe Botanical Garden
6500 South New Hope Road
Belmont, NC 28012
(704) 825-4490
www.stowegarden.org

North Carolina Botanical Garden
University of North Carolina—
Chapel Hill
CB 3375, Totten Center
Chapel Hill, NC 27599–3375
(919) 962-0522
www.ncbg.unc.edu

NORTH DAKOTA

Fort Stevenson State Park Arboretum
1252A 41st Avenue NW
Garrison, ND 58540
(701) 337-5576 / (800) 807-4723
www.ndparks.com/parks/fssp.htm

OHIO

Cincinnati Zoo & Botanical Garden
3400 Vine Street
Cincinnati, OH 45220
(513) 281-4700 / (800) 94-HIPPO
www.cincyzoo.org

Cleveland Botanical Garden
11030 East Boulevard
Cleveland, OH 44106
(216) 721-1600
www.cbgarden.org

Toledo Botanical Garden
5403 Elmer Drive
Toledo, OH 43615
(419) 936-2986
www.toledogarden.org

OKLAHOMA

Myriad Botanical Gardens and Crystal
Bridge
301 West Reno
Oklahoma City, OK 73102
(405) 297-3995
www.myriadbotanicalgardens.com

Oklahoma City Zoo and Botanical
Garden
2101 NE 50th Street
Oklahoma City, OK 73111
(405) 424-3344
www.okczoo.com

OREGON

Leach Botanical Garden
6704 SE 122nd Avenue
Portland, OR 97236
(503) 823-9503
www.parks.ci.portland.or.us/Parks/
LeachBotanicalGar.htm

Mount Pisgah Arboretum
34901 Frank Parrish Road
Eugene, OR 97405
(541) 747-1504
http://members.efn.org/~mtpisgah

PENNSYLVANIA

Morris Arboretum of the University of
Pennsylvania
100 Northwestern Avenue
Philadelphia, PA 19118
(215) 247-5777
www.business-services.upenn.edu/
arboretum

Phipps Conservatory and Botanical
Gardens
1 Schenley Park
Pittsburgh, PA 15213
(412) 622-6914
www.phipps.conservatory.org

Tyler Arboretum
515 Painter Road
Media, PA 19063
(610) 566-9134
www.tylerarboretum.org

RHODE ISLAND

Blithewold Mansion, Gardens and
Arboretum
101 Ferry Road (Route 114)
Bristol, RI 02809
(401) 253-2707
www.blithewold.org

SOUTH CAROLINA

Riverbanks Zoo and Garden
500 Wildlife Parkway
Columbia, SC 29210
(803) 779-8717
www.riverbanks.org

SOUTH DAKOTA

McCrory Gardens
South Dakota State University
Horticulture, Forestry, Landscape &
Parks Department
Brookings, SD 57007
(605) 688-5136
www3.sdstate.edu/Academics/College
OfAgricultureAndBiologicalSciences/
HorticultureForestryLandscapeand
Parks/McCroryGardens

TENNESSEE

Cheekwood Botanical Garden and
Museum of Art
1200 Forrest Park Drive
Nashville, TN 37205
(615) 356-8000
www.cheekwood.org

Memphis Botanic Garden
750 Cherry Road
Memphis, TN 38111
(901) 685-1566
www.memphisbotanicgarden.com

TEXAS

Dallas Arboretum
8617 Garland Road
Dallas, TX 75218
(214) 515-6500
www.dallasarboretum.org

Fort Worth Botanic Garden
3220 Botanic Garden Boulevard
Fort Worth, TX 76107
(817) 871-7689
http://ci.fort-worth.tx.us/pacs/botgarden

San Antonio Botanical Garden
555 Funston at North New Braunfels
Avenue
San Antonio, TX 78209
(210) 207-3250
www.sabot.org

Valley Nature Center
301 South Border
P.O. Box 8125
Weslaco, TX 78599
(956) 969-2475
www.valleynaturecenter.org

Wild Basin Wilderness Preserve
805 North Capitol of Texas Highway
Austin, TX 78746
(512) 327-7622
www.wildbasin.org

UTAH

Red Butte Garden
University of Utah
300 Wakara Way
Salt Lake City, UT 84108
(801) 581-4747
www.redbuttegarden.org

VERMONT

University of Vermont Horticultural
Research Center
Burlington, VT 05405
(802) 658-9166
http://pss.uvm.edu/dept/hort_farm

Vermont Community Botanical Garden
1100 Dorset Street
South Burlington, VT 05403
(802) 864-5206
www.vcbg.org

VIRGINIA

Lewis Ginter Botanical Garden
1800 Lakeside Avenue
Richmond, VA 23228
(804) 262-9887
www.lewisginter.org

Norfolk Botanical Garden
6700 Azalea Garden Road
Norfolk, VA 23518–5337
(757) 441-5830
www.nbgs.org

WASHINGTON

Bellevue Botanical Garden
P.O. Box 40536
Bellevue, WA 98015
(425) 451-3755
www.bellevuebotanical.org

Washington Park Arboretum
University of Washington
P.O. Box 358010
Seattle, WA 98195-8010
(206) 543-8800
http://depts.washington.edu/wpa

WASHINGTON, D.C.

United States Botanic Garden
245 First Street SW
Washington, DC 20024
General Information: (202) 225-8333
Plant Hotline: (202) 226-4785
www.usbg.gov

WEST VIRGINIA

Core Arboretum
West Virginia University
Morgantown, WV 26506
(304) 293-5201
www.as.wvu.edu/biology/facility/
arboretum.html

WISCONSIN

Boerner Botanical Gardens
Whitnall Park
9400 Boerner Drive
Hales Corners, WI 53130
(414) 525-5600
www.countyparks.com/horticulture

Mitchell Park Horticultural
Conservatory ("The Domes")
524 South Layton Boulevard
Milwaukee, WI 53215
(414) 649-9800
www.countyparks.com/horticulture

WYOMING

Cheyenne Botanic Gardens
710 South Lions Park Drive
Cheyenne, WY 82001
(307) 637-6458
www.botanic.org

Page numbers for main entries of specific trees appear in bold type.

Page numbers of illustrations appear in italics.